PRAISE FOR
BE STRONG AND OF GOOD COURAGE

"For those of us who care deeply about Israel and the US-Israel relationship, Ross and Makovsky have done a real service. As Israel's leaders face a fateful choice about the future of the state and preserving its character, they tell the story of Ben-Gurion, Begin, Rabin, and Sharon. It is a story that can provide guidance for today's leaders in Israel and for all of us on the meaning of leadership."

> —Hillary Rodham Clinton, 67th US secretary of state

"The Ross and Makovsky book is a powerful statement on the style and principles of leadership that are critical for shaping the Middle East peace process."

> —Henry Kissinger, 56th US secretary of state

"A brilliant study of the role of moral courage in politics as exemplified by four of Israel's boldest prime ministers, and a passionate plea for similar courage in Israel today. An important work."

> —Rabbi Lord Jonathan Sacks, former chief rabbi of the United Hebrew Congregations of the Commonwealth

"An astute understanding of the policies of real leaders along with insights based on many meetings and close observation provide an important learning experience for readers of *Be Strong and of Good Courage*."

> —George Shultz, 60th US secretary of state

"*Be Strong and of Good Courage* is of great importance to understand the most intimate decision-making process of our leaders during pivotal points of our history, to realize the enormous and courageous struggle to find ways to resolve the Israeli-Arab conflict, the ability to learn from our leaders how they were able to break some of their core and basic ideals for Israel to find its way to be accepted in this region, and to learn and gain insights for Israel's future historic decisions that must be taken."

—Gadi Eisenkot, 21st chief of general staff of the Israel Defense Forces

"This book is a wake-up call to the most difficult decision that the State of Israel has faced since its establishment: preserving a Jewish and democratic identity or losing it. This is not a question of if it happens, but when. The authors clearly point out the great courage required of Israeli leaders to assume responsibility, put Israel's future first, and lead the public to address this challenge before Israel passes the point of no return [to] a binational state."

—Amir Eshel, former commander of the Israeli Air Force

Be Strong
and of
Good Courage

BE STRONG
and of
GOOD COURAGE

How Israel's Most Important Leaders Shaped Its Destiny

Dennis Ross and David Makovsky

PUBLICAFFAIRS
New York

PublicAffairs
Hachette Book Group
1290 Avenue of the Americas, New York, NY 10104
www.publicaffairsbooks.com
@Public_Affairs

Printed in the United States of America

First Edition: September 2019

Published by PublicAffairs, an imprint of Perseus Books, LLC, a
subsidiary of Hachette Book Group, Inc. The PublicAffairs name
and logo is a trademark of the Hachette Book Group.

The Hachette Speakers Bureau provides a wide range of authors for speaking events.
To find out more, go to www.hachettespeakersbureau.com or call (866) 376-6591.

The publisher is not responsible for websites (or their
content) that are not owned by the publisher.

Print book interior design by Amy Quinn.

Library of Congress Cataloging-in-Publication Data
Names: Ross, Dennis, author. | Makovsky, David, author.
Title: Be strong and of good courage : how Israel's most important
    leaders shaped its destiny / Dennis Ross and David Makovsky.
Description: First edition. | New York : PublicAffairs, 2019. |
    Includes bibliographical references and index.
Identifiers: LCCN 2018058189 | ISBN 9781541767652 (hardcover
    : alk. paper) | ISBN 9781541767645 (e-book)
Subjects: LCSH: Prime ministers—Israel—Biography. | Political leadership—
    Israel—History. | Character—Political aspects—Israel—History. | Israel—
    Politics and government. | Israel—Politics and government—Philosophy.
Classification: LCC DS126.6.A2 R68 2019 | DDC 956.9405092/2—dc23
LC record available at https://lccn.loc.gov/2018058189
ISBNs: 978-1-5417-6765-2 (hardcover), 978-1-5417-6764-5 (e-book)

LSC-C

10 9 8 7 6 5 4 3 2 1

To Dan, Michael, and Ben
May you always have good leaders.
    —Dennis Ross

For Sheila and Herb Rosenblum—grateful for your love and
support and in memory of Ruth Elbaum Shane for her warmth
and wisdom.
    —David Makovsky

CONTENTS

Prime Minister David Ben-Gurion looking through documents at his Tel Aviv office, 1959 (Fritz Cohen, public domain). © 2019 National Photo Collection, Government Press Office, Israel.

Prime Minister Menachem Begin speaking on Israel-Egypt peace agreement, The White House, Washington, DC, March 26, 1979 (Sa'ar Ya'acov). © 2019 National Photo Collection, Government Press Office, Israel.

Portrait of Prime Minister and Defense Minister Yitzhak Rabin, 1994 (Sa'ar Ya'acov). © 2019 National Photo Collection, Government Press Office, Israel.

Israeli Prime Minister Ariel Sharon pictured during a defense meeting held at the Pentagon, Washington, DC, May 2002 (Helene C. Stikkel, DoD, public domain).

AUTHORS' NOTE

THE TITLE OF this book, *Be Strong and of Good Courage,* is drawn from the Bible and the injunction that appears several times: *chazak v'ematz.* The Hebrew can be translated various ways: "Be strong and of good courage" or don't waver, maintain resolve, and go forward with success. This is the essence of what we think Israel's leaders will need to show as they face the future, particularly if they are to preserve Israel as a Jewish and democratic state. It is not now a given. The best way to preserve Israel's character—and avoid becoming an Arab and a Jewish state—is to reach a two-state outcome. And there is a compelling logic for it; there are two national movements—the Jewish national movement (Zionism) and the Palestinian national movement—competing for the same space. The only way to satisfy and fulfill these two national identities is to have two states for two peoples, with Israel being the state of the Jewish people and Palestine the state of the Palestinian people.

The two-state outcome would, of course, preserve the Jewish character of Israel by producing recognized borders within which the state's population would remain roughly 80 percent Jewish. Unfortunately, there is little prospect of achieving a two-state outcome anytime soon. The domestic political realities among Israelis and Palestinians do not lend themselves to peacemaking, especially with weakness and division defining the Palestinians and a narrow-based, right-wing government having been responsible for decision-making in Israel. Moreover, leadership succession in the Palestinian Authority is looming, and a succession period is bound to be characterized by competition over who can be more demanding vis-à-vis the Israelis, not who can be more accommodating. For their part, few Israelis think this is the time to take risks, when the region is so unsettled, ISIS remains in the

Sinai, and Iran and Shia militias are entrenching themselves in Syria and along the Jordanian border.

Even the possible ending of the Netanyahu era won't change the way most Israelis view the region and its dangers—and their reluctance to take risks for an elusive peace. Netanyahu's inability to put together a government after seemingly having won a fifth term indicates that his time may be running out. If nothing else, the looming indictment by the attorney general makes him vulnerable.

Yes, removing the dominant figure in Israeli politics for the last decade is likely to be a game changer, but not on the peace issue or the way the Palestinians are perceived. Israelis do not believe that a peace agreement with the Palestinians is possible. Consider that in the last two elections, Netanyahu's main challengers—Yitzhak Herzog in 2015 and Benny Gantz in 2019—did not make peace with the Palestinians an issue. Both understood it was a loser politically, and it was the surest way to be seen as naive.

Still, Netanyahu has been the towering figure whom all other politicians reacted to and were measured against—and he very much set the tone and direction. Even should he win the second election of 2019 and cobble together a new government, he will be more dependent on the right wing. If his legal difficulties produce his resignation, that government would likely act on his call to begin annexations in the West Bank. Even if initially limited to areas that are not controversial in Israel, that will establish a precedent and make it politically harder to stop the drift toward one state for two peoples. Surely, the cost of not acquiescing in the settlers' agenda also will go up.

As such, his successors will face the reality that drift toward an Arab-Jewish state is accelerating—even as it becomes more costly to try to blunt that drift. What compounds this reality is that the prospects for peace are so poor. The legacy of peacemaking over the last twenty years has produced ever-deepening gaps psychologically and substantively between the Israelis and Palestinians. That legacy has also led to profound disbelief on both sides about the prospects of ever reaching an agreement, and that loss of faith has been compounded by the increasing doubt among Israelis and Palestinians that their leaders are up to making historic decisions. In other words, even if the domestic and regional circumstances were to change for the better, it would be difficult to overcome the profound differences between the two sides and their mutual loss of belief.

Neither of us believes that the United States should walk away from the peacemaking effort. Nature abhors a vacuum, and, in the Middle East, history shows that the worst forces will always fill any diplomatic void. We favor an effort that produces sufficient small advances to restore a sense of possibility; real progress on peace has always required both a ground-up approach to show both sides that real, tangible steps can be taken and a top-down effort to put those steps in a larger political context. The ground-up and top-down strategies also fit the mind-sets of both sides: Israelis want to see a process that proves the Palestinians will make commitments and fulfill them, and Palestinians have always wanted to see the end goal guiding the process.

From this perspective, shooting for the ultimate deal stands little chance if the context on the ground and between the parties does not change. At the time of this writing, Donald Trump's peace plan has not yet been presented, precisely because the context is not right. Even if the plan is presented, it is not now designed to be the ultimate deal but rather a plan for having the two sides negotiate such a deal. Having committed so much of our lives to Arab-Israeli-Palestinian peace, we would like to see that happen. Sadly, even the resumption of a negotiating process at this point appears unlikely.

Precisely because the prospects of an ultimate deal are low, we believe that Israel for the sake of its future cannot sit back and do nothing. A policy of inaction will produce an outcome; regrettably, it will be a binational Arab-Jewish state. A binational state is neither feasible nor a promising solution. Israelis will not renounce their state as the homeland of the Jewish people and the Palestinians will not give up on having a state of their own. The Middle East is not post-nationalistic, and the track record in this region of forcing divergent ethnic or sectarian entities into unitary states tends to produce endless bloodshed.

Because a one-state outcome is a prescription for enduring conflict and not peace, we decided to do a book that explains why a big, tough decision in Israel will be needed to avoid such an outcome.

Some might ask why are we focused only on Israeli leaders; don't Palestinians need leaders to make historic choices and decisions? The answer is a resounding yes. But, given Palestinian succession, that is becoming less and less likely—and in the meantime a binational outcome is likely to emerge and be impossible to disentangle. Zionism was always about self-reliance. It was about shaping the Jewish national fate, not leaving it to others. It was about Zionist leaders acting to define the character of the Jewish state by their own actions and not by default.

That Zionist ethos has driven Israel's leadership historically. We believe that looking at the past, when Israeli prime ministers made big decisions, can be helpful in providing a guide to what Israel's leadership in the coming years will need to do.

Our research in those historical cases was able to break new ground because of the declassification of a wide array of documents that were not previously available. In addition to US materials that have been declassified, Israeli state archives have been opened and papers and memos in Hebrew have provided a treasure trove of materials, including, for example, the discussions the Israeli cabinet held over what to do with the territories in the aftermath of the 1967 war. Discussions about what to do with the West Bank—from June 14 to June 19, 1967, culminating in a secret cabinet resolution—were far more extensive than any Israeli government has held since. These and other materials have given us insight into the past cases in which Israeli prime ministers confronted big decisions.

Our hope with this book is to show not just how big decisions were made in the past but also why they were made. And, with that understanding, maybe Israel's leaders will find a pathway to deal with their looming, fateful choice.

INTRODUCTION

ARIEL SHARON WAS a large man. There was something irrepressible about him. Whether he was eating or trying to impress you with his plans, there was a sense of urgency to him. David and I would have different entry points for dealing with him; he as a journalist, beginning in 1989 and throughout the 1990s, and I in the US government, starting in the early 1980s when I was in the Pentagon. Over the years, in and out of government, I would share many meals with Sharon; they were memorable not just for what he could consume but for the discussions that accompanied them. He liked being challenged, but he also liked to make big, provocative points. He did not think small. In one of our last discussions over shawarma sandwiches, he exclaimed: "My generation [of Israelis] is the last one that is not afraid to make big decisions. I fear that the next generation will be led by politicians and they won't decide."

He made the point in response to my challenging him on the logic of just withdrawing from Gaza, instead of making the exit part of a negotiation in which the Palestinian leader, Mahmoud Abbas, could show he had produced Israeli withdrawal but at the same time could be held accountable for fulfilling his side of the bargain. Sharon would have none of this, saying, "We cannot have our future dependent on their irresponsibility."

For him, Israel had to act. He did not trust that the Palestinians would ever be responsible, and Israel's destiny could not be in their hands. There was a risk in acting unilaterally, he acknowledged, but Israel would determine its future and not have it decided by default—or, worse, by Palestinians who might not ever be able to accept anything but a binational state.

That was why he had to decide this, why he had to do it. He could not leave this decision to the next generation of Israeli leaders, because they were "politicians" and would not be up to it.

He meant what he said, deciding to form a new party, Kadima, and leave Likud—a party he had helped found—after the withdrawal from Gaza. He believed that disengagement from most of the West Bank would also be needed if Israel's future as a Jewish and democratic state was to be assured. Otherwise, he believed, given the demographic trends, Israel would become a binational state with roughly equal Jewish and Arab populations. Likud's opposition to the withdrawal from Gaza told him that if he did not remake the political landscape and forge a new centrist party, he might not succeed. Think big, act big—that was his credo—and he did not trust the next generation to do what was necessary.

Interestingly, whatever his disagreements with Yitzhak Rabin and Shimon Peres, Sharon acknowledged that they did not fear doing what was necessary. But Rabin was dead and Peres would probably never be prime minister again. After my meeting with Sharon, I recalled a conversation with Rabin in 1995. He said he was going to build a separation fence—one that Sharon, ironically, would oppose at the time. Rabin's reason: Israel had to secure itself as a Jewish-democratic state, the essence of the Zionist dream and ethic. He preferred to create partition and separation from the Palestinians through negotiations, but if agreement proved impossible, he would secure the future of the Zionist mission by building a fence.

Now Sharon, like Rabin, was saying separation would come from a unilateral Israeli action. But Sharon was also saying that if he did not do it, it would not happen, because the next generation of Israeli leaders could not make big decisions. They were tactical, thought only about their political futures, and would never muster the "good courage" it would take to face down inevitable domestic opposition.

Was he right? Today, it is a fair question to ask. Sharon was not able to follow through on his intentions to disengage from a significant part of the West Bank. It was not political opposition that did him in—it was a devastating stroke. While his successor, Ehud Olmert, intended to implement Sharon's plans, he was unable to do so. The 2006 war in Lebanon weakened him politically, and subsequent police investigations ultimately forced him to resign. Later he would be sent to prison.

But the imperative for Israeli leaders to make a decision has become more acute. Israel's presence in the West Bank has grown to 48,800 Israelis outside of East Jerusalem. It took the force of Sharon's will and personality to press ahead and remove eight thousand settlers from Gaza over serious resistance from the settler community. The challenge in the West Bank would be immeasurably greater. Even if one assumes that settlement blocs and swaps could be adopted—and 77 percent of the settlers could be absorbed in blocs in about 5 percent of the West Bank—the numbers of Israeli settlers living outside of the prospective blocs continues to grow and is now over one hundred thousand. Unless something is done soon to stop that growth, it is hard to see how to prevent Israel from becoming an Arab-Jewish state. Because Sharon withdrew from Gaza, the demographic balance continues to favor Israeli Jews over Arabs in Israel and the West Bank. But even today, the split, according to Israel's leading demographers, is roughly 60/40 Jews to Arabs.

Is this the Jewish state envisioned by the Zionist founders of Israel? Demographic trends will gradually reduce the Jewish plurality over time. Israel is rapidly approaching a hinge point. Perhaps Sharon's claim is wrong. Perhaps, faced with the need to make a big, historic decision, Israel will produce leadership that will act. It has in the past. When it needed a Ben-Gurion, or a Begin, or a Rabin, or a Sharon, they were there. What was it about these men, and what was it about their times, when big decisions were called for, that produced them?

This book will look at each of these leaders, the crossroads they saw, and the big decisions they made in response. It will explore the setting, the challenges, the way they perceived the stakes, the political context at the time, and the scale and depth of the opposition they were prepared to face down. It will dig into their backgrounds—their personal histories and character—and what made them tick. It will explore their assessments and the calculations they made about the choices or the lack of choices available to them. It will offer case studies of times when Israel was not paralyzed in the face of immensely difficult situations and reveal what motivated the actions taken. To be sure, not every big move was wise in hindsight. Ariel Sharon in 1982 believed he could remake the Middle East by removing the Palestine

Liberation Organization (PLO) from Lebanon and installing Bashir Gemayel as Lebanese president, and Israel paid a terrible price for what proved to be a strategic misjudgment. In addition, there were times when not acting proved to be the right policy choice: for example, Levi Eshkol in the weeks before the 1967 war and Yitzhak Shamir during the 1991 Gulf War.

But those choices did not involve the fundamental character of the state. Moreover, avoiding decisive choices when confronted with grave threats or significant opportunities is not the measure of leadership. When Ben-Gurion, against the odds and the advice of those around him, chose to declare the state, or when Begin decided to respond to Sadat, or when Rabin took the risk of dealing with the PLO, they demonstrated vision, courage, and awareness of the stakes—and of the costs of not acting. They also all shared one other attribute: they believed being a leader required them to act.

In this book, we will look at the historic junctures where Israeli leaders rose to the occasion and explain why they did so. What is noteworthy is that, in every case, these Israeli leaders wanted to know where America stood and in most cases wanted American material support and commitments or assurances before they acted.

This is not to say that America was decisive in affecting the Israeli choices and actions—clearly, some Israeli leaders acted believing they would not have American support. David Ben-Gurion may have desperately wanted American support, but he understood it would not be forthcoming. Yet he acted anyway, not knowing that Harry Truman would override his secretary of state, George Marshall, and recognize the new state of Israel. For Ben-Gurion's successors, the United States' position and role would be a key factor in the historic decisions they would make. Indeed, it is not an exaggeration to say that America has loomed large for every prime minister contemplating a major decision since Menachem Begin's time. If Sharon is right that Israeli leaders today are more political and less strategic in their decision-making, America's role will necessarily become even more important as Israeli leaders face big decisions and look for ways to minimize the costs of acting.

And, unquestionably, a historic decision is looming—one, by the way, that both Rabin and Sharon saw very clearly and sought to address. As the prospect of Israel becoming a binational state becomes starker and less abstract, Israel's leaders will have a choice to make. Some will seek to explain it away, denying that anything is changing or that a decision is necessary. They may argue that Israel can expand its hold throughout the West Bank, grant Palestinians limited autonomy on 40 percent of the territory, and perhaps even suggest that the Palestinians can be linked to Jordan. For those making this case, Jewish survival trumps any other consideration, especially that of Palestinian rights or international concerns about those rights.

For others, the choice cannot be avoided. The reality—the increasing parity in numbers of Arabs and the Palestinian demands for rights—cannot be ignored. Even if the world does not insist on acknowledging Palestinian nationalism, Jewish survival requires not surrendering Israel's character by denying another people its rights. Moreover, as some Palestinians increasingly clamor for one person, one vote, they assume the international community will not remain indifferent. Israel will have to decide to stop its settlement in the territories that would inevitably be part of any putative Palestinian state and find ways to separate from the Palestinian population. Those Israelis who see Israel's future this way clearly reflect the considerations that drove both Rabin and Sharon. To be sure, many of them also reflect the fundamental liberalism, in terms of civil and legal rights that must also include the Arabs, that Menachem Begin embodied.

In truth, Israel stands on the threshold of a historic choice—and the choice its leaders make will determine whether it remains Jewish and democratic.

In the culminating chapter of the book, we will assess the political realities and forces within Israel and the pressures for and against deciding to stop the drift toward becoming an Arab-Jewish binational state. We will take a closer look at the arguments the right-wing leaders make for staying on the current path—why they either deny that a binational reality is coming or believe that they can manage a one-state outcome—and then explain why those views are misguided and divorced from reality. We will then outline the specific steps that would be needed to preserve the possibility of Israeli separation from the Palestinians, which is the key to preserving Israel as a Jewish-democratic state even if a peace agreement is not in the cards anytime soon. We will also explain why steps needed for separation will confront Israel's leadership with an extremely difficult decision, given the political weight of the settler movement and the right wing in Israel. Because the decision to keep the option of separation alive is likely to be so hard politically, we will also explore whether the United States can do anything to make the choice easier or at least more manageable for the Israeli leadership. This is not a choice that America can or should make for Israel— only Israelis can make it.

One of the mistakes of the Obama administration was to adopt what a majority in Israel took to be a lecturing posture toward the country, as if America's leaders knew more about what was good for Israel than Israelis did. Nonetheless, Israel's leaders will take the United States into account, and American assurances and assistance have played an important supportive role at key moments in the past. Given that, we will propose what the United States could do to make the looming historic decision more likely. Obviously, the American president will have to care about Israel's choices and the importance of preserving its character, while also recognizing that the United States can influence what an Israeli leader chooses to do. Because shared values have formed the foundation of the US-Israel relationship— and been the source of the instinctive support the American public has had for Israel—we do believe that perpetuating this relationship will depend on Israel retaining its Jewish and democratic character. Indeed, it is hard to imagine American administrations and the American public simply dismissing Palestinian calls for one person, one vote if Israel absorbs most of the West Bank.

In short, we believe that America does have a stake in the decision Israel will make as it determines its future. Israel has always had leaders who were up to historic challenges, and there is value in telling their stories now. Therefore, the book is organized around the big decisions that Israeli leaders made. Many of these leaders, such as David Ben-Gurion, Israel's first prime minister, made several momentous decisions. Ben-Gurion's most significant choice was to declare statehood, knowing that it would trigger an invasion by all the surrounding Arab states and knowing that his fledgling country would have limited external support. Like those of other leaders, some of

Ben-Gurion's decisions were strategic, visionary, and in keeping with the values he felt Israel must embody as a state with deep moral underpinnings. Others choices were not, but rather reflected what he felt was necessary for the Jewish state to survive against formidable odds. All leaders have flaws, but some rise to the moment.

There are those in Israel who believe that at times Israeli leaders may have risen to the moment, but not out of the purest of motives. In the eyes of their critics, for example, Ariel Sharon and Ehud Olmert became peace-makers not because of a higher purpose but because of corruption charges—and their belief that the media and state prosecutors would drop accusations and possible indictments against them to avoid derailing their peace efforts. Like most conspiracy theories, this one is based far more on fiction than fact. While corruption involving Israeli leaders has been part of the political landscape, it has not been a driving force in shaping Israel's evolution. Moreover, as we will show, it is not what motivated Sharon to withdraw from Gaza in 2005. Other factors did, and in other cases where a big decision was made, there wasn't even the hint or scent of corruption. The fact is that big, historic decisions in Israel have been made because Israel had leaders who were not afraid to make them. The question is why. In this book, we will look at what led Ben-Gurion, Begin, Rabin, and Sharon to make historic, transformative decisions.

Of course, not acting can also take both wisdom and courage. Levi Esh-kol in 1967 withstood enormous pressure to launch a preemptive attack in the weeks before the Six-Day War, as Egypt built up six divisions on Israel's border. Because he believed that Israel could not afford to lose American support in the event of a conflict, Eshkol resisted the pressure until it was clear that the United States was not going to do anything. For Eshkol, the lessons of the 1956 conflict, in which the Eisenhower administration threat-ened sanctions if Israel did not withdraw from the Sinai, remained very much in his mind. He believed he must heed the Johnson administration's warnings that Israel would only be alone if it acted alone. Eshkol's judgment was vindicated when President Lyndon Johnson made it clear after the war that the United States would not put pressure on Israel to withdraw from the territories without getting peace in return. Similarly, Yitzhak Shamir in

1991 came under withering pressure from many in the military and his own coalition to retaliate against Iraqi Scud missile attacks during the Gulf War. Shamir decided not to strike back, judging that doing so would alienate the Bush administration and turn a war that had pitted the world against Saddam Hussein into an Arab-Israeli conflict. Both Eshkol and Shamir demonstrated political courage, the kind that real leadership requires.

Real leadership is what will be needed if Israel's government is going to be up to the task of acting to preserve the country's character and identity. It is a decision of enormous magnitude, one that is strategic and involves Israel's basic destiny. It is the type of decision that Ben-Gurion, Begin, Rabin, and Sharon all were prepared to make in the past. For these leaders, the stakes were very high and the consequences of not acting were profound. They understood that. The context and circumstances in which they made their decisions—as well as insight into who they were and what shaped them—can provide lessons for what Israel's current prime minister or his successors must do as they face an emerging and fateful choice about Israel's future. In the end, this book is about seeing whether the factors that led Israeli leaders to make big decisions in the past can provide a guide for helping Israel's leaders decide to preserve the country's Jewish and democratic character in the future.

CHAPTER I

DAVID BEN-GURION

Ben-Gurion's Unswerving Road to Statehood

D avid Ben-Gurion was square-jawed and five foot four. His prematurely white hair conferred an aura of biblical eccentricity. By middle age, as he grew stouter, he would come to be known as "the old man." Israel's foremost novelist, Amos Oz, called him a "walking exclamation mark," projecting "awesome willpower and a volcanic temper."[1] Oz would say about Ben-Gurion that "verbal battle, not dialogue, was his habitual mode of communication." Ben-Gurion also eschewed small talk with a characteristic Israeli scorn, priding himself on discussing issues that mattered. In the pre-state years, these issues were invariably Jewish sovereignty and Zionism.

The founding father of the State of Israel, David Ben-Gurion never deviated from his goal of establishing a state for the Jewish people in their historic homeland. Through the Holocaust, conflict with Palestine's Arabs, disputes with the British, and fierce debates and clashes of personality within the Zionist movement, Ben-Gurion remained committed to his objective, even as he was agile in pursuing his goal. Against all odds, under his watch an ancient state was reborn. His unwavering goal was Jewish sovereignty. Ben-Gurion embraced with singular focus connecting people with the land, a strategy based on Jewish immigration and enlisting a major power to back Zionism

and its push for mass Jewish immigration to Palestine. Indeed, he judged colleagues based on their commitment to this endeavor. Yet despite his unwillingness to cede ground in polemical disputes, Ben-Gurion repeatedly proved
he could adapt and even admit error, when doing so furthered his goals. He
was also a realist, seeking achievable rather than ideal ends. Informing his
realism was a deep knowledge of geopolitics, based on voluminous reading,
setting him apart from the provincialism that beset some of his peers.

Ben-Gurion is known as one of modern history's great autodidacts, and
he kept an estimated eighteen thousand books.[2] Before statehood, while
abroad as head of the Jewish Agency, the proto-government of the Zionist
movement, he spent his meager pay buying books and shipping them home.
Book buying appears to have been Ben-Gurion's lone departure from strict
frugality. The Israeli founding father was also a prolific diarist, recording not
only his personal reflections but also massive amounts of often extremely
precise data, down to the number of rifles possessed by the Yishuv, the pre-
state Jewish community in Palestine, should war break out. His diaries, like
him, were purposeful and focused. He offered few details about his personal life, yet the diaries capture the enormous amount of information he
absorbed to build the Jewish state.

During the 1930s, events in both Europe and Palestine led Ben-Gurion
to four broad conclusions. The first was that Zionism was a far more urgent imperative than he'd originally thought. He foresaw the existential
peril faced by the Jews of Europe and how Zionism offered a solution. After
two thousand years of dispersion and persecution, Jewish power had never
looked so attractive—and a Jewish state never so necessary.

Second, Ben-Gurion understood, belatedly, that Jewish statehood
would come at a steep price. Earlier he had felt the Zionists could evade
major resistance, but his thinking shifted after the Arab riots in Palestine
and Britain's recalculations in light of an impending world war. In 1936,
he admitted publicly that he had failed to properly account for Arab nationalism in Palestine, adopting the view, as a result, that the land would have
to be divided. His talks, though they failed to gain compromise with Arab
leaders in Palestine in the 1930s, were aimed at mitigating Palestinian Arab
hostilities against Zionism.

Ben-Gurion staked out his position based on a belief in the justness of the Zionist cause and a willingness to sacrifice, defying critics to his right, who believed force alone was sufficient, and to his left, who thought pure reason could win out and force was unnecessary. In his worldview, force could only succeed if people across the globe perceived the cause to be just. Ready to sacrifice, Ben-Gurion, before virtually anyone else, prepared for a war with not just Palestinian Arabs but with the cluster of surrounding Arab states as well.

Third, he foresaw a shift by London toward the Arab capitals, whose support the British would need in the looming confrontation with Germany, whereas previously Ben-Gurion had believed British-led diplomacy would guide Zionists to their state—consistent with the Balfour Declaration and the Mandate for Palestine. The coming war, he thought, would supersede the British commitment to the Zionists. Correspondingly, he began to see the United States as the world-power sponsor the Zionists could count on and, in turn, the importance of mobilizing US public opinion to boost governmental support for Jewish sovereignty. He also understood at the end of the 1930s and 1940s that there was great potential for support of Zionism from the vast numbers of newly immigrated European Jews to America. In that, he showed enormous foresight as he traveled America speaking then on behalf of Zionism.

Fourth, Ben-Gurion grew increasingly focused on establishing *mamlakhtiyut*—loosely translated as "sovereignty"—in Palestine. Mamlakhtiyut was a process with two equally important dimensions. One aspect was establishing a Jewish state, creating a political entity in the Holy Land by building new proto-governmental institutions. The other aspect was transforming the consciousness of the Jews who came to Palestine from all over the world and fostering among them a shared political culture and sense of community. Traditionally, Jewish communities in the diaspora were insular in nature, worrying primarily about their physical survival—which was often contingent upon currying favor with local authorities—and the transmission of religious tradition. Now, in Ben-Gurion's vision, the new Jews of Palestine should see themselves as pioneers who would devote their lives to deepening Jewish sovereignty in the Land of Israel. This idea would create pushback among Ben-Gurion's political opponents, who saw this as jettisoning thousands of years of Jewish religious heritage. Mamlakhtiyut would also entail Jewish responsibility over a wide array of aspects of daily life that Jews previously hadn't participated in.

In the short term, Ben-Gurion saw the infrastructure of the state, including a formal Jewish military, as essential, given the inevitability of an armed conflict with the Arabs. During World War II, when the future Israeli leader perceived the Yishuv to be acutely vulnerable to attack, he became even more convinced of the need for such an apparatus. Later, faced with the scale of the Holocaust and a coming war with the Arabs, Ben-Gurion remained steadfast in his focus on the three pillars of statehood: immigration, land, and defense. These he viewed as mutually reinforcing. More immigrants enabled greater defense and greater national security would attract more immigrants.

Democratic values were no less indispensable for Ben-Gurion, who believed a Jewish state must be rooted in universal values worthy of the effort. To be sure, the Middle East region lacked the vibrant democratic traditions of the West, which Ben-Gurion particularly admired in the US and British contexts. Unequivocally, a Jewish state would require a Jewish majority to be truly democratic.

ORIGINS AND JOURNEY TO PALESTINE

David Ben-Gurion was born David Gruen in Plonsk, a small, predominantly Jewish town forty-five miles northwest of Warsaw, in 1886.[3] Both his grandfather, Zvi, and father, Avigdor, engaged informally in legal work, writing petitions to the authorities for townspeople and peasants, as was common in such communities.[4] Zvi and Avigdor believed there was no contradiction between religious orthodoxy and intellectually embracing wider currents of change that were engulfing eastern Europe.* The family was animated by the precepts of the Jewish Enlightenment, or Haskalah, which had unsettled

---

* Avigdor, however, slapped a young Ben-Gurion when he stopped maintaining religious tradition.

shtetl culture in Europe over the previous century. Ben-Gurion's family also embraced Zionism, still a minority position among the Jews of eastern Europe. Avigdor was one of the local leaders of the Hovevei Zion ("Lovers of Zion") group. Growing up in a Zionist family, Ben-Gurion was exposed to the ideology from a young age. From his grandfather, Ben-Gurion learned Hebrew at age three. When Theodor Herzl, the founder of political Zionism, rose to prominence before the First Zionist Congress, held in Basel in 1897, the Gruen household hailed him as the Messiah. Avigdor subsequently wrote Herzl, soliciting advice regarding his brilliant son David, but he received no reply.[5] While still a child, Ben-Gurion declared that he would one day make aliyah (literally "ascend") to the Land of Israel. At age fourteen, Ben-Gurion and his peers founded Ezra, a group that sought to teach Hebrew and Jewish history to children of the religious poor.[6]

At the 1903 Zionist Congress, however, Herzl committed what Ben-Gurion saw as a grave error when he agreed in principle, in talks with British colonial secretary Joseph Chamberlain, to accept Uganda (today's Kenya) as a temporary home for the Jews.[7] Earlier that year, a pogrom in Kishinev had killed dozens of Jews and injured hundreds, adding urgency to Herzl's mission.[8] Herzl considered the measure a stopgap, with the quest for Palestine to be resumed when feasible, but others in the Zionist camp viewed the Uganda plan as sacrilege.[9] In response, the teenage Ben-Gurion decided to set an example by making aliyah.

Thus, in 1906, Ben-Gurion moved to the Yishuv, the relatively small community of primarily young pioneering Jews in Palestine, with a few other Plonsk Jews.[10] Doing so at the time was audacious. (Between 1881 and 1923, approximately 115,000 European Jews immigrated to Palestine, versus the 2.5 million who moved to the United States between 1881 and 1924.[11]) The challenges of life in Palestine included an unfamiliar landscape and the grueling work needed to subsist on agriculture. No doubt, an unwavering ideological commitment guided the small proportion who stayed. Ben-Gurion once estimated that 90 percent of halutzim (pioneers) eventually left for easier lives elsewhere.[12]

Briefly, Ben-Gurion lived on an agricultural settlement in Sejera, in the Galilee, where all work was done by Jews. But his talents lay mainly in political organizing, so he moved to Jerusalem, where he served as an editor for *Ha'achdut,* the newspaper for the socialist Zionist party Poalei Zion.[13] Ben-Gurion had first become involved with Poalei Zion back in Poland, when it was founded in Warsaw during the Russian Revolution of 1905. The speeches calling for freedom and justice during the revolution impressed him deeply. Ben-Gurion, supporting himself by teaching in the Polish city at the time, attended Poalei Zion's first conference and joined the party. He began adhering to several socialist concepts, such as the notion of class struggle between the bourgeoisie and the proletariat and the supposed virtue of the proletariat revolutionaries compared to the iniquities of the upper classes. He envisioned establishing a socialist society within a Jewish nation-state in Palestine. Socialism would remain an integral component of Ben-Gurion's Zionist ideology for decades. As he grew older, his views on the centrality of agriculture and socialism would undergo a subtle but profound change as he realized the primacy of industry and urban life to a new modern state.[14] It was in *Ha'achdut*'s second issue that he first signed his name Ben-Gurion instead of Gruen.[15] Some speculate the source was Yosef Ben-Gurion, a leader during the second Jewish commonwealth as it faced Roman subjugation in 66 CE.[16]

Jewish communal leaders, wherever they lived, understood that, as a minority, local politics required creating relationships with those in power. Herzl had done it by seeking a meeting with the Ottoman sultan. In these early years before World War I, Ben-Gurion believed he could advance the cause of Zionism by lobbying or working with the Ottoman authorities, who at the time permitted minorities to be represented in parliament.[17] Thus, he and his close friend Yitzhak Ben-Zvi moved to Istanbul to study Turkish law.[18] But the Turkish option did not ultimately pan out for Ben-Gurion. Although he stayed in Istanbul for two years, almost completing his studies, the Turkish attitude toward Zionism turned hostile at the start of World War I. Such hostility, amplified by the Young Turks' leadership, was eventually translated into a decline in the population of the Jewish community from eighty-five thousand to between fifty thousand and fifty-seven thousand.[19] Ben-Gurion, despite expressing his loyalty to the Ottoman Empire and support for the Turks and their German and Austrian allies, was deported from Turkey in March 1915.[20]

It was during Ben-Gurion's next stop, in New York, that he concluded the United States, not Turkey, offered the Zionists their best hope for an eventual sponsor. Ben-Gurion was wrong about a potential US role during World War I, but he would revisit this view by the end of the 1930s much more seriously. Yet this realization also coincided with a momentous gesture by Britain. In November 1917, through the Balfour Declaration, the British declared their support for "the establishment in Palestine of a national home for the Jewish people."[21] Now the very government set to take over Palestine amid crumbling Ottoman power had given its official imprimatur to the Zionist project after over 1,800 years of Jewish powerlessness. Ben-Gurion's dream of Jewish sovereignty was no longer a fantasy.

While in the United States, Ben-Gurion also joined the Jewish Legion of the British army, the first Jewish unit to be recognized by a major power.[22] Ben-Gurion still perceived that America was the great Zionist hope, but this was an opportunity for the young Zionist to fight for his cause. In 1918, Ben-Gurion returned to Palestine as Turkish forces were defeated by the British.

In Palestine, Ben-Gurion also endeavored, with his intellectual soul mate Berl Katznelson,* to unite the various socialist Zionist factions.[23] Although eventually failing in this bid, they did start a new party, Ahdut Ha'avodah (Unity of Labor), with a platform that called for both protecting Jews in the diaspora and "international guarantees for the establishment of a free Jewish state in Palestine, which until such time as a Jewish majority was created in Palestine, would be under the aegis of a representative of the League of Nations."[24] The platform was significant for marking Ben-Gurion's early public call for a Jewish state,** which would have been unfathomable before Balfour.[25] Moreover, the Jewish-majority clause made clear the future state must be democratic based on demographics. At the time, Palestinian Arabs far outnumbered Jews, requiring a major immigration push to establish a

---

* While sitting in a hospital in Cairo afflicted with dysentery during his time in the Jewish Legion, Ben-Gurion read an essay by Katznelson, already a Zionist intellectual, entitled "Toward the Forthcoming Days." He immediately realized that he and Katznelson were "of the same mind." Ben-Gurion promptly went to go find Katznelson, who was also serving in the Jewish Legion, in the unit's camp and proposed they join forces. A historic alliance was born.

** Ben-Gurion would make the same call for a Jewish state in New York in 1942.

state.[26] Immigrants would be the raw material that built the state in the Promised Land.

After World War I, rising Arab nationalism led to riots in 1920 and 1921.[27] These events challenged the assumption by Ben-Gurion—who then headed the Histadrut, the nascent Zionist trade union—that working-class Arabs and Jews could cooperate to address common problems and thereby avoid a clash.[28] To this end, Ben-Gurion insisted that "under no circumstances are the rights of these [Arab] inhabitants to be infringed upon."[29] He declared that "the mission of Zionism" was not to dispossess Arabs but rather to "settle in those places where the present inhabitants of the land have not established themselves and are unable to do so."[30] Ben-Gurion genuinely believed Zionism would raise living standards for Arabs as well as Jews. The British, for their part, did not generally expect a conflict either, reflecting the scale of naiveté regarding the clashing nationalist claims that at the time were small but would increase in size.

By the end of the decade, previously optimistic observers were compelled to shed their illusions. Violence was sparked by Palestinian displeasure over the use of screens by Jews at the Western Wall, designed to allow group prayer while separating men from women. (Until then, Jewish prayer at the wall was tolerated by Muslims, so long as it did not involve any infrastructure that implied permanence at a site adjacent to Muslim prayer.) On August 16, 1929, a teenage Jew was stabbed, and ensuing riots on the Temple Mount/Haram al-Sharif caused three Jewish and three Arab deaths on August 22. The next day, in Hebron, Arab attacks killed sixty-seven Jews and prompted more than four hundred to flee, effectively wiping out the holy city's old Jewish community. In all, 133 Jews were killed by Arabs and 104 Arabs were killed by the British, with an additional six Arabs killed by Jews, before the British restored relative calm.[31]

The growth of Arab nationalism created problems not only for the Jews but also for the British administrators in the Palestine mandate. As early as the 1920s, the British had sensed their role in Palestine would entail far more than fostering Zionism as called for under the Balfour Declaration. Instead, they effectively acted as a mediator of competing interests, a shift the Zionists saw as a betrayal of the Balfour promise. Furthermore, since Britain viewed itself as a global power, the government increasingly perceived a national interest in enlisting broad support from the Arabs in the Middle East, which implied a cooling toward Zionism. This dynamic presented a challenge for Zionism. In a world where great powers dictated when (and whether) new states would be established, British support was essential.

Adolf Hitler posed the other monumental challenge to Zionism, a challenge Ben-Gurion identified early on.[32] Indeed, in parallel with uniting and empowering Jews long dispersed around the globe, the Zionist movement also sought to provide a haven for oppressed and threatened Jews.

During the 1930s, Ben-Gurion was rising to greater prominence within the Zionist leadership in Palestine, well beyond his role as trade-union head. But another power center of international Zionism existed in Britain, led by Dr. Chaim Weizmann.

Weizmann was beloved by Jews worldwide, having ascended from the humble world of eastern Europe's shtetls to the highest echelons of diplomacy. Born in the Russian Empire, Weizmann immigrated to Manchester, England, and trained as a chemist. In 1915, at the height of Britain's titanic struggle against Germany during World War I, Weizmann decisively buttressed the British war effort by discovering a fermentation process for producing the chemical compound acetone, used in munitions.[33] This monumental achievement won him prominence and access to the corridors of power in London. Weizmann was subsequently pivotal in getting the British government to adopt the Balfour Declaration and in working with London as it assumed the mandate in Palestine.

Ben-Gurion, sooner than Weizmann, recognized the grave threat the Nazis posed to European Jewry. He declared on July 2, 1932, six months before Hitler came to power, at a meeting of the Labor Party (known by its Hebrew acronym Mapai), that "the ground was burning" under the feet of the Jewish people.[34] "[Jewish] existence," he continued, "is being steadily destroyed, and over whom hangs the threat of physical and spiritual annihilation, decay and destruction."[35]

In late August 1933, Ben-Gurion was at the Munich train station on one of his many European trips when he read Hitler's *Mein Kampf*.[36] In

October, Ben-Gurion would be named head of the Jewish Agency's political department, a precursor to his leadership of the entire agency two years later.[37] In January 1934, at a trade-union conference, Ben-Gurion predicted, in stunning detail, Germany's invasion of eastern Europe and its triggering of another war. He declared: "Hitler's rule places the entire Jewish people in danger. Hitlerism is at war not only with the Jews of Germany but with Jews the world over. . . . Perhaps only four or five years (if not less) stand between us and that day of wrath."[38] (World War II would break out in September 1939, just over five years after Ben-Gurion's prediction.)

In October 1934, in outlining what he considered the right response to the Hitler menace, Ben-Gurion declared that "the mission of our generation was . . . the creation of a powerful Jewish presence in Palestine."[39] A failure of Zionism to rise to this occasion, he later asserted, would be nothing less than a betrayal.

By September 1935, the Nuremberg Laws had been passed, institutionalizing discrimination against German Jews, including stripping them of their German citizenship.[40] In such circumstances, Jewish immigration to Palestine was a necessity. A Jewish majority in Palestine would not only ensure a democratic state, it would also meet the moral imperative of saving lives. "A question of life or death," Ben-Gurion called the situation in a 1936 speech.[41] This existential challenge would be invoked relentlessly by Ben-Gurion during the rise and rule of the Nazis. Zionism could not afford to fail, he was saying, with the stakes for European Jewry as high as they could be. In the early months of 1937, he presciently used the Hebrew term *shoah*, or "catastrophe," with which the Holocaust later came to be associated.[42]

Immediately after Kristallnacht, the pogrom that ripped through Germany and Austria on November 9, 1938, Ben-Gurion sounded the alarm in a letter to British colonial secretary Malcolm MacDonald, asserting that "millions of our people face destruction."[43] In June 1939, just months before Germany invaded Poland, Ben-Gurion stated in a speech, "There may be a war which will visit upon us catastrophe," a war in which Hitler can be relied on to first destroy "all the Jews of Europe."[44] After the German invasion, Ben-Gurion declared that "tens and hundreds of thousands in Poland are doomed to slaughter" and that other countries could be next.[45] As

Ben-Gurion put it, in World War I, "the most important limb of the body of the Jewish people, Russian Jewry, was torn away for a long period [due to Soviet communism]," and now a similar fate would befall the Polish Jews.[46] Transforming the ensuing calamity into a call to action, he declared, "The world war of 1914–1918 brought us the Balfour Declaration. This time, we have to bring about a Jewish state."[47]

EARLY LEADERSHIP CHALLENGES

In these years of foreboding, in part because of a restrictive US immigration statute enacted in 1924, the Palestine option moved from the margins to the mainstream for central and eastern European Jews seeking to escape worsening anti-Semitism.[48] One measure of this shift was the surge in voters at the Zionist Congress. Another was the population of the Yishuv, which would grow from two hundred thousand to four hundred thousand between 1930 and 1936.[49] During these years, 1935 was by far the high-water mark, with the Yishuv welcoming more than sixty-six thousand newcomers.[50] Many of those coming were highly educated, and these refugees would create a middle-class foundation for the Yishuv. The population was no longer just young idealists and religious devotees. With the looming Nazi threat, European Jews from Germany, Austria, Czechoslovakia, and Poland would be integral to the new Jewish national community forming in Palestine. In Ben-Gurion's eyes, the Arabs would not be bought off—even if absentee Arab landowners of estates and resident Palestinian smallholders of land were willing to sell to Jewish land agents for the establishment of Jewish villages, communal settlements, and parts of urban areas. Ben-Gurion and other Jewish leaders did not discount Arab public opposition to Zionism, but these leaders witnessed consistent Palestinian participation in land sales to Jewish buyers. At the end of December 1937, at a meeting of Jewish land experts, with more Arab offers to sell than Zionists had funds to buy, Ben-Gurion told those assembled that acquiring these lands was "nothing less than rescuing the homeland."[51]

Ben-Gurion saw the gathering storm in Europe as providing a reservoir for immigration to Palestine. He would increasingly visit Poland, at the time home to some three million Jews, as well as Germany and surrounding countries. These trips kept him apprised of the fears of European Jews. Some would succeed in getting British certificates to enter Palestine, and some would not. Many attempted to migrate elsewhere. Some still held out hope that Hitler's rule would pass.

The rise of Ben-Gurion, of course, did not happen unopposed. He led the largest movement, Labor, widely considered the leading arm of mainstream, practical Zionism. It favored both political outreach to big powers such as Britain and ongoing internal development, fueled by a pioneering spirit in agricultural settlements. The "new Jew" ethos was an integral part of Labor's ideology—an ideology that sought to create a physical, self-sufficient society divorced from Jewish life in Europe, with its yeshiva bookishness and peddling trades. While working the land, these new Jews sought to enact the principles of socialism in seeking a more just world. The Zionist phrase "to build and to be rebuilt" exemplified this dual desire for sovereignty and for reshaping the Jew as someone who tilled the soil instead of sitting in rabbinical seminaries. Ben-Gurion would seek to mold the character of the new Jewish immigrants, starting down the path of mamlakhtiyut.

The most significant opposition to Labor came from the Revisionist movement, led by Vladimir Jabotinsky, a writer, playwright, and editor originally from Odessa, known as a liberal metropolis in the Russian Empire.[52] Unlike the Labor activists, the Revisionists had a much more jaundiced view of both Arabs and foreign powers. Jabotinsky did not share Ben-Gurion's belief in coexistence through Jewish economic cooperation with the Arabs. Both sides, he contended, would inevitably defend their respective interests and national pride.

In "The Iron Wall," published in 1923 as two essays, Jabotinsky expressed his view that only Zionist military strength could compel Arab acceptance. Only once Arabs acknowledged that the Zionists were here to stay, in his view, could the Jews make concessions based on their military strength.[53] According to this worldview, premature concessions would only encourage Arab demands for more. On the domestic front, the Revisionists rejected socialism, viewing it as antithetical to Zionism.[54]

Ben-Gurion and Jabotinsky were both ardent Zionists. They did agree, in theory, on certain issues: namely, that an increasingly ambivalent Britain and an assertive Arab population in Palestine threatened the Zionists, and that Zionism needed to build up its own defense capability. But Ben-Gurion believed in a more bottom-up, practical Zionism. This meant that Jews couldn't just amass armaments, they also had to cultivate the land. He believed, moreover, that reconciliation with the Arabs must at least be tested. In addition, he thought the Revisionists echoed too closely the militaristic movements of 1930s Italy and even Germany.[55]

Tensions between the two wings flared often, in Europe and within the Yishuv, and at times turned violent. In 1933, Labor blamed the Revisionists for the killing of one of its leading members, Chaim Arlosoroff, who had negotiated a controversial deal* with the Nazis that enabled Jews to immigrate to Palestine with their property.[56] Such an assassination was unprecedented in modern times.** In addition, worker strikes sometimes sparked violent reprisal by the Revisionists. In Europe, meanwhile, speeches by Ben-Gurion to Labor Zionist groups invariably drew jeering opponents from Betar, the Revisionist youth movement.

The Labor-Revisionist divide would preoccupy Ben-Gurion for the entirety of his political life. He unapologetically, and stubbornly, rejected what he perceived as the shortsightedness of the Revisionist worldview. And the Labor patriarch could be vindictive, especially after the state was established. His party blacklisted former Revisionists, then linked to the Herut party, from political leadership positions and refused to let Jabotinsky, who died in 1940, be reinterred in Israel. Moreover, he treated the longtime right-wing

---

* It is worth noting that Ben-Gurion himself was not opposed to negotiating with Hitler over Jewish repatriation and property in the early years of Nazi rule, an indication of how he was tactically flexible in pursuit of his overall goals. In contrast, Jabotinsky was vehemently opposed to any dealings with Germany during this period.

** In June 1934, Revisionist Avraham Stavsky was convicted of killing Arlosoroff and sentenced to death. He then appealed and won the appeal due to insufficient evidence. In 1981, then prime minister Menachem Begin, a Revisionist, called for an investigative committee to revisit the issue, after so many decades. The fact that this issue didn't subside over this period gives a sense of the immense potency of this rare assassination that divided Zionism.

opposition leader Menachem Begin with outright contempt, referring to him in Knesset sessions as the "person sitting next to Mr. Bader" rather than by his name.[57]

Ben-Gurion would not let pressures from the Jewish right and intercommunal hostilities prevent him from pressing for a resolution with the Arabs, at least until the Arab uprising that began in 1936. He saw this as crucial for the Yishuv, especially given the British drift toward the Arab states and his belief in peace and social justice.[58] Exacerbating tensions with the Palestinian Arabs, he reasoned at the time, would only prompt worsening ties with the British. In addition, Ben-Gurion believed that his own "iron wall"— steady, increasing immigration—would compel the Arabs to make a deal. They would have no choice but to accept the Jewish presence in the country. As Ben-Gurion wrote in 1933, "In the course of four to five years we must bring in a quarter of a million Jews and the Arab question will be solved."[59] In prospective conversations with Arab leaders, Ben-Gurion, ever the pragmatist, was prepared to discuss a future Jewish sovereign entity as part of a wider nonbinding Arab Middle East regional federation.

The question he confronted, however, was with whom among the Arabs of Palestine to talk. In the 1920s, the British appointed Hajj Amin al-Husseini, scion of a prominent Jerusalem family, as the grand mufti (a religious leader with considerable political authority) of Jerusalem.[60] Although Husseini was widely and justifiably viewed as a rejectionist who helped fuel the 1929 Arab riots, Ben-Gurion wanted to talk with him anyway. Buffeted by charges that he was capitulating to violence, the Labor leader found support from his close friend Berl Katznelson, who, during a key meeting, mused, "I would say that I would meet with the mufti to discuss preventing pogroms and perhaps even for political negotiations. Is there anyone here among us who can call such a meeting dishonorable?"[61] The term *pogrom* painfully and effectively evoked the Jewish experience in Europe, and in August 1934 Ben-Gurion received the needed authorization from fellow Zionist officials to meet with Husseini to discuss peace.[62]

To get to Husseini, Ben-Gurion worked through Musa Alami, a Cambridge University graduate who had formerly served as personal secretary to the British high commissioner and was now assistant attorney general for the British mandatory government in Palestine.[63] At his first meeting with Alami, Ben-Gurion stressed the economic benefits that would accrue to local Arabs if they worked with the Zionists. But Alami was not impressed. Chaim Weizmann had made the same case to Emir Faisal in 1919 that the Arabs could benefit from the coming Zionist enterprises. As Ben-Gurion reported the exchange, "Musa Alami told me that he would prefer the land to remain poor and desolate even for another hundred years, until the Arabs themselves were capable of developing it and making it flower."[64]

In response, Ben-Gurion demonstrated a keen ability to empathize with the Arabs. He later talked about seeing Zionism "through Arab eyes" and said about Alami, "I felt that as a patriotic Arab he had every right to this view."[65] He would continue to meet with Alami and other Arabs. Talking with Auni Abdul Hadi, the leader of Istiqlal (a pan-Arab nationalist group), in Palestine on July 18, 1934, he said, "We had been compelled to come and settle without the consent of the Arabs and we would continue to do so in the future if necessary, but we would prefer to act on the basis of an understanding and mutual agreement."[66] He offered: "We would agree to support the establishment of an Arab Federation in the neighboring countries and an alliance of the Jewish State with that federation so that the Arabs in Palestine . . . would not a hold a minority position, since they would be linked with millions of Arabs in the neighboring countries."[67] Ben-Gurion made clear that the objective of Zionism "is the independence of the Jewish people in Palestine."[68] In return for Arab support for this proposition, Ben-Gurion promised that the Arabs would not just remain on their land, but that Jews would use their "political influence, financial means, and moral support to bring about the independence and unity of the Arab people."[69]

The Arab federation proposed by Ben-Gurion with Alami would include Iraq as well as Jordan, Arab Palestine, and the new independent Zionist entity; Iraq and Jordan were, like Palestine, ruled by the British at this time. When Alami asked Ben-Gurion if he would curtail immigration to ensure the Jewish population would not exceed one million within the decade, Ben-Gurion demurred. He would not veer from the core principle: unfettered Jewish immigration, which provided the foundation for his new state and national community. He replied that he would prefer "instead of

impeding our growth . . . to work out a plan together . . . to accelerate
Arab development. We would open schools in every village, we would teach
the Arabs new working methods, we would improve their farms."[70] He put
forth a basis for an Arab-Jewish alliance wherein Jews "invested manpower,
organization, technology and money in the development of the Arab economy, as we have done for the development of the Jewish economy. The entire
economic and cultural condition of the Arabs might change. The alliance
between us had to be built on mutual aid and not on mutual hindrance."[71]

Ben-Gurion viewed Arab nationalism as part of a wider Middle East
reality, not necessarily as a particular goal for local Palestinians. Ben-
Gurion argued in a Warsaw speech in October 1935, "For us Palestine is
everything, while for the Arabs it is only two percent of all Arab lands,"
adding that "greater Zionism will find a common language with the future
greater Arab movement."[72] He felt he could finesse the issue with local Palestinians through a combination of economic development and diplomacy,
thereby showing that even with Jewish autonomy, the Jews could contribute
meaningfully to an Arab confederation. Yet Ben-Gurion's views would shift
sharply in 1936, as a result of his conversations with Arab interlocutors and
that year's outbreak of hostilities.

In an April 1936 discussion with the Arab intellectual George Antonius, an Eastern Orthodox Christian who shortly thereafter authored *The
Arab Awakening,* a seminal work on Arab nationalism, the two debated their
competing visions. Antonius was paraphrased by Ben-Gurion as having "understood all the arguments of the Jews, but the Arabs had no other course
but to fight against the 'flooding' of the country . . . which would undermine the very existence of the Arab people."[73] Antonius added, "Mutual
understanding was out of the question, since these aspirations conflicted and
there was no way of reconciling them."[74]

Ben-Gurion retorted, "For even if Palestine, as a result of immigration,
became a predominantly Jewish country, there was no danger to Arab culture or freedom. Even when the Arabs became a minority in the limited
area of Palestine, they would not be a minority as members of the greater
Arab nation."[75] He understood the Arab desire for "Palestine, too, to be
completely Arab." He added, "For us, on the other hand, it might be more

convenient if there were no Arabs there at all. But . . . it was not out of mere emotion or caprice that we were returning to this country. For us it was a question of survival."[76] Ben-Gurion also made his case to Antonius that Jewish autonomy need not involve Arab dispossession. His movement sought, he said, to settle only as many Jews as could "create new possibilities of existence without ousting the Arabs or reducing their ability to support themselves. That was the only restriction we accepted, and we accepted it willingly from conviction, for both moral and political reasons."[77]

Meeting again three days after the outbreak of the 1936 Arab riots, Ben-Gurion and Antonius once more failed to overcome their differences on immigration. Insisting that the Jews and Arabs faced a fundamentally asymmetric challenge in Palestine, Ben-Gurion claimed that "the size of our population in Eretz Israel would determine our fate, but the size of the Arab population in Eretz Israel would not determine the fate of the Arab people."[78]

The focus on Jewish immigration put him at odds with his dovish critic Judah Magnes, an American-born Reform rabbi who became head of the nascent Jerusalem-based Hebrew University. Magnes was associated with the Brit Shalom movement, which advocated a binational Arab-Jewish state. In Ben-Gurion's eyes, there was no worse idea than Magnes's suggestion that Jewish immigration be capped, confining the Jews to minority status in Palestine and denying them their own sovereign home. Ben-Gurion told Magnes in March 1936 that "the difference between you and me is that you are ready to sacrifice immigration for peace, while I am not, though peace is dear to me. And even if I were prepared to make a concession, the Jews of Poland and Germany would not be, because they have no other choice. For them, immigration comes before peace."[79]

Although his talks with Arabs in Palestine had already diminished his expectations about peace, the 1936 riots hit Ben-Gurion like a lightning bolt. He now realized that he had ignored the feeling among many Arabs in Palestine that they constituted a unique Palestinian nation; he had previously thought that they were simply "fragments" of a larger Arab nation. The latter would be compatible with the establishment of a Jewish state in Palestine, because even if such a state were created, the Arabs would still have a state or states in the vast majority of the Middle East. But the former would likely be incompatible, because it might mean depriving the Palestinians of their own state. Ben-Gurion's new understanding would hence require a crucial midcourse correction: acknowledging Palestinian Arab nationalism without yielding in his drive for Jewish immigration as the main method of attaining Jewish sovereignty. Could Jewish and Palestinian Arab nationalism be reconciled?

In remarks at a Jewish Agency meeting in May 1936, Ben-Gurion indicated his dawning awareness of Palestinian nationalism. He explained, "The cause of the Arabs' war today is primarily their fear of Jewish growth in Palestine, in numbers and in strength that can bring about Jewish rule. And then they will face destruction."[80] In a speech to the Histadrut in February 1937, he went further, saying that "the Arab inhabitants of Palestine should enjoy all civic and political rights, not only as individuals, but as a *national* group, just like the Jews."[81]

Ben-Gurion rarely admitted mistakes, but now he was willing to do so. What made it especially difficult for him to acknowledge a Zionist-Palestinian struggle, as opposed to one pitting Jews against the larger Arab community of the Middle East, was that for him Zionism must always be on the side of moral justice, but only so long as this did not negate the pursuit of Jewish sovereignty. The denial of the rights of others, he knew, would challenge that basic precept. Yet while Ben-Gurion recognized the reality of competing nationalisms, his friend Katznelson did not, maintaining that the ongoing riots and killings were spawned by religious fanaticism, not nationalism.[82] Ben-Gurion knew better. "We ourselves, by our very presence and progress, have nurtured the Arab nationalist movement," he said.[83]

Ben-Gurion would not forsake his belief that Zionism must remain a moral movement. Two months into the 1936–1939 Arab uprising, on May 19, 1936, he declared at a Jewish Agency Executive meeting: "I have no doubts about our full right to a Jewish State in Eretz Yisrael. I have perfect faith in its possibility, but I do not believe that it is possible to deny all rights to the Arabs. We have no moral right to do that."[84] In effect, while recognizing the merit of the Arab argument, Ben-Gurion believed his own side had superior merit, built on the looming threat that Hitler posed to European Jews and the fact that the Jews, unlike the Arabs, were stateless.

At the time, Ben-Gurion still hoped that the British could be a fair arbiter in any final agreement, especially given his perception of deep Arab resistance to partition. For this reason, as well as the initially very tough British response to the Arab uprising, Ben-Gurion was keen to avoid conflict with London—yet this, too, was bound to be difficult.

GROWING TENSIONS WITH THE BRITISH AND WITH WEIZMANN

Ben-Gurion hoped and expected Jewish immigration to grow from its peak in 1935 due to the Nazi threat, but he was never complacent, always concerned that the British might impose curbs on entrants in response to Arab resistance and violence. In seeking to counter Arab pressure to kill the Zionist project by shutting off immigration, Ben-Gurion counted on the movement's senior statesman, Chaim Weizmann.[85]

As previously mentioned, Weizmann had cooperated with the British in formulating what became the Balfour Declaration. He had worked tirelessly with Prime Minister David Lloyd George and Foreign Minister Arthur Balfour,* and his efforts yielded a major landmark in Zionism's quest for Jewish sovereignty.[86] This made Weizmann an icon of Zionism, and he was hailed for completing what Theodor Herzl's political Zionism had begun in 1897 by garnering vital support from a major power for the movement. Critically, this also made him an ideal interlocutor with the British.[87]

In his early career, Ben-Gurion revered Weizmann for his unmatched ability to stir widespread Jewish public support for the movement. He made

---

* British support for Zionism was rooted in myriad factors, one of them being the religious idea of restorationism, a belief that the biblical Jews should be returned to Israel as a precursor to Jesus's second coming. Another belief held that the Jews would be a modernizing force, helping the Middle East develop economically following Britain's takeover of former Ottoman territories after World War I. The Jews would also be pro-Western and so would be strategically convenient for the British, who wanted to maintain their control from the Suez Canal to India. Given the politically sensitive idea of tying Britain to the United States, London saw that support for the Zionist cause during wartime would be attractive to US president Woodrow Wilson, a great believer in ethnic self-determination. Britain also feared that Germany was working on its own version of Balfour, and might weaken American resolve during World War I.

all the right arguments and did so with passion. Moreover, Ben-Gurion saw Weizmann as indispensable to keeping Britain on Zionism's side; the Labor leader understood he needed his counterpart.[88] But their relationship would never be easy. Weizmann essentially served as Zionism's senior London-based diplomat—even though he also had a home in Rehovot—while Ben-Gurion engaged in diplomacy, served as a politician in Palestine, and ran development in the Yishuv.[89] Weizmann, whose influence and legacy were secure due to his instrumental role in the Balfour Declaration, was able to dedicate himself to high diplomacy. Weizmann was indeed accountable to a World Zionist Congress and its assorted institutions, but its members were scattered throughout the world. On a daily basis, he had considerable autonomy. Meanwhile, Ben-Gurion had to constantly grapple with domestic opposition from his fellow Zionists in the Yishuv, and he had to determine how or whether to calibrate domestic opinions to be in line with Weizmann. Most importantly, serious fissures emerged over immigration; Weizmann felt the need to manage British sensitivities, while Ben-Gurion hewed to what he saw as an unbreakable principle fundamental to building the state.

In response to the Arab riots of 1936, the idea of limiting Jewish immigration to Palestine gained greater currency. (These same riots would compel the British to later form the Palestine Royal Commission, known as the Peel Commission for its leader, Lord Robert Peel, amid hopes of easing the situation on the ground and navigating a path forward.[90]) In this context, the first serious friction between Ben-Gurion and Weizmann arose when the latter suggested that a yearlong halt to Jewish immigration might indicate Zionist openness to a middle ground.[91] Ben-Gurion responded with fury, believing that such a move would send all the wrong messages by indicating that Arab violence could successfully halt immigration and the Zionist cause. Moreover, he was convinced that what might begin as a temporary suspension would become permanent. Worse still, the desperate Jews of Europe would be denied a haven—and thus betrayed.

An apparent miscommunication added to the bitterness between Ben-Gurion and Weizmann. The former thought he had successfully shut down the immigration pause idea in a meeting with his British counterpart, but in a meeting on June 9, 1936, between Weizmann and visiting Nuri as-Said, foreign minister for newly independent Iraq, this was apparently discussed.[92] During this visit, Nuri also met with British foreign minister Anthony Eden's advisors. On June 20, Eden informed his colleagues of the plan to temporarily halt Jewish immigration.[93] On June 30, the new British official in charge of Palestine, Colonial Secretary William Ormsby-Gore, told both Weizmann and Ben-Gurion that the British would halt immigration while the Royal Commission continued its work in Palestine.[94] Outraged, Ben-Gurion blamed Weizmann for planting the idea with Nuri.[95] Ben-Gurion's red line had now been crossed, and he wrote to his colleague Moshe Sharett (then called Shertok), "Our main struggle now and in the future is immigration. Chaim has already failed us here; he is certainly not capable of future leadership."[96] He added caustically, "I have seen not only the disaster that awaits us now because of this man—the cause of all our political failure in previous years has become clear to me as well."[97] If immigration were halted, Ben-Gurion believed the very oxygen needed to breathe life into a new Jewish state and national community in Palestine would be cut off.

Ben-Gurion, however, would not call for Weizmann's ouster. Instead, he acknowledged the necessity of his colleague's link to Britain, saying simply that Weizmann needed to be "watched."[98] For this, he wanted other Zionist officials to attend meetings in Britain to avoid a repeat of the Nuri affair. Yet when some of Ben-Gurion's colleagues called for a public campaign against Britain, he shot down the idea, cautioning "against alienating the political wing that shelters us."[99] In Ben-Gurion's mind, Weizmann and Britain were inextricable. Still, if Zionism's reliance on Britain were to somehow break, Weizmann's utility to Zionism would greatly diminish.

The riots and the subsequent formation of the Peel Commission were hinge moments for Zionism, both in its relationship to partition and in its view of Britain. Whereas before 1936–1937 the Zionists sought a state including all the Land of Israel, now Zionists were willing to accept half a loaf, rather than all of Palestine for their national home. In essence Britain was declaring a Jewish state possible. Moreover, Ben-Gurion saw partition in a new light and favored it more strongly for additional reasons. First, it could provide justice to both peoples. As early as 1930, Ben-Gurion had asserted on the record that "we wholeheartedly support the right of self-determination for all peoples . . . and that undeniably includes the Arab people of Palestine."*[100] If in 1930 Ben-Gurion thought that Palestinian self-determination could be achieved as part of a wider Arab collective, by 1936 he felt that this formula would be insufficient and that Palestinian nationalist aspirations needed to be addressed independently of those of the Arabs.

Ben-Gurion also saw partition as allowing Zionists to take the high ground in their conflict with the Arabs. In a letter to a British official co-written with Sharett, he explained that "this strength will give us a political victory if England and the world know that we are defending ourselves rather than attacking."[101] Not only important in foreign relations, this high ground would also fortify the Zionists themselves.

Moreover, he did not fear partition would weaken Jewish deterrence—rather, it created permanence, demanding that Arabs come to grips with a Zionist entity. Even if the Arab side failed to accept Zionism now, a strong Jewish state could compel the Arabs to yield over time. Like Jabotinsky, Ben-Gurion believed Jewish deterrence was important, yet he disagreed that this required holding all the land. As he informed his Arab interlocutors, he certainly would have preferred to incorporate Transjordan (modern Jordan), as recognized initially in the League of Nations mandate (but later renounced by Britain in a 1922 White Paper), but he did not see this as critical.

Furthermore, partition would make it possible to maintain British support for Zionism. Ben-Gurion believed such British recognition was a prerequisite for Arabs to ever make their peace with the new reality. If partition was important to London, then the Zionists should rally around it. In 1936, he told his colleagues, "Perhaps in another ten years, the Arab factor will be the most important, but for now, the British factor is paramount." He added, "The key to the political strengthening of the Yishuv is to be found in British policy."[102] He also declared, "We must behave in this manner so as

---

*   Seven years later, Ben-Gurion wrote to Moshe Sharett, "Were I . . . an Arab politically [or] nationally minded . . . I would rebel even more vigorously, bitterly and desperately against the immigration that will one day turn Palestine and all its Arab residents over to Jewish rule."

to attain the trust and assistance of the [British] army for the establishment of an armed Jewish force in Palestine, [and that] if a civil war breaks out in Palestine between Jews and Arabs *on our account,* the first thing to go will be Jewish immigration."[103] He believed the main competing alternative, the Revisionist approach, based on pure force, would have zero appeal for continued British support.

On the fate of European Jewry, too, Ben-Gurion saw the British role as potentially decisive. He told a Zionist forum, "No English commission can determine the fate of the Jewish people forever, but it can determine to a great extent what will happen over the next five years." He continued, "Five years are nothing next to 'eternity,' but not all years in history are alike, and in the next five years the fate of our generation may be decided, if not the fate of generations." He concluded, "The extent of immigration in the coming years is a question of destiny. . . . In determining the principle of immigration [Britain] determines the fate of the people."[104]

Ben-Gurion's analysis led to one crucial and overriding conclusion. The fundamental need for immigration meant that the Zionists were better off having full control over some of the land than partial or no control over all of the land. At one point, Ben-Gurion made clear that the alternative to partition was no Jewish majority. He starkly laid out the two scenarios: "The immediate establishment of a Jewish state in a small part of Palestine or curtailment of immigration and limitation of Jewish settlement to certain areas in accordance with Arab pressure. . . . Partition is a fact." He added, "Only one thing can annul this fact: Jewish consent to remain a permanent minority in Palestine."[105] Counterintuitively, in the circumstances Ben-Gurion faced, partition would do more to facilitate Zionism than an insistence on acquisition of the entire land. Partition represented not a dilution of Zionism, but its realization.

Apart from this, the idea of partition enabled Ben-Gurion to be more explicit than before in reinforcing Jewish institutions within Palestine. In this, he favored separate Jewish and Arab economies, building up Jewish defense capabilities, and transforming the Jewish Agency into a proto-government.[106] For example, the 1936 riots meant the Zionists no longer had access to the Arab-held Jaffa Port and would need to start their own in

Tel Aviv.[107] Moves like this would shape the Jewish state. Partition would, in these ways, become an opportunity to assemble the necessary building blocks of statehood.

THE PEEL COMMISSION AND THE WHITE PAPER

On January 8, 1937, at the Peel Commission inquiry, one of the commissioners, Reginald Coupland, a history professor, declared that if the Jews and Arabs could not agree, it would seem preferable to "split Palestine into two halves, the plain being an independent Jewish state, as independent as Belgium . . . and the rest of Palestine, plus Transjordania, being an independent Arab state, as independent as Arabia."[108] This assessment marked a turning point in the British attitude. Weizmann and Ben-Gurion were thrilled privately, whatever their past divisions over immigration. Six months later, in July 1937, the recommendations of the Peel Commission included a call for partition.[109]

Across the Zionist spectrum, Ben-Gurion faced considerable pushback on the matter of partition. Many feared a bait-and-switch scenario, wherein the Zionists would accept partition and the Arabs would reject it, followed by a dissolution of the entire British mandate, leaving the Zionists with nothing. In making their critique, skeptical Zionists could quote Ben-Gurion himself, who had identified the mandate over all the land as Zionism's greatest achievement. Therefore, it should not be bartered away without a guarantee of getting something in return.

Among even his most highly valued colleagues, such as Berl Katznelson and Yitzhak Tabenkin, a founder of the kibbutz movement, Ben-Gurion faced fierce opposition. Neither Katznelson nor Tabenkin believed in the authenticity of Palestinian Arab nationalism.[110] Moreover, Tabenkin was always suspicious of the British, believing they would trick the Zionists whenever possible. He thought Zionism must continue in the pioneering way, dunam by dunam (quarter acre by quarter acre). Katznelson, for his part, felt a ministate would not be geographically viable. Critics outside the Labor movement included the Revisionists, who thought it was folly to yield land to the Arabs, given the consequences for deterrence. The religious parties, too—though lacking anything like the influence they would acquire in later decades—worried over ceding lands that encompassed biblical patrimony.

This opposition from the Zionist parties put Ben-Gurion in a quandary. Of course, he didn't want to risk losing his allies. But he was a leader who saw the big picture, and he didn't believe the Zionists had the luxury of passing on partition. History would judge them harshly if they did not seize this path to statehood.

Therefore, working with Weizmann to move forward on the concept of partition while simultaneously parrying critics, Ben-Gurion devised language for the 1937 Zionist Congress, indicating that the Peel Commission's proposal was insufficient but that the Zionist supreme body would empower its leaders to engage with the British on the terms of partition.[111] To Ben-Gurion, there were several arguments supporting such a posture. For starters, it would avert a showdown with critics over the idea of partition itself, which Ben-Gurion feared he and Weizmann would lose. In addition, given the zero-sum world that existed between the Zionists and the Arabs, Ben-Gurion believed a too-enthusiastic embrace of partition was tactically unwise and would ultimately require more Zionist concessions in the face of Arab intransigence. As he told a Labor forum at the time, "If this scheme comes up as a Jewish proposal, it is lost. It must come forth as England's plan."[112] Lastly, Ben-Gurion believed the British approach to partition might be too minimalist: Would they include the Galilee in the north or the Negev in the south, or would these go to the Arab side? Worse, according to the Peel recommendations, the British would retain control of the religiously sensitive Jerusalem and Bethlehem.[113] In short, Ben-Gurion thought that accepting the idea of partition was an urgent necessity but that its territorial dimensions required a dialogue with the British.

At the same time, Ben-Gurion understood that partition meant an independent Jewish state, fulfilling Zionism's objective. Once a state existed, the Zionists could open the doors to immigrants and establish a standing army. And the new state could, in turn, facilitate border expansion, with or without Arab agreement. As he wrote to his son, Amos, "I am not in favor of war . . . [but if] the Arabs behave in keeping with [their] barren nationalist feelings and say to us: Better that the Negev remain barren than that Jews settle there, then we shall have to speak to them in a different language. But we shall only have another language if we have a state."[114] In other words, Ben-Gurion did not have moral qualms about potentially redrawing Israel's borders, given the preponderance of surrounding Arab countries and his belief that Arab intransigence would likely lead to the Arabs refusing to compromise, and perhaps even initiating a military conflict with Palestine's Jews. Such circumstances could shape a different Zionist course of action. Without partition, though, the Jews would have neither their small state nor the opportunity to augment it.

There was, however, a real question about whether the British government would stand behind the partition idea. Peel's status as a commissioner certainly suggested so, but the looming threat posed by Hitler led London to assess every commitment according to whether it strengthened Britain in the impending European conflict. The British felt they were caught in a vise between growing Arab nationalist opposition to Zionism and the menace of Hitler. Hitler's anti-Semitism would by definition lead to more demands for increased immigration, which would further alienate the Arabs. The British preferred to disappoint the Zionists rather than the Arabs. The British now put together a panel that would kill the very partition idea that Peel had just approved.

For Ben-Gurion, a retreat from partition would be disastrous. In practical terms, failing to follow through on separate states wouldn't just appease the Arabs, it would also lead to an alternative policy that was gaining ground in British ruling circles. This alternative entailed severely constricting Jewish immigration, dooming the Jews to perpetual minority status. Instead of a Jewish nation-state in Palestine, where Jews would be the majority in a state based in their ancestral homeland, the Jews of Palestine would be a minority, just like they were in the numerous European and other states in which they lived. Therefore, in a larger sense, Ben-Gurion believed a British pullback from Peel would indicate an end to the British commitment to a Zionist state and the Balfour Declaration. Should this occur, he was prepared to upend his loyalties to Britain entirely. He would no longer regard the British as friends, but rather as foes who had forsaken their commitment to the Jews.[115] Choking immigration would be a death knell for Zionism, and it was here that Ben-Gurion drew the brightest of red lines.

The Woodhead Commission, established in 1938 ostensibly to refine the Peel Commission's findings, instead had a very different agenda. The commission members turned out to have little sympathy for Zionism. After the findings were presented to Parliament and published on November 9, 1938—a bitter irony, coinciding as it did with Kristallnacht, when over two hundred synagogues were destroyed across Germany and Austria—the government issued a policy statement that "the political, administrative, and financial difficulties involved in the proposal to create independent Arab and Jewish States inside Palestine are so great that this solution of the problem is impracticable."[116] The Jewish Agency Executive responded that the Woodhead Commission report could not "serve as the basis for any negotiations, either between the Jews and the Arabs or between the Jewish Agency and the [British] government."

The report and the carnage in Europe marked a nadir for Ben-Gurion; both the continent's Jews and Zionism were dealt a blow on the same day. Given this turn of events, Ben-Gurion at last broke from Britain, a move on which he ruminated decades later: "I no longer had any faith in England. At first the English government favored the Peel scheme. They endorsed it . . . but then . . . the government backed down and proposed something which neither the Jews nor the English would hear of. Then I knew the game was up."[117]

After Woodhead, the St. James Conference, held in London in February and March 1939 and involving Jewish and Arab delegations, was designed to address the immigration issue. But the omens weren't auspicious. Because the Palestinians refused to sit with Jews, Britain had to run parallel sets of talks.[118] British deference to the Arabs foreshadowed a coming hard line on Jewish immigration, involving a planned shutoff after low levels of immigration, slated to be a mere fifteen thousand a year for the next five years. Future Jewish immigration would rely on Arab approval, effectively ending the inflow.[119] At the conference, Ben-Gurion pushed back hard: "Four hundred thousand Jews in Palestine would not recognize a law which conditioned the right of immigration to Eretz Israel upon the consent of the Mufti."[120] Only British force, he would say later at the conference, could stop Jewish immigration. Nevertheless, the ensuing British White Paper, issued on May 17,

1939, enshrined the immigration stoppage imagined at the St. James Conference. There was no greater betrayal to Ben-Gurion than the 1939 White Paper. He saw its phaseout of immigration over five years as cutting off the very lifeblood of Zionism.

Even before St. James, in early 1939, Ben-Gurion had sought, in response to the feared immigration restriction, an aggressive promotion of illegal immigration as the best way to save Jews and bolster the Yishuv. This approach would require deftness in eluding British detection at sea.[121] But the Zionist leader's initiative also had a political objective, in that he felt the world media would be sympathetic to refugees fleeing Hitler and settling in Palestine.[122] Therefore, any British effort to attack these immigrants would create a political backlash in London, in turn persuading Britain to reopen the gates. He called his new approach "combative Zionism."[123]

Within weeks of the Woodhead report, Ben-Gurion thus called for "an immigration rebellion, a declaration of war on England—not with guns and bombs, not by terror and murders like the Arabs, but by internal organization of mass immigration to Eretz-Israel, and the transport of thousands of refugees, irrespective of the government's prohibitions, to the shores of Eretz-Israel—an act which would again tie the quest of the refugees to Eretz-Israel."[124] This came to be known as Aliyah Bet (Immigration B), which stood for the Hebrew words for "illegal immigration."

In addition to pressuring Britain directly, Ben-Gurion believed this tactic would rouse support among American Jews, who would urge their legislators to pressure Britain. He proved to be mistaken. His attempts to meet with American Zionists in the United States in January 1939 drew resistance. In light of the Hitler menace, these Jewish Americans countenanced no such campaign against Britain. The British navy simply could not be diverted by a cat-and-mouse game with Jewish immigrants. Many Zionist leaders, too, balked at the idea of placing Jewish immigrants in harm's way, whatever threats they might face in Europe.[125] One can also not discount the discomfort of American Jews drawing public attention to Jewish nationalism at a time when the Nazi threat abroad was coupled with nativist anti-Semitism at home, as espoused by aviator Charles Lindbergh, radio populist Father Charles Coughlin, and other public figures.

Sensing this mood, after his efforts to persuade American Jews fell on deaf ears, Ben-Gurion backtracked from his plan, only returning to it after World War II. Instead, Ben-Gurion famously expressed the paradox of the Zionists: "We must help the British in their war as though there were no White Paper, and we must resist the White Paper as though there were no war."[126] He acknowledged that Britain, the new enemy of Zionism and betrayer of its Balfour promise, was also a great enemy of the enemy of the Jews: Hitler.

All was not lost in Ben-Gurion's effort to court American Jews, though, which initiated a gradual shift in the Zionists' major power alliance from Britain to the United States. The shift carried with it a subtler transformation. Whereas the Zionist-British rapport relied on the inimitable figure of Weizmann, no such counterpart existed in the United States. The exception was perhaps Supreme Court justice Louis Brandeis, but he was eighty-three and could not fully serve the Zionist movement while on the Supreme Court.[127] In fact, Ben-Gurion now wanted something beyond Weizmann or an American equivalent. As noted above, he wanted to cultivate a mass US movement to pressure leaders in Washington, who would in turn pressure London to lift the White Paper, eventually resulting in US support for statehood.

This strategy emerged from his deep-seated belief that Western democracies were responsive to public opinion, particularly amid crisis. His faith in the public resilience of democracies was reinforced during the war, when he subsequently witnessed firsthand in London the stoic response by the British people to the Blitz, an experience he applied when imagining the extent of bombardment the Jewish people could withstand in 1948 in the service of a greater goal.[128]

In the United States, Ben-Gurion was prepared to play a personal role in mobilizing Jewish and gentile support for a resolution to Zionism's predicament. To this end, he spent more than ten months in 1940 and 1941 in America. Ben-Gurion recognized that US president Franklin Delano Roosevelt was too busy dealing with the war to independently concern himself with the Zionists, but he suspected FDR would be receptive to a public groundswell, proclaiming, "The way to win over the American administration is to win over the people."[129] He therefore reached out to labor unions and churches even as he focused on rallying American Jewish organizations, coaxing them toward realizing that Zionism did not threaten their identity as Americans.

Ben-Gurion did not succeed in his efforts to influence US policy. Although Brandeis and fellow justice Felix Frankfurter helped get the Zionist leader introductions with several Roosevelt confidants, Ben-Gurion never met with the president himself. He was stung that Weizmann had a brief meeting with FDR but did not take him along; Ben-Gurion was not even notified of the meeting. At the time, Ben-Gurion had been spending weeks meeting other prominent Americans in order to win support for the Zionist cause in Washington.[130] At every opportunity, he called for US support for a Jewish fighting force in Palestine that could protect the Yishuv while rendering service against Hitler.[131] He emphasized that such a force could be useful should Germany's field marshal Erwin Rommel sweep from North Africa all the way into the Levant.[132] He also thought military training would help build a coherent, effective, post–World War fighting force for the Jews of Palestine. (It is estimated that thirty thousand Jews of the Yishuv enlisted in the British army during World War II. Ben-Gurion wanted the number to be much higher.[133]) Creating such a force would be a fait accompli, establishing an institution—a military—that is essential to any country and thus bringing the Yishuv closer to being a de facto state. Finally, Ben-Gurion believed that Yishuv military involvement would give the Zionists a political chit in postwar deliberations. However, the claim of Zionist military helpfulness was mostly dismissed by the United States and Britain.[134] Yet while he may not have persuaded the Americans to support his concept of a Jewish fighting force, he did win over the Jewish leaders to his broader cause. At the May 1942 Zionist Biltmore Conference, held at the eponymous New York hotel, American Jewish leaders called for a Jewish state and free Jewish immigration to Palestine.

At the Biltmore Conference, Ben-Gurion and Weizmann, as indicated in their speeches, still believed several million Jews would survive the German campaign and immigrate to Palestine at war's end.[135] But by the second half of 1942, news began trickling out of Europe of a systematic

German effort to extinguish the Jews. Indeed, the deportation and elimi-
nation of three million Polish Jews began during the summer of 1942. That
November, sixty-nine Jews who were allowed to immigrate to Palestine in
exchange for German civilians residing in Palestine told members of the
Jewish Agency about the death camps and the plan to wipe out the Jews.[136]
Ben-Gurion, although apparently doubting some of the most horrific details—having recalled efforts to stir up anti-German sentiment with such
stories during World War I—now better understood the scale of the Nazi
plan. The Yishuv leadership declared days of mourning. Even as late as December 1942, after the news had come about the systematic destruction of
European Jewry, Ben-Gurion failed to fathom the scope. At a speech in Rehovot at an economic research institute, he said, "They say maybe Hitler
will destroy two million."[137] At the same speech, he made clear that Zionist
nation builders had to look beyond World War II, saying that there would
be millions of displaced Jews who would not want to return to their homes.*
Therefore, there needed to be thinking about how to absorb these people in
the postwar period.[138]

For Ben-Gurion, the Holocaust was the ultimate reminder of why a
Jewish state was so needed, because no country was willing to take in the
Jews in any meaningful way. He would say, "If a Jewish state was established seven years ago, we would be bringing to this small Jewish state hundreds of thousands, maybe millions, of Jews from Poland and Romania.
And they would be here."[139] But now it was too late. Ben-Gurion believed
that the Holocaust represented a failure of Zionism. Because the movement
had failed to deliver a state by that time, it was able to do very little. It's hard
to imagine that Ben-Gurion had ever felt so powerless. He would mourn
not just the loss of such numbers and the failure of a movement dedicated
to saving Jewish life, but also the loss of European Jews who he believed
held enormous potential to be Zionists. They held this potential, in his eyes,

---

* At the time, he would meet with approximately thirty people of the Yishuv who would
be parachuting behind enemy lines, likely including Hannah Senesh, the twenty-three-year-
old woman of Hungarian descent who sought to assist the rescue of Hungarian Jews about
to be deported to Auschwitz. She would be tragically tortured but still refused to reveal the
details of her mission. Ben-Gurion urged the paratroopers to tell the Jews that they have a
home in Israel after the war.

because their Jewish identity was so central in their lives, they were very well educated, and many had been involved in Zionist youth movements. They had been the heirs to a rich tradition stretching back centuries. Some European Jews had escaped before the Holocaust, but what had essentially been the heart of Jewish civilization for at least a millennium had been destroyed beyond repair.

Ben-Gurion would later write, "European Jewry did not just need a Jewish state but it had all the spiritual and material tools needed to establish it. The Holocaust was more than just a crippling blow to the Jewish people—it dangerously undermined, if not fatefully so, the possibility of the [state's] establishment. More than Hitler hurt the Jewish people that he knew and hated, he sabotaged the state that he didn't see coming."[140]

BEN-GURION AND THE HOLOCAUST

Some Israeli historians are critical of Ben-Gurion's approach to the Holocaust, or Shoah. They argue that he was more concerned with populating the future Jewish state than with doing all he could to save the Jews of Europe, whatever their destination. Those who contend that Ben-Gurion simply viewed Europe's Jews as a means to an end often cite a 1938 speech in which he said his primary "intention [was] to carry out 'the mass return' of 'hundreds of thousands of Jewish youth' to their homeland. . . . If it is ordained that they and we die, they will die here. If it is ordained that they fight, they will fight here, for this is the only place for our war."[141] Indeed, even as the war continued and further atrocities came to light, the Zionist leader maintained similar rhetoric. Later, he stirred suspicions by saying, "It is in our interest that Hitler be wiped out, but since that is not happening, it is in our interest to exploit his existence for the building of Palestine."[142] Wartime speeches by Ben-Gurion, his accusers say, were not aimed at rousing world opinion toward saving Jews. Yet these critics cannot similarly point to a failure of action on Ben-Gurion's part. The truth was, he had deeply limited powers as the head of a non-state entity. He had no air force to bomb the train lines or other German targets, and he lacked a state that could put all its efforts into rescuing Jews[*] and that could open its doors to Jewish immigrants.[143]

Later, an indignant Ben-Gurion would brush aside such caviling, claiming he had dedicated his life to the cause of immigration and statehood. Ben-Gurion chose not to dwell on a perceived failure of the Yishuv to rescue the European Jews, believing such an approach would sap morale. Rather, he articulated Jewish power and statehood as an antidote. He doubled down on his strategic vision even when faced with the genocide, confident that a future state could prevent such a fate from ever befalling the Jews again. As a leader, he was realistic about what he could accomplish: he could not liberate the European Jewry, but he could build the Jewish Agency institutions that would strengthen the Palestinian Jewry; he could not change British attitudes toward constraining Jewish physical or demographic growth, but he could continue to build reluctant American Jewish support for Zionism. He knew his limitations, did not lose sight of the objective for a state, and adjusted his tactics to reach the goal.

AMONG THE SURVIVORS

When the war ended, Ben-Gurion sensed a narrow window to gain international sympathy for Jewish statehood. This was in part because the postwar geopolitical scene was very fluid, and world geopolitical realities could shift starkly, as was later borne out in the Cold War standoff between the United States and the Soviet Union. On a highly practical level, Ben-Gurion knew many Holocaust survivors were in displaced persons (DPs) camps, facing an uncertain future. A large number of these now-stateless individuals yearned for Zion. And whereas Poland was home to Europe's largest prewar Jewish community, many Holocaust survivors saw the Poles as accomplices in the killing of their families. The idea of returning to live among these same antagonists seemed anathema, although a small number did so.

---

[*] During the war, Ben-Gurion would say that 115,000 illegal immigrants made it to Palestine's shores.

Ben-Gurion wanted to meet the survivors, so over a year beginning in the fall of 1945, he made three visits to the DP camps, marking the first time he had engaged with the continent's Jews since the 1930s. It is hard to imagine a more poignant encounter than that between the survivors of the crematoriums and the very leader who had dedicated his life to ensuring Jews would never be powerless again. The moment was unforgettable. Ben-Gurion, who never cried in public, would show much emotion. On October 19, 1945, he arrived in Germany. He visited survivors in the DP camp Zeilsheim—located in the western part of Frankfurt—on that trip.[144] According to US chaplain Rabbi Judah Nadich, Ben-Gurion was mobbed upon his arrival. When he spoke in the camp's auditorium, the survivors broke into "Hatikvah," the Zionist national anthem. Nadich depicted the scene: "As Ben-Gurion stood on the platform before them, the people broke forth into cheers and song, and finally into weeping. . . . His voice choked up, his eyes filled . . . he broke down for a moment. In the sudden quiet one could hear the muffled sobbing from all sides of the auditorium. . . . The impossible had happened. Ben-Gurion was in their midst and they had lived despite Hitler. . . . They had lived despite them all to this day."[145]

Having predicted a burning Europe almost a decade and a half earlier, Ben-Gurion now stood on the scorched earth, facing the survivors.[146] (If Ben-Gurion had any doubt that these people were motivated, the signs on the streets in the camp were called Jerusalem, Tel Aviv, and Bialik, after the person who would be called Israel's poet laureate.[147]) At the St. Ottilien monastery in Bavaria, now converted into a hospital, Ben-Gurion was greeted by eight hundred patients who displayed a blue-and-white Zionist flag wrapped in black.[148] Addressing Auschwitz survivors at another stop, he declared, "What has happened . . . we cannot repair." He continued, "It's our duty to make sure it never happens again. There will not be another Holocaust." This promise, however, depended on "creat[ing] a reality which will not let it happen. . . . Not only your children but we whose heads are grayed with age, will yet live to see the Jewish state."[149]

Ben-Gurion saw the DP camps as having two purposes that could bolster Zionism. First, the camps could function as a pipeline for Jewish immigration. Second, they could serve as an instrument for creating international political pressure for Zionism, particularly as the camps were a human reminder that powerless Jews were defenseless Jews. When it came to the former, Ben-Gurion was concerned that welfare agencies would transfer some of the children out of the camps. He even went to meet Dwight Eisenhower, who was the US allied commander in Europe, and urged that the Jewish state be allowed to send books for the people in the camp and to organize sports activities. It is clear that Ben-Gurion wanted to keep the DPs' motivation high. Eisenhower was open to this and was also open to Ben-Gurion's request that more and more of the Holocaust survivors be funneled to the American occupation zone of Germany.[150]

The demand for resettlement presented by the DP camps, Ben-Gurion knew, could break the 1939 White Paper once and for all. There was no longer any need for incrementalism. Suddenly, the new US president, Harry Truman, insisted that one hundred thousand residents of the DP camps be allowed to come to Palestine.[151] In response, British foreign minister Ernest Bevin balked, calling for the repatriation of survivors to their country of origin. He then charged the Zionist movement with fomenting future anti-Semitism: "If the Jews, who have suffered so much, try to push to the head of the queue, there is a danger of a renewed anti-Semitic reaction throughout Europe."[152] These remarks would spark clashes between the Yishuv and British police.

Addressing the Yishuv in November 1945, Ben-Gurion responded to "Bevin and his colleagues": "We, the Jews of the Land of Israel, do not want to be killed. We wish to live. In defiance of the ideology of Hitler and his disciples in various lands, we believe that we Jews, like Englishmen and others, also have the right to live, as individuals and as a people. . . . We are prepared to be killed but not to concede three things: freedom of Jewish immigration; our right to rebuild the wilderness of our homeland; the political independence for our people in its homeland."[153] Later invoking his experience of the Blitz, during which he taught himself Greek in an air shelter, Ben-Gurion wondered, "I saw the blitz in London. . . . I saw the Englishman whose land and liberty is dearer than his life. Why do you presume that we are not like you?"[154]

Still, even the Holocaust did not prompt the British to ease stringent limits on Jewish immigration, a stance that prompted US-British tensions. Bevin and Prime Minister Clement Attlee sought to hold on to the geo-strategically significant Palestine in an era of decolonization and to curry favor with the Arabs at a time when British power was waning in comparison with that of the United States and Soviet Union. As in the pre-war years, Ben-Gurion found Weizmann too indulgent of British policy. Weizmann's patience would be pointless against London's growing, implacable anti-Zionism. The approach toward statehood instead needed to be *la'altar* (immediate). And this immediacy called for greater militancy, a strategy Ben-Gurion had unsuccessfully debuted in 1939 but now reprised to more-receptive domestic ears.[155]

Launching attacks against British troops in Mandatory Palestine was one of the most controversial decisions made by Ben-Gurion. But in October 1945, believing strikes might move the British closer to Zionist demands, he agreed to have the Haganah, the mainstream pre-state Jewish militia, make common cause with more-militant underground groups—namely the Irgun, led by followers of Jabotinsky, and the group known as the Stern Gang, which sought to facilitate illegal Jewish immigration through violence against the British.[156] Previously, Ben-Gurion had fiercely opposed these groups, calling them secessionists to mainstream Zionism, and he still hesitated to give them any legitimacy. The specific coordination would take place in Paris, allowing Ben-Gurion some distance, given his formal role as head of the Jewish Agency.[157] The focus was on destroying coast guard boats used to stop immigration and sabotaging railroads. The joint militias worked together on many such strikes.[158] For various reasons, the coordination stopped in summer 1946, around the time the Irgun conducted its highly lethal attack on the King David Hotel in Jerusalem, where the British government offices were stationed.[159]

Given their firm opposition to Jewish immigration, the British found ways to resist President Truman's demand to transfer one hundred thousand DPs immediately to Palestine. One technique of Foreign Minister Bevin was to say that the immigration issue must be put in the wider context of a US-British understanding about Palestine's future. But, to Bevin's displeasure, a US-British commission met and agreed that the one hundred thousand should be transferred. To this, Bevin responded by calling for another commission to assess the implementation of the first commission's recommendations. In 1946, this commission, headed by the British politician Herbert Morrison and US diplomat Henry Grady, made transfer of the one hundred thousand conditional on a number of factors that would have ensured Jewish autonomy but no state in Palestine. The Morrison-Grady proposal produced opposition from both Jews and Arabs.[160] The Arabs rejected the plan based on their view that no legitimacy should be granted to the Yishuv, whereas the Zionists felt they were being offered mere cantons and no state. Centrally, this meant no control over immigration.

Responding to Truman's subsequent exasperation toward both the British and the Zionists, presidential aide David Niles contacted Ben-Gurion's advisor Nahum Goldmann in summer 1946 and insisted he visit Washington immediately. Niles, who was Jewish, then offered Goldmann an ultimatum: either the Zionists come up with an alternative to Morrison-Grady or risk losing Truman's support. Such a dilemma echoed the one the Zionists faced after the Peel Commission report: either accept part of the land or potentially get none of it. Ben-Gurion had already made clear that he preferred the former.

In August 1946, the Jewish Agency approved partition in principle, using the following formulation: "The Executive is prepared to discuss the proposal to constitute a viable Jewish state in a sufficient portion of the Land of Israel."[161] Here the term *sufficient* signified partition. Ben-Gurion saw twin political risks in accepting partition, even though he viewed it as essential: a backlash from domestic right-wing critics, who would decry the very legitimacy of splitting biblical land, and an effort by adversaries abroad to further chip away at the Zionist position. A premature territorial concession would not be the ceiling but rather the floor, inviting further concessions, triggering demands from Britain and the Arabs that the Zionists give up more. In remarks that same month, Ben-Gurion sought to put to rest any ambiguity. "It was in this spirit of compromise that we decided to accept Partition, which is the absolute limit to which a Jew and a Zionist can go. Partition is not the Zionist Program; the Zionist Program is a Jewish State in the whole of Palestine.

If nothing comes out of these discussions, we revert, and stand by, our old program. This compromise is our last effort to come to an agreement."[162]

Follow-up meetings between Niles and Goldmann in Washington led to consensus on partition and a "two-state solution" as the terms for an agreement. On August 9, 1946, with "tears in his eyes," Niles momentously conveyed to Goldmann that President Truman would support independence based on such a principle. Before Yom Kippur, which fell that year on October 4, Truman issued a carefully worded public statement to synagogues across the United States that suggested America could support statehood but avoided any absolute commitment.[163] The statement was not only timed to coincide with the holiest Jewish day of the year, when synagogue attendance was sure to be at its peak but also occurred a month before the US midterm elections amid rumors that Republicans would issue a statement of their own. Truman expressed his implicit support for the Jewish Agency's demand for "the immediate issuance of certificates for 100,000 Jewish immigrants." He continued, in reference to the creation of a "viable Jewish state in control of [a part of] Palestine," that it was his "belief that a solution along these [general] lines would command the support of public opinion in the United States. . . . The gap between the proposals which have been put forward is [not] too great to be bridged."[164] The "two proposals" referenced here were those of Morrison-Grady and the Jewish Agency. Truman's declaration was worded to avoid an unambiguous endorsement of a Jewish state; but to American Jews listening, he seemed to be heading in this direction.

That December, the Zionist Congress convened in Basel for the first time since Hitler's genocide. The mood was somber amid the gaping hole left by the destroyed European delegations. In turn, the American representation was greater than in the past.[165] Now Ben-Gurion was burdened with persuading attendees of the necessity of partition. Ben-Gurion, who had sought to thread the needle at the Zionist Congress after the Peel Commission, this time was unequivocal. Yes, the Jews had the right to all the land. However, having rights and exercising them were very different things. As he explained it, "We are prepared to discuss a compromise arrangement if, in exchange for the reduction in territory, our rights are immediately extended and we are granted national independence."[166]

Ben-Gurion was also unequivocal on statehood, fearing that Weizmann might offer unacceptable compromises with Britain on the matter.[167] Indeed, disagreement on this core issue prompted Ben-Gurion, who could be ruthless over principles, to publicly sideline the legendary Weizmann. While petty vindictiveness cannot be discounted in this episode, there's reason to believe that Ben-Gurion sincerely felt that the postwar stakes for Zionism were too high to have two potentially conflicting voices at the helm of the movement. It was an especially sad turning point in the contentious partnership between the two. Weizmann's future role would be confined to ceremony, including his later tenure as the state's president. During the congress, lack of support from Ben-Gurion helped thwart Weizmann's reelection as president of the Zionist movement, and the post remained vacant.[168] Ben-Gurion, meanwhile, was reelected as head of the Zionist Executive, while also earning the defense portfolio.[169] In this latter role, he prepared for independence to exact a high price. Statehood and security were intertwined, he understood, and the movement needed to be prepared for the coming war.

Preparation for War

The seriousness of Ben-Gurion's preparations for war can be traced to an emergency meeting held July 1, 1945, with seventeen American Jewish businessmen at the New York home of oil executive Rudolf Sonneborn. The participants traveled from all over the country, attending without knowing what they'd discuss. In contrast with the public Ben-Gurion, who sought to reassure the Yishuv that Arab nations would acquiesce to the birth of a Jewish state, in private he predicted a dire war once statehood was declared. This declaration, he said, could happen within a year or two, when an exhausted Britain would inevitably leave Palestine.[170] Yet Ben-Gurion's optimism that the British would soon leave was tempered by an ominous warning. He believed the Jews would have to worry about not just the local Palestinian Arabs but also the neighboring Arab states, which would reject a Jewish state in their region. Once again demonstrating uncommon foresight, he explained that the Yishuv was ill prepared for this larger Arab threat, focused as it was on day-to-day struggles.[171]

At the New York meeting, Ben-Gurion then appealed for funds to build and arm a nascent military. Establishing a proper military would not only give the Yishuv a chance of survival against Arab armies but also create an institution fundamental to any sovereign state. At the meeting, Yaakov Dori, chief of staff of the still-unofficial Haganah, who accompanied Ben-Gurion to the meeting, referred to the opportunity to cheaply obtain surplus US weapons, which would otherwise possibly be turned into scrap, from the European theater as operations from World War II wound down. All attendees, subsequently and cryptically dubbed the "Sonneborn Foundation" by Ben-Gurion, agreed to provide support.[172] An immensely grateful Ben-Gurion would later refer to the meeting as one of the three most important events of his life, the other two being his aliyah in 1906 and the establishment of the state in 1948.[173] Years later, he wrote Sonneborn, "I will never forget—I think our people will never forget—that meeting at your home . . . which enabled us to create our military industry."[174]

Thereafter, Ben-Gurion immersed himself in military affairs, history, and policy in what became known as his "seminar."[175] In the months following the December 1946 Zionist Congress, he grilled the Haganah leadership on its readiness for the war ahead, including precise numbers of weapons and ammunition stocks. Two components of the response—just 45,000 soldiers overall and 2,200 in the elite Palmach strike force—did not satisfy him.[176] A new army needed to be capable of larger battle formations. It also required heavy weaponry, which the Zionists lacked. Ben-Gurion meticulously recorded all relevant details and thoughts in his diary while voraciously consuming books by military historians and thinkers, including numerous volumes by ancient Greek scholars. (Ben-Gurion would subsequently assign aides to read Greek military historian Thucydides, whose *History of the Peloponnesian War* Ben-Gurion claimed to have read sixteen times.[177])

Ben-Gurion did not yield to Haganah leaders who doubted his case for heavy weaponry, including airplanes, tanks, and cannons. Such equipment would be needed to vanquish a united pan-Arab army. Imagining such an army, Ben-Gurion explained, "This will no longer be a war of platoons or sections. It is essential to set up a modern army. It is essential to think of the requirement of a modern army."[178] Validating this perception, the Arab League political committee, in September 1947, declared that the Arabs would use all political and military means to prevent the establishment of a Jewish state.[179]

In seeking assets for the future war, Ben-Gurion turned to Yishuv residents who had served in the British military in World War II. These fighters, he believed, could contribute a great deal through their experience with heavy weapons, major formations, training, and the like. But to his dismay, he found that these British veterans were often excluded from the higher ranks of the Haganah expressly because their experience with large-scale war did not match the tendencies of the pre-state militia. About the Haganah, Ben-Gurion would write, "I found two parties: the 'Haganah' party and the 'army' party, with little trust between them."[180] He subsequently made key changes to the Haganah leadership, while also seeking major arms acquisitions. The latter task would have to be accomplished through smuggling, given the British ability to block major imports.

Ben-Gurion, however, saw these obstacles as temporary.[181] Once a sovereign state was formed, he reasoned, it would control its own borders. Meanwhile, the incipient state would need arms immediately in order to be prepared for the battle of its life. To secure these arms, Ben-Gurion summoned Ehud Avriel, a young Vienna-born kibbutznik who had previously helped smuggle Jews from Europe. (Ben-Gurion had met him during World War II to discuss Avriel's efforts as he tried to save Jews in Istanbul and rescued Jews from Greece.[182]) Ben-Gurion took out a wish list from his shirt pocket that outlined the weapons he needed: "10,000 rifles, 2.5 million cartridges, 500 sub-machine-guns, 100 machine-guns."[183] Subsequently, Haganah members began to procure the needed weapons from Czechoslovakia.[184] The sale of weapons to the Yishuv was personally approved by Czechoslovak foreign minister Jan Masaryk. The arms flow actually increased after the Czech coup of February 1948, which transformed Czechoslovakia into a bona fide Soviet client state. The Soviet Union was trying to gain influence in the Middle East by supporting the Yishuv.[185] As Ben-Gurion understood, however, the actual entry of most of the Czech weapons would be prevented by British border restrictions until after the state was founded.[186]

To avoid unsettling the public, Ben-Gurion generally limited his bluntest warnings to party settings. At a meeting in August 1947, he declared:

> Is there a danger to the survival of the Yishuv? . . . It would be a grave, perhaps fatal, error to refuse to . . . *prepare to meet it with all our strength.* We will be facing . . . *not Arab bands but Arab armies.* These armies are not the finest in the world, but they are armies with military equipment, machine guns, artillery, and in some cases bombers and fighters as well. . . . It is not only a question of our own survival, but the survival of the entire Jewish people . . . of the hope and future of all the remnants of the Jews in the world. . . . Our first concern at this juncture must be defense; everything depends on it. Today, in my view, this is the entire doctrine of Zionism.[187]

Ben-Gurion knew that war would be tied to the British becoming sufficiently fatigued to relinquish the mandate. The first concrete suggestions that the British would surrender it reached Ben-Gurion on May 7, 1945—almost three years to the day before he declared a state. He had just met in London with the British colonial secretary Colonel Oliver Stanley. Ben-Gurion later explained, "I understood from him that the British government would not continue with the Mandate much longer. They were unable to decide between the demands of the Arabs and the Jews. They knew that the United States and the Soviet Union supported Jewish demands and the establishment of a Jewish State, a fact which was not publicly known at the time, but they did not want to enter into conflict with the Arab peoples and therefore would soon abandon the Mandate."[188] After the meeting, he noted further, "It was clear to me that we had no one but ourselves to depend on."[189]

Two months later, during his last month as prime minister, Winston Churchill effectively confirmed this British stance in a memo to the Colonial Office and Chiefs of Staff: "I do not think we should take the responsibility upon ourselves of managing this very difficult place while the Americans sit back and criticize." He added, "I am not aware of the slightest advantage which has ever accrued to Great Britain from this painful and thankless task. Somebody else should have their turn now."[190] Bevin, the foreign minister in the incoming Labour government, informed the British cabinet of a similar inclination, although he had not yet devised a plan to exit Palestine.[191] Bevin made clear the British were faced with a "three-sided problem of retaining Arab friendship, assisting Jews, and eliciting American support."[192]

These three largely incompatible needs strained British ties with the United States as well as with the Zionists. Indeed, since the mid-1930s, when it failed to act on the Peel Commission findings, London had viewed the Palestine issue through the lens of national interests. In the postwar period, Britain's economy was devastated and the leadership simply could not afford to sustain its supervision of the mandate, or the chaos. No less important, it believed distance from the Zionists was key to preserving its influence in the Middle East. For his part, Foreign Minister Bevin disliked partition and preferred for Palestine to be administered by a United Nations–run trusteeship, a position Ben-Gurion would learn of in November 1945.* Having famously resisted President Truman's call for one hundred thousand Jews to be transferred from the DP camps, Bevin charged that the United States simply was trying to avoid channeling these refugees to New York. In December 1946, Bevin stated publicly that "after a time, an independent, Arab-majority state would be established."[193] Given Bevin's plainly articulated antipathy, the Zionists saw no value in attending the British peace conferences in fall 1946 and January 1947. The month after the second one, on February 18, 1947, a fed-up Bevin announced that Britain would hand over responsibility for Palestine to the UN.

Three months later, on May 15, 1947, the United Nations Special Committee on Palestine (UNSCOP) was formed to assess the future of the territory. Two months after that, in July, Ben-Gurion offered extensive testimony to a UNSCOP panel, including a lengthy complaint on how the British

---

* The United Nations Trusteeship program was akin to the mandate program under the League of Nations. Under the system, one power (usually a Western one) would supervise the country in question and would be supported by the UN. It was applied to former mandates, colonies, and areas liberated from the Axis during World War II. As with the mandate system, countries held under trusteeship would eventually gain full independence; but, because the timeline for independence was undefined, people wondered if statehood would be postponed indefinitely.

White Paper of 1939 represented an abrogation of Balfour by ending Jewish immigration and constraining the Zionists to a one-third minority or less in a future state.[194] "The White Paper, in destroying the Mandate, has removed the moral and legal basis of the present regime in Palestine," he said, indicating the essence of his objection. "It is contrary to the wishes of the entire [Jewish] population of the country, it causes untold sufferings to our people, it threatens our national existence. It is incompatible with international obligations and good faith."[195]

The mandate, he continued, would now need to be replaced by a Jewish state. And, given that the Zionists no longer depended on a foreign power, nothing could dent their resolve. He summoned Jewish history and universal justice as the twin bases for Zionist legitimacy: "Our entire history is a history of continuous resistance to superior physical forces which tried to wipe out our Jewish image and to uproot our connections with our country and with the teaching of our prophets. . . . We never surrender to sheer physical force deprived of moral validity." Even after millennia of exile, he argued, "unless and until these three disabilities are completely and lastingly remedied, there is no hope for the Jewish people, nor can there be justice in the world. . . . The Jewish people as a whole did not give way, did not despair or renounce its hope and faith in a better future, national as well as universal."[196]

Citing Jewish homelessness as the source of the Holocaust, Ben-Gurion entreated his listeners "to imagine for one second that there were two or three million Jews in the Jewish State of Palestine before the outbreak of the last war. Do you believe that the disaster which overtook our people in Europe would have happened?" Hitler had singled out the Jews, he contended, "because this was the only people without a land of its own, a government of its own, a state of its own able to protect, to intervene, to save and to fight. And now I put the question to you: who is prepared and able to guarantee that what happened to us in Europe will not happen again?"[197] Only statehood and a homeland, he thundered, could offer such reassurance.

He also addressed the Arab component of the conflict extensively. "The Arabs have seven states, the Jews none," he said. "The Arabs have vast underdeveloped territories—Iraq alone is three times as large as England with less than four million people—the Jews have only a tiny beginning of a national home. . . . The most glaring disparity perhaps is that the Arabs have no problem of homelessness and immigration, while with the Jews homelessness is the root cause of all their sufferings for centuries past."[198] He insisted that a war would bring about no Arab dispossession, arguing that in such a conflict the Arabs would "try to deny our right to our country. We do not deny their right to live in this country."[199] In reaffirming majority Zionist support for the Peel Commission's partition idea, Ben-Gurion cited the careful formulation conveyed by Nahum Goldmann to David Niles in summer 1946: "We will be ready to consider the question of a Jewish State in an adequate area of Palestine," even if "we are entitled to Palestine as a whole."[200] He even suggested continued support for a Jewish state as part of a regional confederation, as long as it remained independent and "if this were for the benefit of all the peoples in this region, and if this were the desire of the United Nations." If, however, a confederation meant accepting the status New York State has as "part of the United States," the Zionists would reject such a proposal.[201]

Ben-Gurion saw UNSCOP as an opportunity to expand the borders of a future Jewish state beyond those offered under Peel a decade earlier. UNSCOP would grant the Zionists the eastern Galilee, coastal plain, and most of the Negev.[202] Ben-Gurion was thrilled, writing his wife that if the Bible spoke about the Israelites having the area from the tribe of Dan in the north to Beersheba in the south, now under UNSCOP this would extend as south as Eilat (a port city in the southern tip of Israel): he had exceeded the biblical borders.[203] Using hyperbole, he waxed enthusiastic, saying, "In all of our history the Jewish people have never achieved what we have achieved now."[204]

Ben-Gurion and the Zionists now sought international acceptance of the UNSCOP report. In place of the sidelined Weizmann, Moshe Sharett emerged as their de facto foreign minister and set about lobbying for support from New York. Sharett, who had served as the head of the Jewish Agency's political department until 1948, would become Ben-Gurion's key ally in the struggle for independence and de facto Zionist foreign minister. Geopolitical leanings offered surprises in this context. The Soviets, for example, expressed backing for partition in order to undermine British influence in the

Middle East. The British, in turn, did not know if the vote could elicit the necessary two-thirds majority at the UN.

When, on November 29, 1947, the plan did gain the necessary votes— thirty-three in favor, thirteen against, and ten abstaining—Ben-Gurion did not lead the celebrations. He instead girded for the war he had so long anticipated.[205] The next day, while Jewish crowds thronged the streets, including in the courtyard outside of his office, Ben-Gurion told his daughter Renana, "who knows if among those who are dancing, will also fall."[206] Ben-Gurion was unswervingly focused on the challenge ahead, apparently believing it was a luxury to savor this historic success. Oppositionist Menachem Begin—a young protégé of Jabotinsky—had a grim reaction for another reason: he was outraged over any partitioning of the land. The day after the vote, he announced, "The partition of the Homeland is illegal. It will never be recognized. . . . It will not bind the Jewish people. Jerusalem was and forever will be our capital. Eretz Israel will be restored to the people of Israel. All of it. And forever."[207]

Even as the Zionists prepared for war, they held out hope that it could be avoided, pinning such aspirations on Jordan's King Abdullah. Jordan had gained independence from the British a year earlier, in May 1946, and Abdullah relished his ties to this Western power. The Jordanian Hashemites and the Zionists also had a history of calls for cooperation, including an informal agreement in 1919 between Weizmann and Abdullah's brother Faisal. Separately, Abdullah despised the leader of the Palestinians, the Jerusalem mufti Hajj Amin al-Husseini, and competed with him for the loyalty of the Palestinians.

Among the merits of Jordanian cooperation with the Zionists would be preventing Husseini from a preemptive seizure of territory in Palestine. Further, the inevitable war resulting from such a move would cost the kingdom lives. From the Zionists' perspective, keeping Jordan out of a war was paramount. Abdullah's Arab Legion was the best-equipped and -trained Arab force, in no small measure thanks to British support.[208] Moreover, Jordan held a strategically important location, given both its immediate proximity to the would-be Jewish state and its ability to block Iraqi forces from entering the fray from its east. A neutral Jordan, therefore, could potentially keep itself and another army out of the war.[209]

Despite the suggestion that Abdullah would prefer partition, the reality was highly sensitive. In fact, the Jordanian king did privately inform Bevin that he advocated for this course. Yet considering wide-scale Arab opposition to the idea of a Jewish state, he deemed it too risky to inform UNSCOP officials of this stance, as the Arab-affairs section of the Jewish Agency had requested. (Both sides, of course, knew the Palestinians would reject partition.) To secure Jordanian support, Golda Meir (then Myerson) met with Abdullah on November 17, 1947, two weeks before the partition vote. The meeting took place in the northern border area of Naharayim in the home of Avraham Rutenberg, whose father, Pinchas, headed the Palestine Electric Company and had established close personal relations with Abdullah. Agreeing with the Zionists about the need to prevent use of Jordanian soil for Arab passage to fight Israel, Abdullah also suggested Jordanian acquisition of land the UN would designate for the Palestinian Arabs, an idea to which Meir agreed. Abdullah consented to put this point in writing after the coming UN vote and also agreed to hold another meeting then.

Yet the optimism created by the Abdullah-Meir meeting did not last. The UN vote, when it came, shocked the Arab system, drawing a vociferous response and outright rejection from the Arab League, which declared that "the partition line shall be nothing but a line of fire and blood."[210] The Palestinians insisted on nothing less than full Arab control of Palestine. Meir and Abdullah would not meet again until May, just days before the end of the British mandate.

The UN vote also created a new reality on the ground. A few days after the vote, riots shattered Jerusalem's new commercial center, reflecting the Palestinian sense that only violence could halt the partition.[211] Across the country, roads to Jewish communities, which invariably passed through Arab villages, became perilous. Within a month, 250 Jews had been killed, about half the number killed during the three years of violence that began in 1936.[212] It seems at least 125 Arabs were killed during this period.[213] The

British, having decided to end the mandate, were not keen on enforcing law and order.

Ben-Gurion pragmatically began prioritizing the military situation on the ground, where he knew the future of the Yishuv would be won or lost; in turn, he temporarily set aside the international context, delegating responsibilities in this sphere to his subordinates. He had a gift for prioritizing that which he understood to be truly urgent and pivotal. This shift in emphasis was enabled by the UN partition plan, which had given him the international legitimacy he sought. The partition likewise quieted any doubts that the British would be leaving. No administrative force could prevent the march to statehood—but the coming war would be a great test. Zionism would no longer rise or fall based on the view of external powers, Ben-Gurion, who was now the leader and de facto defense minister, thought. Rather it would be won or lost on the ground. This was a temporary shift for Zionism, which had developed, and in the decades ahead would further define, a twin approach: an ethos of self-reliance when it came to the Yishuv's own defense alongside close political ties with a world power. When it came to the nearing war, the Yishuv knew it would not be receiving military assistance from the United States or Britain.

The international situation grew more complex when, on March 19, 1948, Ben-Gurion demonstrated his newfound ability to contextualize international developments when Warren Austin, the US ambassador to the UN, appeared to suddenly reverse American policy by embracing trusteeship rather than partition. As it turned out, Austin's statement was not authorized by an infuriated President Truman and would later be rendered irrelevant. In real time, Ben-Gurion could not have known this, yet his diary entry suggests a calmer response than that of many of his countrymen. He now knew the Jews controlled their own fate. "The American announcement," he wrote,

> does more harm to the UN—its standing and authority—than it does to us. The change in the American position indicates that the U.S. has surrendered to Arab terror. But this does not . . . impede the establishment of the Jewish State. The establishment of a State does not depend on the UN

resolution of November 29, though that resolution had great moral and political value. It depends, instead, on our ability to emerge victorious. If we have the desire and the time to mobilize all our resources, the State will still be established.

He continued, "We have laid the foundations for . . . a Jewish State. . . . We will not agree to a trusteeship, temporary or permanent."[214]

That same month, Ben-Gurion remained fixated on local military developments, culminating in the opening of the road to Jerusalem.[215] (In December, Ben-Gurion had been part of a motorcade that was fired on when leaving Jerusalem for Tel Aviv. It's unclear if his car suffered a direct hit, but four people in the convoy were injured and a bus was taken out of commission. Ben-Gurion would write in his diary, "We were attacked from the mountain; four were hurt." One person who traveled with Ben-Gurion said, "The attack came from two directions; Ben-Gurion opened the door and jumped out of the car. I thought he was crazy."[216] Apparently, the convoy was rescued by British soldiers who returned fire and the vehicles continued on their way.) The Palestinians had viewed this road as a weak point for the Yishuv, given the proximity between Arab villages and Jewish areas. In fully cutting off the road, the Palestinians believed they could isolate the city's ninety thousand Jewish inhabitants from the main Zionist cities along the coastal plain. From the Zionist side, previous efforts to break the siege with truck convoys carrying water and food supplies failed because of their extreme vulnerability to sniper attacks from Palestinian villages along the Jerusalem hills. Indeed, a sixty-vehicle convoy had stalled for a week at the western end of the Jerusalem corridor.[217]

This was the backdrop for April's Operation Nachshon (also sometimes spelled Nahshon), named for the ancient Jew who was, in the rabbinic tradition, said to be the first to jump into the Red Sea before he knew it would part.[218] Ben-Gurion now considered the situation dire, believing the Yishuv could not survive a full cutoff of Jerusalem and the casualties that would be involved.[219] The fall of Jerusalem would also be devastating because of the city's momentous importance in Jewish history and identity. The Palestinians, Ben-Gurion knew, also recognized the value of Jerusalem. In an all-night meeting with his commanders, Ben-Gurion argued hard that the operation needed heavy support, despite stretched resources on other fronts. Arguing against Haganah commander Yigael Yadin's statement that five hundred troops had been designated, the largest group yet brought together, Ben-Gurion cast the situation in his quintessentially sweeping terms: "At the moment there is one burning question, and that is the battle for the road to Jerusalem. . . . [Yet] the manpower Yigael is preparing is insufficient. Now, that is the decisive battle. The fall of Jewish Jerusalem would be a death-blow to the Jewish community. . . . This time . . . I am taking advantage of my prerogative to issue an order: in two days' time, at dawn, you must concentrate 2,000 combatants at the start line."[220] In the end, 1,500 soldiers were deployed.[221]

In his diaries, Ben-Gurion remarked on the incident, "When I explained the special importance of Jerusalem, each [commander] agreed to allocate half his forces to Operation Nahshon."[222] Fortuitously, that same night the Yishuv received its first load of weapons from Czechoslovakia. These, Ben-Gurion recounted, "were sent immediately from the port to the fifteen hundred men entrusted with the task of opening up the road to Jerusalem."[223] A few days later, Operation Nachshon achieved its "primary objective" with the recapture of al-Qastal, a village on strategically important ground near Jerusalem and from which sniper fire had disrupted Jewish supply routes into the city. Thereafter, on the morning of April 6, twenty-five trucks laden with supplies reached the capital, with several more convoys following in the coming weeks.[224]

The breaking of the siege of Jerusalem was significant for at least three reasons. First, beyond providing relief to an isolated population, Nachshon inspired the troops to believe they could succeed. Until then, the Haganah had been playing more defense than offense. By April 13, Ben-Gurion could credibly write about Operation Nachshon, "The battle is not yet over, but this great operation—the largest of all our operations during the past four months, means that if we want—we can beat the enemy."[225] Second, this was Ben-Gurion's first military victory, a result of his personal decision. Third, in the face of conventional wisdom abroad that the Zionists could not defeat the Arabs, this triumph showed, at a pivotal time, that the

Zionists could hold their own. They were not helpless without backing from a trustee. They could win.

The win, however, was not without complications.[226] Whereas the Haganah had lost some nine hundred soldiers from November through March, between the early-April start of Nachshon and mid-May, another 1,200 died.* Palestinians also suffered high casualties, but precise numbers are elusive. Heavy incursions into Palestinian villages—where snipers were thought to operate—covered areas both inside and outside the November 29 lines set by the UN partition, straining the capabilities of Jewish forces. Yadin at first ordered restraint, but, facing resistance, the Haganah engaged in brutal war acts such as the razing of villages. The Israeli historian Benny Morris, who has written extensively on such episodes, details the scenario:

> Ben-Gurion and the [Haganah General Staff] . . . had set in motion a strategic transformation of Haganah policy. Nahshon heralded a shift from the defensive to the offensive and marked the beginning of the implementation of *tochnit dalet* (Plan D)—without Ben-Gurion or the HGS ever taking an in-principle decision to embark on its implementation. . . . With the Arab world loudly threatening and seemingly mobilizing for invasion, the Yishuv's . . . leaders understood that they would first have to crush the Palestinian militias . . . if they were to stand a chance of beating off the invading armies.[227]

According to historian Tom Segev, Ben-Gurion had a policy of what was referred to as aggressive defense, an approach that was consistent with the commanders' desire not just to defend the borders of the UN, but to have Arabs in the Jewish zone relocate. Nevertheless, Ben-Gurion would be astonished when Arabs of their own volition would leave cities like Haifa and Jaffa.

The operation to open the Jerusalem road came at a time of decreasing British motivation, given their impending exit scheduled for midnight on

---

* This was out of thirty-five thousand soldiers serving in the Haganah at the start of the conflict.

May 15. War was filling the vacuum, and the British no longer resisted. During these early spring weeks, Ben-Gurion filled his diaries with details and terse descriptions of the fighting, including casualties, throughout the country. At one point the troops totaled twenty-nine thousand Yishuv fighters, though Ben-Gurion noted that "only 60 percent . . . are armed properly. There is a shortage of weapons, 3-inch shells, TNT, etc., and we need another four thousand rifles. We are short of vehicles." Ben-Gurion was not surprised by the violence. He had expected it and knew the fight would have to continue.

Moreover, the British exit required the formation of a civil apparatus for statehood to go along with the military one. In spring of 1948, therefore, Ben-Gurion convened institutional bodies and decided on a provisional cabinet with thirteen members and a proto-parliament almost triple that size, to prevail until democratic elections could be held. While Ben-Gurion was laser-focused on military developments that would either ensure or crush the nascent Jewish state, Zionism itself had nurtured civilian institutions from the Balfour period to partition. The movement had built universities, hospitals, trade unions, banks, a sick fund, a pension system, a self-defense force, and a proto-government, the Jewish Agency. As former Palestinian Authority prime minister Salam Fayyad would say seventy years later, "When the Zionists declared the state, they had already built it between 1917 and 1947."[228]

A last major delay to statehood arose with the prospect of a trusteeship imposed by the major powers. Within Zionist confines, all were united on the principle of statehood, but Ben-Gurion needed to persuade his colleagues when it came to timing. The United States, for example, was calling for a cease-fire that would delay the declaration of the state. Some Zionists felt the cease-fire would provide a necessary window to improve the Yishuv's military situation in preparation for an all-out Arab war. Others feared it could be a one-way ticket to UN trusteeship, derailing statehood indefinitely.

The May 8, 1948, meeting between top Zionist diplomat Moshe Sharett and US secretary of state George Marshall thus proved pivotal in testing a US response should the Zionists declare statehood in the next week. Weizmann assisted in the diplomatic effort, and his stature was such that he was able to meet Truman—thanks to the intervention of Eddie Jacobson, Truman's Jewish confidant from their Kansas City days. Yet Sharett, not Weizmann, would ultimately have to make the recommendation to the new provisional government on whether to declare statehood.

Marshall, the US army chief of staff during the war, was enormously popular at home following the Allied victory, and many thought he was even more well liked than the president he served. The Zionists knew that Truman would therefore want the serious-minded Marshall to agree with whatever decision he made. Yet Marshall was dead set against an immediate declaration. In a dramatic White House meeting, he even took the unprecedented step of telling Truman that he might not vote for his re-election if the president were to support independence. Marshall and his top advisors were against statehood for a variety of reasons. They doubted a small Jewish state could survive militarily when surrounded by Arab states and considered the defeat of the Zionist military in a war inevitable. The presupposition of military failure, thus, raised concerns that the Zionists would soon be begging the United States to fight on their behalf, and there was a general conviction that this would be a disaster for US relations with the Arabs.

Marshall and those around him also subscribed to the belief that postwar US foreign policy called for a set of broad alliances aimed at containing the Soviet Union and its communist ideology. These were the early days of the Cold War. Alienating Arab countries would not serve US interests, in this view. Moreover, a postwar economic boom meant increasing US dependence on Arab oil.

Instead of independence, Marshall and his advisors espoused the idea of a truce lasting three months or longer that would lead to a UN trusteeship. The United States hoped, according to this model, that the British might stay in the region to enforce the cease-fire under UN auspices. The duration of the trusteeship was not defined but rather implied to be indefinite, thus suggesting that the prospect of Jewish statehood would fade away.

Sharett did see value in a three-month truce, distinguishing him from Ben-Gurion. A cease-fire would enable the Zionists to better prepare their military, gain more financial assistance from abroad, and once more clear the road to Jerusalem, where deliveries were yet again being prevented by sniper fire. Sharett also saw the value of maintaining American support. He expressed these differences with Ben-Gurion, who was not inclined to compromise on this matter, in a cable to the Zionist leader in early May.[229]

In devising a Zionist strategy, Sharett relied heavily on his May 8 meeting with Marshall, during which he hoped to gauge, first, whether a truce and trusteeship could be unlinked. Sharett could accept a three-month truce but could not live with trusteeship, which he saw as the way to sabotage a Jewish state. Improbable though it may seem today, even the steely Ben-Gurion feared unspecified US military action against the Zionists—as recorded in his diary—viewing US action as a potential existential threat to the Yishuv. The nearing British departure offered a way to assess how determined Washington might be about delaying Israeli statehood. If the British abruptly left Palestine on May 15, no one would be left to enforce the UN cease-fire.

Sharett also wanted to ascertain Marshall's view regarding a deal with Jordan along the lines that Meir had discussed with Jordan's King Abdullah in November, whereby Jordan would take the land that the Palestinians had rejected at the UN partition vote, in return for not invading the new Jewish state. Sharett had heard British colonial secretary Arthur Creech Jones predict that, following the announcement of a Jewish state, King Abdullah would only deploy militarily in areas designated to Palestinians according to the November 1947 partition, thereby refraining from an all-out assault. For the Zionists, this was a very favorable scenario. In addition, such rhetoric from Creech Jones, along with the Meir-Abdullah meeting from the previous November, suggested a British and Jordanian expectation that a Jewish state would become a reality. Marshall, however, was not convinced, believing that the serious coordination between the Zionists and Abdullah that would be required was unlikely. In a meeting with Truman on May 12, one of Marshall's advisors derisively termed it a deal "behind the barn."[230]

Marshall believed the Zionists were engaging in wishful thinking about Jordanian intentions, which could be disastrous if they were unprepared. Marshall likewise suggested to Sharett that the Zionist military commanders might be intoxicated by their successes against Palestinian irregular forces. "Their counsel is liable to be misleading," he warned the Zionist diplomat. No such swift victory would occur against the larger Arab armies.

This warning could not be shrugged off, coming from the US general who just won World War II. A few days later, in his meeting with Truman, Marshall told the president that he had bluntly informed Sharett that the United States would not rescue the Yishuv should it disregard calls for a cease-fire. "If the tide did turn adversely and they came running to us for help," he told the president, "they should be placed clearly on notice now that there was no warrant to expect help from the United States, which had warned them of the grave risk which they were running."[231]

Sharett had attempted to convince Marshall of the importance of the historical moment. The Yishuv, he said, was "on the threshold of the fulfill-ment of the hopes of centuries—a consummation of continuous striving of generations past. . . . To let go now and agree to a deferral without knowing with certainty when this [state] will be established will make us liable at the bar of Jewish history. We could not withstand this."[232] He then posed a "fundamental question" to Marshall*: "What does the U.S. government want?"[233]

In the end, Sharett could not secure assurance from Marshall that Washington would back a state after a three-month truce, stoking the Zion-ist's doubts.[234] Marshall and his advisors argued for the Zionists to postpone the declaration of statehood to avoid a full-on attack by Arab armies.[235] The risks, they said, were too grave. Sharett demurred that "the risk of forfeiting the chance of statehood was graver."[236] The Zionists could not accept a UN mandate that postponed statehood to an uncertain future. Needless to say, Sharett left the meeting deeply upset. He had not gained the minimum as-surances he required to support his own belief in a truce and to make the case to Ben-Gurion for it.

Before he left for Palestine, Sharett received encouragement from an unexpected source, Weizmann. "Moshe," he urged, "don't let them weaken, don't let them swerve, don't let them spoil the victory—the Jewish State, nothing less."[237] He told Sharett to deliver the same message to Ben-Gurion. There was a deep irony in the full embrace by the traditional incrementalist

---

* In the meeting, Sharett would explain that the US embargo on arms was preventing Jewish access to basic tools of self-defense. He accordingly requested the mildest US defense assistance, such as protective armor for buses against snipers.

of his rival's uncompromising approach at this final moment of decision. Weizmann, no longer having to hedge as official London-Jerusalem go-between, was unshackled—and he was unequivocal.

Sharett's disappointment over the meeting with Marshall was tempered by quiet indications that the president had more favorable views toward the Zionist proposals. A friend of Sharett's cited a recent meeting between Truman and Bartley Crum, a US member of the 1946 Anglo-American Committee, during which Crum apparently professed to being "quite optimistic" regarding the US position on a Jewish state. Truman advisor Clark Clifford expressed similar hopefulness regarding the president's stance in a message to the Jewish Agency.[238]

Arriving at Ben-Gurion's home in Tel Aviv on May 11, Sharett reported his findings, which validated the Zionist leader's fears regarding the State Department's tilt toward the Arabs for leverage against the Soviets.[239] Later, Ben-Gurion reportedly recounted his impressions of the encounter: "Moshe . . . gave me a detailed report on his talk with Marshall. He told me of his warnings that we would be annihilated and his suggestion that we postpone the proclamation of the state. At the end of our talk, [Moshe] added four words: 'I think [Marshall's] right,'" a conclusion Ben-Gurion implored his head diplomat to retract.[240] According to historians who have been traditionally sympathetic to Ben-Gurion over time, there would be tension between Ben-Gurion and Sharett, leaving open to question whether Ben-Gurion used those words. (Sharett's main biographer, Gabriel Sheffer, acknowledges the meeting but does not acknowledge the final reported words of Ben-Gurion.)

While Sharett briefed Ben-Gurion, Meir was testing whether King Abdullah still intended to avoid participation in a larger Arab invasion against a Jewish state.[241] Although Ben-Gurion had his doubts that Abdullah could withstand the Arab political pressure, Meir felt the effort was worth a try, especially given their momentous initial meeting the previous November. Ongoing contacts between the Zionists and Abdullah offered some reassurance, but Meir wanted to hear Abdullah's intentions face-to-face.

This time, Abdullah considered it too politically risky to travel to Palestine, so—donning Arab garb—Meir and her aide Ezra Danin went in secret to Amman.[242] During the meeting, Abdullah walked back his earlier commitment. "When I made that promise," he said, "I thought I was in control of my own destiny and could do what I thought right, but since then I have learned otherwise."[243] In addition, the king said the Zionists were too impatient in their quest for statehood and should stop demanding free immigration. Replying, Meir said that a people that had waited two thousand years for a state should not be described as "in a hurry." Likewise drawing an instant rejection was Abdullah's proposal for a "Jewish republic" to exist autonomously for one year but eventually come under his rule. Meir indicated that a Jewish entity within any other country was not the independence the Zionists sought and thus was a nonstarter. Further, Meir made clear that a Jordanian attack would draw a powerful Zionist response that would go beyond the UN partition borders and seek to acquire more land. She voiced concern that the monarch was underestimating Zionist military strength.[244]

In a telling exchange, Abdullah admitted that the Jews, at least then, stood as his "only allies in the region."[245] Yet he still could not back them openly. It was also at this meeting that Danin warned Abdullah of the security risk involved in fellow worshippers kissing the hem of the king's garment, as custom dictated—a warning that proved all too prophetic when Abdullah was assassinated while praying at Jerusalem's al-Aqsa Mosque in 1951.

A JEWISH STATE

May 12 was the day when the Zionists would choose whether to declare statehood or delay. Of the thirteen members of the Zionist provisional government, only ten were present in Tel Aviv. Travel from Jerusalem, where two members were located, was too perilous, and the third was abroad. At the meeting, which would last from 10 a.m. until almost midnight, Meir first imparted her discouraging findings through a scribbled note to the future prime minister.[246] "There will be war," it read.[247] As Meir recounted, "I could hardly bear to watch Ben-Gurion's face as he read the note, but thank God, he didn't change his mind—or ours."[248] The Yishuv leader was not shocked by the news; he had long been dubious that Abdullah could withstand Arab pressure anyway. Meir then would give a full report to the group on her meeting with the king.

On that same day, reports reached those assembled that the Arab Legion had moved preemptively.[249] Hundreds of Arab Legion members, backed by nearby Arab villagers, had attacked an isolated Jewish village between Jerusalem and Hebron called Kfar Etzion, killing 120, including twenty-one women.[250] The religious kibbutz was simply too remote to attract help from the Haganah. Determined and steady in response, Ben-Gurion said there was only one answer: defeat the Arab Legion. Even so, worse news in the form of further casualties would undoubtedly precede an ultimate victory.

Amid the distressing news from Kfar Etzion, Sharett reported on his findings from Washington and spoke at length about his conversation with Marshall, which included disappointment over the secretary of state's preference for the Zionists to delay a declaration of statehood and US calculations on how best to counter the Soviets amid faltering bilateral relations. The US approach, according to a transcript of the cabinet meeting, was aimed at creating a wedge between Russia and the oil-rich Arab states.[251] In reflecting on the State Department's inclination to link trusteeship with a cease-fire, Sharett explained: "The main sting of a cease-fire is not a military sting, but a political sting. It is not stopping war [that is problematic] but the Jews yielding on establishing an independent state." In other words, a stand-alone three-month truce was much less troubling than what it suggested: a prelude to an open-ended UN trusteeship that would divert Zionism from its singular goal of statehood. Sharett wondered aloud if these two ideas—the temporary truce and the subsequent trusteeship—could be decoupled. Here he also shared his sense of the authenticity of Marshall's call for a truce. The general was not, in his approximation, employing a ruse. Sharett praised Marshall's genuine desire to avert a regional war, "a very grave international crisis."[252] Citing his conversation with the secretary, Sharett "saw from [the Americans'] perspective complete candor. . . . They believe the declaration [of statehood] will bring [catastrophe] and it must be averted."[253]

Although Sharett praised Marshall as generally wanting a truce, he reached a dead end with the US official over the latter's genuine belief that the solution was a trusteeship. This was something the Zionists could not accept and was not even debated at this crucial cabinet meeting. Sharett, while acknowledging that the current idea for a truce "needed to be fixed," contended that the Zionists should not rule it out if it could be divorced from trusteeship. To be sure, everyone around the table wanted a state; the question was whether the Zionists could cull the benefits of a truce while extracting a pledge that the United States would favor statehood after that interim period. The participants also measured the risks of defying US wishes at this historic juncture.

Ultimately, Sharett admitted Marshall would give no such assurances about what would happen at the end of three months. This was important to Ben-Gurion, who wrote in his diary that if the United States confronted a new Jewish state militarily, the new state could not survive. Sharett said he could not recommend against declaring a state, even as he sensed that a legal framework for statehood that would be both legitimate under international law and realistically workable should allow some lag time. Such a formulation could, for example, establish an interim government for a number of months, after which a sovereign state could be declared. This approach, he believed, could reduce potential antagonism with Marshall while providing the benefits of an immediate truce—namely, time for the Haganah to prepare for full-fledged war. Yet these ideas he merely mentioned rather than emphasized, in effect staying publicly loyal to Ben-Gurion's vision.

Next, acting commander Yigael Yadin and acting chief of staff Yisrael Galili offered their military assessments at this profoundly historic juncture about whether the state would indeed be born.[254] After Yadin made his presentation, the ministers wanted to know if he felt that a truce was preferable from a military perspective. The duo clearly favored a truce but did not comment on the political dimension of Marshall's idea (that is, trusteeship) due to their professional positions as military men. They were also careful not to emphatically press for a truce, given the controversy. However, they raised broad questions about whether the Yishuv at that very moment in time could withstand a multifront war, given the lack of military preparedness. According to an abridged, declassified Hebrew transcript,* Yadin remarked on his wish for an extra two months

---

* It's unclear if the declassification of the transcript was done without specifying which ministers favored a truce, perhaps to protect them so that they would not be viewed as unenthusiastic about independence.

beyond the May 15 deadline. And he spoke somberly about the prospects of an invasion. Indeed, Yadin had been the one to report the high casualties then being suffered at Kfar Etzion. He and his fellow military leaders had been "mistaken," he said, in believing Arab forces would not strike before a full declaration of war.

Remarking on the Kfar Etzion situation, Galili noted his concern that the Arab Legion's involvement would energize local Arabs regarding the possibility of victory. After Yadin ticked off how many forces each of the Arab armies had, he acknowledged that, while the numbers were not overwhelming, he did feel that the Zionists had to move troops around in order to meet the attack of the Arab armies, and this left certain areas vulnerable. Conversely, the attack could well hinder Jewish morale, which was low due to the news that many Jews had been killed that day in Kfar Etzion and that there had not been reinforcements to save the kibbutzniks. Yadin, who had started off saying that the chances of success for the Zionists were 50/50, modified that statement. Then, when pressed, in assessing the chances for war, Yadin identified the Arabs as having "a considerable advantage."[255] He said, "I would like to summarize and to be cautious, and I would say at this moment the chances are equally weighted. But if I was more candid, I would say that their advantage is great, if all of this power would come and fight us."

This was breathtaking. On the one hand, Ben-Gurion wanted to declare a state, but Yadin and Galili thought the status quo had profound military disadvantages for the Zionists. They clearly wanted a truce. The nascent state was about to fight multiple Arab armies. But some 30 to 40 percent of the Haganah units were not yet armed.[256] They had no fighter aircraft, only primitive planes, and virtually no cannons. The promised new supplies and aircraft coming from abroad had not yet arrived. There was also a fatigue among the units, some of whom had been fighting since partition, almost six months earlier. This also reflected a shortage of manpower: only about a thousand troops, he added, were available to defend the entire southern part of the country.[257] Galili also pointed to an imbalance in heavy armaments, which would lead to "very grave" consequences "if the confrontation occurs during the coming week."[258] Despite their reluctance to comment on political matters, both military leaders were explicit that a cease-fire for a "certain time would be of great benefit for us."[259] There's no doubt that Yadin's overarching point was that a truce would give Israel more time to prepare militarily, to arm itself, and to hopefully integrate weaponry that would come from abroad. He thought a delay would make the Zionists stronger.

The assessments of Yadin and Galili were devastating. The two commanders of the military clearly favored a truce. It was now up to Ben-Gurion to do what he did best: force a discussion toward his preferred decision. Against the commanders' measured approach, he left no doubt about where he stood. While careful not to contradict any of their facts, he refused to waver. It was classic Ben-Gurion, analytical and unambiguous. "I don't see any advantage to a cease-fire," he said.[260] He viewed a cease-fire as a trap, and laid out three possible scenarios. In the first, a cease-fire "hermetically" imposed equally on the two sides would, thanks to Zionist motivation, ultimately spur a Jewish victory: feeling that its back was against the wall, the Yishuv would be able to reorganize and increase its ability to have the upper hand when the conflict recommenced. However, in and of itself, this scenario was insufficient, because the Yishuv would be cut off from support that was beyond its borders, namely manpower and weaponry. In the second scenario, the United States or Britain would lead a blockade against the Zionists, a "very dangerous" situation in which the Zionists would require many miracles to prevail. And in the third, the most likely in his view, a cease-fire would be imposed unevenly, because it could be imposed on the Palestinian Arabs but would never extend to all the surrounding Arab countries. As a result, the Arab states would continue to arm themselves to the detriment of the Zionists.

A declaration of statehood, by contrast, would allow the Zionists to tap their greatest resource—supporters abroad—who could help smuggle weaponry into the nascent country once the British departed. Yes, the Arab states too could rearm, and more tragic attacks, like the one at Kfar Etzion, were bound to occur.[261] General Arab rearmament, however, did not bother him so long as the Zionists could revitalize their own military. The opportunity to do so, prompted by statehood and denied by a truce, must not be missed. Alongside the military advantage was that offered by unchecked immigration, Ben-Gurion's touchstone. Open gates would mean an inflow of greatly needed manpower. With a cease-fire, though, Ben-Gurion argued, "the aliyah will be handcuffed and our ability to bring in weapons will be handcuffed."[262]

Ben-Gurion responded to Yadin. The military leader had said a month and a half ago that the people's morale was not high, and now he was concerned with what happened in Kfar Etzion. There were no reinforcements, and Yadin was worried that morale would fall when people were up against heavy weapons. Ben-Gurion made the alternative case on morale. Victories in Haifa, Tiberias, Safed, and Jaffa, he contended, had boosted the public mood, creating in recent weeks "a feeling of moral ascendancy and military superiority." A cease-fire, he said, would halt this momentum, allowing the Arabs to regroup. While admitting that many thousands of soldiers lacked weapons, he noted opportunities to rectify the situation, such as through drafting fifteen thousand non-enlisted weapon owners.[263] Concluding, he admitted that "the situation is difficult and filled with dangers," yet added that the Zionists could be "decisive" through wise deployment of military resources and enactment of moral values. Thus, despite an evidently weak hand, Ben-Gurion used the sheer power of argument and a vision of victory, tools he'd been wielding for decades, to persuade his cabinet of the merits of declaring statehood. Ben-Gurion was once again decisive and would carry the day.

While no formal vote appears to have been held—perhaps no one wanted to go on the record supporting a delay in statehood—the substance and tone of the speakers during this fateful session are interesting. Six seem to have wanted to declare independence on May 14, while four favored postponement and accepting a truce.[264] The previously ambivalent Sharett was in the independence-now category,* breaking the tie.[265]

---

* The traditional account of the episode is that a formal vote occurred, where six of the Zionist leaders, including Ben-Gurion and Sharett, voted to reject the cease-fire and hence by default declare independence, and four voted to accept the cease-fire. This account is most notably presented in the book *Three Days* by Zeev Sharef, an Israeli civil servant who took the minutes of the May 12, 1948, meeting. However, historian Martin Kramer argues that there was never actually a vote and that it was understood that independence was forthcoming. He does so by pointing to several pieces of evidence, including Ben-Gurion never

The only remaining issue for the moment was whether the declaration of independence would include a reference to borders. Staunchly against such a move because it could seal a geographically fragmented territory, Ben-Gurion cited the US founders, who did not delineate territory in their 1776 declaration.[266] Besides, if the Arabs launched a war, they would cede the moral authority needed to insist on a return to their desired frontier. In this, Ben-Gurion had been consistent since the aftermath of the Peel findings in 1937, when he had written to his son Amos. If the Arabs picked a fight with a new Jewish state, then they would bear the consequences of that decision.

On Friday, May 14, moments before the onset of Sabbath, Ben-Gurion recited the declaration before a jubilant crowd in Tel Aviv.[267] While resolute in public, only in his diary did he allow his worries to show. As after the UN partition vote, he did not celebrate. Now, he wrote, the people's "fate [is] in the hands of the defense forces."[268] Perhaps fittingly, he wrote this very entry in a new diary, as the next chapter of Jewish statehood was about to unfold.

ATTRIBUTES OF A LEADER

Beginning with Hitler's rise in the early 1930s, Ben-Gurion developed a single-minded determination to sustain and grow the Zionist project.[269] The Nazi threat reinforced what he had always believed—that stateless Jews were defenseless Jews—and magnified the urgency of the need for a Jewish state. Events inside and outside of Palestine forced Ben-Gurion to view the pace of the Zionist enterprise as a race against the clock. He increasingly felt the weight of Jewish history hanging on his shoulders.

As such, Ben-Gurion sought to accelerate the timetable of Zionism both in terms of bringing Jews to Palestine and securing a Jewish state. He did not have the luxury of waiting for the mandate to play out indefinitely. This explains why he effectively broke from total reliance on the British in 1939 when they announced they would phase out immigration, preventing Jews from becoming a majority in their own territory while precluding the

---

mentioning such a vote and a vote being mentioned in Sharef's book but not in the minutes on which the book was based.

democratic state from emerging. Similarly, Ben-Gurion accepted the Peel Commission because full control of part of the land, he concluded, would be preferable to no (or partial) control over all the land. This formulation would both allow unlimited Jewish immigration and facilitate the creation of an Arab Palestinian state. He felt he did not have the right to turn down what was offered given the circumstances.

As measured either by convincing the Arabs of the justice of the Zionist cause or by the Holocaust, Ben-Gurion failed. He was unable to persuade Arabs into compromise, and he was fully unprepared to rescue the six million or even a significant portion of them. Both were variables that he could not control but had to manage as best as he and his colleagues could. Yet the leader was intrepid in carrying out the Zionist vision, which he melded into himself.

Tellingly, the first decision made by Ben-Gurion at the session following the Israeli declaration of independence was to abolish the 1939 immigration restrictions. Linking people to the land was essential for Zionist success. Immigration had been Ben-Gurion's North Star since the 1930s, underlying his concept of sovereignty. Immigration would remedy what he perceived as two millennia of Jewish homelessness. And immigration would usher in democracy. The linking of these two ideas—a democratic majority by way of unfettered immigration—formed the very essence of the state, Israel, which had just then come into being. Additionally, he understood that the greater the population, the greater the ability of the Jewish state to defend itself in a hostile environment. When French president Charles de Gaulle asked Ben-Gurion in 1960 what he most wanted for his country, the prime minister replied, "More Jews." And, when de Gaulle asked where they would come from, Ben-Gurion answered: from the Soviet Union, which will collapse in thirty years.*

Ben-Gurion was a visionary. He understood what was necessary for the Jewish state to emerge. His understanding and ability to predict the evolution of international reality—whether foretelling the rise of Nazism and the

---

* Remarkably, he was off by one year, with the USSR collapsing in 1991. But starting in 1989, a million Jews from the Soviet Union would begin immigrating to Israel. Shimon Peres was at the meeting with de Gaulle when this exchange took place and recounted the story.

existential threat it posed to the Jewish people or predicting the collapse of the USSR—was uncanny. He had an extraordinary feel for what was coming, and how to respond to it, and he had the determination and the courage to do what was necessary.

Ben-Gurion would serve as Israel's first prime minister from 1948 to 1953. Moshe Sharett succeeded him, but lasted less than two years. Ben-Gurion would assume the post again from late 1955 until 1963. Only then, at age seventy-six, did he retire to his sparse accommodations at kibbutz Sde Boker in the Negev.

Ben-Gurion's achievements were towering, the inverse of his physical stature. He helped launch a state and served as its preeminent leader over its first two decades. He became the voice and face of the Jewish people worldwide. Even in Israel's early years, when it was impoverished and coping with the terrible losses of the War of Independence, he insisted that Israel must act urgently and open its gates to all the Jews, who came with no resources or possessions, from Middle Eastern countries. There would be opposition to this decision, but he would insist. This was the raison d'être of Zionism, and by dint of Ben-Gurion's sheer determination, Israel roughly doubled its Jewish population within the first three years of the country's existence, with 835,000 becoming citizens based on the Jewish law of return, a definitive slap at Britain's harsh immigration restrictions. If the price of this decision meant that immigrants would have to live in tents in peripheral areas alongside Israel's borders, so be it. The principle was greater: Israel's borders were now open to all Jewish immigrants. Ben-Gurion dedicated all his effort to consolidating and building the infrastructure of the state, while also seeking to cultivate a sense of common identity among the new immigrants who now found themselves living in their ancestral homeland.

Ben-Gurion compromised when needed, such as in accepting German reparations money early in his tenure. It was a highly controversial move, assailed by prominent critics as "blood money," as it occurred so close to the Nazi Holocaust. He reached understandings on religion and the state to avoid internal conflict. And he sought out international allies as a hedge against Arab enmity. While a pitch for US assistance in the 1950s was spurned, similar efforts during the next decade resulted in vital American provision of defensive weapons. Denied the opportunity to have positive diplomatic relations with contiguous neighbors, Ben-Gurion developed a foreign policy of the "periphery" that befriended Turkey, Ethiopia, and Iran. Making these countries strategic friends would benefit Israeli defense strategy for the subsequent three decades. Throughout his career, Ben-Gurion mixed pragmatic methods while being unswerving in pursuit of his overall aspirational goals of statehood and the building of the state. He was tactically flexible while being strategically consistent.

Despite his brilliance, Ben-Gurion was flawed. He was deeply stubborn and very tough on his political adversaries, heaping unrelenting scorn on the right-wing opposition leader, Menachem Begin, and his party. The complete political hegemony of Ben-Gurion's Labor Party from the formation of the state until 1977 engendered bitter resentment among those who did not share Labor's worldview of an Israel guided by secular, eastern European, and socialist Jews. In many ways, Labor has never been able to shake this aura of paternalism. While he was unquestionably idealistic, Ben-Gurion did not foresee the growth of religious influence in the country, therefore failing to reach needed grand consensus with those Israelis who departed from his secular outlook.

Many disagreed with Ben-Gurion at various times, but none could doubt his devotion to building a Jewish, sovereign, democratic commonwealth after two millennia of homelessness. Zionism had many fathers, but Ben-Gurion stood above them all as founder of the state. He was an exemplar of unrelenting dedication to a cause guided by principle, not whim. In 1948, Ben-Gurion made the foundational decision upon which all subsequent Israeli history rests.

CHAPTER 2

MENACHEM BEGIN

The Thin Line: Menachem Begin and the Justice of a Cause

Menachem Begin was born August 16, 1913, in the eastern European city of Brest-Litovsk, then home to about forty thousand people.[1] Situated on the western edge of present-day Belarus, the city was known as Brisk to its Jewish residents, who made up some three-quarters of the population. It spent periods as part of Lithuania, Poland, and Russia, to which it belonged at Begin's birth.[2]

Begin's father, Ze'ev Dov, embraced Zionism with a whole heart and at times defended it with a clenched fist.[3] When the founder of political Zionism, Theodor Herzl, died in 1904, Ze'ev Dov wanted the synagogue opened for a special prayer, but the city's renowned rabbi, Chaim Soloveitchik, refused to honor this request. In response, Ze'ev Dov took an axe to the lock. He was joined in this adventure by Mordechai Scheinermann, the grandfather of future Israeli prime minister Ariel Sharon.[4] Ze'ev Dov was more at home representing the Brisk Jewish community to the Russian authorities than running his father's timber business.[5] He spoke four languages, demonstrating a facility Begin would inherit.[6] Alongside his post as representative for the Jewish community, Ze'ev Dov began in the 1920s working as a journalist for a Jewish newspaper.[7] He also founded a synagogue, Hatechiya (the Revival), as well as a Hebrew-language Tarbut (culture) school.[8]

Among the unusual means by which he inculcated Zionism in his children was speaking to them in Hebrew.[9]

As the synagogue incident suggests, Ze'ev Dov was a man of deep conviction, with a willingness to act on his beliefs. When a Polish soldier tried to humiliate a rabbi with whom Ze'ev Dov was walking by cutting off his beard, Ze'ev Dov struck the soldier with his walking stick.[10] The affair did not end well for Ze'ev Dov, who was beaten on the spot and left to return home.[11] Begin embraced the heroism in his father's actions. "My father came home that day in terrible shape, but he was happy. He was happy because he had defended the honor of the Jewish people and the honor of the rabbi," he later recalled. "From that day forth I have forever remembered those two things about my youth: the persecution of our helpless Jews, and the courage of my father in defending their honor."[12] Begin was similarly inspired by his father's Zionism. "The day will come when we will all be in the Land of Israel," Ze'ev Dov announced in the presence of his son, kindling Begin's desire to transform his life and that of his people.[13]

Begin's mother, Chasia, by comparison, rarely appeared in public. Begin later described her as passive and anxious yet, at the same time, a dependable, comforting presence.[14]

Begin himself, the youngest of three children, was bookish and slight of build. He wore thick glasses and often endured beatings from his Polish peers, an experience that would cement his preoccupation with Jewish self-defense.[15]

A POLISH MODEL FOR THE REVISIONISTS

Until the late 1920s, the only Zionist organization in town was a socialist one.[16] The Begin household participated in this group's activities for a few years, but Ze'ev Dov grew increasingly disenchanted with its emphasis on socialism over Zionism.[17] In 1929, a chapter of the Revisionist youth group Betar opened, providing an attractive alternative.* That same year,

---

* Betar was named for the Jewish last stand against the Romans in 135 CE, as well as for a modern-day hero of the Zionist campaign in Palestine, Joseph Trumpeldor.

the Revisionist founder, Vladimir Jabotinsky, was scheduled to speak at the Brisk theater. Tickets were sold out, but the irrepressible Begin got into the building anyway, nestling himself in the orchestra pit.[18] He was so moved by Jabotinsky's call to stand up for Jewish rights and fight anti-Semitism that he likened his relationship to the Revisionist leader to a marriage.

The appeal of Revisionism to Begin was mostly tied to its brand of Zionism—which rejected socialism while strongly embracing nationalism—but it also held relevance in the context of Polish politics. Zionism, and the Revisionists in particular, shared ideological ground with Polish nationalism and its leader, Marshal Józef Piłsudski (1867–1935).[19] Having unified Poland in 1918, Piłsudski held an inclusive view of the country, acknowledging its different ethnic and religious minorities. His political rival, Roman Dmowski, by contrast, saw Poland as a home only to ethnically Polish Catholics. (On the military front, just as Piłsudski believed the path to Polish independence ran through an autonomous World War I fighting unit, Jabotinsky insisted that the Zionist movement also participate in the war.) From 1919 to 1921, Piłsudski, serving as Polish chief of state, led battles against the newly formed Soviet Union and sought to stanch communist expansion in Warsaw. From 1926 to 1935, he worked to carve out space for Poland and other independent states against the regional powers of Germany and the Soviet Union.

Jabotinsky extolled the Polish leader's achievements, declaring, "I know all the dark sides of this country, but I also know the other side of the Polish nature." He continued, "When the Polish people were on the verge of destruction, on the brink of abyss into which Germany fell a few years later, at that dark hour, Piłsudski arrived with a group of his followers, quietly and without rhetoric; a man who came not out of love for the Jews, and not even for the Poles, but who loved, served and fought for one thing only: fairness. And he saved his country, set in order and planted the seed of fairness within it. Were I a Polish Jew, I would say: My friend, Marshal Piłsudski's group, his faithful followers are your last hope of finding honest allies."[20]

Such rhetoric encouraged Betar members to embrace Piłsudski's legacy, including his successful postwar expansion of Polish territory.[21] While adopting the marshal's emphasis on military readiness along with his affinity for military spectacle, Betar also preached the necessity of immigration to Palestine, favored by all Zionist groups, including the Labor Zionists.

YOUTH MOVEMENT LEADER

In 1933, during his third year as a law student at Warsaw University, Begin was named as one of nine leaders of the fledgling Betar youth movement.[22] In 1935, the year he earned his law degree, he was dispatched to serve as the group's deputy commissioner in Czechoslovakia.[23] He held this role until 1937, traveling to different venues to give speeches and earning a reputation as a stirring orator. Notably, his skills as a public speaker far surpassed those as an organizer.[24]

By 1939, Betar counted some seventy thousand members in Poland alone. Undoubtedly, its rise in popularity owed much to Hitler's leadership in Germany and the continental anti-Semitism he unleashed. Other nativist upsurges were occurring across Europe including from the Dmowski-led bloc in Poland, contributing to an increasingly hostile atmosphere toward Jews in that country. Given the environment, mainstream Zionist leaders and Jabotinsky both sought a variety of avenues to open the British gates to Palestine, including diplomatic approaches. A perverse irony in the shared rise of Betar and Polish nativism is that both favored Jewish immigration to Palestine, although for very different reasons. Some in Poland, in turn, attacked Jabotinsky for playing into the hands of the nativists.

Upon his return to Poland in 1937, Begin attracted attention over two incidents. The first was his six-week imprisonment for leading a protest outside the British embassy in Warsaw over the country's immigration policy in Palestine.[25] Begin fervently believed the British should be issuing more immigration certificates, given the rise of Hitler.[26] This event appeared to herald Begin's transformation from a speaker into a man of action.

The second incident was a public clash in 1938 with Jabotinsky.[27] Like his Labor peers David Ben-Gurion and Chaim Weizmann, Jabotinsky considered diplomatic persuasion to be the primary method of swaying British policy, even as he put a premium on the use of military deterrence. This belief, dating to his own smaller role in Zionist lobbying of the British to issue the Balfour Declaration in 1917, contradicted the common perception of Jabotinsky as a believer in force alone to solve problems. But as his famed 1923 pamphlet, "The Iron Wall," suggested with respect to the Yishuv's Arab neighbors, once deterrence was achieved, territory was no longer sacrosanct. Fundamental security made concessions tolerable. Jabotinsky was also influenced by the nineteenth-century Italian leader Giuseppe Garibaldi, who balanced his nationalism with a belief in democratic ideals such as freedom, progress, and tolerance. Jabotinsky's Zionism was very much rooted in his love of Western civilization. But Begin, during the freighted 1930s, was less open to the liberal elements espoused by Jabotinsky than he would be in later decades. Moreover, the situation in Europe was now a crisis, and the solution required ridding Palestine of its British occupiers. Both of them agreed catastrophe was looming and action must be taken, yet Begin—unlike Jabotinsky—took it further by espousing an approach of concerted violence against the British.

On the ground in Palestine too, many Jabotinsky followers besides Begin were growing impatient with an incremental approach to the British. (Jabotinsky himself had been banished from Palestine by the British years earlier.) These adherents believed fighters were necessary, and in 1931 a group known as the Irgun Zvai Leumi (National Military Organization; Etzel by its acronym) was formed to this end. The Irgun made Jabotinsky an advisor, but the Revisionist leader sought greater restraint than did many of his disciples. Right-wing Yishuv restlessness in the coming years was fueled by Arab riots beginning in 1936 and the Peel Commission report published the next year, which called for Palestine to be partitioned between a Jewish and an Arab state (with a section to be designated as an international zone). In explicit contrast, the Revisionists enshrined the promise of a Jewish state on both banks of the Jordan River, the west (today's Israel and the West Bank) and the east (today's Jordan). Betar did not accept the exclusion of Transjordan from the Balfour Declaration, as outlined in a 1922 White Paper supervised by Winston Churchill, and the refrain of the group made its views clear: "The Jordan river has two banks—this one is ours, and the other one as well."[28]

More galling to Betar than the Arab revolt of 1936–1939 or the Peel report was the British intention to sharpen restrictions on immigration. Begin's willingness to be arrested for this cause showed how seriously he took it.[29] For Irgun fighters in particular, arguing for immigration at the very moment the British were closing the gates seemed futile. They preferred to persuade the British through force of arms. Jabotinsky considered the militant approach equally detached from reality. The Zionists would have no hope of prevailing. The whole issue came to a head at the third World Betar Conference, held in Warsaw in September 1938. There, Begin sided publicly with the Irgun over Jabotinsky, the man he had called "my master and teacher."[30]

Begin did not make this break lightly, and it was likely tied in his mind to the impossibility of Jewish life in eastern Europe under Hitler's dominance. Addressing Begin directly at the conference, Jabotinsky asked, "Explain to me, sir, how you plan to station Betar soldiers in Palestine without the grace of support of the international community." Begin replied, "If a force is created, help from the Diaspora will follow."[31] Begin also wanted to change the language in the Betar oath from "I will lift my arm to use my strength for defense" to "We will fight to defend our people and to conquer the homeland."[32] A piqued Jabotinsky denigrated Begin's oration as the "noise of a creaking door."[33] Yet Begin prevailed in his quest to change the oath, showing his characteristic defiance when a cherished principle was at stake and simultaneously his canny ability to read an audience. The young Betar members in Poland wanted confrontation with the British, not accommodation.

While seeking to make amends with Jabotinsky, Begin also pursued the leadership of Betar in Poland, a goal he achieved in 1939 at age twenty-five. He was so devoted to Betar that he would marry his wife, Aliza, while they were both wearing Betar uniforms.[34] During these tumultuous times, on the eve of world war, Begin had to contend with the broad question of what a Zionist youth movement could accomplish. The group lacked an underground network for smuggling Jews into Palestine, and the British had announced that they were phasing out Jewish immigration to Palestine in the much-reviled 1939 White Paper. Begin's skills as an organizer, as opposed to his vaunted abilities as an orator, would be tested.

BETWEEN NAZIS AND SOVIETS

For Begin and other European Jews, the German invasion of Poland in September 1939 was a watershed. The Nazi attack was massive and sudden, shattering the status quo. Betar effectively ceased to exist. Begin and his new wife, Aliza, along with a limited number of other Betar members, fled to Vilna, believing the city was just beyond Hitler's reach. Apparently, the group expected a warm welcome in Vilna, given the city's large Jewish population. Optimism, however, was soon clouded by reality. Begin biographer Avi Shilon notes that in Vilna Begin was given a firearm to defend himself, the only time in his life he would handle one. In June 1940, Soviet troops occupied the city. Personally, Begin was dogged by accusations of having abandoned his fellow Betar members in Poland, with some saying he should have stayed and aided his community, whatever the outcome.[35] In response, Begin raised the idea with his fellow exiled Betar members of a return to Warsaw but was voted down.[36] Subsequently, Begin defended his relocation, saying the ultimate goal should be to reach Palestine and fight the British. Yet Begin also believed Zionists should fight Hitler; indeed, many enlisted in the British army to do so. All the same, the abandonment charges heightened Begin's sensitivities, and perhaps hardened his lifelong commitment to never letting Jews again become victims.

In late summer 1940, apprehensive about the NKVD, the Soviet secret police, Begin and Aliza sought refuge in a Catholic village outside Vilna. But their plan was soon foiled. On September 20, he was detained by the Soviets.[37] While Aliza initially waited for her husband, she soon continued on to Palestine, using a forged passport and assisted by the American Jewish Joint Distribution Committee. (To assuage a worried Begin, she successfully passed along to him a message that transliterated the Hebrew word *olah,* "immigrating," embroidered on a handkerchief.) During this time, Begin was imprisoned and interrogated frequently. Drawing on his legal acumen, he contended that his involvement in the Betar movement in Poland was fully permissible, refusing on principle to sign a confession statement indicating the contrary.[38] He also engaged in a running discussion with a fellow prisoner, a Trotskyite named Garin, during which he defended Zionist ideology against those who would call it colonialism.[39]

On March 8, 1941, Begin was sentenced without trial to eight years in the gulag for joining the "anti-revolutionary" Betar.[40] Fortunately, he only served around six months. Coinciding with Begin's imprisonment, Hitler abrogated Germany's nonaggression pact with the Soviet Union, prompting an alliance between the Soviets and the Polish government-in-exile against Germany.* (More than a decade after his imprisonment, Begin wrote a book, *White Nights,* to describe his experience, including that of being tortured. He would dedicate this book to the anonymous sufferers of torture, demonstrating an ability to identify with people outside the Jewish tribe and revealing a foundation of his support for civil liberties.)

While at a transit camp in Tashkent, Begin learned of the fate of many of Europe's Jews; not long after the establishment of Israel, Begin would learn that his parents and brother, Herzl, had been killed by the Germans. Of his immediate family members, only his sister, Rachel, escaped. Begin's father and brother were two of the roughly five hundred Brisk Jews rounded up in July 1941 and either shot or drowned in the Bug River outside the city.[41] His mother, hospitalized with pneumonia, was murdered with other patients after the Germans invaded Brisk. On arriving in Palestine in spring 1942, Begin shared the lesson he'd internalized about surviving the bestialities of Europe: "I was not just saved. I have a purpose."[42] This purpose, which would define his life, was ensuring that Jews would no longer be powerless victims.

THE PATH TO PALESTINE

Begin journeyed to Palestine with Anders' Army, the free Polish force commanded by General Władysław Anders. This army traveled from the Soviet Union through Iran to Palestine, where the British waited to assume

---

*   Sources vary regarding the date when Begin was released from the prison camp.

command with the goal of fighting Italy. Begin, like other Jewish Anders' Army arrivals to Palestine, faced a dilemma: whether to stay in the force and focus on fighting the Germans or to stay in Palestine and prioritize the British. The Haganah, the mainstream pre-state militia, unsurprisingly urged the arrivals to take the latter route. Begin himself had doubts about the direct efficacy of a Jewish role against the Germans, but he perhaps also feared once again being tagged as a deserter. He thus briefly remained employed by Anders as a clerk in charge of translations before taking a leave in December 1942.

Around this time, Begin decried the British failure to allow Jewish immigration while the war raged. He held little back in his memoir: "And those who most determinedly shut their ears to the cry of Jewish blood dyeing the rivers of Europe were . . . the British rulers of the Hebrew homeland." He added, "I have no doubt that any honest British statesman who was really informed of the British Government's policy at that time, would admit that the purpose of British policy in Eretz Israel during the war years was to reduce to the minimum the number of Jews seeking to enter."[43]

After assailing the British reversal on Zionism in the 1930s, Begin effectively declared war on the mandatory government: "The British regime has sealed its shameful betrayal of the Jewish people and there is no moral basis whatsoever for its presence in Eretz Israel. . . . There is no longer any armistice between the Jewish people and the British Administration in Eretz Israel, which hands our brothers over to Hitler."[44] In opinion pieces, Begin criticized the mainstream Jewish leadership for its insufficient resistance to the British. Labor leaders during this period still considered it wrong to fight the British when the British were fighting the Nazis. Begin argued, to the contrary, that the Yishuv could attack British governmental and police targets while avoiding military infrastructure being used in the war against Hitler.

In 1940, Jabotinsky's sudden death while making a routine visit to a Betar camp in upstate New York opened up a leadership void in the Revisionist movement. Begin filled it, coming to lead the Irgun militia, which operated along similar ideological lines to another group, known by its Hebrew acronym, Lehi (Lohamei Herut Israel, or Fighters for the Freedom of Israel), and derisively as the Stern Gang.

Begin developed essentially a two-part plan to win over Zionist adherents, drawing on, among other things, his reading of Irish, Indian, and other independence movements. The first step would entail guerrilla attacks on the British. Such attacks would invariably lead to repression, angering local Jews, but Begin believed the British response would necessarily be limited. A slaughter, he said, was out of the question because the "British authorities . . . knew that if they attempted to destroy the civilian population they would launch a desperate war of vengeance in which they would pay dearly in manhood before they could achieve their purpose."[45]

Begin even turned to the Irish playwright George Bernard Shaw, and his remarks on his people's independence movement, in explaining the Yishuv's relationship to the British during World War II: "Mr. Shaw then wrote . . . an Irishman resorting to arms to achieve the independence of his country is doing only what Englishmen will do, if it be their misfortune to be invaded and conquered by the Germans. The fact that he knows that his enemies will not respect his rights if they catch him, and that he must, therefore, fight with a rope around his neck, increases his risk, but adds in the same measure to his glory in the eyes of his compatriots and of the disinterested admirers of patriotism throughout the world."[46]

The second part of Begin's plan involved enlisting the media to boost the Zionist cause. If the world watched as the British suppressed Jewish attempts at gaining autonomy, resulting sympathy for the Jews could spur changes in British behavior. The new Irgun commander put enormous emphasis on rhetorical means to achieve these ends—he read newspapers from safe houses and issued public statements aimed at persuading a wider audience of the justness of the Zionist cause. In turn, he delegated all military operations to his deputy Eitan Livni and, later, to Amichai Paglin.

On February 1, 1944, the revolutionary who had never fired a gun declared a revolt against Britain, aimed at evicting the mandatory force from the country and establishing a Jewish state. Begin personally penned the manifesto for the Irgun, announcing, "No more cease-fire in the land of Israel between the people and the Hebrew youth and the British administration, which hands over our brothers to Hitler." It continued, "The fighting youth will not be deterred by the victims of war and pain, blood, and suffering. They shall not surrender and they shall not rest as long as they are unable to bring back a time when our people had a land of their own, freedom, dignity, bread, justice, and law."[47]

In August 1944, Begin's force attacked three British police stations, in Jerusalem, Haifa, and Jaffa.[48] He recalled, "We simply wanted to take a few arms from the British police. At that time we were leaving military camps alone." This reflected his desire to avoid harming the British effort against Germany.[49] Moreover, the relative modesty of the venture was explained by the tiny Irgun membership: 1,200 in all, only 350 with any training whatsoever, and hardly any arms.[50]

Alongside exempting British military facilities, Begin made clear that he wanted to avoid civilian deaths. Begin proudly recounted how the Irgun would publish preliminary warnings, including English translations, to civilians who might be at risk during Irgun operations.[51] Symbolic targets, those at the heart of mandatory control, were of principal interest. The first targets were the now-empty British immigration offices in cities across the country, epitomizing the British clampdown on Jewish immigration.[52] This issue united large majorities within the Yishuv. Two weeks after the attack on the police station, the Irgun continued with hits on tax offices. Ever mindful of symbolism, Begin publicly warned British soldiers not to interrupt Jews blowing the shofar at the Western Wall on Yom Kippur. Whereas the Palestinian Arab community objected to the Jewish presence at the wall as an attempt to shift the status quo of the holy sites, the Jews saw it mainly as a religious act. Jabotinsky had eschewed an association of his movement with religion, but the traditionalist Begin embraced it, seeing religion as intertwined with rather than distinct from nationalism. Begin would subsequently break from Jabotinsky's son, Eri, largely due to the hotly contested differences between the two over the role of religion in Zionism.

Begin's attempts to sabotage the British put him at considerable personal risk; there was a ten-thousand-pound bounty for his capture. With Aliza and his first child, Ze'ev Binyamin (also known as Benny), he lived incognito in Tel Aviv.[53] He frequently changed aliases, dressing as a bearded ultraorthodox Jew in order to evade capture. At one point, he encountered another militia leader in Hasidic disguise: Yitzhak Shamir, then called Ysernitsky, the leader of Lehi and another future Likud prime minister.

Jewish Underground versus the Mandate

In Cairo, on November 6, 1944, Lehi militants murdered Lord Moyne, the top British official in the Middle East. Lehi had identified Moyne as a leading proponent of the 1939 British White Paper, which had called for an end to Jewish immigration by 1944, ensuring that the Jews would not have their own state. The British reaction to the killing was swift and harsh. Officials insisted that the Haganah, the mainstream Zionist defense arm, turn in all Lehi and Irgun militants. The resulting period came to be known as the "hunting season," or the *Saison*. Indeed, it would be the first time the mainstream Zionists would target and hand over their Jewish brothers. Although resentments had simmered between the Labor and Revisionist wings, particularly in the early 1930s, never before had the mainstream bloc engaged in mass arrests of their kinsmen. One current cause of Labor disquiet was that the Irgun had started its own revolt earlier in the year without getting consent from the mainstream leadership. Begin had received prominent visitors from the Haganah, such as Eliyahu Golomb and Moshe Sneh, who evidently made clear to him that no violent acts would be tolerated. While he likely felt flattered to have received this high-level attention, Begin ignored their warnings against acting unilaterally. For his part, Ben-Gurion saw the Irgun as more of a threat than Lehi, given the former's link to a political platform. He assumed correctly that when a state finally emerged, Lehi would disappear but the Irgun Revisionists would persist.

The collision between the Haganah and Irgun meant, suddenly, no friendly warnings to Begin. Without help from the mainstream Yishuv leaders, the Irgun members were far more vulnerable to British capture. One history of the Haganah recounts that the group gave the British the names of seven hundred members, three hundred of whom were arrested, with others held at kibbutzim.[54] Begin's supporters urged him to push back hard against the Haganah.

But Begin, drawing from the Talmudic dictum that one Jew must never turn against another, insisted on abiding by a cease-fire. Jews, he famously said, must never be riven apart by civil war. Begin would take pride in this stand over his entire life, and it would serve him well for posterity, even as many of his peers at the time disdained his call for restraint. He was characterized as someone who possessed *ahavat yisrael*—literally "a love of Israel," but also widely interpreted historically as a love of the Jewish people. Begin's love of Jews was genuine, but one cannot discount that this also reflected his shrewd political instincts.

At a pivotal meeting of underground commanders during the Saison, Begin laid out his thinking:

> Who are we fighting against? Of course, we're fighting against the British enslavers. And what do the British wish to do? Their answer is short— to destroy us. For this purpose, they are using the Haganah forces. Of course, their plan is to achieve three goals. First, to divert us from our goal—the rebellion. Second, to drag us into a fraternal war. And when the British think that they have eliminated Etzel, and the Haganah is exhausted by this fraternal war, they will engage the Haganah forces and eliminate them as well. When the Haganah realizes its persecutors' plan, it will stop chasing after us, and the way will be open for a joint battle against the British forces of evil. Gentlemen, there will be no fraternal war. And never will a Jew raise his hand to another Jew.[55]

Holding up a slip of paper, he added, "The boundary between purity and contamination is as thin as this sheet of paper. Be careful not to cross it."

Begin's view prevailed, and his stature eventually rose as a result, even as many of his fighters were jailed. While presiding at a cabinet meeting as prime minister almost forty years later, at that point faced with settlers who sought to defy his moves toward peace, he recalled this episode, articulating his hope that avoiding a fraternal war would endure as his greatest legacy.

On avoiding factional enmity, he would also write: "We did not teach the Irgun fighters to hate our political opponents. One sided hatred is obviously a threat to national unity. Mutual hatred brings almost certain civil war."[56] Begin also countered charges from the mainstream leadership that the Revisionists were fighting only to attain political power. To the contrary, he wrote, "We fought in the underground for the establishment of Jewish rule; we were not concerned with power. Our opponents could never believe this of us."[57]

As the world war came to an end, the British hold on Palestine grew ever more tenuous. Now Begin finally had his chance to collaborate with the mainstream leadership against the British. With the Germans vanquished, Ben-Gurion saw an opportunity to hit the British harder, including through violence if needed, with the goal of prying open the doors to Jewish immigration. Even though Ben-Gurion held a low opinion of Begin, seeing him as a demagogue, he conveyed through his aides a willingness to engage in quiet cooperation between the underground groups, with an eye to saving the roughly 250,000 Jews languishing in European displaced person (DP) camps.[58] For Begin, this alliance meant the establishment of the Jewish Resistance Movement, as it was known then, and legitimacy for both him and the Irgun.

This cooperation continued into the first part of 1946, around when US president Harry Truman expressed sympathy for the idea of allowing Jewish DPs to enter Palestine. Despite objecting to this idea, Britain agreed to a joint panel with the United States to consider the option. These developments persuaded Ben-Gurion that the Jewish Resistance Movement had run its course. Now, he felt, militancy could only be a hindrance to immigration. Begin disagreed, wanting to continue the collaboration and believing force would expedite the British withdrawal from Palestine.

In the face of continued operations by the Zionist right wing, the British struck back in June 1946 with a campaign that became known as Black Sabbath. The sweep through Jewish militia sites yielded caches of weapons and documents that threatened to incriminate mainstream Zionists for secretly working with the Irgun and Lehi. Many in the Haganah were arrested, including Yitzhak Rabin, and their sensitive papers were confiscated.

This was the context in which the calamitous bombing of the King David Hotel occurred in July 1946. For months, the Irgun had been agitating to destroy the hotel's wing that housed Britain's military and administrative headquarters, and now the militia had a clear objective: eliminating evidence gathered against the Zionist leadership. In Begin's account, the Haganah itself approved the operation on July 1, with the attack originally scheduled to take place July 19. But Haganah leaders experienced doubts, conveying to Begin that the operation needed to be postponed. The Irgun rescheduled the strike for July 22. Begin believed that a half hour of advance notice would be ample time to evacuate the hotel—preventing any injury—but not so much that the British could take all the documents with them. About fifteen minutes after planting the fuses, the Irgun contacted the French consulate in Jerusalem and the *Palestine Post*. (Begin would claim in his memoir *The Revolt* that a British official had proclaimed upon hearing the warning, "We are not here to take orders from the Jews. We give *them* orders."[59]) But these warnings failed to produce an evacuation. Ninety-two lives were lost in the attack, along with 476 injured, many of them outside the British military. Among those killed were twenty-eight British, forty-one Arabs, and seventeen Jews. Begin, who loved BBC radio, listened to the mournful music as the broadcasters reported on the fatalities. Sinking into his chair, he asked, "What happened, what the hell happened?"[60]

While publicly regretting the loss of innocent lives, especially those with no connection to the British administration, Begin did not entirely disavow the operation. He would later write, "Our satisfaction at the success of the great operation was bitterly marred. Again we went through days of pain and nights of sorrow for the blood that need not have been shed."[61] Yet Begin also cast blame on the British for their obstinate failure to evacuate officials—and felt the sting of what he considered a Haganah betrayal. The Irgun had postponed the attack at least twice at the request of the Haganah, which had provisionally approved it, and now the mainstream militia issued a statement on its radio station denouncing the strike. Still Begin, upholding his principle of solidarity with fellow Jews, did not call out the Haganah, later writing, "We remained silent—for the sake of the common struggle."[62] Nevertheless, the event broke apart the Jewish Resistance Movement for good; no more military cooperation would take place between the groups.

But Begin kept up his anti-British efforts. After a sixteen-year-old Irgun fighter was flogged on December 27, 1946, for holding up a bank in Jaffa, the Irgun responded by capturing and flogging British military personnel in Netanya, Tel Aviv, and Rishon LeZion. The flogging punishment, from both sides, was designed to humiliate. The British retaliated against the Irgun by imposing curfews and making additional arrests. Begin then issued a public threat calling out the "Nazo-British" general Evelyn Barker. "We now warn: if the oppressors dare to injure the body, or the personal or national honor of young Hebrews, we will not respond with the whip: we will respond with fire."[63]

By maintaining his leadership role in the underground, Begin ensured the British would continue to view him as an outlaw. But in August 1947, the newly created UN Special Commission on Palestine, organized in response to Britain's handover of its Palestine burden to the UN, offered the leader another chance at personal validation. While in Palestine on a fact-finding mission, panel members interviewed Begin to ascertain his political views. The secret session, held at the home of poet and Irgun sympathizer Yaakov Cahan, lasted three hours, providing an extraordinary experience for Begin. During this session, Begin made clear that he would dismantle the Irgun upon the founding of a Jewish state, but he likewise asserted that his group opposed a UN partition into Jewish and Arab states.

When, on November 29, 1947, the UN approved this very partition, Begin no doubt had powerful mixed feelings. On one hand, the UN vote paved the way for a Jewish state. This was the consensus dream of the vast majority of Zionists, restoring Jewish sovereignty after two thousand years. On this there was no difference between the mainstream Labor leaders and the Revisionist Begin. The differences were over establishing the state on a relatively small amount of land compared to what the Zionists felt they were entitled to. Ben-Gurion believed the borders would be adjusted if the Arabs attacked and the Jews were able to defeat them. But Begin focused on the injustice of the international system providing half a loaf, thus depriving

Zionism of control over key areas resonant in Jewish history, none greater than Jerusalem. He deplored the internationalized status granted to Jerusalem and believed the division of the land would only lead to later violence. As he wrote on the topic, "Let this be clear: the partition plan is not a plan for peace, despite its inherent renunciation of territory, a renunciation which has no legal validity. The establishment even of this 'ghetto' inside our Homeland will be carried out amidst flames of fire and rivers of blood." He continued, "The partition of the Homeland is illegal. It will never be recognized. The signature by institutions and individuals of the partition agreement is invalid. It will not bind the Jewish people. Jerusalem was and will forever be our capital. Eretz Israel will be restored to the people of Israel. All of it. . . . And we proceeded to explain once again: Partition will not ensure peace in our country."[64] By "illegal," he meant that the UN partition had essentially severed parts of the Jewish biblical patrimony, and he sought to make clear that he would never recognize the validity of these unjust concessions by the mainstream Zionist leadership.

In April 1948, with the civil war phase—which pit Jews against Arabs in Mandatory Palestine without the intervention yet of Arab states—underway for about six months, Begin and his militia experienced what they considered another serious betrayal from the mainstream camp. The context here was a continued focus by the Irgun on targeting British interests rather than those of Palestinian Arabs, on whom members of the militia had long wanted to focus. Begin, for his part, had previously resisted such entreaties, keeping his eyes on the mandate. But now, with the British set to leave the country, he thought differently. The siege of Jerusalem had produced dire shortages and an urgent need to provide relief for residents. Aware of the hilltop snipers blocking provisions from entering the city, Begin sought to enlist the Irgun to do its part, while Ben-Gurion diverted resources to lift the siege.

This was the context in which the Deir Yassin tragedy played out. Deir Yassin was one of a number of Arab villages occupying the strategically important high ground alongside Jerusalem. Capture of the village would allow reinforcements to stream in from neighboring areas to fight for the city. Yishuv leaders also thought the relatively flat terrain in the village would lend itself to an airfield. During talks with the Haganah about creating a unified national defense force once the state was formed, Begin asked David Shaltiel, the Haganah's regional commander for Jerusalem, about a potential Irgun operation to take Deir Yassin. Shaltiel agreed to this idea, asking only that the Irgun hold the village, rather than attacking and then retreating elsewhere. Yet the Irgun—joined by Lehi troops—had no experience in such a maneuver, presaging the meltdown to come. Surprised by Iraqi volunteer units defending the area, the Irgun threw hand grenades at Arab homes without sufficiently warning residents to clear out in advance. According to Israeli historian Benny Morris, who is renowned for his research on the 1948 war, as the Irgun advanced, "a van blared a message calling on the villagers to put down their weapons and flee. But the van quickly overturned in a ditch; the villagers may not have heard the broadcasts."[65] About a hundred Arabs died as a result of the grenade attacks, whereas the Jewish groups lost four members, with thirty-one injured—about a quarter of all the Irgun and Lehi fighters involved.

As usual, Begin had not involved himself in the operational details, leaving it to Mordechai Raanan-Kaufman, an Irgun commander for the Jerusalem district. Yet Begin was the leader of the Irgun and would not distance himself from an operation that could blacken his name. He later wrote of how the rumors of a massacre had so frightened area Arabs that some had been prompted to flee their own villages. At the same time, the event provided a rallying cry for those opposed to Jewish statehood. Deir Yassin became an enduring symbol. The day after the meeting between Golda Meir and King Abdullah in Jordan, Arabs attacked Jews in the Kfar Etzion community to chants of "Deir Yassin."

Debates over Deir Yassin persist until today, but the Yishuv's march toward its state continued. On May 15, as soon as Shabbat ended, Begin welcomed the signing of the Israeli declaration of independence on Irgun radio, having been excluded from the actual event by Ben-Gurion. In his remarks, Begin recited the *shehecheyanu* prayer (literally, "He who has kept us alive"), the traditional Jewish blessing for marking milestones. Yet even after declaring his plans to dismantle the Irgun and incorporate its fighters into the Israel Defense Forces (IDF), Begin would not fully comply with these terms. His deviation centered on Jerusalem, where Irgun fighters had been stationed but were unable to prevent the Arab Legion from gaining control over the Old City, with its holy sites. Whereas Begin could not justify keeping his fighters within Israeli territory, he could justify keeping them outside it, where appropriate—and Jerusalem, internationalized under the terms of the UN partition plan, fit this category.

AN OUTSIDER IN A NEW STATE

On June 1, 1948, with the exception of its units in Jerusalem, the Irgun was folded into the IDF. Begin now believed this gray area would allow for the import of weaponry—made all the more acceptable because it would be delivered to the IDF. But again, the outcome of what turned out to be his misapprehension was tragic. Two days after the state was established, Begin notified key figures in what became the Ministry of Defense that the Irgun had access to incoming weapons, which he was willing to channel to the IDF. In subsequent contacts, he said he wanted some of this weaponry to be dedicated to Irgun fighters in Jerusalem. The vessel for these armaments was a ship called the *Altalena*—named for Jabotinsky's Italian nom de plume, meaning "seesaw"—and the agents responsible for delivering the arms were an unusual coterie of Irgun activists in France, who had successfully persuaded the French government to provide the extra matériel.

Mixed signals sent by Begin to Ben-Gurion's liaisons in the IDF may account for the breakdown that followed. Even the weapons that Begin wanted designated for the IDF, rather than for Irgun units in Jerusalem, he eventually sought to earmark for units that had absorbed large numbers of Irgun combatants. Ben-Gurion could not accept this demand. Complicating matters, a brief UN-mandated cease-fire at the end of May during the war meant a ban on the acquisition of new weaponry.

At the time of the negotiations between Begin and the IDF command, some of the weapons had already been unloaded north of Netanya, at Kfar Vitkin—a quiet port deemed sufficiently distant from the eyes of UN inspectors seeking to enforce the cease-fire. But after clashes began between IDF and Irgun elements, Begin boarded the ship and ordered it to travel to Tel Aviv, where he apparently believed an IDF-initiated confrontation would be less likely in the presence of so many civilians, Irgun supporters among them. But Begin had underestimated Ben-Gurion's resolve to snuff out budding militias after a state had been established. While the boat was still in transit, the Israeli leader, after receiving two cabinet decisions on the matter, ordered young commanders, including Yitzhak Rabin, to fire on the ship. Ben-Gurion would declare, "This is an attempt to destroy the army, this is an attempt to murder the state," meaning the state must maintain the monopoly on weapons and not deteriorate into militias.[66] Sixteen Irgun members and three IDF fighters died in the exchange. Begin was stunned and distraught by the development. But as with his other stands against Jewish infighting, he would be forever proud for insisting that the militia members not fire back. After the captain raised a white flag, Begin waited for the wounded to be treated before making it to shore, avoiding injury. He would subsequently lambaste the government on underground radio for its actions, emphasizing that most of the weapons would have been handed over to the IDF anyway.

Yet Ben-Gurion, too, felt vindicated by his role in the *Altalena* affair. A state could only be established, he contended, when it had established a monopoly on the use of force. He even referred to the weapon that had fired on the ship as the "holy cannon."[67] In taking responsibility for the incident, not to mention refusing to express any regret, the first Israeli prime minister paid what he considered a worthwhile political price. A state simply could not function with competing militias.

Begin's restraint in the affair served him well. He would later write that the threat of a civil war had loomed but that "we swore an oath: 'In no circumstances will we use arms against our fellow Jews.'"[68] He continued, "And so it came to pass that there was no fratricidal war in Israel to destroy the Jewish State before it was properly born. In spite of everything—there was no civil war!"[69] A related story holds that after the *Altalena* incident, Begin had visited the home of an Irgun member who had expressed a desire to assassinate Ben-Gurion. "If you want to kill Jews," Begin reportedly told this individual, "you had better shoot me first."[70] Many wars of liberation, Begin would note, are followed by fratricidal violence, but he had personally ensured this would not happen with his people.

Politically, the long-term threat Ben-Gurion foresaw in the Irgun soon materialized with the creation of the new state. Begin's party was called Herut, meaning "freedom." It contained one wing consisting of Jabotinsky followers, largely based in the United States and including the Revisionist leader's son, Eri. These adherents adopted a kind of libertarian philosophy, focused on free enterprise. The libertarianism aligned with Eri Jabotinsky's secular outlook and entailed a call for Israel to separate itself from the "obsolete ancient civilization" of Judaism.[71] Begin disagreed intensely with this approach, believing Herut must draw its convictions directly from Jewish tradition, which he considered the marrow of his people's history. The party need not consist only of religious members, according to his thinking, but rather should project a broad respect for Jewish tradition, which Begin believed many shared despite the aversion toward religion reflected in Ben-Gurion's Labor Party, known as Mapai. Here, a telling dispute occurred among establishment Zionist groups over whether Israel's declaration of independence would mention God, with a compromise reached to use "Rock of Israel." Begin also believed that respect for Judaism would resonate with traditionally minded immigrants, who were turned off by Labor's insistence on creating a "new Jew." Labor believed in changing the profile of Jews from that of a people who historically saw their lives centered on rabbinical seminaries to one centered on tilling the soil.

Begin's polemical speaking style would elevate Herut's traditionalism over the course of his career. He would intentionally invoke biblical and rabbinical verse to make contemporary points in seeking to connect with his audience. Indeed, if Begin during the pre-state years remained a shadowy figure who feared publicity—in large part because he wanted to avoid capture by the British—he pursued the opposite goal after 1948: the cultivation of a well-defined, entirely distinctive public profile.

Overall, Begin saw Herut as the Jewish conscience of the new state rather than an advocate on discrete issues such as taxation or education policy. Having arrived in the country just five years earlier, he had no particular grasp of the country's range of inhabitants or their overarching needs. He even resisted appeals to outline Herut's party platform in forums like policy journals. In a way, Herut had little choice but to adopt a broad-brush approach. Labor, long before statehood, had consolidated governing authority over trade unions, health care, communal settlements, and other institutions of the Palestine Jewish community. With parliamentary elections approaching in 1949, Herut faced the steep task of simply establishing itself as a credible opposition bloc. It did so largely through appeals to emotion and the familiarity of Jewish tradition. Moreover, where Mapai deviated from Jewish tradition, Herut could act as a check on the majority's power. Begin was well matched to this role, given his oratorical skill and ability to appeal to those outside the Labor Zionist mainstream. Even his tailored suits presented a useful contrast to the open shirts and sandals of the new Jew ethos, signaling sympathy for those Israelis who had not embraced secular and socialist ideals.

Begin, moreover, wanted to ensure Israel was altogether worthy of the Jewish victims of the Holocaust, as well as other Jews who had yearned for a homeland for two thousand years. Whereas Ben-Gurion had not resided in Europe since 1906 and evinced scorn for diaspora traditions, Begin, the recent arrival, would speak thunderously in defense of his European kin. He was a powerful advocate for those who interpreted developments against Israel through the lens of anti-Semitism. His personal experiences—namely the murder of his family by the Germans and his own time in Europe at the start of the Holocaust—gave him the credibility of an eyewitness. He had reason to believe the worst about the Jews' opponents. Taken together, Begin's views were darker than those of the leaders of the Yishuv who were trying to develop a state, even if they had experienced the enmity of local Arabs.

Begin would emerge as the defender not only of European traditionalists but also of the Jewish waves that arrived in Israel from Middle East countries between 1949 and 1951, almost doubling the initial national population—of Jews and Arabs—of just over eight hundred thousand. These newcomers included about 661,000 Jews, as well as others.[72] In allowing Jewish entrants from countries such as Yemen, Syria, Egypt, Morocco, and Iraq—many of whom had been suddenly marginalized as a fifth column in their countries of origin, given Israel's emergence—Ben-Gurion defied some Mapai colleagues who claimed the country simply could not afford to welcome this many arrivals. And, to be sure, the accommodations in *maabarot* (transit camps) situated on Israel's peripheries were little more than Spartan tent cities. Begin, for his part, vocally identified with these arrivals as fellow outsiders—traditionalist Sephardim rather than Mapai socialists from Europe. He connected with them through his invocation of the Jewish traditional experience in the diaspora and by identifying their arrival as fulfilling the end of two millennia of homelessness. Begin reminded the new immigrants that the Irgun had included both Sephardi and Ashkenazi fighters who together had expelled the British. Both in these earlier years and later on, Begin would identify with the outsider status of Sephardi immigrants, charging the Mapai leadership with seeking to socially engineer every Israeli toward an agriculturalist mind-set, rather than allowing immigrants to resume their previously dignified careers as shopkeepers, rabbis, or tradespeople. This rhetoric struck a deep chord.

Begin's emotional speaking style, as many have remarked, seemed like demagogic posturing. His speeches contained, in equal parts, melodrama, searing critique, and sarcasm, and he basked in the adoration of crowds. In response to critics who argued that he should focus on problem-solving, rather than solely on rhetoric that emphasized Jewish themes and unity against external threats to the state, he could be dismissive. In one instance, he retorted: "They should try talking in front of ten thousand people in the square, the crowd standing on their feet, the sun beating down on their heads, and sometimes in the rain, and then they should try to give a scholarly lecture."[73] Such expressions revealed his stubborn streak. His refusal to bend often exacerbated national divisions.

"BLOOD MONEY"?

A defining moment for Begin and his rhetorical limits occurred during the debate over German reparations. During the early 1950s, while absorbing masses of immigrants, the country was experiencing profound economic austerity, with virtually no foreign reserves. This explains why, in 1951, Israel petitioned the powers occupying Germany, noting that the new state had resettled approximately half a million Holocaust survivors. In March 1952, negotiations began between Israel and West Germany, later joined by the World Jewish Congress, and a deal was struck in September 1952 making Israel heir to Holocaust victims who lacked survivors. In the agreement, West German chancellor Konrad Adenauer pledged to provide Israel with three billion German marks (around six billion dollars in 2018 terms) over the next twelve years, with the money to be invested in national infrastructure, thereby helping build Israel.

Begin rejected not only the terms of this deal but the entire premise of the reparations, calling the proposed payments "blood money"—essentially offering absolution to Germany for the atrocities it had perpetrated. Begin was not alone in holding this view; the pro-Soviet Mapam party, often at odds with the establishment Mapai, also considered it unthinkable to accept German money.

For Begin professionally, the reparations debate came at a key moment. He had felt himself somewhat adrift after a poor showing by his Herut party during the 1951 Knesset vote, and he had announced his intention to resign. He also began studying for the bar, so that he could practice as an attorney, and composing what would later be *White Nights,* his memoir about his time in the Soviet prison.[74] But the reparations question drew him right back into public life. Begin regarded negotiations with West Germany as a direct assault on the Jewish people and on his immediate family. Yohanan Bader, a fellow Herut parliamentarian who had served with Begin in the Irgun, sought to coax his friend out of his retirement: "Menachem, this is not just a historical issue. This is your moral obligation to your family, your duty toward your murdered mother."[75]

The reparations issue once again revealed core philosophical differences between Begin and his rival Ben-Gurion. Whereas Begin focused on the victims of the Holocaust, the prime minister kept his emphasis on the need to build the state, which housed Holocaust survivors, among others. But the brand of Zionism embraced by Ben-Gurion took a more strident approach to the concept of *shlilat ha'golah,* or negation of the diaspora. His insistence that Israelis hebraize their names implied a distancing from their European past, even a repudiation. (Menachem Begin's name remained unchanged from his birth name.)

In the postwar years, furthermore, Ben-Gurion saw the diaspora as a competitor to the new Israel. While desiring the diaspora's economic assistance, he simultaneously sought to avoid the suggestion that Jewish life outside Israel was just as legitimate, ideologically, as that within the new state. In something of an irony, Begin, the fervent nationalist, experienced no such qualms. He instead saw greatness in the diasporic legacy over two millennia, even if he preferred that Jews live in the Land of Israel. The Jews had no doubt suffered during their exile, but they had also survived, staying intact as a people. Over those years, Jewish religion and culture had flowered thanks to the Talmud, religious scholarship, and resilient communal structures. Another difference between Ben-Gurion and Begin was that the prime minister saw Zionism as a revival after two millennia of displacement since the last Jewish commonwealth was destroyed by Rome in 70 CE, while the oppositionist considered it a link—albeit a special link—in a continuous chain of history. Every link in this chain mattered to Begin, the German calamity perhaps foremost among them. All Jewish memory and identity, in Begin's view, depended on honoring the people who underwent unthinkable horrors in the recent past, especially in a country that tended to repress them. Politically, this allowed Begin to burnish his image as the guardian of Holocaust memory and of future Jewish survival.

To assail the reparations deal, Begin spoke at two rallies, on January 5, 1952, in Tel Aviv and on January 7 in Jerusalem. In these speeches, Begin drew on all his rhetorical skills while abandoning any hint of restraint or statesmanship. At the Tel Aviv demonstration, attended by some ten thousand people, Begin called on citizens to refuse to pay taxes should the reparations deal go forward.[76] Asserting that Ben-Gurion would be judged for his "crimes," Begin urged his audience to attend his upcoming speech in Jerusalem, to be held near the provisional Knesset building downtown. During that address, before an even larger crowd of about fifteen thousand, Begin invoked the Bible in discussing the "abomination" of the talks. He thundered, "They say that Germany is a nation and not what it actually is: a herd of wolves who devoured our people as prey. . . . And thanks to our people's blood Ben-Gurion became prime minister, that small tyrant and great maniac. . . . How will we look when our disgrace is exposed, as we turn to our fathers' murderers to receive money for their spilled blood?"[77] Begin then led the crowd toward the building, personally ascended the podium inside the chambers, and proceeded to violate all norms of civic discourse.

Invoking the *Altalena,* and pointing at Ben-Gurion, he raged, "When you fired your gun at me I commanded: No! Today I will command. Yes!" He then added ominously: "I am telling you, there will be no agreement with Germany. . . . This is one of those things for which we will give our lives; for this we will die. We will leave our families and say goodbye to our children so that there will be no negotiations with Germany."[78]

Begin's incendiary oration spurred riots outside the building, with his acolytes hurling rocks at the Knesset windows. The police used tear gas in response, allowing Begin to draw opportunistic comparisons to the gas chambers. When all was said and done, some 140 protesters were arrested and hundreds of police and protesters were injured. Begin lost the Knesset vote for which he'd been lobbying, sixty-one to fifty. For advocating violence and insulting the prime minister, he was suspended for three months from his Knesset seat. Begin, in the aftermath, briefly mulled fighting on, even suggesting to an old Irgun peer that he'd consider resuming life in the underground. Yet the peer did not offer to join. Begin soon realized he had erred and stepped back from such suggestions. This was a sovereign country, not a pre-state entity.

The reparations crisis was a low point for Begin. The country was in its infancy. Its democratic institutions were not yet fully formed when Begin declared he would defy all limits. Though his own sense of restraint would eventually prevail, this restraint came too late. Begin should have known better. The risk of strife was high and only luckily was it averted. In later years, Begin never brought up January 7, 1952. It was no source of personal pride. He is not known to have ever apologized for his incitement, but he did resume his former opposition to violence against fellow Jews, irrespective of policy disagreements.

ARABS AND CIVIL LIBERTIES

Begin's views on Arabs, in the early years of statehood, would vary based on the area in question. On Israel's claims to Jordan, he was fairly clear. Biblical land was not a chip to be bargained away but rather an inheritance to be adamantly defended. This explained his disapproval of the UN partition in

1947. When an armistice agreement was reached with Jordan in July 1949, Begin submitted a no-confidence motion against the government, saying, "This is an agreement with a country that has no right to exist."[79] After the armistice, he publicly called for a further round of hostilities to take Jordan, an idea that attracted little support following the heavy costs of a war against five Arab nations.[80] Up until 1964, Begin and his Herut party would put "Jordan" in quotes in their writing.[81] This sort of posturing made it easy for Ben-Gurion to marginalize him as an extremist.

On Arab-Israeli relations in general, Begin regarded Ben-Gurion's actions as too solicitous toward the US position, which favored a more accommodationist stance. The Suez crisis, which occurred in 1956, was a case in point. When Ben-Gurion agreed to withdraw from the Sinai following the threat of sanctions by US president Dwight Eisenhower, Begin bristled. Yet unlike in Jordan, the reason here involved not Jewish inheritance—the Sinai in his view was not part of ancient Israel—but strategy. He believed the United States, a world power, would continue to exert unrelenting pressure on Israel unless the Jewish state resisted. During the first few years of the state, Begin did favor neutrality between the Americans and the Soviets when it came to the superpower competition.[82] However, his position evolved; he stopped questioning the fundamental idea that Israel needed to ally itself with the United States. This view was solidified when he learned that the Soviet Union was providing arms to Egyptian president Gamal Abdel Nasser.

While he took a hard line on the Arabs over issues relating to territory, Begin argued that Israeli Arabs should enjoy equal rights with their Jewish compatriots. Jewish nationalism, he believed throughout his life, was compatible with civil liberties for all Israeli citizens, a position that later placed him at odds with party colleagues. Thus, in 1962, he publicly opposed keeping the Israeli Arab population under martial law amid security fears—the national policy that prevailed from statehood until 1966. He also objected to the idea that Arabs' exemption from military service should somehow dilute their rights, calling this a "strange claim" during one Knesset session. The exemption, he explained, was a product of Israel's "own free will and I believe that the moral reason for it is valid. Should war break out, we would not want one Arab citizen to face the harsh human test that our own people had experienced for generations."[83] Likewise, the Qibya attack in 1953, led by twenty-five-year-old Ariel Sharon in response to Palestinian cross-border operations, drew Begin's displeasure because it claimed innocent Arab lives.

According to Begin's sense of liberty, the state should never trample on individual rights. Indeed, given the predominance of the governing party, he had long feared being treated unfairly by the Mapai leadership. As an antidote, he counted on the courts to check what he considered an overzealous wielding of the state apparatus by the majority. Even when faced with an unfavorable court ruling, Begin took solace in the role of the courts as a check on executive power. Still, there were limits to his advocacy. Begin was among those to push early on for an Israeli constitution, but he was unwilling to confront the religious Israelis who feared such a document would curb their prerogatives.

MINISTER WITHOUT PORTFOLIO

Over the first two decades of Israeli statehood, Begin remained a political outsider while seeing few challenges from within his party. Herut lost election after election, yet the former Irgun leader commanded loyalty from his fellow party members even while shut out of power. In May 1967, however, the threat of war against Egypt, Jordan, and Syria changed the calculus for Begin. During this tense period, national leaders were questioning whether Prime Minister Levi Eshkol, who served simultaneously as defense minister, was up to leading Israel in battle. Underlying such anxieties was Eshkol's lack of a military background or involvement in the pre-state underground.[84] The reality is that Eshkol had dispatched an envoy, Foreign Minister Abba Eban, to win political backing in Washington, London, and Paris for Israel's position after Egypt sent six divisions into the Sinai and to Israel's border.[85] However, this diplomacy, along with the subsequent trip of Mossad chief Meir Amit, was not discernible to the public. The public mistook Eshkol's low-profile, active efforts to avert war as indecisiveness in the face of Nasser's amassing of troops. In a dramatic departure, Begin even made a visit to his nemesis, Ben-Gurion, urging him to come out of retirement and replace Eshkol. Yet here Begin observed that Ben-Gurion lacked his former command of policy detail. On June 1, to deal with growing unease within the country, Moshe Dayan became the new defense minister in Eshkol's government. But Begin's party was also invited to join a national emergency government, with the opposition leader serving as "minister without portfolio." In this moment of national crisis, Begin was, at long last, empowered.

On June 6, the second day of the war, Begin called for the IDF to take the Old City of Jerusalem amid rapid progress in the larger fight. For Begin, the lover of symbolism and ceremony, opportunities abounded. The Irgun's last campaign during the 1948 war, for instance, had been an unsuccessful attempt to take the Jewish Quarter. Now that effort could be redeemed. Moreover, Begin advocated that once the area was seized, the entire cabinet— along with Israel's two chief rabbis—go to the Western Wall and read the Psalms passage invoking the return to Zion, as well as the shehecheyanu.[86] Begin, ever the stickler with language, insisted that Israel use the term "liberated," not "captured," but ultimately agreed on the formulation that the Old City "is in our hands." This is precisely how paratrooper leader Mordechai "Motta" Gur put it on seizing the Temple Mount/Haram al-Sharif.[87]

With the ultimate victory over the Arab states, though, came steep challenges for the Israeli leadership, and for Begin in particular. Israel now controlled triple its prewar land, having won the Golan Heights from Syria, the Sinai Peninsula and adjoining Gaza Strip from Egypt, and East Jerusalem and the West Bank from Jordan. The government needed to articulate a coherent plan.

Later in June 1967, while in New York for a session of the UN Security Council, Israeli foreign minister Abba Eban planned to meet separately with US national security advisor McGeorge Bundy to discuss Israel's newly acquired territories. Having a strategy about how to deal with the recently won lands and conveying this to the United States, in Eshkol's view, was crucial. So in preparation for this Bundy-Eban discussion, the Israeli cabinet conducted a series of highly secretive meetings between June 14 and June 19, 1967. An Israeli debate of such scope and detail on territory, as indicated in hundreds of pages of declassified minutes, has not occurred since those days. The minutes reveal that a ministerial subcommittee on the matter was

established and Begin was a member. Notwithstanding clear ideological differences among the participants, they developed a consensus on the future
of the Sinai and Golan Heights: in exchange for peace, these lands in their
entirety could be returned to Egypt and Syria. In other words, in return for
peace, Israel's future borders with Egypt and Syria should be the international border.

Begin saw neither the Golan Heights nor the Sinai to be part of ancient
Israel. This is illustrated by their absence from the seals of both the Irgun
and later the Herut party.[88] Still, Begin voiced skepticism about whether
Nasser would agree to restrictions on the Sinai, such as demilitarization,
or to transit for Israeli ships through the Suez Canal, let alone sign a peace
treaty with Israel. But in a larger sense, Begin was ready to negotiate.[89]

The cabinet also agreed that East Jerusalem should be annexed. The fact
that Israel had had no access to this holiest area for Jews between 1948 and
1967 was certainly one factor. The deeper historic resonance, for Begin and
the others, also weighed heavily. The cabinet would decide not just to annex
but to expand the municipal boundaries of the city.

The major area of dispute was the West Bank. But even in this debate,
Begin was far from a lone maximalist. An overall consensus did emerge on
the importance of the Jordan River serving as Israel's eastern border, although
whether as a "security border" or a "political border" was a dramatic and historic point of debate. Here, a well-known distinction crystallized between
the views of Yigael Allon, a Labor minister and former general, and Moshe
Dayan.[90] Eshkol, initially cool to the idea of a Jordan River border, eventually expressed sympathy when the security role was highlighted. Begin—in
listening to Allon, who had established his reputation as the daring commander of the pre-state Palmach fighting force—began to see the advantages
of settling the West Bank, with a special emphasis on the strategic importance of the Jordan Valley. This area, on the territory's eastern perimeter and
adjacent to Jordan, had come under attack from the east in both the 1948
and 1967 wars. In later years, Begin would tout the value of settlements, less
for strategic reasons than as an embodiment of historic Jewish rights.

In these early postwar meetings, the idea of Palestinian autonomy in
the West Bank also first surfaced. While not opposing this idea in principle,

Begin thought it tactically unwise to raise it now, given the torrent of international pressure that he believed was certain to follow. A decade later, though, Palestinian autonomy would become an organizing principle for him.

The postwar exuberance, and desire to expand territory, drew warnings from other quarters within the Israeli leadership. Whereas in 1967, Israel included 2.4 million Jews and around four hundred thousand Arabs, now the country stood to welcome an additional estimated 1.3 million Arab inhabitants from the West Bank, Gaza, and East Jerusalem.[91] Given the higher Arab birth rate, these numbers contained plenty to worry about.

The declassified Hebrew minutes point to a very tense and extensive set of discussions over a few days, which are fascinating in foretelling much of the Israeli debate over the West Bank until this very day, when the same decision still hangs in front of Israel. Health Minister Yisrael Barzilai thus declared, "We are trying to do something that cannot go. We want a lot or not a lot of territory but the new territory [should be] without the people who live there."[92] When some ministers suggested Gaza could be annexed to Israel, Eshkol asked what would happen to its four hundred thousand Palestinian Arab inhabitants, later asking the same about the eight hundred thousand West Bank Palestinians as well as the one hundred thousand living in villages around Jerusalem. A West Bank withdrawal linked to peace with Jordan, according to leaders who offered these demographic concerns, would shift responsibility for these Arab civilians away from Israel. Justice Minister Yaakov Shimshon Shapiro argued that a failure to discuss Israel's intentions regarding the newly occupied lands would open up the country to international criticism and undermine a constructive postwar partnership with the United States, which was eager to know Israel's intentions.

Begin did not equivocate in response to these concerns: "I say, simply, Western Eretz Yisrael is all ours. What is the fear to say this?"[93] Shapiro had a blunt reply: "In the not-too-distant future, we will become a binational state. And in a bit longer . . . we will be a minority." In calling for the West Bank to be returned to Jordan, he contended that "otherwise, we are done with the entire Zionist enterprise and we will be a ghetto."[94] Eshkol shared these concerns, saying, "I don't want more land and I don't want more Arabs. When will we be a minority in this country?"[95] Concurring were Tourism Minister Moshe Kol and Finance Minister Pinchas Sapir, who added that the further acquisition of land would raise international expectations for Israel to solve the Palestinian refugee problem on its own.

In response, Begin made a familiar-sounding case when he said, "We have to penetrate public opinion [to make the point] that we are here in western Eretz Yisrael not because might makes right but because right makes might."[96] This was his signature worldview: rights and not force are the source of policy decisions. But even he recognized that this rhetoric was insufficient to address the reality of an additional 1.2 million Arab inhabitants on Israel-controlled land.* Thus, in those days of June 1967, Begin would concede that the population issue constituted "one of the most serious problems of our future."[97] A future Arab majority, he knew, was unacceptable. Begin would even advocate that expulsion of Palestinians should be forbidden and that ultimately Palestinians should be able to vote in East Jerusalem, the West Bank, and Gaza. This idea that West Bank Arabs should vote in Israeli elections was nothing short of astonishing. Nobody on the mainstream Israeli left, let alone the right, favored giving West Bankers a vote. They saw this as potentially suicidal, diluting the voting Jewish majority. In promoting this position, Begin cited the 1871 German-French dispute over Alsace-Lorraine, where the newly formed German Empire settled its own citizens but also offered citizenship to the region's French inhabitants. He believed this formulation would allow Israel to remain both Jewish and democratic while granting civil liberties to all its residents.

How could Begin's position be reconciled with the actual numbers of Palestinians? Begin suggested that the Palestinians should be residents first and only gain citizenship after a seven-year period, citing the five-year span for immigrants in the United States. Those seven years, Begin believed, could allow Israel to reach a sustainable demographic advantage. To achieve this, he proposed that the Jewish Agency, nominally independent of the

---

* In the 1960s, it was common for Israeli politicians to refer to Palestinians as "Arabs living in the West Bank" instead of as "Palestinians." Begin always insisted on referring to them as "Arabs of the Land of Israel," thereby refusing a distinction between Arabs living inside Israel and those living in the West Bank. Even as Israeli politicians increasingly referred to these West Bankers as Palestinians, Begin stuck to his description for many years.

state, offer financial incentives for Jewish mothers to have additional children. In addition, he argued that a united Jerusalem would attract Jewish tourism, in turn boosting Jewish immigration. And in a show of prescience, he held out hope that the Soviet Union would open its doors—allowing Jews to emigrate—although this would not happen during the time frame he envisioned. He likewise hoped Israel and Jordan could cultivate closer economic ties, making the latter more attractive to the West Bank Palestinians and facilitating a kind of voluntary emigration in pursuit of Jordan's economic potential. Yet his ultimate view was that Palestinians should have the right to Israeli citizenship. Thus, the right-wing Begin espoused an idea in the early postwar cabinets that was shared only on Israel's leftward fringes by those supporting a binational state.[98]

Begin did not force a vote on this issue, as none of his colleagues endorsed the idea of granting gradual citizenship. But he could claim foresight in having argued that the "Jordan solution" to the Palestinian dilemma was inadequate—though he himself had proposed a modified version of this option. The anxieties expressed by leaders such as Eshkol, Shapiro, Barzilai, Sapir, and Kol never coalesced into an action plan or policy. Thus, the lack of a decision became the decision. The template for the decades that followed flowed from that historic decision to postpone making fateful choices. Israel would control the territory, even without annexing it. Early on, the only issue on which the government could reach agreement was the need for a military government in the territory to ensure order. The Palestinian question has remained Israel's most vexing challenge and is still unresolved. At the time, Begin's instincts told him that Israel should keep all the West Bank, while his values indicated that the Arabs must also have rights.

A LIKUD PRIME MINISTER

For Begin, being in the government was a mixed blessing. On one hand, it fulfilled his craving for approval from the political establishment, which he first tasted when joining Ben-Gurion in the short-lived alliance against the British in the 1940s. On the other, he could no longer be a channel for public dissatisfaction with the ruling coalition. After the October 1969 vote,

Begin's Gahal bloc—a merger between the Herut and Liberal parties forged four years earlier—held twenty-nine seats in parliament, against fifty-six for Labor and its allies. That February, Levi Eshkol had died while still in office, and Golda Meir had replaced him. Begin appreciated the hawkish new prime minister, calling her "a proud Jewess."[99] Toward the end of 1969, when US secretary of state William Rogers put forth a peace plan calling for Israel to give up virtually all its new territory for something less than peace treaties, it unsurprisingly garnered little support from either Meir or Begin. Although Meir was certain to reject the deal, Begin chose to leave the ruling coalition at this time. Why? On an immediate level, he did not like the government's adoption of UN Security Council Resolution 242, passed after the 1967 war, which dictated that Israel would have to yield land for an uncertain peace. Moreover, he was undoubtedly more comfortable in the opposition. One could speculate that the longer he was part of the government, the harder it would be to stake out a position in contrast to the dominant Labor, in keeping with his historic role as outsider, before the next election.

During its eight years in existence, the Gahal bloc succeeded in softening Begin's edges as an extremist. Then, in 1973, Begin welcomed the freshly retired general Ariel Sharon and other small parties into the fold, refashioning it as Likud (Unity). Sharon's decision was significant, considering that until then Labor had held a virtual monopoly on generals in a country that worshipped them. Before him, after the 1967 war, Ezer Weizman, nephew to the Zionist eminence Chaim Weizmann (but who spelled his name in English differently) and head of the Israeli Air Force, had joined Begin's party.

The timing of Sharon's association was fortunate for Begin. The next month, after the surprise Arab attack on Israel during the solemn Jewish holy day of Yom Kippur, Sharon came out of retirement to turn the tide of the war. For this, he was hailed as a national hero. But the overall sentiment after the war ended was one of dismay. Yes, Sharon's forces were approaching Cairo at the time of the cease-fire and additional Israeli units stood just outside Damascus. But Israel had lost a crushing 2,800 lives. Everyone knew someone who had died, and an unforgiving Israeli public was demanding answers.

The quest for those answers was carried out by a legal commission led by Supreme Court chief justice Shimon Agranat. Even though the Agranat Commission, as it was known, did not call for Meir and Moshe Dayan to resign as prime minister and defense minister, respectively, both did so anyway under public pressure. But the broader question lingered: Was it really natural for a single party to have held power since the state's founding? Suddenly, Begin's Likud looked like a credible alternative.

Labor, alongside its association with the 1973 war debacle, faced corruption scandals and internal divisions. The next year, the political novice Yitzhak Rabin took Meir's place atop the party hierarchy. His chief rival, Shimon Peres, a longtime aide to Ben-Gurion known for his savvy political instincts, would be named defense minister. To undercut Rabin, and against his wishes, Peres supported those settlers seeking to build outside the strategic Jordan Valley. These settlers answered to a rather extreme coterie of religious authorities while scorning the National Religious Party, whose leadership they regarded as insufficiently nationalistic. These settlers did feel some kinship with Begin and his invocation of "Judea and Samaria," the biblical name for the West Bank.

Begin saw additional political opportunities in autumn 1975. Following the agreement between Rabin and US secretary of state Henry Kissinger on a second military pullback in the Sinai, Begin ridiculed Rabin for doing what he considered to be the US secretary's bidding, declaring that Israel should not yield an inch in incremental pullouts until it had achieved peace treaties with both Egypt and Syria.[100] Even though Rabin would secure major American commitments, including military aid, as part of Sinai II—as talks at that time were known informally—Begin effectively portrayed this interim deal as a giveaway: land for nothing.

Further challenges to Rabin arose in 1977, when the new US president, Jimmy Carter, signaled his intention to break from Kissinger's incrementalism. He wanted a grand Middle East peace conference, one almost certain to result in calls for major Israeli territorial concessions.[101] Into this discussion, Carter inserted the new element of a homeland for the Palestinians. Jordan, by largely sitting out the 1973 war, had in effect forfeited its role on the Palestinian question. Now the Palestine Liberation Organization (PLO), based in southern Lebanon after having been kicked out of Jordan following the 1970 Black September events, stepped into the fray. At the 1974 Arab League summit in Rabat, the PLO received a mandate to negotiate for the West Bank. Much of Israel saw PLO leader Yasser Arafat as a terrorist. And whereas Carter was careful not to negotiate with Arafat or the PLO, he appeared willing to move in that direction. If Rabin could not sway Carter, Begin argued, Israel needed to put forth a tougher interlocutor.

Separately, a scandal in which Leah Rabin, the prime minister's wife, had kept open a bank account in US dollars—to which she was entitled when Yitzhak served as ambassador to Washington from 1968 to 1973—reinforced the idea of an entrenched, corrupt Labor leadership that was disconnected from the public. Refusing to cast blame on his wife, Rabin resigned. This development, coupled with the Rabin-Peres division and the taint of the 1973 war, further battered a party that had held power for twenty-nine straight years. A split in Labor ensued, with a prominent group of Labor-leaning Israelis, such as Yigael Yadin, putting forward a parliamentary list of those critical of corruption in Labor.[102] But rather than consolidating national support, the splinter group strengthened Begin in the 1977 prime ministerial campaign.

The whole mood of corruption played to another area of strength for Begin: his honesty and frugality. Even detractors of the Likud leader generally believed in the sincerity of his motives and lifestyle. As described in a CIA profile prepared before his maiden visit to the White House, Begin was regarded as a "highly principled" man with "strong beliefs."[103] He lived in a very modest two-room apartment, opened his home every Shabbat afternoon to strangers, and was deemed altogether incorruptible.

Beginning with the Sephardim whom he had visited in the *maabarot* in the 1950s, Begin stitched together a coalition of outsiders who saw him as one of them, a traditional Jew the establishment disdained. Begin had widened his constituency by adding the national religious bloc—which, propelled by the settlement movement, had moved sharply right—along with a new generation of native-born Israelis who lauded Begin's focus on historic claims to the land. This would turn out to be a key shift with profound implications down the road. Another group, the ultraorthodox, also sensed that the traditionalist Begin, as opposed to the avowedly secular Labor, would be more generous in providing the resources they sought for a network of schools. These backers, moreover, believed Labor had been too entitled for too long.

In the elections of 1977, the Likud (including a two-member faction led by Ariel Sharon, which joined the coalition) earned forty-five seats to Labor's thirty-two. A journey of decades had reached its pinnacle. Begin had arrived. He was no longer an outsider; he was now the leader of Israel. It was telling—Begin celebrated his astonishing victory after decades of being in the political wilderness by going to the Western Wall, and putting on a *kippah*, and saying the blessing that is declared at a time of milestones, just as he had done after 1967.

EARLY DAYS IN OFFICE

Begin, from his first day in office, aspired to project the persona of an Israeli leader who was proud of his Jewish roots and did not shun religion. To this end, he visited Rabbi Zvi Yehuda Kook, the son of the pre-state first chief rabbi and now the de facto spiritual leader of the settlement movement. At the Western Wall, Begin prayed for Israel to realize the goals he had personally advocated during the Six-Day War campaign. Shortly thereafter, he hoisted a Torah scroll outside the Palestinian city of Nablus, pledging that more such settlements would blossom in what he termed "liberated," not occupied, territories.[104]

US officials were stunned by Begin's victory. Three months before the election, a CIA assessment had cited the possibility of a Labor-Likud unity government, likely led by Shimon Peres, but had not entirely ruled out a Begin victory.[105] The latter scenario, according to the assessment, would require massive US pressure to produce peace negotiations. William Quandt, who served as President Carter's Middle East advisor on the National Security Council, later conceded, "We didn't know where he was coming from. We weren't prepared for [his election]."[106] The reality now felt harsh. Having known only Labor leaders, with their familiar approach favoring compromise, the United States faced a new Israeli premier who spoke without equivocation and would press historic claims in the West Bank. Because of his militant role in the pre-state years, media reports sometimes referred to him as an "ex-terrorist."

Egypt, by contrast, was moving toward conciliation with the United States. Having expelled Soviet military advisors in 1972, and after seeing that the bilateral alliance had failed to restore the land lost in 1967, President Anwar Sadat had now made overtures to the United States. These bore fruit in Kissinger's two Sinai disengagement deals in 1974 and 1975. But warmer relations with the Americans did not rescue Egypt's foundering economy, which led to Sadat's announcement of liberalization measures. With Sadat's decision to implement the reforms recommended by the International Monetary Fund (IMF), in return for eventual IMF and World Bank loans to alleviate the country's debt burden, Sadat was required to terminate basic state subsidies for bread, rice, flour, and cooking oil. These measures caused a 50 percent spike in food prices, creating immediate stress for average Egyptians. From January 18 to 19, 1977, bread riots engulfed Egypt's cities, leaving seventy-nine dead and more than five hundred injured. The return of demobilized soldiers made the crisis all the worse—while apparently persuading Sadat that peace with Israel could indeed be the ticket for easing his people's economic suffering.

PRELIMINARY TALKS WITH PRESIDENT CARTER

On April 4, 1977, Carter and Sadat held their first meeting at the White House. According to a State Department memo on the conversation, Sadat proclaimed, "The Soviets are furious when I say that 99 percent of the cards are in the U.S. hands, but it is true." Sadat then defined the peace he sought with Israel: "The question of the nature of peace is very crucial. They want open borders. But after 29 years of war and of hatred, no one can agree suddenly to open borders and to free exchanges. This is mostly a psychological problem. What I see is that I will sit at Geneva, and that we will sign a peace agreement that will end the state of belligerency, we will normalize the situation, and both we and the Israelis will fulfill our obligations under [UN Security Council] Resolution 242 [which ended the 1967 war]."[107]

Carter, in turn, asked Sadat for greater specificity on how a potential treaty, in which Israel yielded land, would affect diplomatic and trade relations. Sadat hedged a bit before offering a tantalizing hint regarding his mind-set: "I don't know if in a peace agreement we can add a clause on normalization in five years or so. Or perhaps you could guarantee the normalization. When peace is achieved, and there are guarantees, this issue should not be a problem. But you should be there as a witness."[108] The leader of the Arab world's largest state was signaling, in principle, that he could accept peace with Israel. The suggestion was historic—even though Sadat, at this point, still viewed peace as part of a larger regional endeavor. He mentioned his belief to Carter that he could persuade Syrian president Hafiz al-Assad to go along with this plan. Yet simultaneously he voiced suspicion of Assad, who favored a unified Arab delegation at a comprehensive Middle East peace conference in Geneva, rather than separate teams from the respective states. Assad, the Egyptian leader explained, "insists on [one delegation] to reduce my room to maneuver, so that he can veto my moves. This reduces my flexibility and it will create problems."[109]

Begin was unaware of the substance of the Carter-Sadat meeting, but he stood to be its beneficiary as Sadat embarked on the road to peace. Even so, the Israeli prime minister would not be apprised of the new Egyptian thinking for several months, at least judging from a memo by Moshe Dayan, who had been rehabilitated after his 1973 resignation and was now serving as foreign minister in the Likud government. It was a political coup for Begin to attract someone who so embodied the Labor mainstream establishment of decades and was a bona fide hero despite the 1973 war debacle. Dayan was a reassuring presence that signaled that Begin was no radical.

In Dayan's memo dated June 24, 1977, just three days after Begin took office, Dayan outlined Israel's interests for the prospective outcome of a Geneva peace conference. The text indicated Dayan's assumption that a peace treaty with Egypt would be impossible under any circumstances.

In the opposition, Begin was a critic of the Rabin-Kissinger incrementalism, where Israel would yield parts of the Sinai and the Golan for less than full peace. Yet, he felt Israel should only make territorial concessions for a full treaty. He was a believer that peace with Egypt was possible.

According to his son, Benny, Begin would point to the intelligence briefings he received in the opposition as evidence that there was change underway in Egypt toward Israel. Clearly, Begin was not oblivious to the fact that Sadat was a partner to two disengagement agreements and had flipped sides from the Soviet Union to now be part of the American orbit. Begin would put in motion a series of back-channel discussions with Romanian leader Nicolae Ceaușescu and would authorize a channel through Morocco's King Hassan II. These would prove to be critical milestones on the way to Sadat's electrifying trip to Jerusalem that November. It is an enduring source of irritation to the Begin family that He has never received the international accolades that were given to Sadat, when in fact these preparatory meetings were key to Sadat's decision to go it alone.

The Dayan memo, more generally, was meant to prepare Begin for his upcoming meeting in July with Carter, an introduction with all the makings of a disaster. Carter's pathbreaking call for a Palestinian homeland in the West Bank, along with the PLO's recent elevation at the 1974 Arab League summit, put the US president seemingly at odds with Begin. The new prime minister was clearly unsympathetic to Palestinian nationalism, given the threat he saw it posing to Jewish biblical patrimony in the West Bank.

Temperamentally, too, Begin and Carter were hardly a natural fit. The Israeli leader was a melodrama-inclined former commander of the Jewish underground, with the Holocaust having claimed much of his family, while the US president was a reserved Georgia peanut farmer and former engineer who had served on a nuclear submarine. Indeed, before the summit, differences surfaced between US advisors on how Carter should even receive Begin. National Security Advisor Zbigniew Brzezinski thought Begin would respond to a tough-minded approach, whereas the US ambassador to Israel Samuel Lewis, who would later develop a close rapport with Begin, believed Carter was more likely to succeed "with honey, not vinegar."[110] Carter took Lewis's advice, at least initially.

When Begin finally arrived at the White House on July 19, 1977, he was eager to share with Carter his narrative of Jewish history and Israel's place within it. Yet Begin also appeared to have sought common ground with the US president, focusing on Israeli security needs vis-à-vis its Arab neighbors, rather than historical claims. Notably, Begin did not assail Carter over the new US position on the Palestinians, even as he could not resist offering the Jewish narrative of the conflict.[111] He even brought with him an official Israeli proposal saying that his government favored the convening of a Geneva conference. For this, he wanted an opening ceremonial session that would quickly break out into separate working groups between Israel and the individual Arab states: Egypt, Syria, and Jordan. He was comfortable with US attendance at these bilateral meetings. And, if the parties balked at a direct meeting with Israel, Begin said he could accept shuttle diplomacy wherein US representatives would travel between meetings in Israel and the Arab capitals. He further voiced support for peace negotiations based on UN Security Council Resolutions 242 and 338, the latter having been adopted after the 1973 war.

Israeli acceptance of these resolutions, rooted in the principle of land for peace, was, as Arab leaders explained to Carter, a prerequisite for their participation in any peace talks. Begin was ready to accept Resolutions 242 and 338, but he had his own definition and emphasized to Carter that the language in 242 required withdrawal from territories, not *all* territories. Carter was well aware of Begin's opposition to an Israeli return to the 1967 lines and to a Palestinian state, but he chose not to harp on those issues. Like Begin, he wanted a good meeting, believing that could help get them to Geneva and that once negotiations were launched, the parties could find a way to overcome their differences.

The one issue that Carter did not try to finesse was settlements, and he asked Begin to avoid construction until after Geneva was convened. Begin was noncommittal in reply. He was, however, adamant about the PLO: Begin vigorously opposed any PLO participation in the Geneva talks, including the idea of incorporating PLO officials within the Jordanian delegation. Carter did not resist, saying that PLO participation would depend on its accepting "242 publicly and [acknowledging] the right of Israel to exist in peace." Then, he said, "we would talk to them and listen to their position."[112] In later summarizing shared US-Israel views on the talks,* Begin said he

---

* Carter was also sympathetic in other parts of the discussion to Begin's specific proposals about assisting Jews in the Soviet Union, Syria, and Ethiopia. Follow-up suggestions were exchanged.

was pleased both sought a peace treaty as an end goal. Carter, presumably to keep things cordial, agreed to Begin's request that the United States omit public mention of its policy calling for a return to the 1967 borders with minor adjustments.

In addition to their two discussions focused on procedural matters, Carter and Begin met alone following a state dinner that same evening, July 19. During this session, Begin removed a sheet of paper clarifying Israel's position on withdrawal, and he then declared, "Regarding Egypt: In view of the large area separating the two countries, Israel is prepared, within the framework of a peace treaty, to make a significant withdrawal of its forces in Sinai." On the Golan as well, he said Israel would withdraw forces, redeploying them to a point agreed upon as part of a peace treaty. Although he did not specify the point, this marked the first time Begin, as prime minister, had agreed to the principle of withdrawal. He would not show similar flexibility on the West Bank, declaring instead that "Israel will not transfer Judea, Samaria and the Gaza District to any foreign sovereign authority."[113] But he also said that Israel would settle the area, not annex it.

Begin was trying to show he could be flexible in some areas, but not in others. In the meetings, as if to describe who he was and what motivated him, he recalled the incident in which his father had struck the Polish sergeant who had tried to cut off a rabbi's beard. His father, Begin explained, "had defended the honor of the Jewish people and the honor of the rabbi." He continued, "Mr. President, from that day forth I have forever remembered those two things about my youth: the persecution of our helpless Jews, and the courage of my father in defending their honor."[114] As Begin remembered it later, "I wanted him to know from whence I came and what kind of a Jew he was dealing with."[115]

Carter would later write that he felt the meetings with Begin had gone well, and he sent Secretary of State Cyrus Vance to the region two weeks later to prepare the parties for going to Geneva.

SECRETARY VANCE ABROAD

In Alexandria, Vance discovered that Sadat was ready to move. The Egyptian president furnished the US secretary with a draft treaty document, which the two reviewed paragraph by paragraph. This document included a fallback option should ideas vetted with the United States be unacceptable to Israel. Sadat also suggested to Vance that each country should submit a proposed text to the United States and that it should finesse the differences prior to convening at Geneva. Vance cabled Sadat's proposals to Carter and Brzezinski. Vance conveyed one other interesting point in the cable: Sadat wanted the Americans to "tell Dayan that he (Sadat) is ready to conclude peace with him. He commented that he is pleased Dayan is Foreign Minister, as he believes he is flexible and wants to make peace."[116]

At this juncture, Sadat remained hopeful. He thought that Assad would support his preferred Geneva format, and he believed that Arafat would recognize Israel's existence, thus allowing the PLO leader's participation. To this end, Sadat said he would soon invite Arafat to Alexandria. Vance would ask Sadat something Carter had not: If Syria and Jordan were not ready to go along, "was he prepared to make a separate peace with Israel?"[117] Sadat gave an unqualified yes, making it clear that he would go his own way and not be tied to the need for an inter-Arab consensus. This was a remarkable departure from traditional Arab positions—and seemingly suggested that the Egyptian and Israeli positions might be bridgeable.

In ensuing stops in Jordan, Saudi Arabia, and Syria, however, Vance found almost no convergence with Israel—or for that matter with Egypt. In fact, the more explicit he was with his Arab hosts, the further this distance grew with Israel.

The widening gap between plans for Geneva and the realities also reflected a basic gap between Jerusalem and Washington on the contours of peace, most notably over full withdrawal to the 1967 lines with minor modifications. In talks between Vance and Begin on August 9–10, 1977, the differences between the two sides became very clear. Only now, Begin did not avoid clashing with his US counterpart. The pleasantries of the inaugural US-Israel meeting had given way to the imperative, Begin believed, of protecting the Israeli people.

After applauding Vance for getting the Arab states to pursue peace treaties instead of nonbelligerency agreements, Begin raised strong objections to US positioning. In a tone of outrage, he referred to the indication by a State Department spokesperson that if the PLO accepted Resolution 242 with modifications, the US would agree to a PLO interpretation of the resolution. In response, Begin read from a section of the 1964 PLO covenant that negated Israel's right to exist and called for the expulsion of Jews who had arrived in Palestine after 1917. He noted further that during the first seven months of 1977, the PLO had launched ninety attacks against Israel. Given this track record, a US conferral of legitimacy on the PLO—a "genocidal organization"—would be "one of the most regrettable developments from the moral point of view."[118] Begin felt that if the PLO wanted legitimacy, it needed to change its charter, an outcome he did not expect. He was convinced that the PLO rejected Israel, and "Israel [would] not discuss its self-destruction." The language needed to be "is excluded forever." Only with Israel's agreement, he said, could the proposed composition of Geneva be changed. And this simply would not happen.

Begin's verbal attack against the PLO had the unintended effect of temporarily pushing Vance toward the Syrian position, wherein Arabs would negotiate under a single umbrella such as the Arab League. This arrangement, Vance mused, could allow for easier incorporation of Palestinian voices, while also permitting bilateral working group discussions. But Begin rejected this proposal out of hand.

Begin also raised another concern with Vance: Carter's commitment not to call publicly for an Israeli return to the 1967 lines. As Begin observed, if American officials were conveying this point privately in Arab capitals—and Vance had done so in every single one—then this would compromise Israeli negotiating leverage. Begin was making clear that Israel would not be compelled to act against its will and the interests of its citizens.

Maybe the most significant development during Begin's discussions with Vance, however, was the prime minister's suggestion that Palestinians be granted "cultural autonomy." He had first broached a similar idea after the 1967 war but had refrained from pressing it for tactical and security reasons. Now, a decade later, Begin raised a version of this concept, as well as his support for eventual Israeli citizenship for Palestinian Arabs. According to the prime minister, cultural autonomy would mean this: "Israel would not interfere in [Palestinians'] lives. They would have schools based on their own heritage. They should have the free option of citizenship in Israel. Now in Judea and Samaria the Arabs are citizens of Jordan. Israel will not force citizenship on them, since that would be wrong. But Israel is prepared to give them options. If they ask for Israeli citizenship, Israel will grant it. They will be entitled to vote in the Knesset and will have full equality."[119]

This was a remarkable position for an Israeli leader to take; given the demographics, this might actually have led to a binational state. But Arab leaders were not impressed when Vance communicated the idea to them. These leaders accepted the secretary's term "interim agreements" as applied to the temporary status of the West Bank and Gaza, but they wanted no Israeli role in the matter. Arab leaders were obviously no more pleased when Vance shared with them the message that Begin opposed a PLO seat in Geneva as well as a return to the pre-1967 lines.

BACK CHANNEL IN MOROCCO

While Begin engaged Vance, a potentially larger move on the chessboard had been initiated by Morocco's King Hassan, entailing historic secret encounters between Egypt and Israel. These meetings seem to have been in the works even before the first Carter-Begin discussion on July 19, and Sadat's reasons for agreeing to them remain obscure. According to Carter, Begin alluded to the Morocco rendezvous during their evening discussion on July 19, mentioning "tentative plans for direct meetings with Sadat."[120] Also, while much attention has focused on a session in September in Rabat, the initial meeting actually happened in late July between Mossad head Yitzhak Hofi and his Egyptian counterpart, Kamal Hassan Ali, who then ran the Egyptian intelligence service. In this earlier exchange in Casablanca, Hofi apparently provided intelligence connected to a plot by Libyan leader Muammar al-Qaddafi and the PLO to assassinate Sadat.[121] This meeting laid the ground for the later one between Dayan and Egyptian deputy prime minister Hassan Tuhamy, one of the Egyptian Free Officers who, along with Nasser and Sadat, deposed King Farouk in 1952.

Tuhamy, an eccentric with an affinity for mysticism, was a confidant of the Egyptian president. On the Israeli side, Dayan was the natural interlocutor; his stature as foreign minister was bolstered by his impressive war record, which Arabs implicitly respected. As early as 1949, he had held secret talks with Jordan's King Abdullah. Dayan's eventual meeting with Tuhamy, held on September 16 at King Hassan's palace, likewise hinted at Sadat's implicit belief in Begin as a potential peacemaker. He must have trusted that Begin would not leak news of the meeting, a development that could deeply wound Sadat in the Arab world.

Decades later, a declassified eight-page Mossad summary would reveal the main exchanges in the initial Tuhamy-Dayan meeting. Tuhamy promised a handshake between Sadat and Begin as soon as Egypt recovered the land lost in 1967.[122] King Hassan interjected that Sadat would meet Begin even earlier, after the Israeli leader had committed to returning the land. As a compliment, Tuhamy then said the Egyptian president sensed Begin and Dayan were "strong and brave leaders [who we believe] would dare to accept fateful decisions for full and fair peace."[123] Perhaps just to flatter his counterparts, Tuhamy added that Sadat did not have the same faith in the previous Israeli government.

Tuhamy then got further into how Sadat wanted to proceed, saying that Sadat preferred to avoid working with the Soviets, who were slated to co-chair the conference. Even more surprising was Sadat's preference for the Israelis and Egyptians to work out the terms of the deal bilaterally in advance of Geneva. "We are suggesting between us here, with the help of the King in the process, to finish here before Geneva all the matters that pertain to us." Tuhamy added that "this will have great weight for the President of Syria, who will join the agreement that would already be done between us."[124] Tuhamy made clear this was all contingent on Begin committing to withdrawal.[125]

Tuhamy did not specify whether a peace deal would hinge on Begin's vowing in advance to return only lands seized from Egypt or whether territory won from other Arab countries would also have to be included. He likewise refrained from setting conditions on Jerusalem, whose value to the Arabs he nonetheless made clear. "He wants peace without surrendering," Tuhamy said of Sadat, characterizing the Egyptian president as a soldier whose lands had been captured and who was seeking an "honorable peace."

In reply, Dayan expressed uncertainty about whether Begin could give a prior commitment to withdrawals, adding his sense that Begin would want to meet the "highest-level official" on the Egyptian side. Nor did Dayan commit to an Israeli withdrawal from the Sinai, the southern part of which, around Sharm el-Sheikh, the foreign minister famously believed Israel must retain for strategic reasons.*[126] No evidence suggests the prime minister would have authorized this promise anyway. According to US ambassador Lewis, "I am sure that Begin would not have authorized Dayan to make any such secret commitments."[127]

Nonetheless, in his meeting with Tuhamy, Dayan voiced confidence about the Israeli ability to solve problems with Jordan and Egypt, while simultaneously ruling out a sovereign Palestinian state. Dayan told Tuhamy, "We trust Sadat. We don't trust the president of Syria. However, we have discussed matters seriously and immediately. I accept your proposal to exchange peace documents as soon as possible for reciprocal evaluation."[128] This exchange is what probably led Tuhamy to report positively about his expectations on Israeli withdrawal.

Begin, in communicating with his cabinet about these talks, evidently provided just enough information to fend off the potential accusation that he was hiding serious contacts. On September 4, for instance, the prime minister relayed to his ministers that he had met a few days earlier with Romanian leader Nicolae Ceaușescu in Bucharest and that Sadat had agreed in principle to a senior-level meeting between Egyptian and Israeli officials. He did not similarly note the Dayan-Tuhamy exchange.

THE ROAD TO JERUSALEM

Dayan meanwhile, traveling to Washington after his September Rabat meeting, delivered to US officials his draft of the peace treaty as a basis for Geneva. But there is no evidence that he disclosed his meeting with Tuhamy. Either Tuhamy did not want the meeting disclosed or maybe the Israeli leadership did not trust the Americans to safeguard the extremely sensitive information. Secret though it was, the Rabat meeting appears to have shifted

---

* "Better Sharm el-Sheikh than peace without Sharm el-Sheikh," Dayan had said years earlier.

Egyptian and Israeli thinking toward the idea that Geneva would simply be a venue for signing a peace previously worked out through bilateral talks.

On the Egyptian side, Foreign Minister Ismail Fahmy's visit to Washington overlapped with Dayan's. On September 21, signaling the change in thinking, he shared with Carter his view that Geneva would be a good place for talks to both begin and end, implying the substantive negotiating would happen elsewhere.[129] The next day, Fahmy told Brzezinski, "If the Arabs at Geneva refuse to be logical, we'll face them in an Arab summit and will go alone to sign a peace treaty."[130] This was a suggestion by Egypt that it might sign a separate treaty with Israel.

A week later, on September 28, frictions between Egypt and Syria came into view after the Syrian foreign minister, Abdel Halim Khaddam, told Vance that his country's insistence on a unified Arab delegation went beyond a ceremonial opening at Geneva. It must last for the whole conference, he said. The next day, Fahmy expressed his indignation to Vance, suggesting that Syria wanted to "block any progress." He continued, "They fear that Egypt may be able to go ahead and make an agreement. That is why they want one delegation."[131] Whatever confidence Sadat may have earlier had about Assad was now gone.

Further rankling Egypt, as well as Israel, was a joint US-Soviet statement on October 1 calling for a comprehensive Middle East peace, ending the exclusion of America's Cold War foe from the process. This was a sharp departure from the last US peace broker, Henry Kissinger, whose organizing principle was to marginalize the Soviet Union in the Middle East. This, the clearest expression yet on this matter, convinced Begin that Carter was intent on forging an imposed peace that could, if needed, be nudged along by withholding US military and economic aid. Carter appeared to confirm such intentions when he imparted to Arab officials in meetings his sense that the unfolding nature of the Geneva talks would cause world opinion to turn against any unforthcoming party—which, he made clear, meant Israel.

Thereafter, in a lengthy, extremely tense October 4 meeting among Carter, Vance, and Dayan, the president alternatively threatened Israel and sought to allay its fears—Israel did not, for example, have to accept the October 1 US-Soviet statement as a basis for attending Geneva.[132] Dayan, questioning the feasibility of a comprehensive peace, contended, "My attitude is that for the first time Egypt is ready, and the others may not be. 'If you take one wheel off a car, it won't drive.' If Egypt is out of the conflict, there will be no war."[133] The Arab states, Dayan was saying here, could not fight Israel without Egypt.

Sadat, meanwhile, reaffirmed Egyptian intentions in a letter delivered October 4 through Fahmy. This letter, according to Carter's diaries, urged "that nothing be done to prevent Israel and Egypt from negotiating directly, with our serving as an intermediary either before or after the Geneva Conference is convened."[134] The favored US format, this note argued, would likely fail in Geneva. The Syrian delegation would object loudly to separate Egypt-Israel talks and therefore obstruct the path to peace.

Geneva was now looking like a ticket to nowhere, thanks to the rigid format favored by the Syrian leadership and Carter. Yet even as the president's dream of a regional conference was crumbling, he persisted. On October 21, in a personal note to Sadat, Carter admitted that US attempts were faltering and asked the Egyptian leader for assistance in salvaging Geneva. But Sadat did not reply favorably, instead visiting three other countries in late October and early November: Saudi Arabia, Romania, and Iran. From the leaders of the latter two, he sought approval for shattering the ultimate historic taboo: a direct peace with Israel. Sadat was now going to untether himself from Carter and go his own way. He wanted to test his ideas with a very select group of leaders.

The Romanian head of state, Ceaușescu, was unique in being the only Eastern Bloc leader to maintain ties with Israel; he also had relations with Egypt. Begin had viewed Ceaușescu as a key to securing a Sadat visit to Israel, and he later recalled making this specific request to the Romanian leader during an August 26, 1977, visit to his summer retreat. Ceaușescu, according to the prime minister, had also vouched for him as a peacemaker when later talking with Sadat. "When Sadat met Ceausescu, he asked his host two questions," Begin wrote. "'You've met Begin, so tell me. First, do you think he wants peace? And secondly, is he a strong man?' Ceausescu answered both of Sadat's questions in the affirmative."[135] He further told Sadat, "Once he agrees to something [Begin] will implement it to the last dot and comma."[136]

In an indication that Israel was receiving reports on Sadat's travels abroad, Dayan traveled to Tehran immediately after Sadat's visit with the shah.[137]

Yet another step in the Egypt-Israel dance occurred November 3, when Begin first mentioned the possibility of bilateral contacts to a US official, even as the earlier Dayan-Tuhamy exchanges went unacknowledged. Speaking to Ambassador Lewis, the Israeli prime minister noted Sadat's consent, working through Ceaușescu, to dispatch his vice president to Bucharest to meet Dayan in mid-November.[138] Six days later, on November 9, Sadat created a political earthquake by announcing to the Egyptian parliament, "I would go to the end of the world to spare an injury to one of our men, much more the death of one." He added, "Israel must be greatly surprised to hear me say that . . . I am even ready to go to the Knesset and discuss with them."[139]

Perhaps inevitably, a flurry of confusion followed this announcement. The question on everyone's lips was: Would Sadat actually visit? CBS News anchor Walter Cronkite dramatically brought the leaders together via a video conference on satellite television, confirming Sadat's intentions and Begin's willingness to host. Begin issued a verbal invitation, but this was followed, at the Egyptians' request, by a written one conveyed through Lewis and US ambassador to Egypt Hermann Eilts. Begin, who loved ceremony, then took the next step; as Lewis recalled, Begin "handed [it] to me to deliver to Cairo in a very public, flamboyant, dramatic ceremony in Begin's office at the Knesset."[140] Excitement bubbled across the world, except, notably, in Arab capitals and at the White House. The Carter administration reacted coolly, seeing this as undercutting its preferred comprehensive approach. But, with domestic and international excitement building around the Sadat visit, this position was not sustainable.

Suddenly, a solution seemed within reach to the Arab-Israeli conflict, with former premier Golda Meir likening Sadat's impending arrival to that of the Messiah. When Sadat touched down on November 19, 1977, later sharing laughs on the tarmac with his erstwhile adversaries Meir and Sharon, Israelis were riveted. For Begin personally, the visit marked an enormous triumph; having been vilified for decades as a warmonger, he now had achieved a major symbolic step toward peace after just five months in power. Begin, despite assertions to the contrary, yearned for the approval of others.

Now he basked in it. The Sadat visit was indeed a high point, and many difficulties would follow. Begin would be tested later regarding whether he was up to the challenge of peace.

To begin with, questions hovered over the strategic meaning of the visit. IDF chief of staff Mordechai "Motta" Gur feared Sadat was setting up Begin, that he would ultimately claim that he failed to persuade the Israeli leader to give up the land won in 1967, thus providing the pretext for another war. (Gur even suggested implausibly that Sadat's arrival could serve as a military ruse aimed at wiping out the Israeli cabinet right there on the tarmac.) Dayan meanwhile saw the Egyptian president as engaged in a balancing act between advancing his country's interests by pursuing peace and staying faithful to the broader Arab community.

Indeed, when Sadat addressed the Knesset on November 20, he expressed elements of both views. He took an uncompromising line on the need for Israel to return land taken in 1967, including East Jerusalem, and for Palestinians to have their own state. Going further, he made clear that Israel's retreat from occupied lands was the key to peace, and those missing this unique opportunity to make it would never be forgiven: "Expansion does not pay. To speak frankly, our land does not yield itself to bargaining. It is not even open to argument. To us, the national soil is equal to the holy valley where God Almighty spoke to Moses—peace be upon him. None of us can, or accept to, cede one inch of it, or accept the principle of debating or bargaining over it. I sincerely tell you that before us today lies the appropriate chance for peace, if we are really serious in our endeavours for peace."[141]

At the same time, Sadat asserted that peace meant Egyptian acceptance of Israel and Israelis. In responding to Sadat in the Knesset, Begin emphasized that Israel relied on force only for self-defense: "No, we do not believe in might, and we have never based our relations with the Arab Nation on force. On the contrary, force was exercised against us. Throughout all the years of this generation, we have never ceased to be attacked with brute force in order to destroy our Nation, to demolish our independence, to annul our right. And we defended ourselves." He added, "We do not believe in might; we believe in right, only in right. And that is why our aspiration, from the depths of our hearts, from time immemorial until this very day, is peace."[142]

Often lost in the symbolic elements of the Sadat visit—the two Knesset speeches, the stops at the al-Aqsa Mosque and Yad Vashem—was the substantive meeting between the two leaders, which lasted several hours. According to Dayan's memoirs, there was one key discussion between the two leaders. "He and Begin had only one basic talk, at which no protocol was taken, where the two leaders agreed to three principles: No more war between the two countries; the formal restoration of sovereignty over the Sinai Peninsula to Egypt; and the demilitarization of most of the Sinai, with limited Egyptian forces to be stationed only in the area adjoining the Suez Canal, including the Mitla and Gidi Passes."[143] During their discussion, Sadat said many things to assuage Begin. He said that Egyptian forces would not need to be stationed beyond the Sinai disengagement areas, marked by the Mitla and Gidi Passes. Further, he suggested turning the Straits of Tiran into an international waterway, obviating a repeat of the Nasser blockades of 1956 and 1967, which contributed to two wars. While calling for a Palestinian state, Sadat sought to reassure his counterpart by saying it would not be a threat to Israel, but instead be consumed by infighting.[144]

AFTERGLOW AND STALEMATE

After Jerusalem, both Begin and Sadat projected near euphoria. Sadat was greeted by cheering throngs upon his return to Cairo, and Carter remarked that he envied Begin's post-Jerusalem polling numbers. A corresponding result was increased political capital for each leader, which would be needed to make concessions. For the moment anyway, Sadat could shrug off the epithets being hurled at him over purportedly abandoning the larger Arab cause. In a cable sent by Eilts immediately upon Sadat's return, the US ambassador noted that Sadat had never imagined such an enthusiastic response, either at home or around the globe. Feeling like the "national hero" of not just Egypt but also Israel, Sadat characterized the trip as his "greatest victory, even greater than the [1973] Oct[ober] War."[145] Sadat was particularly moved by praise from Israel's defense minister, Ezer Weizman, for his role in the 1973 war. Reciprocating the goodwill, the Egyptian leader pledged no more wars. Sadat even asked Eilts whether an Israeli diplomat might be posted to Cairo at the US embassy to deal with day-to-day bilateral issues.

In broad terms, Sadat was hopeful that direct Egypt-Israel engagement on military and political relations would gain momentum. Amid this expansive sense of possibility, Sadat even mused about a transitional UN custodianship for the West Bank and about establishing a Palestinian state not just in Gaza but also around Rafah, in the northern Sinai, where Israeli settlements such as Yamit were situated.[146]

Begin was no less ebullient in his debriefing with Ambassador Lewis, while simultaneously striving to reassure Carter that a separate Egypt-Israel peace had not come up in discussions. Rather, as Begin explained, the two leaders had agreed to work toward a comprehensive peace and regarded Geneva as a place to sign agreed-upon deals. Moreover, Begin believed he and Sadat shared common ground in seeking to keep the Soviet Union at a distance and expressed his sense that Sadat now better appreciated Israel's security concerns.

In the afterglow of Sadat's visit to Jerusalem, whatever the divergence on details, a different Begin began to emerge, one who sensed the historical moment. Now everyone wondered whether he was up to the task. Could he actually make peace with Sadat, who had just shattered a spate of taboos, including flying to Israel and putting forward peace terms while addressing Israel's parliament in the contested city of Jerusalem? The challenge was complex. Both Sadat and Carter believed success would require that Israel give up the West Bank, reinforcing a sense that the Palestinian issue must be resolved, even amid murmurs of a separate peace. Begin considered the West Bank historical land not to be bargained away, but still he saw a middle course: maintaining maximal territory while granting civil liberties to Palestinian Arabs in the territories. In his interpretation of Revisionism, rooted in liberal democracy, the refusal to yield land went hand in hand with giving Arabs equal rights. In a larger sense, Begin was starting to see how, during his years in the opposition, lambasting the government was easy enough to do. Now, leading the majority, wielding power consistent with his values constituted a far more difficult task. The question was how the resulting proposals would be received by his negotiating counterparts.

Begin worked on his autonomy plan in December 1977. According to it, Israel would not cede West Bank land but would extend as many rights as possible to the area's Palestinians. Begin did not go so far as to acknowledge

Palestinian nationalism—perhaps surprising, given the centrality of Jewish nationalism to his worldview. Instead, he referred to Palestinians as "Arabs of the land of Israel" or "Arabs of Judea of Samaria." By regarding West Bank Arabs as individuals rather than a group, Begin could rationalize recognizing their rights. That did not mean national rights, however.

Seeking to implement his autonomy plan, Begin, "in his handwriting on a little piece of paper," presented fifteen points to his attorney general, Aharon Barak. These points would ultimately be transformed into the legal foundation of the proposal later presented to Sadat.[147] Remarkably, the resulting document contained many of the details that would appear in the September 1978 Camp David Accords (which comprised twenty points). As Barak would explain years later, "The idea of autonomy is a political idea that comes from the stomach of Begin." He added, "The autonomy proposal reflected Begin's values—the idea of giving the Arabs a right to vote was a way to bridge the gap between Begin the liberal democrat and 'Eretz Yisrael Hashlema,'" a reference to the ideology of recovering the entire Land of Israel. "It was a balancing act."[148]

Among the concessions palatable to Begin was abolishing Israel's military government in the West Bank, with the forces to be redeployed to fixed locations within the West Bank but away from urban areas. Further, in return for the Israeli right to buy West Bank land, Arabs in the territory would be allowed to purchase land in Israel, as well as vote in Israeli elections following a five-year transitional period, during which self-rule would be established. Virtually nobody across the Israeli political spectrum, left or right, was then advocating for either of these, particularly as they were viewed as paving the way for a binational, rather than Jewish, state. For Begin, it was a potentially costly compromise because earlier in the year he had campaigned on the idea of applying Israeli sovereignty in the West Bank. Now he realized this would be impossible. The trade-off for preventing "foreign sovereignty" in the territory was forswearing Israeli sovereignty—at least during the transition period, and likely thereafter. This marked a major shift for Begin, who had viewed the sovereignty issue as an important element of his political persona.[149]

Whatever the risks, Begin took pride in his full proposal, which encompassed a mix of Jewish values and pragmatism on controversial topics from the West Bank to the Sinai. His core team, consisting of Dayan, Weizman, and Barak, along with Meir Rosenne, a lawyer in the Foreign Ministry, encouraged him to keep the momentum going. Among these advisors, Dayan had experience with Arabs and keenly understood Israel's military needs; Weizman, beginning with Sadat's Jerusalem visit, had quickly developed strong chemistry with the Egyptian leader, who appreciated the defense minister's freewheeling style; Barak, the future chief justice of Israel's Supreme Court, would eventually be regarded as the country's greatest legal mind; and Rosenne had a strong grasp of international law, later serving as Israel's ambassador to the UN.

Around this time, on December 2–3, 1977, Dayan returned from a second meeting with Tuhamy, this time at King Hassan's palace in Marrakesh. He sensed an uphill climb ahead. At these sessions, the two sides quickly deadlocked on details surrounding an Israeli withdrawal from the Sinai. Moreover, Tuhamy made clear that not a single Jewish settler could remain in the Sinai and that Egypt would demand a Palestinian state in the West Bank.[150] More troubling still, he made no mention of a separate peace should the other Arab states stand back from a comprehensive negotiation, even after earnest Egyptian efforts to enlist them. Dayan, citing his belief that Jordan's King Hussein would fear Syrian radicalism, voiced pessimism that the monarch would join the circle of peace.[151]

On the autonomy proposal, Begin believed it essential to gain Carter's buy-in for Sadat to consider it seriously. This was part of the reason the Israeli premier traveled to the White House on December 16–17, where he briefed the president on his vision for peace talks. A week later, Begin would be traveling at last to Egypt, where he planned to unveil his autonomy plan to Sadat. Although he would have preferred an invitation to Cairo, given the symbolism of an Israeli leader speaking in the Arab world's most populous capital, Begin had settled for Ismailia, a city on the Suez Canal. Cairo had proved too politically risky for Sadat, who had also floated the Sinai—inconveniently still in Israeli hands—as a potential meeting place. Dayan would write in his diary that he was disappointed that there were no welcoming Israeli flags like there were Egyptian flags when Sadat came to Jerusalem.

As for Carter's impressions during the Begin visit, it was the high-water mark. Carter especially valued the specific policy steps Begin had outlined, along with the maps showing what Israel could do, as opposed to his verbal explanations in July of what it couldn't do.

On the future of the Sinai, Begin explained to Carter that the two sides had agreed to demilitarized zones, to be established in two phases with restrictions on the Egyptian military presence. The Israeli withdrawal from the territory would be coordinated along with the phasing in of diplomatic relations. Begin, reiterating his message to Sadat in Jerusalem, assured Carter that, likely after a five-year period, "Israel will ultimately withdraw to the international border. The Sinai will go under Egyptian sovereignty."[152] Begin also did not intend to keep Sharm el-Sheikh, despite Dayan's famed public declaration that the area was more important for strategic reasons than peace. As long as Sadat committed to free navigation of the Straits of Tiran, the port city could be returned to Egypt. And Sadat had vowed no country could close the straits without unanimous consent from the UN Security Council, where the United States held a veto.

Carter was highly optimistic in response. "In my opinion," he said, "there is nothing in your proposals that Sadat could not accept." But he had failed to absorb two likely complicating elements: Israel's desire to maintain two air bases on the peninsula and the Israeli settlers who lived in the northern Sinai.[153]

As in most of the exchanges between the Israeli and American leaders, Carter had focused on the Palestinian issue to the exclusion of details on the Sinai. On this topic, Begin had attempted to outline what he meant by home rule in the West Bank and how the Palestinians would be empowered during their five years of transition. The abolition of military government, Begin explained, meant "there will not be Israeli rule in Judea, Samaria and Gaza." He continued, "There will be local rule with free elections to the administrative council. The residents will have free options on citizenship. They can be Israeli or Jordanian citizens."[154] Begin also shared his plans for allowing reciprocal purchases of land—Arab purchases in Israel and Jewish purchases in the West Bank. When pressed, he said the Palestinian administrative council would have authority to expropriate land and manage immigration, although he immediately qualified this statement by saying such actions would be coordinated with Israel to ensure public order.[155] At one point, Begin said he could envision an administrative council working with Israel and Jordan to discuss issues of common concern.[156] In the West Bank, Begin went on, the central focus would be on security. The area was so narrow that nearby Arab states or other antagonists could lob ordnance at Israeli cities or fire rockets at civilian aircraft using Israeli airspace. But the Israeli military would strive to retain only a residual presence, while trying to stay out of Palestinian cities. Begin explained finally that he could not accept the notion of foreign troops deployed in the West Bank to protect Israel: "We do not want to be protected Jews. . . . We want to sustain our independence and to end the persecution of Jews. . . . We want to live as a normal nation."[157]

Regarding the administrative council, he preferred that it be located in Bethlehem. He mentioned Ramallah as an alternative but opposed East Jerusalem as a site. On December 17, day two of this particular round of talks, Begin again broke new ground when he astonishingly detailed his thoughts on the Jerusalem holy sites: "My idea, which will require further consideration, is to have international religious councils take care of the holy shrines. The Muslim shrines should have a committee consisting of Jordan, Egypt, Syria, and Lebanon, along with Saudi Arabia, Iran, and Morocco. This committee would take care of Muslim shrines, and they would have full autonomy and could guarantee free access to those shrines."[158]

In responding to Begin's various proposals, Carter and his advisors showed considerable attention to detail. They wanted, for example, to understand the specific powers of the proposed administrative council. Here, based on the Carter team's questioning and the larger context, Begin sensed a US desire for the five-year interim period to evolve into full Palestinian rule in the West Bank and thus Israeli withdrawal. Of course, US officials would never seek a final-status commitment on this issue, understanding the futility of such a request to Begin at this point. Nonetheless, the president and his team remained pleasantly surprised with the Likud leader. Carter even told Begin that he had called Sadat and remarked on the prime minister's "constructive actions." The self-rule idea, Carter admitted, "could be seen as very positive," pending details on the council's powers. Finally, Carter thanked Begin for his flexibility, about which he had generally harbored doubts, and his friendship.[159] Carter would perhaps never again summon this level of generosity toward the Israeli leader.

The White House meetings buoyed Begin. On returning to Israel, he referred to Carter advisors and members of Congress by name and to the positive reception they had given him. Indeed, Begin could not resist making clear in public remarks how delighted he was by the favorable reception his ideas had received in Washington. He deemed his proposal "a plan that is praised by anyone who sees it."[160] In contrast, the Carter White House followed its initial public support for Begin's ideas with more neutral comments, making clear that the specific issues must be worked out by the parties. Begin, meanwhile, sought to convey similar confidence in Sadat's intentions. "In two or three months," he mused, "we want to sign peace treaties. You should not exclude the possibility the Egyptian-Israeli peace treaty will come first."[161] Simultaneously, the Israeli leader tried to quiet fears that Sadat's peacemaking could threaten his rule, citing the claim by Dayan and others that the Egyptian army stood behind him.

The Ismailia talks, held on Christmas Day, lacked the drama of Sadat's Jerusalem visit, but the event felt historic to Israelis nonetheless. After all, this was the first time an Israeli leader had set foot on Egyptian soil. Perhaps, as Dayan commented, the subdued reception reflected Sadat's hesitancy over whether the Egyptian people would really welcome an Israeli leader. Yet Israelis were still impressed that Sadat used the occasion to swear in his new foreign minister; Ismail Fahmy had resigned after Sadat announced his Jerusalem visit. In Ambassador Eilts's subsequent cable to Washington, he remarked that Sadat had described Begin as "fair, strong, and decisive."[162] Evidently, Sadat also took heart in Begin's message that the Israeli cabinet had agreed to an IDF pullback to the international border in the Sinai.[163] Yet this concession glossed over the issue of the settlements and the two Israeli air bases in the territory.

On the West Bank issue, wide gaps remained. Sadat could not embrace the autonomy proposal, believing he could not sell it to the Arabs inside and outside of Egypt. While he admitted that this proposal represented a step forward, he called on Begin to accept the concept of Palestinian "self-determination," an effective path to statehood. On this point Begin demurred. (Separately, one surprise to emerge from the talks was Ezer

Weizman's quiet support for outside pressure to be applied on Begin. This was made clear in Eilts's cable to the State Department: "Such pressure [according to Weizman] should come from the United States, Western Europe and international public opinion. It will make it easier for Begin to make the right decisions, which he cannot do in one step."[164])

Following the meeting in Ismailia, Begin unveiled elements of his autonomy proposal in a speech to the Knesset on December 28. He argued that both Israelis and Arabs should suspend their sovereignty claims on the territory or else face an impasse. He also discussed the "logic" and moral correctness of allowing Palestinian Arabs to have Israeli citizenship. The speech was a major moment for Begin in that he assailed the idea that Israel could keep land without providing political rights for its inhabitants. Moreover, he made clear that Zionism and "apartheid" were incompatible. This was critically important, especially coming from the leader of the Israeli right. Following twelve hours of often-acrimonious Knesset debate, Begin raised the example of Rhodesia, which had denied rights to its black citizens. Israel does not want to be like Rhodesia, he averred, contending that his proposal demonstrated "decency" and "goodwill." A country could not ethically control land without granting rights to all its citizens. He continued, addressing world opinion, "We never wanted to be like Rhodesia. And this is a way to show our fairness to all men of goodwill. . . . Here we propose total equality of rights—anti-racialism. . . . Of course, if they chose such citizenship . . . we do not force our citizenship on anyone."[165]

Begin faced a backlash from the right. This domestic threat was not one that Carter and Sadat appreciated. They believed Begin was strong as the champion of his political bloc and perhaps didn't view Israelis to his right as having much political clout. Instead, Carter and Sadat were far more preoccupied with the Arab backlash against Egypt, especially given the geopolitical value of oil. But Begin faced a painful challenge, with one prominent settler accusing him of making his proposal to win a Nobel Peace Prize. In his Knesset speech, the prime minister struck back at the settlers—so recently his allies—for having a "messiah complex."[166] This would prove an extremely rare instance in the Israeli milieu: a right-wing leader publicly chastising his allies, especially in such biting terms.

The settlers were not the only critics. Likud members, including Shmuel Katz, who had attended the prime minister's July meeting with Carter, charged that yielding the Sinai would compromise Israel's strategic depth. Another Likud member, Moshe Arens, who would later serve as ambassador to Washington and defense minister, made a similar case.

Still another bloc within the Israeli cabinet, led by Ariel Sharon, believed Sadat could simply live with the settlement enterprise in the northern Sinai. According to Begin's cabinet secretary, Arye Naor, Sharon wanted to test what was possible on the Sinai settlements with additional building.[167] For Sharon, either this added infrastructure in the northern Sinai would elicit no rebuke from Sadat or it would be a bargaining chip to be quickly tossed away. Unfortunately, when combined with announced Israeli plans backed by Begin to expand settlements in the West Bank, these actions repelled both Carter and Sadat. The Israeli actions produced a devastating backlash against Begin. Carter and Sadat happened to be meeting at the time, early January 1978, in Aswan. Most immediately, the developments punctured the amicable relationship Begin had built with Carter, causing the US president to believe Begin would never waver in his attachment to the West Bank. Holding the territory for security purposes could be justified, but settlement expansion suggested Begin intended to stay indefinitely. For his part, Sadat reacted by adopting a new strategy based on getting Carter to force an early Israeli decision to return to the 1967 borders.

Here, personal dynamics with Carter began to move even more in Sadat's favor. Whereas Carter viewed Sadat as bold, warm, and charming, he largely saw Begin as rigid, lecturing, legalistic, and lacking Sadat's imagination. He further considered Begin far tougher than any of his advisors and Sadat the most open-minded among the Egyptians.

On the Sinai settlements in particular, Sadat expressed the view that Israel was not reciprocating the goodwill offered in Jerusalem and Ismailia. In early January 1978, therefore, he suspended bilateral talks with Israel. Talking with Carter by phone, he said of the Israelis: "They prefer land to peace. They shouldn't have raised the issue of settlements. They think I want peace at any price."[168] As Sadat saw it, he had already taken enormous risks with his overtures to his Israeli neighbors, and Israel's response had put his initiative in peril. Carter agreed entirely with Sadat's assessment.

In mid-January 1978, US officials, such as National Security Advisor Brzezinski, coalesced around the view that Begin's policies would thwart the push for peace. Early the next month, in a rare gesture, Carter invited Sadat to Camp David to discuss a US strategy for moving forward. In these meetings, Brzezinski proposed an extraordinary step: colluding with Sadat to form a common approach for pressuring Begin. This view was favored by William Quandt, an advisor on the National Security Council, who wrote, "Both Carter and Vance were disinclined to use such manipulative techniques of diplomacy, but the idea began to be seriously considered as the more straightforward methods seemed to be leading nowhere."[169] According to US thinking, Sadat would put forward a proposal with "one or two maximalist demands which we would subsequently publicly disown. This would enable us to take issue with the Egyptians, and to use the subsequent Egyptian 'concession' as the point of departure for joint public pressure on the Israelis. I further developed this thought in a memo, with which the President expressed agreement."[170] The plan embraced by Carter required Sadat to say that his peace initiative was being threatened by Israeli settlements and Begin's resistance to applying UN Security Council Resolution 242 and its principle of withdrawal to the West Bank. Under these circumstances, they believed they could put pressure on Begin and sustain it domestically in the United States.

But Sadat did not play his role as Carter and others had envisioned. He chose not to say publicly that the initiative was being endangered by Israeli settlements and a lack of respect for Resolution 242. Still, the Brzezinski approach was based on creating a showdown with the Israeli prime minister, and that would come in Carter's meeting with Begin on March 21–22. The meeting had been delayed by the Coastal Road terrorist attack in northern Israel, which killed thirty-eight, followed by Operation Litani, a cross-border Israeli retaliation into Lebanon. The deaths of Israeli civilians in these events drew no real sympathy from Carter.

The president zeroed in on Begin's vagueness regarding what would follow his proposed five-year transition period for the West Bank. All Begin would commit to, after this period, was the choice by West Bank residents to become either Israeli or Jordanian citizens. He would not similarly agree to allow Palestinian elections to determine the fate of the territory, an outcome that would satisfy the US administration. Begin, as well as Dayan, felt such a commitment would cede too much in determining Israel's future. US officials contended that Israel had no genuine intention of using the five-year period to test Palestinian self-rule; instead, all the Israelis wanted was to expand their settlements and their territory. As Brzezinski put it to Begin, "We have to have an agreement that is satisfactory to you on security grounds, but which is politically realistic. If you want genuine security while giving the Palestinians genuine self-rule and identity, that can work. Security—yes, political control—no."[171] By agreeing to withdraw to fixed military positions, Brzezinski reasoned, Israel could scale back its West Bank authority and demonstrate a credible distinction between security and political control.

Despite his growing skepticism, and his aides' desire to create a showdown, Carter at least initially tried to foster a favorable climate for his discussions with Begin. The president and first lady hosted a dinner for Begin and his wife. During the meal, Begin discussed his parents' and brother's death in the Holocaust and his own imprisonment at the hands of the Soviets. Afterward, the two leaders met privately for about ninety minutes. But instead of renewed warmth, Begin felt the chill that had set in since December, when Carter had shown such receptivity to his autonomy plan. According to Carter's diary, Begin said he was "wounded in the heart" by this change. As for the details, when Begin insisted Sadat wanted a Palestinian state, Carter answered he knew for a fact this was untrue.[172] Ambassador Lewis would later say that Begin "wanted Carter to admire him, but he realized that Carter did not like him as much as he admired Sadat." The sensitive Begin was hurt by this, but he was not prepared to change to earn Carter's approval.[173]

In formal talks the next day, Carter was icy toward Begin. The president, apparently casting aside whatever personal efforts had been made the previous evening, attacked the prime minister with "disdain in his voice and fury in his eyes," in the words of one Israeli participant. He enumerated what he would refer to as Israel's "six no's":

> Mr. Prime Minister, the Israeli position, as I understand it, is that even if there were a clear statement by us *against* a total Israeli withdrawal from the

West Bank and *against* a Palestinian state and even if this were to be accepted by Egypt, Israel would still not stop building new settlements or the expansion of settlements; Israel would not give up the settlements in Sinai; Israel would not permit an Egyptian or UN protection over the Israeli settlements in Sinai; Israel will not withdraw its political authority from the West Bank and Gaza; Israel will not recognize that Resolution 242 applies on all fronts, including the principle of withdrawal from the West Bank; Israel will not give the Palestinian Arabs, at the end of the [five-year] interim period, the right to choose whether they want to be affiliated with Israel, with Jordan, or live under the interim arrangement. This is my understanding of the present situation. If I am correct, the likelihood that the peace talks can be resumed with Egypt is very remote. There are no immediate prospects of a substantial movement toward a peace agreement.[174]

While enduring this tirade, Begin looked "ashen," according to more than one attendee. Carter, he felt, had not granted him credit for the distance he had traveled.[175] Thus, Begin reiterated Israel's willingness to withdraw to the international border in the Sinai, as well as his support for Palestinian self-rule in the West Bank, free of Israeli interference. "Our forces will be in designated camps in Judea, Samaria and Gaza," he explained. "The question of the future sovereignty of these areas shall remain open."[176] Yet he pointedly avoided engaging on the settlements issue.

Seeking to put pressure on Begin, Carter called the members of Congress—including Jewish members—whom the prime minister was about to meet, to report on the failure of the talks, attributing this failure to Begin's "six no's." Hearing from those he met in Congress that the president was actively lobbying against him added to Begin's disquiet and anger.[177] Lewis, who accompanied Begin during his congressional visits, subsequently recalled, "When Begin left town to return to Israel, he was really mad, unhappy, angry and feeling very much abused. The press coverage was as Carter wanted it. It did depict Begin as quite intransigent."[178] Once back home, a dejected Begin did not share details with the Israeli public, but he also did not paper over his differences with Carter. Addressing the media, he said, "Always remember that what is, admittedly, a matter of important policy for the mighty United States of America, is for us a matter of life and death."[179]

Amid the sharp tensions with Washington, Begin was reinforced in his view that a separate Egypt-Israel peace offered the only path forward. He and Carter, he believed, would never reach a common understanding on the West Bank. For outreach to Egypt, the obvious envoy was Weizman, given his rapport with Sadat. Soon the defense minister received an invitation to Cairo. Within Israel, however, Weizman faced skepticism from members of the cabinet, who saw him increasingly taking Egypt's side in debates. To assure critics of his impartiality, he brought with him to Egypt Attorney General Aharon Barak, who had a reputation for directness as well as legal brilliance. For these reasons, Begin held Barak in high regard. As such, Barak's participation gave Weizman political cover.

But in these talks with the Israeli delegation, held on March 30–31, 1978, Sadat made clear he would not agree to forging a separate peace, believing this would undermine Egypt's standing in the Arab world and strengthen the Soviet position in the region. According to Barak's notes of the meeting, which also included Egyptian defense minister Mohamed Abdel Ghani el-Gamasy, Sadat explained: "If there will be a separate peace, everyone will be in shock. The Soviet Union will say, 'Sadat made a separate peace and he leaves all the Arab states to their fate. He has a secret agreement with the United States and Israel.' This will not serve me nor you."[180]

While refusing to discuss a strictly bilateral deal, Sadat showed some give on the West Bank. Echoing Carter from a week before, he declared, "A Palestinian state must wait."[181] He also acknowledged that a new Palestinian entity would need a link with Jordan, as well as with Israel; here he consented for the first time to Cairo potentially replacing Amman in this role, should the Jordanians bow out. (Jordan's King Hussein was privately open to Egyptian peace talks with Israel but didn't know if they would succeed; therefore, he didn't want to publicly stand apart from the Arab world in opposition to the Sadat initiative.) In other words, Egypt would not be party to a separate peace, but it would fill the void left by a key Arab state. Israel, Sadat continued, would even retain a veto on major security-related issues in his plan, which he admitted would apportion relative power over the Palestinians to existing states. He elaborated, "We should go back to the situation before 1967. The West Bank will be tied to Jordan and Gaza to Egypt. In these two circumstances, you will have an active role in protecting your security." Israel would later rue not giving the troublesome Gaza back to Egypt.

In an apparent first, Sadat also disclosed his failed attempts—made through Jordan and Saudi Arabia—to engage the PLO in the initiative and have it recognize Israel: "I have taken the PLO out of my dictionary," he said, indicating his displeasure. "They have taken themselves out by their behavior during the negotiations." Still, reflecting his growing distrust of Begin, Sadat did not want his updated views on Palestinian statehood or the PLO imparted to the prime minister. If Begin learned of his disavowal of a Palestinian state as a goal or the PLO as a partner, the prime minister—a captive to Israeli politics, in his view—would be compelled to declare these statements publicly, creating problems for Cairo. Separately, in response to Begin's comments that the settlements would stay, Sadat evidently felt "insulted." At one point, Israeli defense minister Weizman gently urged Sadat to meet with Begin in person to explain Egypt's views, because the Israeli leader felt "out of the picture."

In the talks with Weizman and Barak, Sadat focused especially on Egypt's predicament with respect to its Arab peers. To this end, he repeatedly stressed the need for Israel to publicly declare its intention to leave the West Bank and only stay in fixed military locations within the territory.[182] In addition, the settlements could remain but they could not grow, and Palestinians could be allowed to sell their private land to Israelis.

The separate talks that followed between Barak and Gamasy would be a turning point, in the attorney general's estimation. "I came back from Egypt and told Begin the gaps were definitely bridgeable," he later recalled.[183] Such a conclusion suggested Begin had been wrong about the necessity of a separate peace. Israeli and Egyptian stances on Palestinian self-rule were narrowing, Barak sensed, providing a cause for optimism. But neither the Egyptians nor the Israelis chose to share the detailed results of their talks with Washington, perhaps because Sadat believed he could gain better terms from a US proposal. From Begin's perspective, direct talks with Sadat could yield more than going through the White House.

On May 1, 1978, around the time of Israel's thirtieth anniversary, Begin again visited the United States. The visit corresponded with Carter's announcement that the United States would open a Holocaust museum, a gesture the president may have perceived as outreach to Begin. In his diary entry about their meeting, the president wrote, "I told him that peace in the Middle East was in his hands, that he had a unique opportunity to either bring it into being or kill it, and that he understood that the Arabs genuinely wanted peace, particularly Sadat. He had seen the expression on the faces of people in Cairo, Ismailia, and Jerusalem when they exchanged visits, and there was no doubt in his mind about it. . . . My guess is that he will not take the necessary steps to bring peace to Israel—an opportunity that may never come again."[184] For Carter, Begin was the impediment to peace, not Sadat.

Formal Egypt-Israel negotiations had been suspended since January 1978 due to Sadat's anger over settlements. Sadat said he was only willing to resume them if the United States would present its own proposals. By June, though, State Department officials made clear to Sadat that a US plan would only follow a peace proposal by Egypt, so that the United States could apparently be the bridge in the aftermath of failed Israel-Egypt negotiations. Cairo now appeared to be emboldened. On July 3, the Egyptians released a plan that, in Israeli eyes, signaled a hardened position. Whereas the Aswan Carter-Sadat statement in January had called for Palestinians to "participate in the determination of their own future," the new Egyptian proposal stressed "the right of the Palestinian people to determine its own future." The updated language also called for dismantling all West Bank and Gaza settlements and omitted all references to peace treaties and normalized relations. A legal analysis produced on July 11 by Rosenne, the Israeli Foreign Ministry official, was withering in its criticism.[185]

After the release of the Egyptian document, the United States, guided by Vance and Brzezinski, held back from releasing its own, despite its implicit promise to do so. One reason was a desire not to antagonize the Israelis, who sensed collusion, given the proximity of the US and Egyptian positions. Instead, US officials thought they could wait things out, serving in a mediator role while Israel and Egypt worked to bridge their differences.

Now, even as formal talks remained in limbo, driven largely by Sadat's anger over settlements, Egypt's president agreed that Israeli and Egyptian officials could hold talks on political issues in July. In the interest of finding common ground, Vance pressed for a meeting of foreign ministers, hoping to maximize Dayan's pragmatism while sparing Sadat and Begin an awkward personal exchange.

The location agreed upon for the July 17–19 conference was unimpeachably neutral: Leeds Castle in Kent, England. In this quiet venue, the thinking went, the parties could reengage away from the media spotlight, which was apt to exacerbate differences.

On substance, the dominant point of contention remained the future of the West Bank. Dayan, who had a penchant for exploring creative solutions before he was authorized to do so, approached Vance at Leeds with a compromise that he had devised on his own. In this formulation, Dayan asked whether the final status of the West Bank could be delayed until the end of the five-year transition period. Vance, who well understood that Begin would not commit now to Arab sovereignty, recalled, "I told Dayan that I would not rule out an arrangement such as he was suggesting. He then offered his personal opinion that if the Israeli peace proposals were accepted, Israel would be prepared to discuss the question of sovereignty at the end of the five years and that an agreement could be reached at that time."[186]

Dayan then offered his personal opinion that if the Arabs would present plans to divide the West Bank, as opposed to calling for a full Israeli withdrawal, Israel would consider that option. Dayan hadn't consulted Begin, and he later recalled his trepidation in using the term "territorial compromise"—even from a personal standpoint—because the country identified this position with the Labor Party, with which Dayan had formerly been affiliated. On learning what his foreign minister had broached, Begin did not castigate Dayan, instead publishing the Leeds summary in full, including the renegade proposal. But this was because he believed the Arabs would only accept all or nothing, dooming the idea.

In the end, the Leeds conference, for all its hints of progress, did not herald a breakthrough. Vance, now convinced that the bilateral approach had run its course, called for State Department official Harold Saunders to begin "drafting the document which, after many permutations, was to form the basis of the Camp David framework for a comprehensive settlement."[187] For Begin, the refusal to define Israel's position in final-status talks had the additional benefit of exempting the prime minister from having to spar with some of his own advisors, who questioned ideas such as letting Palestinians vote in Israeli elections or purchase land inside Israel.

Later in July, Sadat implied threats that suggested the bilateral frictions could deteriorate into a crisis requiring dramatic US intervention. The particular issue at hand involved Egyptian permission for Israeli military officials to remain in Cairo, which had been granted despite the absence of active Egypt-Israel military talks. Now suddenly Sadat was insisting that they leave. Furthermore, Sadat had held some fence-mending sessions with radical Arabs, as if preparing to bolt from the peace talks. On July 31, Carter wrote in his diary, "I'm concerned that Sadat might precipitate a conflict in October, as he has hinted several times."[188]

CAMP DAVID AT LAST

Now, only a summit involving the two leaders, Carter believed, could drive the process forward. Only the principals could make the toughest decisions. After toying with the idea of holding the conference in Europe or even Morocco, Carter settled on Camp David, resolving that this would allow him access to an unobstructed stream of intelligence. As at Leeds, a central idea was to keep the media away, forcing the leaders to focus on the issues and eschew grandstanding. With Vance assigned to personally deliver the president's handwritten invitations, Carter insisted that Begin receive his first, to avoid the impression of a conspiracy against him. Indeed, when Begin met Vance in Jerusalem, the prime minister accepted the invitation immediately but, according to the US secretary, "was apprehensive about our intentions . . . worrying that he would be caught between Carter and Sadat."[189] Indeed, Sadat saw Camp David as the moment when the United States would at last offer a set of proposals favorable to Egypt.

A Camp David peace summit would attract the attention of the whole world. The president of the United States was using all his prestige to reach a breakthrough in a high-stakes summit at his personal retreat. The possibilities were great, but so were the risks—for all three leaders. For Carter, an unsuccessful gamble on peace could hurt his presidency and his chances of being reelected. He wanted a foreign policy victory partly as a basis for reelection. Moreover, a failure would mean an all-out confrontation with the American Jewish community, especially if Carter identified Begin as the culprit. Failure for Sadat could be construed as a repudiation of his Jerusalem journey, possibly putting him on a trajectory toward conflict. And Begin, given the closeness between Carter and Sadat, felt sure he would shoulder the blame for failed talks. Beyond these risks, Israeli relations with Egypt could revert to their former hostility, worsened by the threat of future war, a refrain Carter voiced to Begin. US-Israel ties could fray as well, isolating Israel as Washington and Cairo drew closer. This isolation would hold profound risks for Israeli military and economic strength, not to mention the warm US-Israel societal relationship built over decades.

For Begin, the stakes were high for both his country and him personally. He knew he'd be exiting his comfort zone. On the West Bank, he could justify his autonomy proposal because it fit within his carefully developed worldview, maintaining ties to biblical territory while granting civil liberties to its inhabitants. Yet in other areas, Camp David would require making clear ideological concessions in exchange for the promise of peace. These concessions, impinging upon an ideology shaped over a lifetime, fell into four main categories: yielding the West Bank, now or later; recognizing the existence of Palestinian nationalism; dismantling Jewish settlements in the Sinai, thereby setting a precedent for removing those in the West Bank; and freezing further construction of Jewish settlements in the West Bank. Another set of issues did not challenge Begin's core beliefs but did challenge his inclinations, namely, the question of relinquishing Israeli air bases in the Sinai.[190]

On all four ideological questions, Begin started the summit intending not to compromise. He adopted this stance despite a feeling that Sadat and Carter were allied against him, despite his not having communicated with Sadat in months and the nadir in personal relations with Carter, precipitated by the settlements issue. Begin couldn't even rely on ideological or cultural unity from his own delegation, which consisted of Dayan, Weizman, and Barak, among others. During one Friday evening meal at the summit, as recalled by Elyakim Rubinstein, a Dayan aide, "Begin wanted to sing songs of the Irgun, but virtually nobody on the Israeli team knew the words."[191] The only ones present who did were there to support Begin in a personal capacity: his wife, Aliza, and his longtime personal aide, Yechiel Kadishai.

As a matter of strategy, the United States believed it could leverage Begin's desire for a bilateral deal with Egypt to produce progress on the West Bank. Brzezinski explained the endgame as a "joint agreement, to be achieved by a subtle combination of U.S.-Egyptian pressure on Israel to make the necessary concessions with regard to the West Bank in order to achieve that which Israel particularly wanted, a separate accommodation with Egypt."[192] The essence of US strategy thus rested on Israel's yielding much of the West Bank in exchange for the prize of a peace treaty with Egypt.

Still, Begin was not without leverage. He knew that Carter wanted a peace breakthrough for his own presidency and therefore would perhaps be willing to settle for a bilateral peace with Egypt while deemphasizing the West Bank. Begin also knew from the March visit by Weizman and Barak to Cairo that his concept of Palestinian self-rule might be reconcilable with Sadat's. The question would be whether this self-rule would represent an interim point on the way to full Israeli withdrawal or an endpoint.

On September 7, 1978, the third day of the summit, Begin made his case to Carter for keeping the Sinai settlements, following what he perceived as an uncompromising line drawn by Sadat at the start of the summit. (Begin suspected Egyptian coordination with the Americans, and indeed Sadat had informed Carter of his fallback position at the outset of the talks.) Sadat's initially stated terms included not just full evacuation of settlers from the Sinai, but also full withdrawal from the West Bank and East Jerusalem. But according to Begin, these Sinai communities represented a tiny carve-out in an enormous territory, close to Israel's border. Begin had even articulated an intention to retire at one of them, Neot Sinai. Angered by the prospect of giving up the settlements, Begin told Carter that in Israel there was a "national consensus . . . that the Sinai settlements *must* stay."[193] Sadat contested that the settlements were no small accommodation and that no

Egyptian could live with Israeli settlements on Egyptian land, which was nonnegotiable. At a meeting with all three leaders held the same day, Sadat shouted at Begin, "Security, yes! Land, no!" Begin felt the anger was unwarranted, given his own agreement to give up the strategic southern tip of the Sinai, Sharm el-Sheikh.[194]

With tensions mounting, Sadat claimed the entire Arab world would refuse to accept the maintenance of the Sinai settlements. "My initiative has come not out of weakness, but out of strength and self-confidence," he said. Begin retorted that two thousand Israeli settlers in thirteen Sinai settlements posed no threat, and that Sadat could easily make them Egyptian permanent residents. Shortly thereafter, Sadat rose to leave, saying he saw no basis for further talks. Only Carter's intercession kept him from acting on this threat. Then the US president told Begin he believed the Israeli people would prefer peace to a handful of settlements. To this, Begin answered that dismantling the settlements would cause his government to collapse. If he believed in the cause, Begin continued, he would be willing to pay the price—but he did not.[195]

For Carter as a mediator, this exchange was a watershed moment. The talks would not be easy, and those between the leaders would be nearly impossible. Not once, over the course of the summit, would Carter again try to convene a three-way exchange, given the gaps on positions and personal acrimony. Yet during a follow-on meeting that evening, Carter told Sadat that he believed giving up the Sinai settlements was "extremely painful" for Begin, whatever the US view. In turn, Sadat agreed with Carter's suggestion that any Israeli withdrawal from the settlements would come with a phase-in lasting two to three years.

On September 8, day four of the summit, Begin argued in a session with Carter that the Sinai settlements served as a buffer between Egyptian forces in the Sinai and Palestinians in Israel-held Gaza. Carter disagreed, citing the restrictions on Egyptian offensive capabilities in Sinai areas closest to Israel and Gaza. Yet Begin still urged Carter not to include this stance in a proposed US draft framework for peace. Altogether, Begin feared what became known as a "US paper" that could set baseline terms unfavorable to Israel. Put another way, the Egyptian positions could never be more flexible than the American ones. Still, the prime minister issued a tantalizing hint regarding settlements in a rather offhanded manner, without elaboration. He stated he could "never personally recommend" dismantling them, which implied he might not block the move if proposed by others. Carter called Begin's turn of phrase "extremely significant."[196] The president did not underestimate the challenge faced by the Israeli leader. "I understood his dilemma," he wrote. "He was the one who was being pressured to change the private and public commitments of a lifetime."[197]

Days later, Aharon Barak offered a different perspective to Carter, suggesting that precedent mattered most to Begin. A key concession on the Sinai settlers would open the floodgates for future negotiations, especially given Begin's stature as a lead ideologue. If a right-wing Israeli prime minister was willing to demolish settlers' homes in the Sinai, his successor might do the same in the West Bank. And when it came to the West Bank, Begin thought yielding settlements—then home to just 3,200 or so residents, not including East Jerusalem—would be not only misguided but illegitimate. (The settlement population in the late 1970s was minuscule compared to today.)

About a week into the summit, Carter tried to finesse Sadat on the settlements issue. If Jews could live in Cairo or Aswan, a prospect to which Sadat consented, then why couldn't they similarly stay in the Sinai as Egyptian citizens? To this, Sadat gave his own finessed reply. "Some things in the Middle East are not logical or reasonable," he said. "For Egypt, this is one of them."[198]

Whatever the complications on the Sinai, the West Bank remained the more fraught topic for negotiation. Sadat voiced his desire to deliver an Arab victory on the territory. Meanwhile, in his talks with Begin, Carter grew exasperated at the Israeli leader's refusal to delineate the post-autonomy contours of his proposal.[199] Recollecting his anger, Carter wrote: "I accused Begin of wanting to hold onto the West Bank, and said that his home-rule or autonomy proposal was a subterfuge. He resented this word very much and brought it up many times in our subsequent discussions."[200] That same evening, in a private talk with Sadat, Carter tried the opposite position, offering that "Begin's proposal for home rule on the West Bank does provide a basis for resolution of problems during a transition period."[201] The future beyond self-rule, Carter continued, would require a realist approach from Egypt, given that effective responsibility for the West Bank would ultimately fall to Jordan. This marked the first indication that Carter would defer to Sadat on the Sinai but perhaps offer more limited support on the West Bank.

Still, in these early days of the summit, Sadat took a firm position on the territory, demanding a full Israeli withdrawal and calling for a treaty to include non-acquisition of territory by force. Here, the "non-acquisition" language echoed the preamble to UN Security Resolution 242, implying that Israel would have to return strictly to the prewar 1967 lines. But Begin pushed back on several fronts. He reiterated that Resolution 242 called for withdrawal from "territories," not "*the* territories," referring to the English draft of the resolution. Further, he contended that the preamble did not constitute the operational part of Resolution 242. And he argued that, in 1967, Israel had engaged in a defensive war after Nasser had blockaded a key waterway and poured troops into the Sinai unprovoked. If the "non-acquisition" clause as invoked by Sadat was applied retroactively to all of Europe's wars, Begin protested, the continental boundaries would surely have to be entirely redrawn. Even Carter, hardly a reflexive backer of the Israeli leader, said the same to Sadat.

On Sunday afternoon, September 10, the sixth day of a deadlocked summit, Carter sought to breathe life into the talks by taking the participants to the Gettysburg battlefield. The symbolism was evident. An inability to resolve differences peaceably could lead to disaster. This would be the only time between their heated exchange on day three and the end of the summit when Begin and Sadat would see each other. In a breathtaking moment, while Carter was addressing attendees, Begin began reciting the Gettysburg address—first just with his lips, then more audibly. He appeared to know it by heart.[202] For Begin, the address evidently represented the power of rhetoric in the hands of a true leader.

The return from Gettysburg marked a new phase of the summit. For the first time since the Sadat visit to Jerusalem, the United States proposed its own written, full-blown peace plan—not just verbal suggestions, as it had offered throughout. But as week two of Camp David wore on, the question lingered as to whether the Americans would press equally hard on the Sinai and the West Bank. For Carter, taking a hard line on the West Bank could have domestic costs, given the public clash it would guarantee with Israel. The alternative would be to push harder on the Sinai issue, with all its prospects for a breakthrough, while permitting an unclear endpoint after a West Bank transitional period. Carter, who prided himself on pursuing the tough policy road over the expedient one, decided to leave his options open. Yet he maintained the viability of the second approach by making a key procedural move. He insisted the parties agree to two separate accords: one focusing on the bilateral issues and the other on establishing a framework for further negotiations on the West Bank. For the second, the hope was that it could be achieved with Jordanian follow-up. To facilitate progress on the bilateral track, Carter sought to work with empowered top officials on each side, rather than the leaders themselves. Barak, given his legal acumen and his influence over a prime minister who was similarly guided by the law, seemed a good pick on the Israeli side. Osama el-Baz, a top national security advisor who had studied at Harvard Law School, fit the bill for Egypt. (Barak had also done a year of research at Harvard Law.)

Back at Camp David after the Gettysburg visit, Carter impressed upon Begin the strategic benefits Israel would accrue by giving up its Sinai settlements. But, focusing on the West Bank, the Israeli leader homed in again on the "non-acquisition" clause and how it could not be applied to territory won in a defensive war. The climate eventually grew desperate. Sensing that consensus would remain permanently elusive, Begin beseeched Carter to simply end the summit then and there, allowing Egypt and Israel to negotiate separately. A seething Carter answered that the leaders would hardly be motivated to make concessions once they'd stepped away from the summit and its sense of expectation.

On Thursday, September 14, the tenth day, Sadat agreed to meet with Dayan, who Carter apparently thought could influence Begin on the Sinai.[203] Indeed, Barak would later affirm that this is why he believed Dayan was chosen by Carter.[204] During their meeting, the Egyptian leader was struck by the Israeli foreign minister's sense that Begin would not budge on the settlements. The next day, reprising earlier threats from both sides, Sadat informed his team that he was leaving. This development prompted Carter to lay everything on the line. He proclaimed that all the progress, all the relationships built over the past year, would be lost if Sadat walked out.

Carter's plea worked, at least for the moment. Sadat stepped back from the ledge, agreeing to stay at Camp David. Then, in a letter addressed to both leaders, the US president identified Sunday, September 17, as the final day of the summit. The talks could go on no longer than that. Carter had been absent from his other presidential roles for nearly two weeks. The parties should therefore push relentlessly for a deal over the next three days. Preparing for the alternative, Carter asked his team to draft a speech admitting failure, specifying that the Sinai settlements and a refusal to endorse Resolution 242 as the basis for West Bank negotiations had doomed the talks.[205] In other words, Israel was at fault—an apportionment of blame Weizman and Dayan had long feared, and one that could bring the United States and Egypt closer still, at the expense of the US-Israel bond.

Moreover, the Dayan-Sadat meeting on Thursday, September 14, and one between Weizman and Sadat the next day made clear to the Israelis that evacuation of the Sinai settlements would be required to secure Sadat's signature to a deal. Carter had been saying this for days, and he reiterated it when meeting with Dayan and Weizman on Friday. Carter also restated the enormous benefits to Israel of an agreement: full diplomatic relations, opening of the Suez Canal, and removal of Egypt from the Arab military coalition that had existed against the Jewish state since 1948—accepting the conventional wisdom that no Arab state could wage war against Israel without Cairo.

The question now emerged for Dayan and Weizman of whether political cover could be provided for Begin to cede the Sinai settlements. Avraham "Abrasha" Tamir, an Israeli military advisor present at Camp David, introduced the idea of enlisting Ariel Sharon toward this end.[206] Earlier in the decade, Sharon, while serving as head of the IDF Southern Command, had himself built the Sinai settlements in order to slow a potential Egyptian advance in the northern Sinai and prevent contiguity between Egypt and Gaza. In a phone call on September 14, the general directly told Begin he did not perceive a military reason to avoid evacuating the settlements, assuming this was the last obstacle to peace. Sharon evidently had shared such a view with Tamir prior to the talks. On the last day of Camp David, Begin described the phone call, saying that Sharon told him, "You know my views on the settlements. Write down that any decision that you take, I will support."[207]

Weizman, following his meeting with Sadat, had told the Israeli delegation, "We don't have any other choice," adding that "we have to choose between a peace agreement and the Israeli settlements in the Sinai."[208] Perhaps Begin harbored some doubts about Weizman's advice, given his susceptibility to Sadat's charisma.

Nevertheless, the time had come for a decision. Begin's team of non-ideological advisors made clear that he would indeed be making a painful decision, but not one that would betray his essential beliefs. At a very momentous meeting with Carter held late Saturday night—just before Carter's deadline the next day and also attended by Vance, Dayan, and Barak—Begin agreed to pass the Sinai settlements issue to the Knesset for a vote. "If what is holding up peace are the Sinai settlements . . . I shall submit the matter to the decision of the Knesset and honor whatever the Knesset decides," Begin said, as recounted by Weizman.[209] To eliminate a final sticking point, US secretary of defense Harold Brown and President Carter agreed to provide three billion dollars in soft loans for Israel to rebuild its Sinai air bases on Israeli soil.[210] The path was now cleared for a bilateral deal.

Prospects for the West Bank were murkier. Israel had already agreed earlier in the week to a second round of negotiations aimed at determining the final status of the territory. This round would be held toward the close of the five-year transitional period. The question was whether the land-for-peace concept enshrined in Resolution 242 would be the basis for those final-status talks. Begin, believing that this formulation would prejudice the outcome, was adamantly opposed. Sadat, having already conceded earlier in the week on no explicit mention of the non-acquisition-by-force terminology in the 242 preamble (instead, the whole resolution appeared as an annex to the peace accords), took the opposite stance. The resulting compromise was artful, essentially saying that 242 applied to the bilateral Israel-Jordan talks, thereby fuzzing the issue of whether it applied explicitly to the West Bank or not. This amounted to creative ambiguity, wherein each side could contend the text justified its own point of view.

On the Sinai, Begin knew he had adequate political support at home. Even if some Likud members opposed the deal, the vote could pass with Labor backing. This near assurance of a positive outcome likely provided steady motivation for the prime minister. Still, the move carried heavy risks. Sometime down the road, as Barak had made clear to Carter, Arab leaders would invoke the precedent to push for a comparable dismantling of Israeli settlements in the West Bank. And they would cite the full withdrawal from a territory to call for a similarly complete evacuation of the West Bank and the Golan Heights, claimed by Syria.

Also arising at the September 16 meeting with Carter was the issue of Palestinian rights. Whatever Begin's professed belief in civil liberties, he had been consistent in not acknowledging the national rights of Palestinians. Earlier, he had referred to Israel's neighbors as "Palestinian Arabs," "Arabs of Eretz Yisrael," or "Arabs of Judea and Samaria." Now he finally made a significant conceptual concession in accepting the "legitimate rights of the Palestinian people." This meant that the notion of Palestinians had entered his public worldview. Begin had been brought to this point in part by Barak, who had convinced him that all rights were "legitimate," even as Begin avoided the term "national rights."

Yet the issue of the West Bank settlements remained unresolved. According to Barak's notes, Carter and Vance tried to get Begin to agree to an open-ended moratorium on settlements over the five-year period of self-rule, with Carter citing Sharon's expressed hopes of reaching one hundred thousand settlers to justify the freeze. But Begin would not be moved. The only moratorium he would agree to covered the prospective three-month interim period to finalize an Egypt-Israel treaty. Even this brief pause would need to exempt one new settlement scheduled to be built in the Jordan Valley for the IDF military-agricultural program known as Nahal. Begin made clear to Carter that a long-term freeze would create a political problem. As Carter would write, "It was obviously very painful for Prime Minister Begin, who was shouting words like 'ultimatum,' 'excessive demands,' and 'political suicide.'"[211]

After midnight, on what was now Sunday, September 17, Carter offered a formulation on settlements without a time frame. Perhaps the late hour explained the subsequent lack of clarity surrounding the issue. Begin said he would think it over and respond the next day. He also agreed to postpone the Nahal deployment in the Jordan Valley. Yet later on Sunday, Carter told Sadat that Begin had actually agreed to an open-ended freeze on all West Bank settlements, a claim the Israelis would dispute even decades later. Indeed, the lone comprehensive notetaker at the event was Barak. After Camp David, Begin would instruct Barak to contact Carter to read what he had written down.[212]

Despite this and other side areas of contention, the parties departed Camp David and announced their breakthrough at the White House late Sunday night, September 17, 1978. Suddenly, the tensions that had built up over the previous two weeks evaporated. Begin and Sadat, who days earlier couldn't even tolerate being in the same room together, embraced at the ceremony. Brushing aside the bitterness of the negotiating sessions, Begin lavished praise on Carter. The Israeli leader recalled earlier that day visiting Sadat's cabin and thanking the Egyptian leader for his friendship. (Sadat also was effusive in his praise of Carter, but did not mention Begin.) Begin, not one for historical understatement, proclaimed Camp David to be "one of the most important" conferences since the 1814–1815 Congress of Vienna, which set the boundaries of Europe after the French Revolution and Napoleonic Wars.[213]

WINNING KNESSET APPROVAL FOR CAMP DAVID

Now Begin faced the major challenge of marketing the breakthrough at home. For the most part, the Israeli public embraced the agreement. The teachers' union, in solidarity, called off a planned strike. Shimon Peres, leader of the opposition Labor Party, said his bloc would back the accords in the Knesset. Peace Now, founded in March 1978 to call for Israeli concessions to Egypt, organized a rally in support of the very prime minister it had demonstrated against before Camp David. Amos Oz, the novelist who led Peace Now, wrote Begin to praise him, saying a change in conviction after so many years could not have been easy. Begin wrote back loftily that he had dreamed of peace with the Arabs since the UN partition vote of 1947, reminding the author that the British had been his main opponent in those days, not the Arabs.[214]

The harshest reactions, unsurprisingly, came from the right. The prime minister had opened the door to future concessions in the West Bank, some in this camp charged, even as the Palestinian leadership still refused to accept the existence of Israel. Begin thereby had failed to uphold Jabotinsky's "iron wall," having offered concessions to the Arabs before they had fully recognized Jewish national rights. Demonstrators took to the streets carrying black umbrellas, a reference to British prime minister Neville Chamberlain's appeasement policies against Hitler in 1938. Sinai settlers—and their supporters—blocked roads with tractors. Protesters called Begin a "traitor." For the prime minister, all this stung.[215]

Among the most painful lashings came from Rabbi Zvi Yehuda Kook, spiritual head of the Gush Emunim (the Block of the Faithful) settler movement. Just a year earlier, following his election triumph, Begin had sought a blessing from Kook. Now the rabbi denounced the Camp David agreement as a "desecration of the sacred name of peace."[216] Kook, along with Likud parliamentarian Geulah Cohen and many others, believed that in agreeing to Palestinian self-rule in the West Bank, Begin had betrayed his foundational principles and sealed the fate of the territory as a Palestinian land. He had, furthermore, forsaken Israeli sovereignty over Jewish biblical inheritance.

Amid the admiration and the uproar, Begin had promised his negotiating counterparts to bring the full Camp David accords to a Knesset vote within two weeks. He kept his word, scheduling the balloting for September 28. Begin saw an advantage in acting quickly, given international elation over the deal. Yet the good feelings were not shared universally within the Likud. Of the forty-five Likud members in the Knesset, twenty-nine supported the deal, while seven opposed and nine planned to abstain. Among the Likud abstentions were longtime partners from Begin's underground days, including Eitan Livni, head of the operations staff in the Irgun; Dov Shilansky, a fellow demonstrator against the reparations deal with Germany;

and Yitzhak Shamir, the former Lehi leader, who would succeed Begin as premier. Begin needed a simple sixty-one-vote Knesset majority to gain approval, and support from other factions within his bloc, including religious parties, would not get him there, necessitating votes from the opposition Labor Party.

After Begin began addressing the room, the firebrand Geulah Cohen spoke up. She had joined the Irgun in 1942, later switching to Lehi, for which she served as an underground broadcaster. Now she flatly called on Begin to resign, referencing his former eviction from the Knesset for his principled, albeit highly provocative, opposition to reparations. When asked by the Knesset speaker to leave the plenum for interrupting, she declared, "I respect the dignity of the house, so I will leave."

"But," she quickly added, "I do not respect the dignity of the premier," who she claimed was "not bringing peace or security or honor. He is bringing us the repartition of Eretz Yisrael."[217] She inveighed, "One compromises on things that are marginal, not on the central issue, not on the very heart of the Land of Israel," adding that "Zionism is readiness to sacrifice something now for the sake of the Land of Israel, and not to sacrifice the Land of Israel for something now."[218] Later, addressing a reporter, Cohen explained, "I am nothing compared to what Begin would be like if the Labor Party had made the Camp David agreements. He would be 1,000 times stronger: he would demonstrate, have people throwing themselves on the streets, refusing to leave territories. He once said he would never send a Jewish soldier to expel a Jewish settler. He did everything he said he wouldn't do. He has even recognized the claim of Palestine for their rights. Now it is in our hands. In five years it will be theirs."[219]

Moshe Shamir, another Likud parliamentarian of Begin's generation, invoked a different pillar of the prime minister's ideology: standing up for the defenseless Jew. During the Knesset debate, he excoriated Begin for agreeing to dismantle the Sinai settlements. This act, he contended, was a "blow to the Jew who has stood up straight and been prepared to fight back. . . . I have the impression that by making this decision this government has returned to a state of receiving the charity of others, of begging for handouts, of bowing one's back to those who are one's benefactors."[220] Likud member

Moshe Arens suggested withdrawal would make Israel more vulnerable to military attack from the Sinai rather than more secure.

But Begin was undeterred by such critiques. Now he saw members of his own party grandstanding, just as he had done during his years in the opposition, free from the burden of actually governing. Difficult decisions required compromise, and he had come to understand this. The deal had been completed, and it must be defended on the level of Israeli interests as well as values. Grounded in a realism that had often eluded him in the past, he declared that if Israel wanted peace, it had to relinquish the specific settlements. There was simply no alternative. He also defended his resolve as a Zionist: "I had to decide. . . . The peace treaty was on one side of the scales and the settlements on the other. According to every moral code to which I subscribe the scales tipped on the side of the peace treaty. There is no other way. With the pain, the insults, the shouts—no other way. To my dying day, I will believe that this is the right choice." He added, "There is no evasion here, no flight from responsibility."[221] A failure to compromise at Camp David, Begin reasoned further, would have isolated Israel from the United States, American Jews, and world Jewry, creating untold, profound stresses for the state.

The deal also presented an opportunity to end the virtually constant threat of war looming over Israel during its first three decades. "We don't want there to be war every five years," he said. He commended Israel's soldiers, saying their fortitude had convinced Egypt that peace was preferable to future military engagement. "Peace is born, first and foremost, of our blood," Begin said solemnly. "For this peace we have sacrificed 12,000 of our best boys, in five wars, one war after another, one battlefield after another. We want to put an end to that. This is the opportunity; this is the chance." After invoking the Holocaust, he pleaded again on behalf of peace. "Now is the hour," he said.[222] It may have been Begin's finest. There seemed to be a direct line going back to the Saison—which lasted from the end of 1944 through the first several months of 1945—when Begin raised the thin piece of paper and declared that every ideology has to be subordinate to a focus on the national interest. When one makes such a judgment, it opens him up to later accusations that he is not fervent enough in his beliefs. But Begin understood that he had to answer to a higher authority: his concern for people who did not share his ideological convictions. When Begin was at his best, this was the mantra that guided him. He saw this desire to restrain himself on behalf of the national good as something that linked him to a historic chain of leaders, which gave him responsibility for all Jews and not just Jews who shared his convictions.

After seventeen hours of debate, at 4 a.m. the Knesset approved the Camp David framework by an eighty-four to nineteen vote, with seventeen abstentions. On March 26, 1979, following another six months of diplomatic sparring, the first treaty between Israel and an Arab state was signed on the White House lawn.

LEGACY OF CAMP DAVID

Over forty years later, the peace endures. Egypt and Israel have not engaged in war since. Nor has any other Arab state attacked Israel. The country faces its most daunting military threats from non-state groups such as Hezbollah and Hamas, as well as from Iran. The deal also survived the tragic assassination of Sadat in 1981 and, three decades later, the brief tenure of a Muslim Brotherhood government in the wake of the Arab Spring. Today, Egypt and Israel cooperate in rooting out Islamic State militants in the Sinai, containing Iran, and exchanging information to maintain security in the Gaza Strip. Israel has been able to diversify its budget away from a singular military emphasis. To give an idea: in the mid-1970s, approximately 30 percent of Israel's GDP went to the military; now that figure is less than 5 percent.[223] Today this amounts to a savings each year of over one hundred billion dollars, which Israel has been able to invest in education, health care, and infrastructure.

Egypt, too, has gained from the accords. It has been spared costly wars and, since 1979, has been one of the world's largest beneficiaries of US military and economic assistance, only after Israel. Despite the recent national volatility and US objections to Egypt's human rights record, the country has remained the top American ally in the Arab world. Of course, the peace between Israel and Egypt has remained a very cold one at the people-to-people level. However, it has endured and presently the two governments cooperate more than ever on issues of common security concern, as well as on free-trade initiatives.

Finally, the peace deal has carried strategic advantages for the United States. In its Cold War competition with the Soviets, the United States emerged as the unmistakable peace broker in the region. The treaty likewise enabled America to maintain close ties with both Israel and its principal regional ally, Egypt. All this played out as another alliance, between the United States and Iran, was collapsing amid the 1979 Islamic Revolution. Egypt would thereafter replace Iran as a strategic pillar in the region.

A little more than a decade later, an Israeli-Palestinian breakthrough would occur, although it remains preliminary and fraught. A peace deal with Jordan, signed in 1994, would prove as sound as its Egyptian predecessor. And in 2005, Israel would unilaterally withdraw from its settlements in Gaza. Such developments would ultimately soften the sometimes-contradictory pulls between the United States' traditional support for Israel and for the Gulf Arab states.

In assessing Begin's leadership at Camp David, memoirs by Carter and his advisors published very soon after the administration left office suggest the Israeli prime minister succeeded by defining his priorities narrowly as compared to Sadat. His central priority was achieving a separate peace with Egypt. Even so, the corresponding failure to resolve the Palestinian issue must be regarded as a substantial missed chance. Decades of international displeasure, two Palestinian intifadas, and numerous failed rounds of negotiations have followed. To be sure, some might say Begin would have winked at the massive settlement expansion that has followed in the West Bank. After all, Israel has created ample facts on the ground for a future division of territory, if and when it comes. But Israel, on so many levels, has suffered from having held the territories all these years, a fact Begin would acknowledge.

On the Jordanian option for the West Bank especially, many Israeli officials look back and rue a lost opportunity. The Hashemite kingdom would have gained control of the Palestinian land, while Egypt would have had responsibility for Gaza. And all this would have happened a few short years after the Arab League summit when the PLO was anointed master of its own fate. Israel would have been unbound from a perpetual future burden.

Yet Begin—a nationalist who was often accused of demagoguery—perhaps deserves more credit than he gets for opening the door to a West Bank under something other than Israeli sovereignty. Just after leaving power in the 1980s, Carter and his advisors were among the strongest voices claiming Begin had refused any accommodations with the Palestinians. But a different message emerges from the Israeli side. Since the 1993 Oslo Accords, which established the Palestinian Authority, virtually every Israeli prime minister has cited Begin to validate their dealmaking with the Palestinians. In other words, Begin's acknowledgment of the "legitimate rights of the Palestinian people" opened a political space that had not existed beforehand. His move gave political cover to people across the Israeli political spectrum to recognize that Israel had to deal with Palestinian representatives regardless of their ideology.

Begin might be seen as a nineteenth-century European liberal democrat living in the twentieth-century Middle East. This context helps explain his view of nationalistic Zionism as being compatible with civil liberties, a theme that was no less important for him than the necessity, after World War II, of preventing Jews from ever again being victims. Given the often harsh positioning of today's Israeli right, one can reasonably wonder whether Beginism, with its emphasis on extending civil liberties, is vanishing, and in what sense or circumstances it might be revived.

Appearances aside, the Irgun commander who became a peacemaker didn't actually deviate from his key principles. His vision remained consistent for most of his life. To the extent that he evolved, he did so from an overwhelming sense of national responsibility. Even when difficult decisions in Israel's interest threatened his political support, alienating him from some of his oldest and closest comrades, he showed he could make them.

Of course, signing the Egypt-Israel treaty in March 1979 did not mean all challenges were behind Begin. Over the next three years, he needed to be firm when settlers in the Sinai resisted evacuation. The same held after Sadat was assassinated by an Egyptian militant in 1981, when domestic critics charged that there was too much uncertainty to complete the withdrawal.

But Begin saw it through, a testament to his commitment to principles and to his character. The prime minister made other bold decisions, including the bombing of a nuclear reactor in Iraq. Yet Camp David was the one decision that would require political courage from a man who spent a lifetime carving out both a deeply felt ideology and a political base that he was called on to defy.

Unfortunately, in the waning years of his leadership, Begin would demonstrate the limits of his resolve, acceding to adventurism in Lebanon. After the Egypt-Israel peace treaty, he was overcome by his desire to avoid being attacked further, as well as by his poor physical health, especially after the death of his wife, Aliza. The hundreds of Israeli fatalities during the Lebanon War likewise burdened him. Dan Meridor, who served as his cabinet secretary in his second term and was one of those closest to him, concurred that Lebanon exacted a heavy toll on Begin. He grieved for the Israeli victims. Contrary to some reports, however, Meridor denied that Begin was clinically depressed at this time.[224] Meridor, who visited Begin weekly in a reclusive retirement until the former premier's death, said he recalled a conversation in 1985 about the Lebanon War. While keeping with a lifelong practice of not publicly blaming his comrades for mistakes, Begin did blurt the following about the war: "[Ariel] Sharon and Raful [former chief of staff Rafael Eitan] presented us with fait accomplis."

Perhaps one of the lowest moments for Begin would come in the aftermath of the massacre of Palestinians by Christian militants at Sabra and Shatila after the PLO's withdrawal from Lebanon in September 1982. Begin condemned the attack but denied that Israel was complicit. This would create an international furor.

But the Begin of Camp David—surrounded by advisors largely untainted by ideology—was driven by a sense of national responsibility rather than the credo of the rejectionist right. He seized the opportunity to avert war and bolster relations with the United States.

In truth, Begin's views carried more nuance than a mere focus on Jewish strength, mainly of the military sort. Yes, he believed in military might as a necessary means of power, but he was likewise devoted to principles such as historical rights, basic equality for Jews and Arabs, and a refusal to allow

Israel to be isolated in its own region or distanced from the United States. For Begin, isolation from the United States and dashed prospects of peace with the largest Arab state would diminish Israeli power, not enhance it.

Once convinced of the justice of a cause, Begin could be compelled by a broadened definition of national strength. And his principles led him to see, as he told his comrades during the Saison, that a very thin line separated a just cause from one that must be repudiated. Judgment would always be required, and Begin's own assessment enabled him to avoid extremism while maintaining the faith of his public. He could also embrace political realism, based on weighing the risks of action versus inaction. At Camp David, he weighed the risks, and he decided. Israel's national interests mattered more than the attitudes or the anger of those in his own political camp. Leaders made decisions, even when it was painful to do so. Fundamentally, he understood that the anger he faced would eventually dissipate, as the strategic benefits of the treaty he helped to craft would endure.

CHAPTER 3

YITZHAK RABIN

Mr. Security Accepts the PLO and Oslo

Henry Kissinger, who would deal extensively with Yitzhak Rabin during the Richard Nixon administration, captured his essence: "Taciturn, shy, reflective, almost resentful of small talk, Rabin possessed few of the attributes associated with diplomacy. Repetitious people bored him and the commonplace offended him. . . . He hated ambiguity, which is the stuff of diplomacy. I grew extremely fond of him though he did little to encourage affection. His integrity and his analytical brilliance in cutting to the core of a problem were awesome."[1] They were. But there was another attribute that singled out Rabin: he was honest to a fault. He could not lie. After he made a secret commitment to withdraw from the Golan Heights, if an Israeli journalist had known exactly how to ask him about Israel's withdrawal and what specifically he had told the Americans, Rabin would not have lied to him.

Of course, to protect a secret, he could say things that were technically true and still misleading. However, he would never say something that was untrue—he simply couldn't. While an admirable quality, what was even more impressive is that he was honest with himself and would admit when he was wrong. Because he was so intensely analytical, when he had thought through his position there was no prospect of convincing him otherwise.

But if you disagreed with him, if events or reality proved him wrong, he never hesitated to acknowledge that he had been incorrect.* Few leaders possess such a quality, but he did.

Rabin faced reality and understood the consequences of denying it. That is who he was. What shaped him? What other characteristics came to define him? Where did he come from?

EARLY YEARS

Yitzhak Rabin would learn to assume responsibility from an early age. His parents, Rosa and Nehemiah, were activists. They came to it naturally.

His mother, nicknamed "Red Rosa," was born in Russia to a wealthy family, but she eschewed its money and Orthodox Jewish traditions and pursued a secular education at a Russian polytechnic school. She very much identified with the poor and needy and favored radical change in a time of great upheaval, war, and revolution in Russia. After the Bolsheviks came to power, she ran into trouble when, not seeing the regime as sufficiently committed to the workers, she refused to join the Communist Party and was fired from her position running a munitions factory—a firing that led the workers to go on strike.[2] Though not a Zionist, she had an uncle in Jerusalem and, according to Rabin, when she encountered a group of young Zionists who were about to board a ship for Palestine in 1919, she "decided—somewhat impetuously, I imagine—to join them."[3]

His father, Nehemiah, was born to a poor family in Ukraine and, to escape the pogroms in 1905, made his way to America. There he became a tailor. Soon thereafter, he became active in the Jewish Tailors' Union and also

---

* Dennis had many experiences with Rabin that reflected this characteristic. Several examples could be cited, but one stands out. In December 1987, when Rabin was defense minister and Dennis was serving on the National Security Council staff, he was in the meeting Rabin had with Colin Powell, then the national security advisor to President Reagan. Rabin explained why the Palestinian rioting, which would become known as the intifada, would end soon, and Dennis challenged him, saying his impression from traveling through the West Bank recently was that resentments had built up and the rioting might prove very difficult to stop. Several months later, when Dennis saw him in a meeting, Rabin told him that he had been right and he, Rabin, had been wrong.

joined the Poalei Zion party—a party very much guided by the ethos of so-cialist Zionism. Of his father, Rabin would say that the Balfour Declaration "fired his imagination," and Nehemiah would respond to the British call to join the Jewish Legion to help the British liberate Palestine from the Turks.[4]

His parents would meet by chance in Jerusalem, with both rushing to respond to Arab rioting in the Old City in 1920. They would marry and, after Yitzhak was born in 1922 in Jerusalem, move to Tel Aviv. Quite apart from their work responsibilities, both were committed to the cause of build-ing the state: His mother was an accountant for Solel Boneh building con-tractors and also became a member of the Tel Aviv municipal council. His father worked for the newly founded Electric Corporation and became ac-tive in the metalworkers' union as well as the Electric Corporation's workers committee. As Rabin points out, with his parents so involved outside the house, he "was trained from an early age to assume responsibilities at home: making beds, washing dishes, sweeping floors"—as well as taking care of his younger sister, Rachel, who was born in 1925.[5]

For Rabin, this simply reflected his parents living "with a sense of mis-sion that permeated the atmosphere at home. One did not work merely to satisfy material needs; work was valuable in itself. Public activity was not a way to further personal interests; it was a duty owed to the community."[6]

In his biography of Rabin, Itamar Rabinovich points out that Rosa was the dominant parent with "a powerful personality."[7] At the age of six, Rabin's parents sent him to the School for Workers' Children. Rabin would later write that "Mother had no time to ease me through those first days of school, or perhaps she believed it was better for me to find my own way." He would do so in a school that placed "inculcating values before impart-ing book learning. Responsibility, involvement, concern for the welfare of the school and its pupils were of cardinal importance. We cooked our own meals, washed our own dishes, cultivated a vegetable garden, and worked in the carpentry shop."[8]

The only family time was reserved for Friday night. Other nights, meet-ings would be held in the home, often involving members of the Haganah. While there was great activity and a deep sense of purpose, there was also, in Rabin's words, a grim aspect to his childhood: "My mother suffered from a heart ailment, and I was dogged by fear that it would bring her to her grave. Whenever she had a heart attack, I would run as fast as I could to call the doctor, terrified that I would return to find her dead."[9] In fact, she would die when Rabin was fifteen, in 1937. At the time, he boarded at the Kadouri Agricultural School, which "was then the center for youngsters who planned to establish new agricultural settlements." In his words, this "was something of a national passion in those days, especially for youngsters who had been raised on the principles of the Labor movement. It was our way of laying claim to the land in the most literal fashion possible."[10]

At the Kadouri school, his readiness to assume responsibility was further developed, perhaps along with his instinct for honesty. As he would later write, "We lived by the honor code (teachers would leave the classroom during an examination) and followed a strict schedule packed with responsibilities."[11] But it was also at Kadouri that he began to be trained militarily. With the Arab revolt beginning in 1936 and the school being attacked several times, he was initiated into "military matters." Initially, given their age, he and the other pupils were used only as messengers between defense positions. Then they were trained in the use of small arms, and their instructor was Yigal Allon, one of Kadouri's graduates.

Allon, who would become the commander of the Palmach, would shape Rabin's early career. It was Allon who told Rabin at the end of World War II that it was "out of the question" for him to take a scholarship to study hydraulic engineering at the University of California at Berkeley. Rabin had deferred it upon graduation from Kadouri because, in his words, he was "incapable of leaving the country, and my friends, during wartime." (For much of the war, and certainly before Rommel was defeated, the threat from the Germans, with Arab support, was perceived as a real danger to the Jews in Palestine.) But in 1945, with the war over, Rabin considered continuing his studies. However, Allon was preemptory, telling him he could not leave because "the world war has just ended, but our war is only beginning."[12]

By this time, Rabin had already risen in the ranks of the Palmach, thanks largely to Allon's recognition of his talents. He had been recruited into the Palmach shortly after he graduated from Kadouri and had joined the kibbutz Ramat Yohanan, near Haifa. In 1941, the Jewish Agency had decided to establish special units of "permanently mobilized volunteers" within the framework of the Haganah; they would be strike or assault units and they became known as the Palmach. As Rabin later observed, while he did not know why he was recruited in the kibbutz dining hall, "the fact remains that the invitation to join the Palmach changed the course of my life."[13]

In 1941, his first mission was to go thirty miles into Lebanon by foot and cut down the telephone lines to prevent the Vichy French from being able to rush reinforcements to the area where Australian forces were to deploy. The only reason this mission became well known, Rabin would later note, was because Moshe Dayan lost an eye during it. But it was from this night that the Palmach became Rabin's "full-time occupation," and it would remain that way until its units were disbanded and integrated into the Israel Defense Forces (IDF).

Rabin was appointed first as an instructor and then as a platoon leader in 1942. His platoon quickly became "one of the best in the Palmach in supplying covering fire." He was asked at one point to lay on a fire display before Haganah senior officers, and in the course of the exercise one of the mortar shells did not explode. Lacking shells for his platoon's mortars, he decided to take the one that did not fire and put it in his shoulder bag. He also decided that on the way back to their camp after this exercise he would separate from the platoon, believing that if the British stopped him and arrested him for possessing such a weapon, he would "take the blame on my shoulders and not involve the platoon in the 'crime.'" While it turned out that the British did not pose a problem, he nonetheless had one. Given the paucity of arms it possessed at the time, the Haganah was keeping track of every weapon, gun, and shell—and there was one not accounted for, the one he had taken. A week after the firing exercise, his company commander approached him and said a shell is missing. "Did you take it?" Another man might have dissembled in response to such a query. Not Rabin. As he said in his memoirs, "I could not tell a lie."[14] He was reprimanded on the spot and subsequently disciplined with the punishment of no promotions for a year.

Here was Rabin, the one who instinctively assumed responsibility and who also could not lie. As it turned out, the incident did not hold back the advancement of his career. By early 1945, his punishment was a thing of the past, and with the blessing of Allon—who saw in Rabin an exemplary instructor and an extraordinary planner—he became the chief instructor for the First Battalion of the Palmach, effectively the number two in the battalion. When the Palmach created a national section leaders' course, he was placed in command and led it.

With the British trying to stop Jewish immigration into Palestine, Rabin would be called on to plan and lead operations to free Jewish detainees—actually survivors from the death camps who had made it to Palestine, only to be locked up by the British with the aim of returning them to Europe. One of his early operations involved freeing two hundred such detainees from British control in a camp at Atlit, south of Haifa. Rabin's plan addressed every aspect of the operation but overlooked that these survivors would not be separated from their bundles (their only possessions) or their children. Rabin stayed behind until all were out of the camp and had reached trucks to take them away, and he even carried one of the children, whom he described as "paralyzed with fear," on his shoulders for several miles to safety. Other missions involved disrupting the logistics and movement of British forces, which included cutting rail lines.[15] He would be arrested with other Palmach and Haganah officers on what became known as Black Sabbath in 1946 and released months later.

David Ben-Gurion would assume the defense portfolio in the executive of the Jewish Agency in early 1947. Rabin later described how Ben-Gurion brought a new spirit and determination to prepare for a war on a scale not previously envisioned. That was hugely important, but for Rabin it came late and reflected a misplaced priority. While Rabin respected Ben-Gurion's "breadth of vision," he believed that he had made a fundamental mistake, starting in 1942, by emphasizing that Jews in Palestine enlist in the British army instead of building an independent Jewish force there. He compounded this mistake, in Rabin's eyes, by later giving preference to British veterans over homegrown commanders. Yes, they would be part of the emerging Israeli forces, and Ben-Gurion would devote all his time and energy to overcoming the military shortcomings, but the needs of the Palmach were left unaddressed for far too long. As a result, on the eve of the UN vote on partition, Palmach numbered only about 2,200 troops, including women and men unfit for combat. Moreover, its weapons stockpile at this time was not only small in number but contained no cannon, artillery, or anti-tank weapons and relatively few mortars, an inventory that meant, according to Rabin, that "we were sorely unprepared."[16]

Rabin believed that, "if the Yishuv's leadership had given priority to the creation of an independent force, the outbreak of the War of Independence would have found the Palmach with five thousand or even ten thousand troops equipped with better arms . . . [and] the course and outcome of the War . . . would have been appreciably different."[17] These words, written in his memoirs, were informed by what he experienced as a commander during the war and the terrible price his troops paid.

THE SEARING IMPACT OF THE FIGHT FOR JERUSALEM

Yigal Allon would decide that he needed Rabin more as his deputy and operations officer than as a battalion commander and brought him to Palmach headquarters. Beginning around the time of the UN's vote on partition in late 1947, Rabin's responsibility at the headquarters was to plan the convoys carrying material supplies—civilian and military—to the substantial Jewish population in Jerusalem. This was a herculean task. There were ninety thousand Jews living in Jerusalem at this time, but it was isolated from the other centers of Jewish population in Palestine. Worse, the situation strategically was, in Rabin words, "ideal for the Arab forces, since whoever controlled the road up from the sea to the crest of the Judean Hills held Jerusalem in thrall. Needless to say, the Arab plan was to hold that road and choke Jerusalem's ninety thousand Jews into submission."

Rabin would devise ways of protecting the convoys with troops, but the price would be high; the road ran through areas controlled by Arabs and the terrain meant that Arab fighters were firing down on the narrow and windy road. To preserve morale, he would join the convoys and promised that homemade armor cars were being developed and produced. His efforts at organizing the convoys and having them protected by troops worked for a while but ultimately broke down in March 1948. There was no choice but to seize control of key Arab areas. As he would later write, out of this need to change the strategy came Operation Nachshon, "which was designed to employ the largest concentration of Haganah forces ever fielded under a single command." It would succeed in capturing many strongholds and a number of Arab villages, and "three convoys succeeded in getting through in the context of this operation."[18]

On April 15, 1948, Rabin was appointed the new commander of the Harel Brigade. He was still responsible for getting convoys through to Jerusalem, but with information that the British were preparing to abandon key strategic positions in the city before the end of the mandate on May 15, he was also ordered to move the brigade to Jerusalem and aid in its defense. He would be ordered by Ben-Gurion to carry out a plan to capture the northern and southern sectors of the city. Though largely outnumbered and fighting Arab irregulars backed by Iraqi reinforcements, his forces prevailed. Unfortunately, the Jewish Quarter in the Old City was totally cut off. Subsequent attempts to regain a foothold there succeeded, but the intervention of the Arab Legion—Transjordan's army, which was armed by the British and led by seconded British officers—shifted the balance dramatically. Moreover, Rabin was asked to commit the Harel Brigade to what he saw as an ill-considered plan of the Jerusalem Brigade to break the siege. Notwithstanding his objections to the plan, he felt he must commit his forces—and they overcame steep odds and were successful in their mission. However, the promised reinforcements from the Jerusalem Brigade never materialized and his forces could not hold out and were ordered to withdraw.

On May 28, Rabin "went up to Mount Zion, where I witnessed a shattering scene. A delegation was emerging from the Jewish Quarter bearing white flags. I was horrified to learn that it consisted of rabbis and other residents on their way to hear the legion's terms for their capitulation. That same night the Jewish Quarter surrendered to the Arab Legion."[19]

The war carried many shattering scenes for Rabin. While his forces helped ensure that the new state of Israel would hold much of Jerusalem, the price had been staggering. He would later describe that his brigade had suffered more than one hundred dead and four hundred wounded, and that one of his "battalions had lost so many men that I was obliged to reinforce it with a platoon of Gadna troops [youth detachments]. I very much wanted to spare these fifteen-and-sixteen-year-olds the horrors of battle, but I was left with no choice."[20]

Several days after David Ben-Gurion declared the new state of Israel—a declaration his forces were too exhausted to celebrate—Rabin asked himself searching questions about why his forces were so undermanned and poorly armed: "This was for me a bitter day, a day of soul-searching. During the period of the convoys, in the days of fierce fighting in Jerusalem, prior to and after the invasion of the regular Arab armies, I was bothered by the question, why has this war caught us so ill prepared? Was it necessary?"[21]

Rabin throughout his life would ask himself hard questions. His experience in war contributed to his instinct to see things as they were, not as he might like them to be. In fact, his whole career in the IDF shaped him and his outlook. But nothing had more of an impact on him than his experiences in Israel's War of Independence in 1948. The casualties in the Harel Brigade had totaled nearly 50 percent of his troops. Years later, in speeches, he would return to the theme of the terrible price that had been paid, reflecting on how this was etched in his memory: "But as long as I live, I will never forget the rows of bodies riddled by bullets, bodies that had once been my beloved friends, the brave fighters of the battalion near Kibbutz Kiriat Anavim in 1948. I remember the cars in flames on the road at Bab-el-Wad, whose drivers gave their lives trying to break the siege of Jerusalem."[22]

Similarly, in speaking to the US Congress in 1994, he referred to the ruins of the convoys that had been preserved on the road to Jerusalem, saying, "For me and my comrades-in-arms, every scrap of cold metal lying there by the wayside is a bitter memory. I remember, as though it was yesterday, the youngsters who died inside those metal heaps. Their screams of pain still echo in my ears. In my mind's eye, I can still see the blood draining out of their bodies. And I am still haunted by the deathly silence which followed."[23]

In his memoirs, written two decades before that speech, Rabin lamented what he felt was "the bloody price of years of neglect. Now I knew for certain that my assessment prior to the War of Independence had been correct: the Yishuv leadership had not prepared enough weapons of the quality required, and combat forces had not been sufficiently trained. No other people has charged so few, so poorly armed, with gaining and safeguarding its independence."[24] He personally set about to correct this. He would stay in the military and develop it; he would forgo his dream of studying hydraulic engineering. Instead, he would fulfill what he described as a "profound sense of moral responsibility, a kind of debt of honor toward the men whose courage and whose very bodies had blocked the Arab advance."[25] He would now dedicate his life to "ensuring that the State of Israel would never again be unprepared to meet aggression."[26]

He would fulfill that mission, doing much to build the IDF. As Rabin rose through the ranks of the IDF, he initially had major responsibilities for training and the development of doctrine. Later, he held nearly every operational command, culminating in becoming the chief of staff of the IDF, with the rank of lieutenant general. He was known for his careful planning and attention to detail. He spent time in the field with the troops. He engaged them and drew them out, being teacher as much as a military leader. As Itamar Rabinovich wrote, "Famous for his awkwardness and impatience with long-winded discussions in staff meetings, Rabin displayed unusual patience and calm grace when talking to soldiers."[27] He was shaped by the IDF, and he also shaped the institution and its approach to its array of missions. In the words of Yisrael Tal, the general who developed Israel's armor corps, Rabin was "the highest intellectual authority on military matters."[28]

Rabin, as the chief of staff of the military, was the architect of the IDF's plans and preparation for the 1967 war and its sweeping victory. When asked to deliver an address on the Mount Scopus campus of the Hebrew University after the war, it was "the well-springs of the IDF's spiritual and moral strength" that he stressed. The IDF, in his words, "was the army of a nation that desired peace but was capable of fighting valiantly when enemies force it into war. It was an army that displayed all the splendor and virtues of that people whenever it faced difficult trials. It was an army that proved its unrivaled prowess in combat yet even in the heat of battle preserved its humanity."[29]

It was now time for him to leave that military, and his service as its head, and he faced a decision on what to do next. He chose to move to the political world, but he sought a transition first and asked Prime Minister Levi Eshkol to appoint him as the Israeli ambassador to the United States.

He would serve Israel and at the same time acquire experiences that would broaden him as he entered the world of Israeli politics.

RABIN'S MIND-SET

Certain core elements of Rabin's worldview emerged from his experience in war and in the Israeli military—and, of course, from Arab rejection of Israel and the conflicts of 1948, 1956, and 1967. Not surprisingly, power lay at the center of it. As he would say while still chief of staff, "The analysis of the facts proves that essentially what has assured Israel's existence, and will continue to do so, in the face of hatred all around it and the will to destroy it, is primarily Israel's comprehensive power, with military might as a decisive element."[30]

Similarly, in his eyes, even peace depended on Israeli power and an Arab understanding that Israel could not be defeated. In a 1976 interview, he said, "Our future power will determine the chances for peace in our region. Weakness is not a recipe for negotiations. If our neighbors come to realize that Israel is not weak, they will eventually see the rationale for mutual compromises, reconciliation, and peace."[31] After the Gulf War in 1991, Rabin, speaking to military cadets, said that "no Arab ruler seriously will consider the peace process as long as he can toy with the idea of achieving more by way of violence."[32]

Seeing the role of Israeli power for deterrence and for peacemaking would remain, not surprisingly, a constant of Rabin's views over time. But he was also acutely aware of the limits of military power and what it could achieve. Moreover, he saw the territories that Israel had occupied as a result of the 1967 war as something to be traded to get peace in return. Neither the military instrument nor the lands seized in the Six-Day War were, in his eyes, ends in themselves. At the same time, Rabin understood that at some point hard decisions would be required of Israel.

Speaking to the National Security College in 1981—a frequent venue for his talks—Rabin said: "The use of military force is intended to achieve a political goal and it is not a competition in airplanes and tanks."[33] Of course, he knew that the quality of weapons could affect the outcome of any battle, and Israel needed qualitatively superior arms, given the reality of having quantitatively smaller forces than its Arab neighbors, but here he was making the point that it was essential to have a clear objective in war and one that was politically achievable. He was convinced that force should be used to defend the nation, to destroy the armies and weapons that were being deployed against Israel, and to prove the futility of waging war against the Jewish state.

At the same time, he felt history demonstrated that broad, ambitious political objectives could not be achieved by the use of force. In a 1988 lecture entitled "The Limits of Force in the Preparation and Conduct of War," Rabin declared, "I do not see any constraints on the use of military force by the state of Israel to attain two defense objectives: guaranteeing the national political survival and ensuring the security of the state. An Israeli military force that is not capable of performing these tasks places the very existence of the state in peril." But he went on to ask whether the use of force could achieve "far-reaching political objectives," such as "bringing the war to an end, imposing peace, or establishing a new political reality more convenient to Israel?" He used history to show why it could not: "If you were to attempt to learn from two wars [the Suez War of 1956 and the Lebanon War of 1982], they had far-reaching political objectives that were not attained. Was this a coincidence? Was it an accident?" No. "There is a fundamental error in the approach that uses military might to achieve the total imposition of our political will over an Arab state or a group of Arab states."[34]

A few years later, he drew a similar conclusion by making a different point: Israel could destroy Arab armies, but "they undergo a rapid refurbishing of the military . . . [and] I cannot remember a war where the country defeated by us did not subsequently improve the quantity and quality of its arms."[35]

For Rabin, the military could safeguard Israel and give the Arabs a reason to make peace, but it could not impose it on them. Here was Rabin the realist. Power mattered, and if Israel did not have it, the state would be imperiled—and indeed peace would never be possible because the Arabs would have no reason to adjust their behavior and accept Israel's existence. But peace could not be imposed and the acquisition of territories would not produce it.

Rabin held this view consistently; early on, he understood that territorial concessions and compromises were necessary. As he wrote in 1983, during the time of the Lebanon War, "We must view the territories that we conquered as bargaining chips for negotiations with our neighbors for the attainment of peace or for the advancement of political objectives aimed at amelioration of the Israeli-Arab conflict. . . . That is what I thought then in 1967 and what I think today."[36]

He acted on that recognition in negotiating an interim agreement with Egypt, Sinai II, in 1975. And, later, he supported the Egypt-Israel peace treaty in 1979, in which Israel would agree to withdraw from the whole of the Sinai. Even though he became prime minister only shortly after their completion, he took a very active role in the 1974 negotiations that were a part of Kissinger's thirty-two-day shuttle, brokering the disengagement agreement between Israel and Syria. Yet Rabin rejected an interim agreement with King Hussein. Although he saw the benefits of dealing with Jordan when it came to the Palestinians, the king required extensive Israeli withdrawal on the West Bank even for a limited interim agreement—and Rabin faced the opposition of a majority of the ministers in his cabinet to such a deal. Moreover, he wanted to bring the National Religious Party into the coalition and he knew that they, too, would reject such territorial concessions on the West Bank.[37]

Political factors and his own hesitancy to take bold risks during his first tenure as prime minister from 1974 to 1977 explain, at least in part, why Rabin chose not to make a deal with King Hussein, even though he favored the Jordan option for resolving the conflict with the Palestinians at this time. There is, however, another reason why Rabin was reluctant to move at this juncture in a far-reaching way on peace and especially on the West Bank. For him, the time was not right; it was still too close to the 1973 war. The Arabs, Rabin was convinced, believed Israel was weak and they were strong,* particularly with their use of oil as a political weapon and the unmistakable American vulnerability to it.[38]

---

* On a number of occasions, President Nixon created a clear link between the oil weapon and the American need to press for peace. At one point during the oil embargo, he told a group of visiting governors that "the only way we are going to end the embargo is to get the Israelis to act reasonable . . . to get them to behave." Later, after the embargo was lifted, he

For Rabin, the context had to change, especially if Israel was to contemplate concessions on territory—which, after all, he was prepared to do in return for achieving peace. By definition, he believed that Israel must negotiate from a position of strength. And, in 1976, he told Shlomo Avineri, who was then the director general of the Foreign Ministry, that Israel's strategic position even three years after the Yom Kippur War was still too precarious to make significant concessions on territory. Israel must become stronger psychologically, diplomatically, and strategically before it could actually negotiate peace agreements. According to Avineri, Rabin said, "My task is to improve the morale and equipment of the army, to strengthen United States support for Israel, and to get out of Arabs' heads that a weak Israel is willing to make concessions. Only in another five years, when we have reached a position of strength, will Israel be in a position to make compromises."[39]

In other words, Rabin understood that concessions, difficult concessions, would be necessary. But context mattered. Israel should be in no rush. And, in the 1970s, he was convinced the time was not right for peace agreements, even saying at one point that "our most sensible policy is to stall."[40]

Unlike those on the right in Israel who believed in stalling in order to avoid ever having to surrender territory, especially in any part of the Land of Israel, Rabin was coming from a very different premise. He did not see the territory in ideological terms. He viewed it strategically through a security lens. In the 1970s, he had no problem building small settlements in areas of strategic value, such as the Jordan Valley or the Golan Heights, but he was fundamentally opposed to building in populated Arab areas. To do so would needlessly provoke the Palestinians and complicate Israel's options for the future—and do nothing for Israeli security. In fact, he belittled the settlements' role in security, implying they were a burden on the IDF.[41]

Not surprisingly, he did not see the settler movement, which was pushing for massive building everywhere in the territories, as heroic or carrying on the spirit of the pioneers of Zionism. On the contrary, he saw the settlers,

---

was "confident that the progress we are going to continue to make on the peace front in the Mideast will be very helpful in seeing to it that an oil embargo is not re-imposed."

particularly those who made up the Gush Emunim settlers, as a threat to Israel's democracy. In a press interview, at a time when the Gush's leaders were pushing for building in Qadum in the West Bank, he did not mince his words: "A settler movement . . . is like a cancer in the social and democratic tissue of the state of Israel, a group that takes the law into its own hands. . . . With historical perspective, people will question what Israel was doing in 1976, and in what a lousy and unimportant place. A mystical debate focused on the existential problem of the existence of Israel. It's unbelievable. . . . What is settlement anyway? What sort of struggle is it? What does it mean?"[42]

He made this statement on the record. But Rabin gave other off-the-record interviews at the time that were very similar in content and made clear in blunt terms the consequences of the Gush Emunim's actions: "I do not believe one can exist over time if one does not want to get to apartheid with a million and a half Arabs inside the Jewish state. Over this, I am willing to go to elections."[43]

In other words, over this, he was willing to put his political future on the line; over this, he was ready to make tough, politically difficult decisions. For Rabin, the extremist settler movement posed an existential threat to Israel over time. Even in the near term, he saw settler pressure to build in places that made no strategic sense as damaging to Israel's interests. Not because he was ready to make territorial concessions at this time; he was not. He was, however, ready to make them at some point. He understood that peace deals would require extensive territorial concessions, and he was prepared for them, but only when the conditions—strategically and diplomatically—were right. In this sense, what emerges in the 1990s when Rabin was prime minister for the second time should not be seen as a fundamental departure or change in his attitudes. It was not his views on territorial compromise, settlements, or peace that changed; it was the circumstances, context, and Israel's geopolitical position—and the way he saw them—that made it possible for him to adopt different policies and approaches and to be ready to make historic decisions.

That said, there is an area where Rabin's attitudes do evolve. On the Palestinians, the Rabin of the 1990s is very clearly not the Rabin of the 1970s.

RABIN'S EVOLUTION ON THE PALESTINIANS

In his memoirs, written after he resigned as prime minister in 1977, Rabin addresses the Palestinian problem, saying there is "really no ideal solution" to it.* Unlike Golda Meir, who in 1969 denied that the Palestinians were a people, Rabin was not one to deny history or reality. He acknowledged that a "terrible human tragedy has taken place" in reference to what had happened to the Palestinians. But, in his words, "we believe that it was created by the Arab countries in 1947–48, when they rejected the United Nations' partition plan and continued to struggle . . . against the very existence of the State of Israel." Nonetheless, that did not relieve Israel of the responsibility "to become an active partner in seeking a solution to the problem, for unless it is resolved the chances are poor that comprehensive peace will ever be realized in the Middle East."[44]

At this time, he outlined three options for dealing with the Palestinians. First, the option "advocated by Palestinian extremists": "create a sovereign Palestinian state in the West Bank and Gaza Strip." Second, the option promoted by then Israeli prime minister Menachem Begin and his Likud party: grant the Palestinians limited autonomy in the West Bank and Gaza, and they can choose either Israeli or Jordanian citizenship. "But regardless of the citizenship of its Arab residents, the West Bank and Gaza will become an integral part of the sovereign state of Israel." Or the third option, the one Rabin and the Labor Party favored: create a Jordanian-Palestinian state. Within the original borders of Mandatory Palestine—which included Israel, the West Bank, and Gaza—and Jordan, Rabin said, "there should be two states: Israel, basically a Jewish state (though not all Jews will live there and not only Jews will comprise its population), and to the east of it, a Jordanian-Palestinian state that would include considerable portions of the West Bank and Gaza Strip. . . . This Jordanian-Palestinian state will allow for the expression of the unique identity of the Palestinians in whatever form they choose to exercise their right of self-determination."[45]

---

* Leah Rabin had a foreign bank account, which at the time was not legally proscribed. Though permitted when they were living in Washington, she had not closed it on their departure. He had not known about it but took full responsibility and resigned—a factor that added to his credibility with the Israeli public.

Rabin did not pretend this was the perfect solution. It was, in his eyes, the only practical one. Absorbing the Palestinians in sovereign Israel was a nonstarter for him; later, he would explain clearly that to do so would change Israel's Jewish character and make it either a binational Arab and Jewish state or an apartheid one. And yet Rabin also believed that there was no alternative to permitting the Palestinians to express their "unique identity" in some politically acceptable fashion. But an independent Palestinian state in the West Bank and Gaza was also not acceptable to him at this time, because he was convinced it would constitute a mortal threat to Israel—not primarily because such a "mini-state" could not "absorb the almost million and half Palestinians who currently reside outside of these two areas," but rather because such a state would be ruled by the PLO, "the most extreme faction in the Palestinian political spectrum."[46]

For Rabin, the PLO's declarations of intent should be taken seriously: "The leaders of the PLO have declared—and I believe them—that they view such a 'mini-state' as but the first phase in the achievement of their so-called secular, democratic Palestine, built on the ruins of the State of Israel."[47]

The PLO's active commitment to terrorism seemed to reflect its determination to achieve its publicly declared long-term aims—and no doubt added to Rabin's perception of the organization. Interestingly, for Rabin, terrorism was a serious security issue but not a strategic threat to Israel's existence. In an interview when he was the head of the IDF, he said the PLO was a tool of Arab states and did pose "a greater danger to Jordan" but that Fatah, the largest faction within the PLO, "is not large and maybe it is not a very serious organization, but its harassment function could be severe in the future."[48]

He did not want to lend credence to the PLO and its agenda. In addition, while he recognized there might be no comprehensive peace without dealing with the Palestinian issue, he did not want the focus to shift to the Palestinians and away from the Arab states. In his eyes, the Arab nations constituted the strategic threat militarily to Israel—not the Palestinians—and, at least until the 1990s, he preferred to deal with the Palestinians through the Arabs. In speaking to a joint session of Congress in 1976, Rabin went so far as to say, "Those who believe the Palestinian issue is the obstacle to peace are mistaken. We have to settle this problem as part of the permanent peace settlement, but those that claim it is the key to peace, the formula for peace, the means to achieve peace . . . are simply misreading reality."[49]

He did not misread reality. Even more importantly,* he saw in the Gerald Ford administration a push to make the Palestinian issue the centerpiece of the conflict.[50] For him, it was a mistake to "transfer the locus of the confrontation between ourselves and the Arabs, from Arab states to Palestinians." Why? Because "diverting the focus of a solution . . . to the Israeli-Palestinian level" would lead to Israel having to deal with the PLO.[51] Rabin made this latter statement in 1988, after the first Palestinian intifada had erupted.

While the intifada would induce him to change his thinking on the Palestinians, one can see from this statement that it did not alter his approach to the PLO. Before the intifada, Rabin was convinced that the Palestinian issue needed to be addressed, but that could only be done by dealing with the Arab states. It was not just the imperative of not dealing with the PLO that guided Rabin; it was also his perception that the Palestinians were too weak to speak for themselves or command his respect. In 1981, he had a revealing conversation with Yoram Peri, a former Labor spokesman who had tutored Rabin on Labor Party politics.** After acknowledging that Rabin would not deal with the PLO, Peri asked him why not conduct talks with moderate Palestinians from the territories. Rabin's response:

> There's no point. When I speak to one of them, he tells me he has to consult with the King [Hussein of Jordan]. When I speak to another, he says he has to consult with the president [Mubarak of Egypt]. When I speak

---

* In congressional testimony, Harold Saunders, the US deputy assistant secretary of state in the Bureau of Near Eastern Affairs, stated that the Palestinians were the heart of the conflict. Saunders acknowledged that the United States did not yet have a "framework for negotiation involving the PLO, but it is obvious that thinking on the Palestinian aspects of the problem must evolve on all sides. As it does, what is not possible today may become possible." This, despite the MOU—which was part of the Sinai II accord and in which the United States promised not to deal with the PLO unless it renounced violence, recognized Israel, and accepted UN Security Council Resolution 242.

** Peri joined a small team that worked with Rabin when he returned from Washington in 1973 and entered the world of Labor Party politics. He would have many candid conversations with Rabin over the years.

to a third, he has to consult with the other president [Assad of Syria]. The fourth says that he has to consult with the chairman [Arafat of the PLO]. So what's the point of speaking with proxies? It is better to speak with those who have the power to decide.[52]

As Peri points out, Rabin was not ideological about the Palestinians; like on all issues, he was practical. The intifada changed his view of the Palestinians from the territories. They were no longer weak. They would no longer let others speak for them or represent them. But his previous view of them as incapable of standing up for themselves also affected how he perceived the intifada when it initially broke out in late November 1987. It was why he was convinced that a tough response would bring the rioting to a quick end. Why he, as defense minister, would take his scheduled visit to Washington in early December, shortly after the demonstrations and related violence had spread from Gaza to the West Bank. Why he would say "no one dies from a beating," believing those in the territories would not want to sustain the uprising in the face of the IDF inflicting very real punishment.

But the intifada did not end. Palestinians in the territories organized themselves and sustained the intifada even as the IDF quarantined villages, made sweeping arrests, imposed economic penalties, and implemented Rabin's initially harsh order. Rabin had become defense minister in the national unity government (NUG) that emerged after the 1984 elections, and he would remain in that position until 1990, when the government would not survive a no-confidence vote. As the defense minister, he had the responsibility for dealing with the territories and the intifada.

He had expected the Palestinians in the territories to give in to the physical pressure; he did not think they could endure pain or deprivation. When they did, Rabin, ever the pragmatist, was prepared to adjust his views and the policy. Pressure and force alone would not work, and by March 1988 Rabin was acknowledging that the policy must have a political as well as a military leg: "Any policy supported by only one leg will never bring about a solution."[53]

He understood a balance was needed. Palestinians must have a sense that the occupation could change, but they must also understand that violence would not produce the outcome they wanted. That is why Rabin began to say that "while we cannot solve it [the intifada] by military means only, they cannot solve it by violence or terror or wars."[54]

He searched for ways to create incentives and disincentives for the Palestinians from the territories to end the intifada. He employed economic strategies, as both reward and punishment, explaining, "We have to strike a balance between actions that could bring on terrible economic distress and a situation in which they have nothing to lose, and measures that bind them to the Israeli administration and thus prevent civil disobedience."[55]

Rabin realized several weeks into the intifada that something was different with the Palestinians. He needed to understand better what was driving them. As a result, Itamar Rabinovich writes, Rabin convened an "unusual gathering" to discuss what was going on; the meeting included army generals, current and former officials from the civil administration in Gaza and the West Bank, and specialists in Arab affairs and the Middle East from both the government and academia. Rabinovich reports that the most compelling presentation was made by Professor Shimon Shamir, who showed that Western societies dealing with popular insurrections in territories under their control rarely if ever succeeded in using force to end them. The only effective answer was to use political methods that led to a political settlement. According to Rabinovich, Rabin was impressed enough with Professor Shamir's presentation that he sent an aide to request a copy of it in written form.[56]

Over the year following the outbreak of the intifada, Rabin would adjust his position on how to deal with it several times. Initially, given his perception of the Palestinians, he believed that they could be coerced into stopping the rioting. Seeing that would not work, he thought a mix of economic and political inducements, along with the continued use of force and economic penalties, could work. When that, too, failed, he came to the conclusion that "the solution can only be a political one."

It was not just the difficulty of quelling the intifada that influenced Rabin. The political and psychological challenges it created also had an effect on him. Unlike the second intifada (2000–2004), in which Israel proper was the subject of attacks from a large number of suicide bombers, the first intifada did not involve bombs and for the most part did not involve guns;

it was led by "the children of the stones" and mostly involved rioting and stone throwing against the IDF and settlers. But because the IDF is a citizen army, the intifada still affected Israeli society.

For Rabin, two developments were particularly troubling. First, the image of the IDF, and its well-armed forces, suppressing and at times beating Palestinian teenagers was terrible internationally. Israel took a beating in international public opinion, even as the literal beatings seemed only to fuel the Palestinian anger that gave rise to the intifada in the first place.

Second, and even more important for Rabin, was the terrible impact the policing function was having on the Israeli military. The damage to morale was real—Israeli soldiers did not like going after kids. Even worse, there were signs of a breakdown in discipline and order in an atmosphere where thrown stones and Molotov cocktails often led to the use of excessive force in response.

Eitan Haber, one of Rabin's closest aides, would later describe how the impact of the intifada on the IDF, as well as the corrosive effect of occupation made more visible by the intifada, affected Rabin and produced his change toward the Palestinians:

> First, there was the recognition that it was not possible to suppress the intifada by force. After that, he gradually recognized that we would not be able to continue to rule two and a half million Palestinians against their will. The indications of moral deterioration that had appeared as part of our rule over the Arabs in the territories led him to recognize that we must not continue to dominate another people. The scenes of what the occupation was doing to the IDF and the behavior of soldiers at roadblocks or in the pursuit of demonstrators concerned him greatly. After a large number of court-martials of soldiers from elite army units and officers, some of high rank, for violent and illegal behavior, Rabin understood that the IDF was in deep trouble.[57]

Rabin's earlier acknowledgment of the Palestinians' "unique identity" and his belief that there needed to be a solution to the Palestinian problem reflected his understanding that Israel could not rule another people indefinitely. The intifada highlighted the costs. It led him to begin not just to speak of the need for a political solution but also to outline his thoughts on what that solution should be and how to pursue it.

While the Palestinians in the territories might have paid lip service to the PLO, Rabin saw that these Palestinians had led the struggle on their own for the first time, and he hoped they would be "strong enough to be masters of their own fate" and "ready to negotiate." He envisioned elections after a three-to-six-month period of calm; the purpose of the elections would be to produce negotiators who could then work out the terms of "expanded autonomy or an administration for self-rule which would conduct [Palestinian] daily affairs."[58]

Rabin would spell out his idea of autonomy and its relationship to negotiating a permanent solution more fully in the early days of the George H. W. Bush administration in 1989. Basically, Rabin favored the original Camp David framework that Begin had accepted in the Egypt-Israel peace treaty of 1979. But he modified it so that elections would produce Palestinian negotiators from the territories to be Israel's partners in the talks. In addition, because Rabin opposed absorbing the Palestinians, he envisioned a different final-status agreement. In a March 26, 1989, speech, he pointed out that Labor differed from Likud on the goal of final-status talks. Labor understood that controlling "the complete land of Israel" threatened "a Jewish Democratic state," because of the consequences of ruling "over a million and a half Palestinians." Likud did not. He would go on to explain his guiding principles toward ending the conflict with the Palestinians:

> Opposition to a Palestinian state between Israel and Jordan. Therefore no negotiation with the PLO. . . . It therefore seems to me that we should come up with a proposal, that I have presented. . . . I believe it can also be agreed and coordinated with the US. . . . The policy should be based on the following phases: Restoration of calm, elections, negotiation over a transitional period of five years and no later than three years a final status negotiation begins. . . . This move must be predicated on the Camp David accords. . . . The second thing is to continue with the policy of using force against violence. . . . The third thing, is coordination with the US.[59]

This speech was quintessential Rabin. First, he explained his differences with Likud and Menachem Begin. Unlike the Likud position, Rabin made clear that Israel could not occupy the Palestinians or absorb them without losing its identity as a Jewish and democratic state. Second, the PLO could not be a partner for Israel because that would mean accepting its agenda of statehood. Third, there must, nonetheless, be a way to end the occupation of the Palestinians, and, for Rabin, the Camp David approach was the right one: there should be a five-year transition period in which Palestinians from the territories would gain autonomy or self-government and then negotiate the issues of final status to resolve the conflict. He saw the Palestinians in the territories as being Israel's natural partners, for they were the ones under occupation and had an interest in ending it. Elections were his innovation because they could be used to produce the Palestinian negotiators and invest them with the legitimacy they would need to be able to represent and speak for the Palestinians in talks.

To be sure, the Palestinians from the territories must also see that violence would achieve nothing for them. Hence, Israel, while being ready to pursue a political outcome, must continue to use force to show the Palestinians they would pay a price if they did not adopt a period of calm and follow the path of negotiations.

Rabin's last point, on coordinating with the United States, was a fundamental part of his mind-set.

THE CENTRALITY OF AMERICA

Much like David Ben-Gurion, Rabin believed deeply that Israel must have the backing of a major power. In a world shaped by the balance of power, Israel needed the unmistakable support of one of the world's most powerful countries. Nothing was more central to his beliefs.

During the Korean War, at a time when the Truman administration feared the spread of the conflict to Europe and the Middle East, Ben-Gurion would go so far as to offer not just Israel's bases but also all its forces to the United States in the event the conflict spread. With the Eisenhower administration, Ben-Gurion saw the United States trying to organize the Middle East into an alliance against the Soviet Union, and he was ready to join—only President Eisenhower and his secretary of state John Foster Dulles feared any connection to Israel would prevent Arab states from joining the alliance.

It was during this period that Israel drew close to France. France would be Israel's main supplier of weapons and would even help build its nuclear reactor at Dimona. Shimon Peres, director general of the Defense Ministry, was the key player in acquiring arms from the French and getting them to help establish a defense industry in Israel. Rabin, from the perspective of the IDF, was not a fan of the French connection (or for that matter Shimon Peres, with whom he would clash repeatedly throughout his career). He much preferred American weapons—and the implied commitment they would provide. Until the John F. Kennedy administration, US arms were not an option, but they became one at that time. Moreover, when the Kennedy administration agreed to have a strategic discussion with Israel in 1963, Rabin, then deputy chief of staff of the IDF, came to Washington in a small Israeli delegation and took part in three days of talks about the region—an event that deepened his attachment to the United States.

The ongoing debate with Peres over the American versus French connection was settled by the 1967 war. At that time, French president Charles de Gaulle canceled arms contracts with Israel and walked away from French commitments that had been made at the time of the 1956 Suez War. For Rabin, there was only the American option. The United States was the superpower. During the Cold War, the Soviets were the other superpower, and they consistently built up the arms of the Arabs and posed an existential threat to Israel. Only the United States could provide the counterweight.

To get a sense of how important American arms were to Israel (and, at least indirectly, to Rabin's sense of the necessity of building Israel's relationship with the United States), note how Rabin described Levi Eshkol's legacy as prime minister: "Levi Eshkol's most historic decision was to intensify our campaign to break into the American arms market. Even if that had been his only accomplishment during his prime ministership (which it certainly was not), it would have sufficed to secure his fame in the chronicles of modern Israel."[60]

Rabin's desire to become the Israeli ambassador to America was heavily influenced, in his words, by his appreciation for "the role that the United States played in our region and the need to coordinate our policies with the Americans. It seemed to me that strengthening our links with the United States was our greatest political challenge—not to mention a vital condition for maintaining the power of the IDF."[61] In a memo he wrote to the Foreign Ministry shortly before going to Washington, he identified four objectives he would pursue as ambassador:

(1) Ensuring that Israel was provided with her defense requirements; (2) coordinating the policies of the two countries in preparation for eventual peace negotiations or talks on a political settlement in the Middle East— or, at the very least, preventing the emergence of too wide a disparity in policies; (3) securing American financial support to cover our arms purchases and buttress our economy; and (4) ensuring the American use of their deterrent force to prevent Soviet military intervention against Israel in the event of another war.[62]

His time in Washington only deepened his belief in the importance of the US-Israel relationship. Already he saw the United States as Israel's only reliable friend internationally, and the 1973 war validated that perception. European countries, including the United Kingdom and Germany, fearing Arab wrath and the use of their oil weapon, refused to allow America to use their bases and ports for the resupply of Israel during and immediately after the war. As Rabin would say following the war, "We had only one friend in the world and that was the United States."[63]

Surely, the massive US air and sea lift of military resupplies to Israel, starting the second week of the war, was not just critical to the IDF's counteroffensives in both the Golan Heights and the Sinai but was also a reminder of how much Israel depended on the United States. When Golda Meir explained to her military chiefs why Israel must accept a cease-fire because the United States was insisting on it, she reminded them that the weapons they had today, they did not have yesterday.[64]

Some longtime observers of Rabin, such as Efraim Inbar, have argued that the prime minister actually agreed to the Sinai II accord and its territorial concessions not because he saw it as a stepping-stone to peace with Egypt but because he wanted to prevent a deterioration of relations with the United States. Inbar is correct that Rabin at the time feared that the image of Israel was not strong enough in the eyes of the Arabs, but it is an exaggeration to say he did the deal only because of his concern with the US relationship.

Rabin could say no to the United States when he felt Israel could simply not do what it was asking. For example, he would not accept Kissinger's proposal at the end of his March 1975 shuttle to try to broker an agreement on Israel's pullback in the Sinai. Rabin felt he needed more from Sadat in terms of nonbelligerency to justify withdrawing beyond the Gidi and Mitla Passes—the key strategic choke points for moving through the Sinai. Despite great pressure from Kissinger, which included a letter from President Ford threatening a fundamental reassessment of America's policy toward Israel and the region, Rabin rejected the Americans' proposed deal, even as he explained to Kissinger in very poignant words why he did not make the decision lightly: "I am fully aware that the situation is fraught with dangers . . . and that is not just a political problem for me. I regard every IDF soldier as my responsibility—almost as if he were my son. You know that my own son is in command of a tank platoon on the front line in the Sinai. My daughter's husband commands a tank battalion there. In the event of war, I know what their fate might be. But Israel is unable to accept the agreement in the present terms, and there is nothing I can do but carry that heavy burden of responsibility—the national as well as the personal."[65]

Kissinger was not moved by Rabin's words, and following the breakdown of his shuttle effort and the administration's threats about the consequences for Israel of the policy reassessment, Rabin actually fought back. He let Ford's threatening letter be leaked, and he encouraged Israel's friends on Capitol Hill to produce a letter to the president signed by seventy-six senators—a letter that called on the administration to meet Israel's urgent military and economic needs and to stand with the country in the search for peace. That, the letter declared, should form the basis of the administration's "reassessment."

Still, instinctively Rabin wanted to be as closely aligned with the United States on policy matters as possible. He would conclude the Sinai II agreement on September 1, 1975, and he essentially backed off what he had earlier been seeking from Sadat on nonbelligerency. At the same time, however, he also received a great deal from the United States in the memorandum of understanding (MOU) he concluded with Kissinger as an annex to the agreement. In the MOU, the United States made new commitments to meeting Israeli defense needs, including significant increases in military assistance, and also made a number of important policy promises. Specifically:

- The United States committed to presenting no initiatives on Middle East peace without first discussing them with Israel.
- The United States understood the importance of the Golan Heights to Israeli security and, should America ever adopt a position on the final status of the Golan Heights, it would give great weight to the Israeli position there.
- The United States promised not to deal with the PLO unless it recognized Israel and accepted UN Security Council Resolution 242.

In Rabin's eyes, these commitments "turned the tide in Israeli-US relations."[66] Indeed, on issues that Rabin regarded as critical to Israel's well-being, the United States was not only committed to a "no surprises" policy but would take Israel's interests and concerns very much into account. While it may be an exaggeration to say, as Inbar suggests, that Rabin only made the Sinai II agreement to prevent a problem with the United States, there can be little doubt that Rabin felt he was gaining extremely important assurances from the Americans—and those security and policy commitments made the concessions to Sadat palatable. Indeed, Rabin saw these US commitments as binding the country to Israel in a way that had never been true before, and, as such, they were profoundly important to Israel's future.

But binding the United States to Israel also meant that Israel must be mindful of US interests, and that could constrain or affect Israel's choices. As Rabin himself acknowledged, the practice of coordinating with the United States might well require Israel to adjust its policies and make concessions, but the benefits of the relationship made any such compromises worth it. In fact, for him, if Israel was going to take an initiative of any sort, it should only do so with US support. Only the United States could invest such initiatives with weight, particularly because rejecting Israeli proposals was easy for the Arab states, but it was not a simple matter for them to reject a US-supported position. In his memoirs, Rabin would say: "I had always believed . . . that prior to embarking on any political initiative, it was imperative for our two governments to reach an understanding, even though in order to do so we might be called on to make certain compromises. Naturally, in the course of hammering out a coordinated policy, differences of opinion and tensions may well arise . . . [but] once the discussions were completed, we would have a common strategy with the United States—no minor achievement for a small nation in today's world."[67]

Once, when he was ambassador, Rabin went so far as to tell Kissinger that he was surprised that an Israeli raid had just been conducted in Lebanon, particularly because Prime Minister Meir was due to arrive shortly in Washington. As he confided to Kissinger, he could not understand why Meir had authorized it, admitting that "when I was the Chief of Staff whenever we were trying to achieve something from the United States in the political arena, I piped everything down."[68]

Rabin lived by the maxim that if Israel wanted America to take its interests into account, it, too, must take America's into account. He understood that the United States saw the pursuit of Arab-Israeli peace in the region as a way for America to manage its relations with the Arabs, even as it supported Israel. With that very much in mind, Rabin felt it was imperative to show the Americans that Israel was genuine in its readiness for peace and would negotiate in good faith whenever there was an opportunity to do so. At one point, he tied this directly to US military assistance to Israel, saying, "The US will aid us, if it finds Israel displaying a willingness for peace."[69]

This attitude came strongly into play at the outset of the first Bush administration. President Bush was attracted to the idea of convening an international conference to push diplomacy on the Arab-Israeli conflict. Prime Minister Yitzhak Shamir was dead set against it, but so was Rabin, the defense minister. Both saw it as a way for Arabs to avoid recognizing or negotiating with Israel. Instead, it was likely that the Arab nations would gang up against Israel and the most extreme position among the Arab parties would become the lowest common denominator.

Given the American president's interest in an international conference, James Baker, the secretary of state, conveyed to the Israelis that Prime Minister Shamir needed to come with ideas when he visited President Bush early in the administration.[70] Rabin was already thinking of the need for a political initiative, and it was Rabin who shaped the elections part of the idea that Shamir presented to President Bush.*

It was not just that the idea was Rabin's and Shamir went along; it was vintage Rabin in the sense that he had been convinced for some time of the virtue of presenting initiatives that the United States could embrace and promote. If nothing else, it kept the Americans comfortable with Israeli policies. It showed that the United States and Israel were aligned—something he was convinced enhanced Israel's deterrent capabilities—and made the United States far more inclined to be responsive to Israeli military and economic requests.

Rabin was right, and until the NUG collapsed in the spring of 1990, both President Bush and Secretary Baker trusted Rabin and felt it useful to be responsive to requests he made. Indeed, even as both came to be increasingly dubious of Shamir's aims with regard to the initiative he had brought to Washington, they correctly saw Rabin presenting ideas to salvage it.**

Having come up with the election idea, Rabin embraced the US suggestion that there should be a preelection dialogue with Palestinians from the territories to help produce calm and create the conditions and terms for the

---

* Shamir would explain that the initiative had several parts: expand the circle of peace by having other Arab states engage with Israel, mobilize international financial support to reconstruct the refugee camps and transform them from being incubators of the conflict, and hold elections to produce Palestinian partners from the territories for talks with the Israelis. While agreeing that all these ideas were good, Baker would tell Shamir that the only one he felt he could convince the Europeans and Arabs to embrace at this stage, in place of an international conference, was the elections idea.

** Dennis was the private channel through which Rabin would convey his ideas and get US responses. Because Dennis was dealing with Rabin discreetly, Baker and the few people around him who knew about the channel would refer to Rabin—a chain smoker—as "the man who smokes." Margaret Tutwiler, Baker's press spokesperson and one of his inner

elections. The sticking point came to be who would represent the Palestinians in this dialogue, and the PLO, through the Egyptians, sought to have a Jerusalemite and a Palestinian from outside the territories on the delegation. Even if the PLO could not take part, it wanted to signal its imprint on any dialogue with these conditions. Not surprisingly, Shamir rejected them and the negotiations were stuck. Rabin, ever the problem-solver, came up with the idea that the Israelis could accept on the delegation a dual addressee (someone who was a resident outside of Jerusalem but would be seen by Palestinians as a Jerusalemite) and a Palestinian the Israelis had deported but allowed to return.*

When Rabin raised these ideas, Baker, wanting to be sure there was no misunderstanding, double-checked with Shamir and he confirmed what Rabin said, including that the Americans should see if the Egyptians could accept these new terms. But when Baker subsequently got a yes from the Egyptians, Shamir began to stall—and then asked Baker to see Moshe Arens, the foreign minister. Even though Shamir had not informed Arens of what he had allowed Rabin to do, Arens agreed to work out a formula that was consistent with the Rabin ideas and with what the Egyptians had accepted. However, when this formula was brought to a vote in the Israeli cabinet, Shamir voted against it. This led Shimon Peres, the finance minister in the government and the head of the Labor Party, to push for a no-confidence vote in the Knesset, and the government fell. While Peres thought he had the votes to form a new Labor-led government, Likud was able to thwart his efforts, and after a three-month period a narrow, right-wing government was formed without the Labor Party.**

Rabin was no longer defense minister. A year earlier, Rabin had publicly forecast such an outcome if the NUG collapsed, even saying, "Of course,

---

circle, coined this euphemism and would often come to Dennis and say, "What are you hearing from the man who smokes?"

* Rabin identified many Palestinians who fit the "dual addressee" definition, living outside of Jerusalem but clearly considered by Palestinians as coming from Jerusalem and being identified with the city.

** The day of the vote in the Knesset, there were defections of two members of the religious party Aguda, and Peres was unable to form a new government.

we can leave the government. And what will happen? An extreme right-wing government will be formed, Likud and the Orthodox. And what will happen after three years? What happened in the settlements during the last years will be multiplied."[71]

Clearly, Rabin was not happy about bringing the government down. He would not defend Shamir's behavior, but continued to believe that it might be possible to find a way to work with him and, in any case, felt it was worse to have an ideologically driven right-wing Israeli government. Ironically, the collapse of the government also put Rabin in a position to challenge Shimon Peres, his longtime rival, for the leadership of Labor in advance of the next election in the spring of 1992. He would win and now be the leader of the Labor Party.

With the collapse of the NUG and the formation of a narrow-based government led by Yitzhak Shamir in June 1990, the Bush administration was poised for a crisis with Israel. Had Saddam Hussein not invaded and occupied Kuwait on August 1, there is little doubt that the administration would have moved to support an international conference on the peace issue and Shamir would have rejected it, creating a crisis in the relationship. Instead, Hussein's invasion and absorption of Kuwait became the main preoccupation of the Bush administration, and the peace issue was put on hold.

Problems with Shamir would emerge after the war, when he pushed for ten billion dollars in loan guarantees to absorb the large number of Soviet émigrés now permitted to come to Israel. President Bush was not prepared to provide the loan guarantees without a freeze in Israeli settlement activity, lest the guarantees finance a policy he opposed. The image of conflict with the United States—especially in the aftermath of the Gulf War and the collapse of the Soviet Union at the end of 1991—cost Shamir and the Likud party in the 1992 election. Yitzhak Rabin, a leader who had come to personify security—given his experience in the IDF, commentary on military matters, and service as defense minister—became Israel's prime minister for the second time.

RABIN THE PEACEMAKER: THE CONTEXT HAD CHANGED

It was not only the differences with the United States over the loan-guarantee issue that contributed to the defeat of Likud and Shamir. Shamir was a very hesitant peacemaker at a time when it appeared to the Israeli public there was an opportunity for peace. He had agreed to go to the Madrid Peace Conference reluctantly and immediately compensated his settler political base by authorizing new building, which added to his difficulties with the Bush administration. Moreover, his approach to negotiations made clear that little was possible.

The Madrid Conference had launched bilateral negotiations between Israel and Syria, Israel and Lebanon, and Israel and a joint Jordanian-Palestinian delegation, as well as multilateral talks with a wider circle of Arab states. It looked increasingly like Shamir could not respond to this opportunity, and, in failing to do so, he would be unable to stop the intifada—which had eased but not ended.

For his part, Rabin made clear he saw the new opportunity and even promised during the course of the election campaign to produce an interim agreement with the Palestinians in nine months. He was not just posturing; he genuinely saw a different world. And he understood the importance of taking advantage of opportunities, which by definition were always fleeting.

Rabin's own analysis led him to think this was a moment to be seized. To begin with, of course, he saw the collapse of the Soviet Union in broad geopolitical and geostrategic terms. The Soviets had consistently armed and rearmed the Arabs, making the threat of war a constant. Even before the Soviet Union's collapse, he saw the change with Mikhail Gorbachev and his unwillingness to support Hafiz al-Assad's pursuit of "strategic parity" with Israel as an indicator that the immediate threat to Israel was reduced.

When Baker came to see Rabin in July 1992, shortly after he had formed his new government, the secretary of state told him that Assad was ready to make a peace deal much like the one that Egypt had made with Israel. Rabin responded by saying he was fully ready to test what was possible and would not shy away from making big decisions with the Syrians or the Palestinians.

He said this in Baker's second meeting of the visit. In the initial one, Baker, still channeling President Bush's attitudes on settlements, had taken a tough line on the loan guarantees. To be fair, Rabin had told Baker at the outset that he was still trying to add parties to his coalition and did not want to get into specifics on issues at this time, but he did want to resolve the question of the loan guarantees. At the time, Dennis was one of Baker's chief aides and had gotten to know Rabin well during his time on the National Security Council staff in the Reagan administration. In between meetings, Rabin saw Dennis in the elevator, and in his deep, gravelly voice, said, "Tell Baker he is now dealing with a different Yitzhak." Baker understood the message that Rabin was not intransigent like Shamir, and the second meeting, even on loan guarantees, changed in tone and character, with Rabin making his point on being ready for historic choices.

At that time, the Bush administration did not truly grasp how Rabin saw those choices and the backlash he expected domestically. Nor did the Americans fully understand his determination to proceed in the face of the opposition he expected. His fundamental assessment, and why he was determined to test what was possible on peace, was that in this moment Israel was strong, but that would change at some point and Iran and possibly Iraq would emerge as threats with unconventional weapons in the coming decade. Israel needed to see if it was possible to transform the region in the meantime. As Rabin explained in a subsequent private meeting with Dennis, that is why he was determined to move on the Palestinians. He said, "I can do things; it won't be easy." He expected opposition, even violent opposition, from the settlers, but that would not stop him. Fortunately, he said, "The entire leadership of the IDF was made up of my boys." They had been with him throughout their careers, he had promoted them, they were the best the IDF had produced, and they were "completely loyal" to him. Asked if what he saw ahead was close to a civil war with the settlers and others, his unequivocal answer was yes. "It will get ugly."*

Rabin did not envisage total withdrawal from the West Bank or negotiations with the PLO. But he had decided he would make historic decisions if the opportunity presented itself. He would not sacrifice Israeli security;

---

* This conversation took place with Dennis when he returned to Israel shortly after Baker's visit in July 1992.

he still saw that as the underpinning of peace. For him, there would be no peace without security, and he never accepted the trite formula that peace was the best guarantee of security—not in the Middle East, where power determined reality, where acceptance of Israel was driven by a perception of Israeli strength, and where threats to Israel would continue to come from those who rejected Israel's right to exist.

Even before he began his second term as prime minister, Rabin's instinctive pragmatism had led him to probe the possibilities with the PLO, well before he crossed that threshold and made the decision to pursue Oslo. Efraim Inbar points out that, in the mid-1970s, Rabin's friend and former member of the Israeli General Staff, Matti Peled, persuaded Rabin to let him try to produce discreet understandings with Arafat. As Rabin expected, Arafat would not deliver on any of the understandings. Similarly, a decade later, when he was defense minister, Rabin used Shlomo Gazit, former head of Israeli military intelligence, to meet PLO representatives in order to gauge if there were any possibilities. Had these meetings leaked, the explanation was going to be that the talks were about Israeli soldiers missing in Lebanon.[72]

Later, after US secretary of state George Shultz made the decision that the PLO had met US conditions for a dialogue and one was established in the waning days of the Reagan administration, Rabin would ask if the United States could convey messages from him to Abu Iyad, the putative number two in the PLO. In this case, he operated through Oded Eran, who was the deputy chief of mission in the Israeli embassy in Washington. Rabin thought Abu Iyad was more serious than Arafat and might be someone who would actually do business—and in any case he was more connected to those leading the intifada in the territories. Here again, one sees Rabin's practical orientation; he was looking for ways to deal with the intifada and thought outreach to Abu Iyad might offer a pathway to do so, as well as serve as an interesting test of the PLO.*

Low expectations about, and even hostility toward, the PLO would not preclude outreach when Rabin thought it could potentially be useful. Before

---

* The channel was Oded Eran to Dennis, and he conveyed messages and questions for Abu Iyad to the US embassy in Tunis.

investing all his chips in the Oslo channel that was being run by Shimon Peres, Rabin chose to explore alternatives. He would use Ephraim Sneh, a former general and former head of the civil administration in the West Bank and Gaza, with PLO member Nabil Sha'ath as an alternative channel, to see whether the PLO would accept an interim approach to resolving conflict. Rabin used the Egyptians as yet another channel. Arafat had even sent him a letter via Egypt.* The letter intrigued him because in it Arafat agreed to defer Jerusalem and the issue of jurisdiction on land and settlements— issues that, in the official negotiations in Washington, the Palestinian negotiators from the territories were insisting on dealing with immediately. Deferring these issues was important to Rabin as a measure of Palestinian seriousness about doing an interim deal. Still, his fundamental doubts about Arafat remained and were not easy for him to overcome. Rabin might have been pragmatic and nonideological, but his suspicions about Arafat ran deep and made it emotionally difficult for him to envision dealing with the PLO leader and negotiating with the organization. Of course, he also knew it would be highly controversial with the Israeli public, given the PLO's responsibility for so many acts of terror against Israelis.

No doubt because of his reluctance to deal with Arafat, he suggested in March 1993, during his first visit to Washington after the election of President Bill Clinton, that the United States propose that Faisal Husseini become head of the Palestinian negotiating team. This was a remarkable, if subtle, suggestion by Rabin. He understood that, by bringing in Husseini, the scion of one of the most prominent Palestinian families from Jerusalem, the city would be introduced into the negotiations.** But he also wanted to satisfy himself that there was no alternative to negotiating directly with the

---

* After Dennis was named the American envoy for peace in the Clinton administration in June 1993, Rabin showed him the letter when they met privately.

** Prior to Madrid, Shamir had made it clear that, because Jerusalem was not up for discussion at least at this stage, there could be no Palestinians from Jerusalem on the joint Jordanian-Palestinian delegation. To get around this issue, Dennis proposed and Shamir accepted that on the joint delegation there could be a Jordanian who had originally come from Jerusalem. Baker, who had been meeting with Husseini as the representative of Palestinians in the territories, instructed Dennis to tell Husseini that, if they were to get to Madrid, he could not be on the delegation.

PLO. Once the administration made the proposal, Arafat summoned Husseini to Tunis and then refused to let him leave for Washington for the talks. Rabin had his answer.

Later, in explaining his decision to deal with the PLO, Rabin said in the Knesset: "During the course of the negotiations—in fact from the very onset—it became clear that the one and only address for the delegation's decisions was PLO headquarters in Tunis. It would have been possible to behave like ostriches. We could have hid our head in the sand and lied to ourselves; we could have deceived ourselves and claimed that Faisal Husseini and Hanan Ashrawi and others represented the inhabitants of the territories, and that we didn't know and didn't want to know who stood behind them."[73]

Rabin was no ostrich. Despite his reluctance and genuine unease, he would bite the bullet and deal with the PLO. Rabin was not going to forgo the possibility of a breakthrough.*

CROSSING THE THRESHOLD

There were clearly many factors and developments that convinced Rabin that the time was right to take a chance on peace. The Soviet Union was gone. The United States had reacted to Iraqi aggression and defeated Saddam Hussein, demonstrating that America would use its power; it paid to be America's friend and cost to be its foe. With Iraq—the country that had been the leading rejectionist, radical Arab state—defeated, the political space for other Arab leaders to act on peace would be far greater.

It is noteworthy that in Rabin's inaugural speech to the Knesset, introducing his government in 1992, he emphasized the changes in the international landscape and Israel's position:

---

* Rabin probably made the final decision to go with the general understandings worked out by Peres's aide Uri Savir with Palestinian negotiator Ahmed Korei after testing whether Syria's president Hafiz al-Assad would respond to his conditional offer to withdraw fully from the Golan Heights. The offer was conveyed through US secretary of state Warren Christopher. While Assad acknowledged the offer was serious, he immediately began to negotiate on the Israeli conditions—the content of peace, the security arrangements, and the timetable for withdrawal. Rabin understood from Assad's reaction that there would be no quick breakthrough with Syria, and he was not going to give up an understanding with the PLO for something that might not materialize with Syria.

In the last decade of the 20th century, the atlases and history and geography books no longer present an up-to-date picture of the situation. Walls of enmity have fallen, borders have been erased, great powers have crumbled and ideologies collapsed, states have been born and states have perished. And even the gates of immigration to Israel have opened. It is our duty . . . to see the world as it is now—to discern its perils, explore its prospects, and do everything necessary for the integration of the State of Israel in this changing world. We are no longer of necessity "a people who dwelleth apart," and no longer is it true that the "whole world is against us." We must join the international campaign for peace, reconciliation, and cooperation that is currently sweeping the globe. Otherwise, we shall be left behind, all alone.[74]

For Rabin, the threats to Israel had diminished, and that made it less risky to pursue peace. With the world changing, Israel should not be out of step; it should not forgo new possibilities. He did not dismiss the risks of pursuing peace or the need for security. Indeed, even as he spoke of the changes taking place and why Israel must take advantage of them, he reminded Israeli military officers that they had a special responsibility in this new era: "In the face of the new reality of a changing world . . . this is the hour for making changes; for opening-up, for looking around us, for engaging in dialogue, for integrating, for making friends, for making peace." The world is "no longer against us," but, "as commanders of a first-rate army, you must seek excellence in all spheres of activity, for you are the line which stands between the Jewish, Zionist, democratic strong State of Israel, and the dangers which await it, even in an era of movement towards peace."[75]

Rabin saw an opening to transform the Middle East. The enemies of peace were weaker and Israel's neighbors were threatened by the same fundamentalist Islamists that threatened Israel. He wanted to capitalize on this possible convergence, or at least test to see if it was real, by seeking a breakthrough with the Syrians or the Palestinians.* A breakthrough on either one would trigger basic changes in the region and Israel's ability to develop

---

* He would tell President Clinton, Secretary Christopher, and Dennis that he felt the political traffic would not bear moving on both at the same time, even as he would explore both.

relations with a wider circle of Arab states. If that happened, he believed Israel could insulate itself and have regional partners to deal with the threats Rabin foresaw coming, principally from Iran. In March 1993, when he met President Clinton early in the administration, he explained both his personal stake in pursuing peace and his analytical assessment of why it was so important to see if it was possible: "I am seventy-one. I have seen many wars and their price and I am willing to take risks for peace. There is a certain period of time before fundamentalism peaks and before Iran obtains weapons of mass destruction and missiles. Many ask me what is the point of making peace in the inner circle while the external circle behaves the way Iran does. My answer is that making peace in the immediate circle will reduce the risk in the external circle. For Israel it is also important to preserve the Hashemite regime in Jordan."[76]

He was not as specific or even as personal as he was with President Clinton in private, but he would offer the same basic analysis in public. He would flag the danger of Iran and the need to take on the problems of the Middle East before the threat from Iran became far more severe. In a speech in December 1992, Rabin declared, "Today Iran is the leading disseminator of fundamentalist Islam in the region. Iran has replaced Iraq in its megalomaniacal ambitions in empire-building. Within seven years, this will be a threat in the Middle East. We have this time in which to resolve the problems."[77] Rabin's words then seem no less relevant today; more than anything else, they reflected his conviction that Israel must not sit on its hands. From his days in the IDF, he understood the importance of anticipating threats. But he also understood the importance of taking advantage of openings, and he saw a moment to be seized. In this sense, Rabin was motivated as much by his perception of the danger of not acting as he was by his belief that peace might be possible.

A number of other factors also drove him, among them his concern about the corrosive effect that the occupation was having on the IDF. This was his beloved institution. The soldiers would do their job, and maybe there would be no choice, but as an institution, it was better to get the IDF out of the policing role in the territories. Apart from the impact on morale and performance, Rabin also worried about distraction from the main military mission of protecting the state from external threats.

Rabin was not convinced that the public had the staying power for additional conflict. He saw signs of fatigue, driven by the desire for the good life, and he spoke of how "we have changed" and "softened." He made these comments in describing how tens of thousands of residents had left Tel Aviv during the Iraqi Scud missile attacks in 1991. He drew a contrast with the 1948 war, when Egyptian bombing of the city was producing thirty casualties a day and yet had little or no impact on daily life in Tel Aviv.[78]

Dalia Rabin felt there was another even more personal factor that drove her father's pursuit of peace. In an interview after his death, she said, "My dad hoped in the past that we, his children, would not have to fight, and the moment his grandson put on a uniform and went to the same wars, I believe it did something to him."[79]

Rabin himself would speak about being a grandfather and his concerns for casualties. When visiting Israeli soldiers in what was then Israel's security zone in southern Lebanon—where his grandson was also serving—he said, "I feel like any grandfather. I have overall responsibility for the life of each one serving there, but naturally I have greater sensitivity to my own grandson."[80] In fact, Rabin would often express his concern over casualties, how they weighed on him and the special responsibility he felt for each one. After he accepted the Nobel Peace Prize, he reflected on the men and women of the IDF: "I served in the military for decades. Under my command, young men and women who wanted to live, wanted to love, went to their deaths instead. . . . However, I was compelled to resort to the gun." Then, referring to seeing the cemeteries and those who filled them, he mournfully said, "And of all the memories I have stored up in my seventy-two years, what I shall remember most, to my last day, are the silences."[81]

Rabin was at his most moving when he spoke about the deaths of Israeli soldiers, often saying, "We feel the pain of the death of those who were dear to us and we share the sorrow of the bereaved families, whose pain the passing years do not dull, nor do they heal the wounds inflicted by this tragedy."[82] If he could end the wars, particularly now in his second chance to be prime minister, he would. Indeed, in his very last speech at the peace rally on November 4, 1995, shortly before he was murdered, he explained why he chose this path and was determined to see if it could be realized: "Peace entails difficulties, even pain. For Israel there is no path without pain. But the path to peace is preferable to the path of war. I say this to you as one who was a military man and minister of defense, and saw the pain of the families of IDF soldiers. For their sake, for the sake of our children and our grandchildren, I want this government to extract every particle, to exhaust every possibility, to promote and reach an inclusive peace."[83]

Rabin's sense of responsibility to the soldiers, and "to be able to look in the eyes of their mothers," created an emotional driver for him. What made him able to cross a historic threshold with the Palestinians and the PLO— and to be willing to cross a similar one in terms of offering full withdrawal from the Golan Heights to Syria—was this feeling of responsibility, particularly at a moment of perceived opportunity.

Of course, his responsibility to the state may have been the most important factor of all. When he publicly explained the emotional difficulty he had shaking Arafat's hand, it was this larger obligation he cited:

> I [knew] that the hand outstretched to me . . . was the same hand that held the knife, that held the gun, the hand that gave the order to shoot, to kill. Of all the hands in the world, it was not the hand that I wanted or dreamed of touching. But it was not Yitzhak Rabin on that podium, the private citizen who lives on Rav Ashi Street in Tel Aviv; it was not the father of Dalia and Yuval, who both completed their army service, or the grandfather of Yonatan, a grandfather who does not sleep too well at night and worries like all parents and grandparents in Israel. . . . I stood as the representative of a nation, as the emissary of a state that wants peace with the most bitter and odious of its foes, as a state that is willing to give peace a chance.[84]

It was this higher responsibility of preserving the state and its character that he saw as a duty. Even in the 1970s, he was conscious of the need to preserve Israel as a Jewish and democratic state and worried about the threat that those in the Gush Emunim and the settler movement posed to Israel's future. By the 1990s, this had become more of an imperative—and he made it more of an issue. Explaining the Gaza-Jericho Agreement to the Knesset in May 1994, he said: "It is not a coincidence that the territories were not annexed, even when the country and the Government were led by the supporters of the Greater Israel policy. Alignment and Labor governments knew then, and know today, that the annexation of 1,800,000 Palestinians would cause the State of Israel to lose its Jewish and democratic character."[85]

His language would be even stronger a few months later, speaking to a group of Israeli writers, about the effect of the occupation and the stakes for Israel's future. It was, in his words, a question of values and of preserving Israel's character:

> We will have to choose, on the one hand, between the road of zealousness, the tendency toward dreams of grandeur, the corruption of Jewish values as a result of ruling over another people, the blind faith, the hubris of "I am, and there is no one else beside me"; and on the other hand, the road of maintaining a Jewish, democratic, liberal way of life, with consideration for the beliefs of others, even among ourselves, as well as side by side with us, with everyone living their lives according to their own faith. . . . The battle over the nature of the Jewish state in the twenty first century has begun.[86]

Similarly, when Bill Clinton asked Rabin why he made the decision to do Oslo and deal with Arafat, he answered: "Beyond my family and friends, my country is my life." Rabin continued, "We have to decide what it will be like if we don't share the future, including the land, with the Palestinians. Then very soon we will either no longer be a democracy or we will no longer be a Jewish state. Either decision would violate our solemn obligations."[87]

He was clear then. He was clear when he spoke to the Knesset to present the interim agreement in October 1995—an agreement that would have the Palestinian Authority govern all the major cities in the West Bank—and he reminded the elected officials in Israel's parliament that the Labor Party's position in the last election was stated repeatedly: "We preferred a Jewish state, even if not on every part of the land of Israel, to a binational state, which would emerge with the annexation of 2.2 million Palestinian residents of the Gaza Strip and the West Bank." Rabin continued, saying, "We had to choose between the whole of the land of Israel, which meant a binational state, and whose population, as of today, would comprise four and a half million Jews and more than three million Palestinians, who are a separate entity—religiously, politically, and nationally—and a state with less territory, but which would be a Jewish state. . . . We chose a Jewish state because we are convinced that a binational state with millions of Palestinian Arabs will not fulfill the Jewish role of the state of Israel, which is the state of the Jews."[88]

Earlier in 1995 in a private meeting, Rabin explained that he had given instructions to the minister of police, Moshe Shalal, to study and prepare the ground for building a "separation fence" if a final settlement with the Palestinians could not be negotiated. While he preferred an agreement, and would try to reach one, he said, "If we cannot do so, we will separate from the Palestinians. One way or the other there has to be a partition [of the land] because we will not become a binational state."[89]

Rabin knew the personal risks he was running in either reaching an agreement with the Palestinians or separating from them. The demonstrations against him were ugly. The right wing attacked him mercilessly and its rhetoric justified violence. He was dismissive of the threats—perhaps because he did not believe a Jew would kill him, or perhaps because living with risk was not new for him. In any case, he would not be deterred by the threats; he had his mission. Whether as a soldier or a leader, he would try to fulfill it.

In his March 1993 meeting with President Clinton, when Rabin told Clinton that he had a mandate to take risks for peace, the president said, "If you're going to do that, my role is to minimize those risks."[90] Clinton was thinking about external threats, not necessarily internal ones.

From Rabin's standpoint, the context was now right to take the risks that action required. He was ready to make big decisions. He was ready to cross thresholds in pursuit of peace. Not to do so would, in his eyes, be irresponsible. He was not acting only because he saw an opportunity or because he was trying to preempt the external dangers that he saw looming over the horizon. He was acting ultimately because he saw that it was his responsibility to do so: it was his responsibility to safeguard the IDF from the consequences of occupation, to seek peace if it was possible, to reduce the potential for pain that every parent and grandparent faced in Israel, and to ensure that Israel would retain its values and its Jewish-democratic identity.

The one characteristic of Yitzhak Rabin that superseded even his instinct for problem-solving was his sense of responsibility. He never shied from assuming it. Once the planes were launched in the raid on Entebbe to free the Israeli hostages in 1976, he told his aides he had prepared his letter of resignation in case the daring rescue effort failed, with a likely terrible loss of life. When casualties were sustained in Lebanon during the partial Israeli withdrawal to the south in 1985 or later in the security zone, he would explain the event and take responsibility for the loss.[91] In October 1994, when Corporal Nachshon Wachsman was kidnapped by Palestinians and killed in the rescue raid, Rabin immediately went on Israeli television explaining that he, not the forces or commanders involved, was responsible.

Yitzhak Rabin was responsible. That innate sense of responsibility required him to act to preserve the country he had served his whole life. The circumstances in the 1990s gave him the reason he needed to do so. But on November 4, 1995, an assassin's bullet would cut short his quest.

CHAPTER 4

ARIEL SHARON

A Leader Who Tells the Settlers to Give Up the Dream

Ariel Sharon was a man of contrasts. He was a man of incredible personal discipline who prepared intricate, meticulous plans and knew every inch of terrain—whether directing a military operation or settlement construction. Yet, he could never discipline his eating habits. He was the driving force behind building Israeli settlements in the territories seized in the 1967 war. Yet, later, he would be the Israeli leader who actually dismantled the settlements in the Sinai and Gaza.

He would declare that giving up any territory taken from the Arabs would signal Israeli weakness, and yet he was the prime minister who withdrew unilaterally from Gaza. He excoriated Yitzhak Shamir for not retaliating against Iraq for the firing of Scud missiles into Israel during the 1991 Gulf War, and yet he would agree with President George W. Bush to not respond if Iraqi missiles struck Israel during the American invasion of Iraq in 2003. He was merciless in criticizing Israeli leaders for not being tough enough in dealing with Palestinian terror, and yet in response to the suicide bombing of the Dolphinarium, an attack on the Tel Aviv nightclub in which many teenagers were killed, he, as prime minister, declared that "restraint is also strength." He was devoted to the Israeli military, and yet rarely got along with his superiors in the Israel Defense Forces (IDF); he was nearly drummed out of the military at least three times.

He did not trust "Arabs" and yet always had Arab workers on his ranch, whom he employed for years and with whom he typically shared meals in his home. He would not shake Yasser Arafat's hand at the Wye River negotiations in 1998, and yet, after becoming prime minister, he sent his son discreetly to meet the Palestinian leader and instructed him to be respectful and treat him with dignity. He long opposed a Palestinian state in the West Bank and Gaza, seeing it as a mortal threat, and yet he was the first Israeli prime minister to embrace Palestinian statehood publicly in these areas.

Sharon was not a rigid ideologue. He was a pragmatist and a realist. To be sure, what drove him through much of his career was a deep belief that he knew best when it came to Israeli security. He could and would challenge others who he felt did not measure up or who stood in the way of Sharon achieving a place where he had the responsibility for making decisions. He might claim he did not have great political ambitions, because he was happiest working on his ranch, but from the time he entered politics until he became prime minister, few escaped his withering criticisms—including prime ministers who gave him ministerial positions. The reason: Sharon wanted to put himself front and center and weaken those who might contend for power.

For Sharon, becoming Israel's prime minister was his ultimate ambition. Not to hold power for its own sake; rather, he wanted to make decisions and serve the interests of the country. Making decisions and assuming responsibility defined the essence of leadership in his eyes.

WHO WAS ARIEL SHARON AND WHERE DID HE COME FROM?

Ariel Sharon was born in Kfar Malal in 1928. Kfar Malal was a moshav, or cooperative village. His parents, Samuil and Vera, came to Palestine from Russia. His father was trained as an agronomist and was convinced that he knew best about how to farm the land, including what to plant, how to fertilize, and when to water. A moshav, unlike a kibbutz, allowed each family to own land; it was not shared. But decisions on farming or deciding whether to turn over land for a new village were made collectively.

Samuil and Vera went their own way. Samuil would not plant the crops that the rest of the moshav agreed to, and the two of them would reject the vote within the moshav to surrender part of their land to a neighboring moshav. They fenced off their land and grew their own orchard. When a fence was erected on the part of their land that was to be given to the new village, Vera cut a hole in it and preserved what was theirs. Years later, Sharon would say his mother's militant action "symbolized an uncompromising stand, a battle for borders and a sense of enterprise and initiative."[1]

His parents were difficult people and were largely shunned by the rest of the moshav. As Sharon described them, "My parents did not wear their hearts on their sleeves. What my parents did exude was strength, determination, and stubbornness." These were the qualities, Sharon went on to say, "they were famous for . . . their stubbornness set them apart, often far apart."[2] Sharon would also say that his father "was by nature unable to compromise. . . . If he thought something was wrong, he came out and said it. And, if he was convinced of his position, he would not give in, not if a majority was against him and not if everyone was against him."[3] As for his mother, she "would do what had to be done without asking too many questions about it."[4]

These qualities of his parents—thinking they knew best, being prepared to go against everyone else's views, doing whatever it took without asking too many questions—would come to characterize Sharon over the years. He was very much their son, and being isolated from the community in which he was growing up only deepened these traits. One of his neighbors at the time, Yossef Margalit, later observed how the family's alienation in Kfar Mala affected Sharon: "There's no doubt that his parents' rift with the rest of the moshav—and there really was an all-out battle—played a big role in shaping Arik's personality. The house felt like it was under siege . . . and a sense that they were surrounded by enemies. . . . Arik took the struggle to heart."[5]

There was, to be sure, another struggle that he took to heart: the struggle for security against threats from the neighboring Arabs. Sharon was socialized to think of terror and security from a very young age. In his autobiography, he would write, "As a child of five, I travelled with my mother on a bus from Tel Aviv to Jerusalem for treatment of a chronic eye problem. The entire trip I spent hunched down, peering out the window and scanning the Judean Hills for signs of Abu Jilda, a famous terrorist of those days whose specialty was ambushing Jerusalem-bound traffic."[6] Security was a preoccupation, and guard duty for protection from Arab thieves or attackers was a shared responsibility on the moshav.

Samuil would make it a duty for his young son to guard the family plot. Later, by the time he was thirteen, Sharon would guard the fields. In his words, he would be "sitting in the dark armed with a club and wearing the engraved Caucasian dagger my father had given me for my Bar Mitzvah."[7] His former neighbor Margalit would say that "Arik wasn't afraid of doing guard duty, even though it meant staying quiet, in the dark, all alone."[8] He was fearless.

His preoccupation with security and what it took to produce it was further developed when he joined Gadna, a youth paramilitary organization, as a teenager. Margalit would say it transformed Sharon physically and mentally, leading him to test himself and "to know what he wanted of himself."[9] He would become a trainer and then an instructor in Gadna; it put him in a position of authority for the first time, where he was able to direct others—as opposed to being shunned by them—gain approval from those older and more senior, and strengthen this "young commander's firm belief in the might of the fist."[10]

His parents imparted three other beliefs that he would carry with him throughout his life. First was a profound commitment to hard work. "I listened," he would later write, "to my parents talk about the nobility of physical labor. By the time I was old enough to have any thoughts of my own on the subject, the work itself was in my bones."[11] Sharon could never be idle; he could never satisfy himself with talk. He was a doer; he got things done. This was all part of an ethic of work that had been imparted by his parents. When his mother died at the age of eighty-eight, he said, "I remember her: a woman of labor. Up until a year ago, she worked 18 hours a day. She planned orchards, grew tobacco, milked cows and goats, plowed, guarded. She never rested a minute."[12] And neither could he.

One of his friends described him, saying, "He is not a regular politician, who lives off of politics. Arik's a warrior and a rancher and wants to work. It kills him not to have a real task. He's not built to wake up in the morning and attend meetings where people just talk and talk and nothing ever gets done."[13] When he became the minister of agriculture in the first Begin government and he laid out his plan for building the settlements, he said, "I am the only Mapainik here," meaning he was the only Labor Zionist among those in the cabinet, and they should know if they approved what he was proposing, he would do it and not simply talk about it. Work clearly fed his sense of purpose and sustained him through what would be devastating personal losses: the loss of his first wife to an automobile accident and the death of his firstborn son, Gur, when he was ten years old to an accidental gunshot. Years later, when he was prime minister, Sharon was asked in an interview about the accidental death of his son and whether he felt guilt. "No, not guilt," he responded. "You know you debate yourself. Afterwards, it continues to strike at you all of the time. If you ask me there isn't one day that I don't remember it. But when you are busy doing things—and I don't know what it is like for those who aren't busy and wallow in their bereavement— but when you are busy creating things, it helps you overcome."[14] He would always be busy doing things, working like his parents.

Second, his father in particular emphasized the need for unity among Jews. His father would pick out articles for him to read about internal Jewish strife and warring factions and explain the consequences for the Yishuv. Given his father's isolation within the moshav, this may seem strange. But it was his constant theme, especially after the assassination of Chaim Arlosoroff, a Labor Zionist and head of the political department in the Jewish Agency in Palestine. While Sharon would certainly create his own divisiveness in later years, he consistently favored governments of national unity; when he became prime minister, he formed one with the Labor Party.

Third was a deep distrust of the Arabs. His mother, Vera, slept with a rifle under her bed her entire life. She was shaped by the reality in which they lived, and no doubt by the experience during the Arab riots of 1929, when word came that thousands of Arabs were massing in nearby Qalkilya to come and overrun Kfar Malal. She took her two toddlers (Ariel and his older sister, Yehudit) and hid in a cowshed that night as the men of the moshav prepared to defend the village at all costs. Fortunately, the attack never came, but it was a night of terror nonetheless. Later, when Sharon was in Egypt after the peace deal and phoned his mother from Cairo, she exclaimed, "Do not trust them! Do not trust them!"[15] In truth, he never fully did; as Oren Magnezy, one of Sharon's former aides, confirmed, "He did not trust the Arabs; it was embedded in him. But he also said we must respect as well as suspect them."[16]

At the Wye River negotiations between the Benjamin Netanyahu–led government and the Yasser Arafat–led Palestinian Authority in 1998, there was one memorable outburst by Sharon, who had recently become Israel's foreign minister. When the two sides were close to agreeing on the terms of the security package of obligations for the Palestinians and Israel's responsibility to transfer more territory to the Palestinian Authority in the West Bank, Sharon asserted that there could be no transfers until the Palestinians had fulfilled all their security obligations. US secretary of state Madeleine Albright said the whole point was to create simultaneous or parallel moves so that both sides could see the other was living up to its obligations. In response, Sharon blurted out that the Palestinians were all "thieves and liars." Israel, he said, could not depend on their word, but must first see Palestinian performance.

Sharon's Tumultuous Military Career

By all accounts, Sharon was an extraordinary soldier. From the War of Independence in 1948 until after 1973, he would play a prominent military role in every conflict: the counterterror operations in the early 1950s, the Suez campaign (1956), the Six-Day War (1967), the War of Attrition (1968–1970), and the Yom Kippur War (1973). He nearly died in the battle for Latrun in 1948, and he drew basic lessons from the failure of that operation. At the time, Sharon was twenty and a platoon commander of the Alexandroni Brigade. As he waited to launch the attack, he wrote a letter to his parents describing how a convoy of trucks had "stopped next to us and unloaded new, foreign-looking recruits. They looked slightly pale. . . . They'd come to us through blocked borders, from Europe's death camps. . . . Not one of them cried out: Let us breathe the free air after the years of terrible suffering. It is as if they have come to the conclusion that this is one final battle for the future of the Jewish people."[17]

For Sharon, the stakes were clear and the image of untrained recruits from the death camps served as a reminder of not only what he was fighting for but also how unprepared many of those thrust into the battle were. Sharon's platoon would be isolated in the assault, not knowing they were alone—or that forces they thought were on their flank had been withdrawn and reinforcements were not coming. He would describe the battle as being against regulars from the Arab Legion and irregular Arab forces who had the high ground and came in waves against his men, who were exposed to the elements: "Each time we drove them back, choking on the stench of cordite mixed with the smoke billowing over us from the fires in the wheatfield. . . . Between the fighting, the sun, and the hot wind coming across the plain, we were dying of thirst. . . . Our people there were gone—dead or withdrawn . . . the Arabs stooping over them were looting and mutilating the bodies. Then I understood the silence. We were alone in the field. The other units had been ordered back."[18]

During the fighting, Sharon was badly wounded in the stomach and somehow Ya'akov Bugin struggled over a considerable distance to get him to safety. With the legionaries and irregular Arab forces all around them, Sharon told Bugin to leave and save himself, but Bugin said later that "in my heart, I'd reached the conclusion I would not let this man die."[19] For Sharon, it was as if he had been saved for a reason, for a higher purpose. He would tell the journalist Uri Dan—a lifelong friend of Sharon's—that the battle "marked" him.[20]

As he spent weeks in the hospital afterward, he drew lessons that would guide him in the years ahead. First, "I thought about how we had been left out there alone. Why hadn't one of the commanders been there to see what had happened and get us off the field? As badly as we had been hurt, we had driven off one Arab attack after another. The more I thought about it, the more I was convinced we could have kept going until nightfall. If only we had not been abandoned. If only someone had been there to make the decision."[21] Nothing would be more basic to Sharon from this time onward than the necessity of having senior officers at the front. In his words, "The need for a commanding officer in the theater of operations who is capable of making decisions according to the real evolution of the situation rather than relying on occasional radio-transmitted messages."[22]

Second, given that Sharon had seen wounded Israelis "massacred" and others mutilated—"many with their ears missing, some with their genitals cut off and stuffed in their mouths"—he resolved to never leave a soldier in the field of battle. As he said, "It became an unbreakable rule for me: the wounded are not to be abandoned in the field."[23]

No doubt these experiences added to his distrust of the Arabs while also influencing his attitudes toward what might be done in battle against them. As a commander, Sharon displayed little concern about the casualties his soldiers would inflict. While other battalion commanders would ask their superiors, "Where do we train?" Sharon's question was "Where can we fight Arabs, where can we kill Arabs around here?"[24] At a time when there were near-daily fedayeen terror attacks in Israel—notwithstanding the armistice agreements that had ended the formal war—such an attitude did not disqualify Sharon for command. Quite the opposite: David Ben-Gurion believed that ongoing Arab infiltration and terror attacks would not stop unless Arab leaders came to believe they would pay a high price. It was this belief that led to the creation of Unit 101, a commando force that would operate behind enemy lines and largely outside of any rules.

Sharon was recruited by Mishael Shacham, commander of the Jerusalem Brigade, to create, organize, and build Unit 101. It would be separate from the IDF but had the full blessing of Ben-Gurion and Moshe Dayan, chief of staff of the military. Sharon would bring his attention to detail, to preparation of every aspect of each mission, to rigorous training, and to understanding the terrain of the route to and from the targets. Dayan would say about Sharon that "when [he] studies a map, he studies it like a conductor studies a concert score."[25]

In essence, Unit 101 was about making Arabs understand that they could not infiltrate Israel and kill its citizens with impunity. The missions were dangerous, carried out at night, and always in neighboring Arab states.

It took an unusual leader to command the absolute following of his men—and Sharon did. One of those men, Shimon Kananer, said that Sharon seemingly cast a spell over those in the unit: "When I first came to the unit and met Arik I couldn't sense anything special about him. But after a week in his presence it was clear to me, and to anyone in the 101st, that he would change the course of history."[26] He would often have that effect on those under his command.

While Unit 101 would conduct many raids, it would become notorious because of its attack on Qibya, an Arab village in what was then Jordan. The operation into Qibya in 1953 was designed to retaliate for a terror attack in the Israeli town of Yehud, where a mother and her two infants were murdered. The attackers had come through Qibya, a village that was close to the border and the site of nearly continuous terror incidents. According to Sharon, his mission was "to inflict as many casualties as I could on the Arab home guard and on whatever Jordanian army reinforcements showed up," and then "blow up every major building in the town."[27] There was a firefight with the Arab home guard before getting to the village, but upon entering the village itself, Sharon's forces found it largely deserted—or so they believed. A boy and a girl were discovered and removed and then after briefly going into the homes to yell warnings, the houses were blown up. But the mission went awry, as sixty-nine civilians, mostly women and children, were killed. There was an international outcry in response, and Prime Minister Ben-Gurion denied knowing anything about the raid. Later, Sharon would explain: "For years, Israeli reprisal raids had never succeeded in doing more than blowing up a few outlying buildings, if that. Expecting the same, some Arab families must have stayed in the houses rather than running away. In those big stone houses where three generations of a family might live together, some could easily have hidden in the cellars and back rooms, keeping quiet when the paratroopers went in to check and yell out a warning. The result was the tragedy that had happened."[28]

While Sharon refers to it as a tragedy, there is little sense of remorse. In fact, though he never denied the civilian losses, he would speak about the value of this raid and its consequences: "The Qibya raid was also a turning point: After so many defeats and demoralizing failures it was clear that Israeli forces were again capable of finding and hitting targets far behind enemy lines."[29] Even though Ben-Gurion found it expedient to deny knowing anything about the raid—and would even disband Unit 101 after Qibya—he would tell Sharon, "It doesn't make any real difference about what will be said about Qibya around the world. The important thing is how it will be looked at here in the region. This is going to give us the possibility of living here."[30] Dayan, too, after heeding the instruction to merge the unit with the Paratroopers Brigade, declared that it is "not in our hands to guarantee each water line against sabotage, each tree against uprooting. It is not in our hands to prevent the murders of workers in the field and families in their sleep. But it is in our hands to fix a high price for our blood, so high the Arab community and the Arab military forces will not be willing to pay it."[31]

Sharon would take the Dayan logic one step further. For him, traditional deterrence did not fit Israel's reality with the Arabs. The price had to be prohibitive in terms of how the Arabs measured it. This belief would guide his concept on the use of force against Israel's neighbors: "I came to view the objective not simply as retaliation or even deterrence in the usual sense. It was to create in the Arabs a psychology of defeat, to beat them every time, and to beat them so decisively that they would develop the conviction that they could never win." He felt Israel's small size and population made a balance of power unacceptable; instead, the Arabs needed to see that "aggression would bring them nothing but humiliation and destruction."[32]

The context of daily threats led to Sharon being granted a broad license to conduct the raids as he saw fit. One other factor contributed to his unit's lack of oversight: Unit 101 was outside the formal structure of the IDF, contributing to its anything-goes style. Moreover, Dayan's orders were often vague, which gave Sharon, in his words, the "widest freedom of action." In fact, as Sharon would say, "Dayan's predilection for ambiguous orders combined with my determination to accomplish what I understood was needed, was to make for more than one controversy, and more than one incident with international repercussions too."[33]

Controversy continued even after Unit 101 was merged with the Paratroopers Brigade. Only later would Dayan and Ben-Gurion, Sharon's protectors from the senior officers in the IDF, have problems with some of his actions. In 1956, before the Suez War, Sharon was responsible for an ambush of Egyptian soldiers in which twelve were killed, including a medical team. Dayan was livid, believing that "Sharon was conducting his own independent policy."[34] Similarly, after an October 1956 raid in Qalkilya, Dayan again believed that Sharon had gone too far and even accused him of indifference to Israeli casualties, needlessly risking soldiers' lives in order to kill greater numbers of Arabs and score "fuller" victories.[35]

This charge of needlessly endangering the lives of Israeli soldiers would gain greater weight after the Suez War. Israel would lose thirty-eight soldiers and have 120 wounded in the Mitla Pass. Sharon was blamed for pushing to go into the pass without knowing whether the Egyptians had laid a military trap. Sharon kept pressing to take the Mitla Pass, asking when will the troops "stop guarding and start fighting" and "why are we, the best fighters, not in the fighting."[36] In response to his pushing, he was authorized to send in a small reconnaissance probe.

Instead, under the guise of a patrol, he sent in a battalion led by Motta Gur, with, in the words of journalist David Landau, an "ill-defined force with its ill-defined mission."[37] Twenty percent of all Israel's fatalities in the war were suffered in this battle because the paratroopers were caught by surprise. Gur would later charge that Sharon was nowhere to be found once Gur's forces were basically trapped in a killing zone—one they would fight valiantly to escape and inflict heavy losses on the Egyptians in the process. He charged that Sharon was not functioning for hours on end and that "he was panicked, presumably because he'd acted against orders and because the casualty figures scared him. . . . The brigade commander was totally out of it."[38]

Gur, who would go into the Labor Party and be a long-term opponent of Sharon's, might have had an axe to grind, but what is clearly true is that even though Sharon had pushed to take the pass, he himself had stayed outside of it. Later, in reviewing what had gone wrong, Sharon would claim that his position outside the pass was necessary to manage a number of other pressing needs: organizing the rest of the brigade, preparing a landing strip to medevac the wounded, hunkering down to defend against an anticipated Egyptian armor attack, and feeding in reinforcements as necessary.

The problem with his later explanation is that it seemed to belie one of his basic principles: the need for the commander to be on the scene in order to know the actual situation and be able to make the right decisions. Indeed, Gur explained that because he knew of Sharon's extraordinary ability to read the battlefield, he was especially angry that he was unreachable, saying, "If he'd have been in contact with us, everything would have ended differently."[39]

After the war, the issue for Dayan was not that Sharon had been unavailable for Gur, but that he had defied orders and then lied about it. As Dayan put it, "My complaint against the paratroop command was not so much over the battle itself as over their subterfuge in terming the operation a 'patrol' in order to 'satisfy' the General Staff. This made me sad, and I regretted that I had not succeeded in molding such relations of mutual trust that if they had wished to defy my orders, they would have done so directly and openly."[40]

Sharon playing fast and loose with the rules was one thing; his not being truthful was another. Though it might also reflect his sense that what he was doing was for a higher purpose, and that others found it convenient to create deniability for themselves, the fact remains that Sharon developed a reputation for lying. Ben-Gurion, his ultimate defender, raised this with him, at one point asking, "Have you weaned yourself of your off-putting proclivity not to tell the truth?" When Sharon assured him that he had, the prime minister would record in his diary, "He admitted that he had not told the truth on occasion in the past, but he said he doesn't anymore."[41]

Because of the damage to his standing and reputation after the 1956 war, Sharon had a problem. The head of the Central Command, Zvi Tsur, under whom Sharon would be serving, wanted him out, and Tsur's views were not unique among the senior officer corps. Tsur and others argued that Sharon's lack of discipline and respect for his superiors—as well as what some saw as his "unbridled ambition"—required he be separated from the service. Dayan, despite his problems with Sharon, still looked at him as embodying the daring, skill, creativity, and extraordinary ability to lead men in battle that the IDF needed. So he finessed the issue by working out an arrangement in which Sharon would go abroad and take a yearlong course for mid-level officers at the Royal Military Academy outside of London.

Even more than Dayan, Ben-Gurion revered Sharon's bravery and unconventional mind, and he felt a way must be found to keep Sharon in the military. Later, after Sharon returned from his study abroad in 1958, he sought Ben-Gurion's help in getting a command. The prime minister spoke to Haim Laskov, who had replaced Dayan as the chief of staff of the IDF, and he, too, felt it would be better to end Sharon's military service. Ben-Gurion told him that Sharon had "negative characteristics and blessedly positive ones. I'd like him to be given a chance to right himself because he is an important soldier." Laskov would only agree to give Sharon a staff position.

He would lose it a few months later when he clashed with General Yosef Geva, the head of training. Geva fired him for failing to show up at a meeting and then lying about the reason for missing it. Once again, Ben-Gurion stepped in and protected Sharon, explaining that "he is brave, original, and resourceful." To which Geva said, "Yes, but he's not disciplined, and he doesn't tell the truth."[42] Geva reluctantly agreed to give him another chance as the commander of the army's infantry school. Sharon would describe this position as being in "exile in the wilderness," but he threw himself into it, revamping the training course and introducing the "instructional procedures I had developed with the paratroops."[43] At the same time, he was made a commander of a reserve mechanized brigade and also enrolled in the armor company commanders' course. He learned all about tank warfare, impressing the lead instructor with his innovative ideas.

This would lead to his being given command of a reserve armor brigade in 1962. But Zvi Tsur, who had now replaced Laskov as chief of staff, was not prepared to make him a general and give him an active command. Still, Ben-Gurion was not done being Sharon's advocate, and upon resigning in 1963, he went to Yitzhak Rabin, the soon-to-be head of the IDF, with a request about Sharon. Rabin later recounted that Ben-Gurion "opened his heart to me and said you know I have a special regard for Arik Sharon. I see him as one of our best military men and one of the finest fighters the State of Israel has had. If he would only tell the truth, that would help him get ahead. I'm asking you please don't treat him the way he's been treated until now."[44]

Rabin decided to give him a chance. During his first week as the chief of staff in 1964, Rabin called Sharon in and told him, "Everyone knows you're a superb military man. Your trouble is, though, that people tend to believe you're not a decent human being. I don't know you well enough to say. I want to promote you, but I've got to be sure that your accusers aren't right. I am going to appoint you for one year as deputy commanding officer at the Northern Command. If at the end of the year your direct superior, the CO of Northern Command, says that you behaved like a decent human being, then I will promote you to general."[45]

Sharon got along well with General Avraham Yoffe, the head of the Northern Command, and Rabin would later write that Sharon "passed the test without a shadow of a doubt."[46] Rabin promoted him to major general, appointing him as the director of military training and commander of a reserve division. In his position as director of training, he played a critical role in preparing the IDF for the war it would fight in 1967, and as the commander of a division that was mobilized in the days before the fighting began, he also played a leading role in the military campaign in the Sinai.

But the Sharon style—that is, he knew best and the rules did not apply to him—once again manifested itself in the run-up to the war. As Landau points out, the problem was not just his criticism of his superiors, both military and civilian, to his subordinates, but also his readiness to challenge the civilian government. At the time, Israel's prime minister, Levi Eshkol, and his cabinet appeared hesitant and uncertain in response to a series of highly threatening moves by Gamal Abdel Nasser that put Israel in a perilous position.*

Eshkol's hesitancy to respond to Nasser's aggression was driven by his belief that Israel must avoid a repeat of what had happened in the 1956 war, when the United States opposed Israel's invasion of the Sinai and President Dwight Eisenhower threatened sanctions if Israel did not withdraw. Eshkol

---

* Nasser would demand that the UN Emergency Forces leave the Sinai and its blocking position between Egypt and Israel, move six divisions to Israel's border, mine the Straits of Tiran and blockade Israel's Red Sea port of Eilat, and declare to his parliament that—having reversed the results of the 1956 war—he would now reverse the results of 1948, meaning Israel's existence.

believed he must show America's leadership that Israel had done everything it could to avoid a war. With President Lyndon Johnson repeatedly conveying that "Israel would be alone only if it acted alone," Eshkol argued for letting the United States see if it could defuse the crisis. In truth, the American approach was always too limited, focusing only on getting the Straits of Tiran reopened and not on the presence of six Egyptian divisions on Israel's border—a reality that would have required the continued mobilization of Israel's reserve units and brought the Israeli economy to a standstill. Still, Eshkol felt, if war was required, Israel must have America's backing and could not afford its opposition.

He may well have been right. But because he let the crisis linger for several weeks once Nasser's forces moved into the Sinai on May 15, the Israeli public felt an existential fear. Israel was mobilizing its reserves but holding the military back from striking, even as bloodcurdling threats emanated from the Arab world—with Arab leaders who had been Nasser's rivals now declaring their fealty to him and their readiness to join his forces to avenge Palestine and meet in Tel Aviv. Israelis began to dig trenches around the cities, vast areas were set aside for cemeteries for the expected casualties, and Eshkol compounded matters by giving a radio address in which he stumbled over his words. It was a speech designed to reassure the public; it did the opposite.

In this setting, with his efforts to launch a military strike having been rebuffed by the cabinet, Rabin asked for the ministers to meet the generals. He began by warning of a threat to Israel's very existence, and Sharon then accused the ministers of ensuring that the military would now have to pay a high price in an inevitable war: "Because of [your] hesitation and foot dragging we have lost the key element of surprise."[47] Eshkol angrily rejected his accusation.

Years later, a story would emerge that Sharon suggested a soft coup to Rabin. By one account, Sharon, after the meeting with the ministers, advised Rabin to detain the cabinet and declare war in their stead.[48] Sharon's own version is not too different: "I said [to Rabin] that if we had got up at a certain point and said, 'Listen, you lot, your decisions are endangering the State of Israel. And since the situation is extremely serious, you are hereby requested to go into the adjoining room and stay there while the chief of staff goes to the national radio station and broadcasts an announcement.' In my judgment, if we did that they would have accepted it with a sense of relief and liberation."[49]

In fact, whatever Sharon may have hoped for or been prepared to do, Eshkol would lead an inner group of ministers to authorize the launching of the war three days after this meeting. Sharon's division would have the responsibility of defeating the formidable defenses at Abu Agheila-Umm Katef—defenses that, once overcome, were the springboard to taking the rest of the Sinai. He would devise a complex divisional assault based on simultaneous attacks on multiple axes at night, and would direct it with extraordinary skill and precision. In 1956, it had taken the Israelis three days of difficult fighting to overcome this highly fortified set of positions; Sharon would manage to achieve the same result in one night.[*]

Once again, Sharon had demonstrated his unusual command in war and the devotion of his soldiers to follow his lead. Sharon was a charismatic commander. He exuded the qualities of leadership to all the soldiers who served under him. He emerged from the war with a much higher public profile in Israel thanks to his exploits and the very favorable press coverage of him. To his critics, he loved and craved the limelight. Sharon did value publicity and may often have sought it, but always with an eye to putting himself in the positions where he could make decisions. In the aftermath of the 1967 war, he saw the need for action in the territories that Israel now controlled. Sharon the strategist perceived an opportunity to change Israel's circumstances and overall security position.

Others were thinking about how to use the territories to leverage peace with the Arabs. The cabinet would adopt a secret resolution on June 19 in which Israel would offer to withdraw to the international borders with Egypt and Syria in return for peace.[**]

---

[*] His battle plan and course of action would be studied in military academies around the world.

[**] Dayan—who had become defense minister on June 1, as Eshkol reluctantly saw the need to restore the confidence of the Israeli public before the war—insisted that no decisions be

Sharon had his own ideas. He saw the value of retaining the land for security purposes. Once his reserve division was deactivated and he returned to his job as director of military training, he moved quickly to create footholds in the newly occupied territories. With little oversight and a clear purpose in mind, he began moving the training schools from within Israel to the West Bank. He would later explain that, even while he was still in the Sinai, "as soon as I heard that Samaria and Judea had been liberated, I had cabled instructions to the commander of the infantry school to move from the base in Netanya to a captured Jordanian army camp near Shechem [Nablus]. That was the first one I moved. But within a few months I was able to transfer quite a number of them: the infantry school, the engineering school, the military police school, part of the artillery school, the main basic training school for new recruits, the paratrooper recruit school, and others."[50]

Because of the cost involved, he faced some opposition from Chaim Bar-Lev, who succeeded Rabin as the chief of staff of the military. But Sharon, believing that these areas were essential for Israel's defense, was relentless. "The basic fact," he argued, "was that these areas were an integral part of the country that had been captured by the invading Arab armies in 1948. Now we had come back to them." There was no interest, he said, in taking Arab agricultural lands—"we did not want or need them"—but "I was just as certain that we did need the important road junctions and the high controlling terrain. The hills of Samaria overlooked Israel's narrow coastal plain. I myself had grown up there in the shadow of Arab towns like Qalkilya, which had served as staging areas for Arab armies and bases for the gangs that for decades had terrorized Jewish farms and villages."[51]

Sharon was staking out what he believed Israel had to retain for security purposes. It would be a guiding principle later for him on where to build settlements. He was not waiting to create an Israeli hold on the territory, given the means he had available as the director of training. Those means turned out to permit him to occupy "almost every single one of the old Jordanian

---

made on the West Bank and Gaza without a thorough review of the options. He also took the lead on the ministerial group formed to consider the future of these territories.

military positions and outposts outside of the cities"—all of which were in strategic locations.[52]

Despite riding high after the war, Sharon's remaining time within the military would be marked by disagreements with two additional chiefs of staff—Chaim Bar-Lev and David Elazar—and by another extraordinary military operation, which changed the course of the 1973 war.[*]

With Bar-Lev, the differences stemmed from how to respond to the War of Attrition that Egypt launched against Israel in 1968. Nasser wanted to raise the costs to the Israelis of occupying the Sinai and, in particular, of maintaining a forward line of defense along the Suez Canal. To that end, his forces began to use artillery and tank fire—as well as daily sniper attacks across the canal—against the Israeli positions. Bar-Lev, after a review of the options, settled on building a series of fixed hardened positions along the canal. He believed this would allow the Israelis to withstand the Egyptian strategy yet preserve their forward position of limited forces. Sharon was vehemently against this, saying Israel should not have a fixed-point defense, especially with small numbers of troops. It would always be vulnerable; it made convenient targets for the Egyptians and would be incapable of defending against a large-scale Egyptian assault across the canal. Instead, Sharon argued for a withdrawal from the forward positions and the employment of a mobile defense against any Egyptian crossing, exploiting the vulnerable points of the attacking forces.

Sharon would later write that their differences became increasingly heated, especially after a surprise Egyptian artillery barrage on the Israeli positions caused severe casualties in September 1968. In Sharon's words, "Our relations, never good, now strained toward the breaking point."[53] By early 1969, after a "particularly acrimonious exchange," Bar-Lev set up a meeting later that day that Sharon thought was supposed to be a discussion of the continued efficacy of the static defensive line. Instead, he discovered

---

[*] Tragedy would strike a few months later, when his son Gur was shot and killed accidentally with his own shotgun in front of Sharon's house while he was inside. Though it was never clear if Gur had accidentally triggered the blast or if a young neighbor had been playing with the gun when it went off, Sharon would never accept that Gur, whom he had taught how to handle the gun, could have been responsible.

that it was a tribunal to throw him out. Dayan, still defense minister, was there and denied this was the purpose of the meeting, arguing that Sharon could affect what would be discussed. Nevertheless, Sharon soon felt he was effectively on trial and walked out of the meeting; shortly thereafter, Bar-Lev moved to force him out of the military.

Sharon sought the intervention of both Dayan and Prime Minister Golda Meir, but neither came to his aid. Ben-Gurion was gone. At this point, he began to think about a political career. A friend of his, Joseph Sapir, was the head of the Liberal Party and had long urged him to consider going into politics after the army. He now called Sapir and told him he was ready to do so. More importantly, he said he was ready to join the opposition—which was made up of Herut, led by Menachem Begin, and the Liberal Party—because their views on holding the land taken in the 1967 war were closer to his than those of the Labor Party. An enthusiastic Sapir suggested a meeting with Begin.[54]

Sharon would agree in the meeting to join the Herut-Liberal alliance but almost immediately had misgivings. He was losing control, he had un-characteristically not thought this through, it was happening too fast, and he did not want to be seen as someone's puppet. The next day, the Israeli press was full of his impending political move, and that only added to his disquiet. As luck would have it, Sharon was not completely out of protec-tors. Pinchas Sapir, no relation to Joseph, was the finance minister and the strongman of the Labor Party apparatus. He called Bar-Lev, whom Sharon described as "the military's most prominent Laborite," and told him to find a place for Sharon and keep him in the military—lest he undermine Labor in the upcoming election of December 1969.[55] Bar-Lev did so. Because there was no place for Sharon in any command positions, Bar-Lev gave him a special duty to go around the world and visit American and allied military bases to discuss Israel, its military situation, and the Middle East more gen-erally. The tour would last nearly two months, and when it was over the Southern Command had opened up and Sharon became its new chief. Now he had one of the major commands in the IDF.

While it would not end his disagreements with Bar-Lev, the position was something Sharon wanted, and he managed his relationship with the chief of staff. He focused on preparing necessary infrastructure, including roads in the Sinai designed to bring in reinforcements and enable Israeli forces to counterattack in the event of an Egyptian crossing of the canal. His preparation also included identifying points where Israel could carry out its own crossing of the canal in the event of war.

This would not be the first time—or the last—that Sharon would be greatly critical of a superior and then accommodate him so that he could operate in a position that he regarded as important. As head of the Southern Command, Sharon had responsibility for dealing with not only Egypt but also Gaza, as well as terrorists infiltrating from Jordan. He would counter terror in both areas aggressively. To deal with infiltration from Jordan, he adopted passive measures (barriers and listening devices) and active ones, including having Israeli patrols lie in ambush in Jordan along the routes the infiltrators typically took. He went back to the tactics he employed first in Unit 101, and infiltrations did in fact drop. He appeared to have similar success in Gaza in 1971, where he would isolate neighborhoods from which those committing acts of terror came, kill those responsible for the terror, and be ready to deport those who supported them. Meir Dagan worked for Sharon in Gaza at that time and said later that they carried out a targeted assassination and deportation policy in Gaza.* Regardless of whether there were other factors at play, terror within and from Gaza declined dramatically in 1971.

Sharon would also weigh in on how to respond to what was an urgent American request to come to the aid of King Hussein of Jordan in September of 1970. This was Black September, when Hussein finally had had enough with the Palestinians building a state within a state in Jordan. Following an assassination attempt against him and the Popular Front for the Liberation of Palestine's hijacking and destruction of three civilian airliners, the king launched a campaign to wipe out the armed Palestinian presence in the country. The Jordanian army killed thousands of Palestinians and began driving the Palestine Liberation Organization (PLO) out of Jordan. Syria intervened with a significant armored thrust into northern Jordan, threatening

---

* Dennis first met Meir Dagan in the 1990s, and in one of the initial meetings Dagan spoke about Gaza. As prime minister, Sharon would appoint him to head Mossad.

the Hashemite monarchy. The Nixon administration asked the Israelis to mobilize forces on the Golan Heights in order to deter or stop the Syrians.*

Sharon was the only member of the IDF General Staff to oppose the US request, because he was against rescuing King Hussein and the Hashemite regime. He argued that if the Palestinians took over Jordan, it would solve Israel's Palestinian problem.

His colleagues challenged his view, saying, "You think a Palestinian government in Amman will just calmly agree to let us stay on the River Jordan?" He answered, "No. But at that point, the discussion will be about where the border should be. We will no longer be dealing with the issue of Palestinian identity and about their right to a political expression of their identity."[56]

Sharon's position is remarkable: he was recognizing a Palestinian national identity. Even though Prime Minister Meir had denied that the Palestinians were a people in 1969, Sharon understood that they were. Much like Rabin at the time, Sharon recognized that the Palestinians had a national identity, that there would be pressure to give it political expression, and, if not addressed, it would be an existential challenge to Israel; it "would weigh heavier and heavier over our heads as the years went by."[57] True, a radical regime in Jordan would add to Israel's security problems, but for Sharon that was essentially a tactical challenge. One could fight over the border, but the only way to avoid competing claims over the land was for the Palestinians to have a state. For Sharon, that state should be Jordan—otherwise, it would probably be in the West Bank and Gaza, and he viewed that as a mortal threat.**

He was also arguing to reject the American request to save Jordan, an American friend led by a moderate leader, from a radical Arab regime armed

---

* When the Israelis mobilized two brigades on the Golan Heights, Hafiz al-Assad, the chief of the Syrian air force, refused to commit his forces to the battle in Jordan. Without air cover, the Jordanians beat back the Syrian armored incursion.

** Sharon would not alter his position on Jordan and Palestine until 1997, when he was asked by then prime minister Netanyahu to go meet with King Hussein and mend the friction in the relationship caused by the Israeli effort to assassinate Hamas leader Khaled Meshaal in Amman. Sharon succeeded in doing so and became committed to the relationship with Jordan as a Hashemite kingdom not as a Palestinian state. It did not hurt that King Hussein gave him the red-carpet treatment and accorded him unmistakable respect.

by the Soviets. At the height of the Cold War, after having lost King Idris and the American air base in Libya the year before to Qaddafi, the Nixon administration felt it was essential to prevent another Soviet win in the region. To turn down the Americans in this context was bound to affect the Nixon administration's view of Israel and US connections to it. By contrast, being responsive was going to not only preserve a less threatening neighbor—and one that tacitly cooperated on security—but also show the strategic value of Israel to the United States in the Middle East. Sharon was not dismissive of the effect on the United States, but in his mind this was a case where Israeli and American interests diverged. For Sharon, Israel's needs had to come first. In fact, for much of Sharon's career prior to becoming prime minister, he did not feel the need to be overly solicitous of America. Only when he became prime minister would that change.

Sharon was, however, far from being Israel's prime minister at this time, and his tenure in the military was destined to end soon too. David Elazar was not a fan of Sharon and, upon becoming the chief of staff in 1972, he informed Sharon that he would be retired upon the completion of his term in July 1973 as the head of the Southern Command. Two months before his scheduled retirement, the Egyptians carried out a large exercise that looked like a prelude to an invasion. Israel mobilized its forces and Sharon prepared the defense against an attack across the canal, which included bringing the entire command to a state of readiness and concentrating water assault equipment for an Israeli crossing. As Sharon put it, "I planned to surprise the Egyptians with a crossing of our own."[58]

During the Israeli response to the Egyptian exercise, Sharon went to Elazar and argued that the forward defense positions in the Bar-Lev line needed to be evacuated immediately in the event of a large-scale Egyptian assault. The small number of troops deployed in those fixed positions could not defend themselves against a large-scale attack, and, as Sharon pointed out, the effort to rescue them, with Egyptian forces likely to be in "firing positions . . . would cover our approaches" and would put the incoming Israeli forces at great risk.[59] Elazar agreed and Sharon thought that meant that the order would be given to withdraw immediately should the Egyptians invade. Five months later, Sharon discovered that Elazar had changed his mind.

In the meantime, Sharon asked—in light of what he perceived to be an increased chance of war with Egypt and his belief that his replacement, Shmuel Gonen, lacked the experience to be the commanding officer—if he could postpone his retirement and extend one more year in his position. Elazar said no. Once again, Sharon asked Dayan and Meir to intervene, and once again they would not do so. However, Dayan, over Elazar's objections, did agree to Sharon's request to be given command of a reserve division. He would retire from the military in mid-July.

Of course, Sharon could not retire the way others had done. He would do it his way. He would not go to the dinner given at the General Staff for every retiring general, nor would he allow the IDF to arrange a farewell press conference held only with the military correspondents. Instead, he would hold a going-away dinner with officers at his home and hire a hall to meet with the press—including all the political correspondents, not just the military ones.

At his dinner, he launched a blistering attack on the chief of staff and the "top echelon of the defense establishment," which, as David Landau wrote, "embarrassed the many serving officers present." As for the press conference, it would be his opening salvo in politics. In 1969, he had not been truly prepared to take a leap into Israeli politics, but now he was ready. Four years had gone by; had he thought he might have been appointed chief of staff of the IDF, he would have deferred such a move. But that was not in the cards. So now, at his press conference, he spoke of going into politics and making a difference. He proclaimed that a "loyal opposition is not good enough." An effective democracy needed an opposition with a "realistic prospect of changing the government. It is totally wrong for one party to rule for decades on end, without facing any serious danger of being replaced." He proposed that the opposition parties unify in a bloc in order to achieve that purpose: "Herut, the Liberals, the Free Center, the State List, and if possible the Independent Liberals too. These are the potential partners in an alignment of centrist parties that will stand against the Labor alignment."[60]

Sharon was as good as his words. On September 13, after nearly two months of wrangling, Sharon, the political neophyte, succeeded in forging the new party of Likud out of all the opposition parties, with an agreed single list of candidates for the upcoming election. He was now an opposition politician, and he commenced campaigning immediately.

Over the next few weeks, he was busy running the Likud campaign. On Friday, October 5, he was called to the Southern Command to look at the intelligence, and he knew that "this time it is war." The massing of crossing equipment and the huge deployment by the Egyptians was, in his words, "quantitatively different from the exercises we had gotten used to watching." The next morning, only a few hours before the Egyptians and Syrians launched their coordinated attack, he was mobilized and headed to his reserve division's base camp.

Sharon's arguments against the strongpoints of the Bar-Lev line proved to be correct, but Elazar and Gonen still believed that it was possible these positions could hold until Israeli forces arrived and pushed the Egyptians off the east bank of the canal. As Dayan would later write, "The strongpoints were strongpoints as long as the east bank of the canal was in our hands. Now they became traps for the units caught inside them and surrounded by Egyptian forces."[61]

THE YOM KIPPUR WAR AND ITS AFTERMATH

After being mobilized, Sharon arrived at his base camp to discover a chaotic situation. He organized what he could but did not wait to get to the front in the central Sinai. Israel's losses were staggering: two hundred of its three hundred first-line tanks disabled in the first twenty-four hours, and eight hundred in all knocked out of commission in the first week of the war. Colonel Amnon Reshef's armored brigade had to deal with the massive Egyptian onslaught in support of the fixed hardened points of the Bar-Lev line. When Reshef reported to Sharon the next day, he "explained that opposite each company of mine an entire Egyptian division had crossed. By the time my tanks reached their firing positions, Egyptian commandos were waiting for them with anti-tank weapons. Arik didn't cast blame, and he didn't complain. There wasn't time for that. The situation was catastrophic. He was focused, businesslike and constructive."[62]

Sharon's initial focus was to get the strongpoints evacuated—he pressed Gonen and Elazar but to no avail. Failing that, he then pressed to organize a concentrated counterattack consisting of two divisions to defeat the Egyptian Second Army—only two divisions, Sharon argued, would be sufficient to break it. Elazar was against concentrating forces, believing that they had to be held in reserve to protect against an attack across the Sinai into Israel. Sharon correctly understood that the Egyptians would consolidate their hold across the canal and not stretch their forces or get out from under their air cover by moving toward Israel, but Elazar's mind was made up. To make matters worse, the next day Gonen ordered Sharon's division to pull back eastward and then move fifty miles south in a move that Sharon argued against, given the current battlefield realities. Gonen insisted, telling Sharon if he did not follow the order immediately, he would be dismissed. Sharon pleaded with him "to come down and look for yourself." Gonen rejected this as well. Feeling he had no choice, Sharon took his forces south away from the fighting, only to be ordered to return three-and-a-half hours later to where they had been.[63]

With the initial efforts at counterattacks failing at a high cost, former chief of staff Bar-Lev was now brought in to run the Southern Command, with Gonen serving under him. But Sharon was not standing pat. Instead, always looking for the weak points to exploit, he pressed hard to take advantage of what Reshef's forces had discovered: there was an opening between the Second and Third Egyptian Armies that would permit the Israelis to get to the canal, cross it, and exploit the rear areas of the enemy forces on the Egyptian side of the canal.

Sharon pressed Gonen to seize the initiative and to prepare for the crossing by "bringing assault rafts down . . . and preparing the bridging equipment. In parallel with Adan's division, we could [then] grab the whole area and push across. Why just sit back and wait for the Egyptians to discover the seam and close it up? In the northern sector we would have to fight our way to the canal. But here the whole thing was already in the palms of hands."[64] Gonen not only rejected any attack at this point but also ordered that Sharon's forces pull back from the canal and assume a purely defensive posture.

Landau writes that this order convinced Sharon that Elazar, Bar-Lev, and Gonen simply did not want him to cross the canal. They wanted Avraham Adan or another general to get that credit.[65] Sharon could not otherwise explain not seizing the opening Reshef had created. For their part, Elazar and the others felt that, with Egypt's two armored divisions having not yet crossed the canal, it was best to wait for them to do so and allow for more time to prepare for the crossing. They were as suspicious of Sharon as he was of them. They felt he simply wanted the glory and was pressing before the forces were ready to make the crossing.

What would later be called the "war of the generals" revolved very much around the issue of when to do the crossing and who should get credit for the move that would change the course of the war with Egypt. Sharon kept pushing to exploit the opening and be allowed to cross. He was given orders principally to shore up Israeli defensive positions and then to widen and protect the bridgehead on the eastern side of the canal while General Adan's forces crossed. Bar-Lev's frustration with Sharon's readiness to ignore some of these orders led him to press Elazar to fire him, but the minister of defense, Moshe Dayan, would not permit it.

Through it all, Sharon's actions paved the way for the crossing and moved some of his forces across even before the full bridging equipment was in place. The scope of what he could do was, however, limited by Elazar and Bar-Lev. Abrasha Tamir, one of Sharon's military aides at the time, described how "the Southern Command forbade us to transfer more of our forces across the canal" after the initial crossings. According to Tamir, the Southern Command "wanted the only attack to be accomplished by Bren [Adan] and Kalman, while we stayed with the bridgehead. . . . All in order that Arik shouldn't strut around as though he were the victor."[66]

Tamir would not defend all Sharon's actions during the war—his tantrums, his blatant disregard of certain orders, his not answering the radio when Gonen and others would call—but his key point was that many orders given to Sharon were politically motivated. Dayan lent credence to this charge when he responded to Gonen's accusation that Sharon was fighting his own private war, saying, "There are those who say it is this war room that has been infiltrated by political considerations."[67]

Asher Levy, who was a brigadier general during the war and served in the Southern Command, was not a fan of Sharon's. He was critical of some of Sharon's decision-making, believing he produced needless casualties late in the war by attacking Ismailia, and also accused him of chafing early after the crossing because "all the glory was over there and Arik was sitting over here [on the eastern bank]." That said, he also believed that there would have been no crossing without him. According to Levy, "Arik Sharon with his tenacity and perseverance determined that Israel crossed the canal. No one can take that away from him, ever. Whoever denies it is simply not telling the truth."[68]

In a terrible war in which Israel was taken by surprise and forced to pay a very high price, Sharon understood early on what was necessary and was responsible, ultimately, for the actions that provided the turning point in the conflict with Egypt. It further cemented his belief in his own judgment; he again saw that his superiors simply did not get it. Worse, they tried to prevent him from doing what was necessary, while also denying him the credit he rightfully deserved.

Even Moshe Dayan, whose relations with Sharon might best be described as ambivalent, suspected political considerations affected at least some of the orders given to him. Sharon, having just gone into politics, was perceived as a "Likud general." Bar-Lev was a Laborite. Perhaps, that played a part in the so-called war of the generals and the controversies that wafted around Sharon at the time. But the reality is that controversy always seemed to follow him. Challenging authority was not new for him. Believing he knew best was part of his DNA. Playing by his own rules had gotten him in trouble before, but his protectors had helped him survive because they, too, understood what he offered as a military commander. An outsize personality made him a general who necessarily had a following. Soldiers who saw him or heard his voice on the military radio transmitting orders in the difficult first days of the war spoke of how reassuring his presence was. A soldier who had been trapped in one of the strongpoints opposite Ismailia said there was "a moment of exultation when we heard Sharon had arrived. If we'd had champagne, we'd have opened it. Just his voice on the radio was like salvation."[69]

Sharon's desire for glory may well have grown out of his ambition—an ambition that reflected his desire for leadership and his own deeper sense that he had been saved at Latrun for a reason. Whenever he faced a crisis, he would often recall that he had "risen from the dead" in Latrun. It is almost as if he believed he was destined for greatness and had a responsibility to fulfill that destiny.[70]

Taken together, all these factors tended to create in Sharon a belief that the ends justified the means. That belief did not come out of a vacuum. Israel needed to create its own security because of the rejection and enmity of its neighbors. Nothing would be given to it. Israel's early leaders needed those who understood this. In the mid-1950s, Dayan said to Sharon, "Do you know why you're the one who does all the operations? Because you never ask for written orders. Everyone else wants explicit clarifications. . . . You just do it."[71] Just do it. Just get it done. For Sharon, this became a credo.

As long as he succeeded in the military, his controversies could be managed. As long as he could point to the results, Israelis would turn a blind eye to how he produced them. In his political career, Sharon's belief in creating results continued to mean that the rules should not necessarily apply to him. Those above him could not count on his loyalty any more than his superiors in the military could count on him following their orders. He would forge different political alliances and create partnerships that served his immediate needs, all in the service of what he was trying to achieve or to help carve out a political niche for himself. While he was rarely loyal to those above him, he was different with those who worked for him. This, too, seemed to flow from his military experience, in which having troops commit themselves completely to him required a sense of his commitment to them. Dov "Dubi" Weisglass, Sharon's lawyer long before he became his chief of staff in the prime minister's office, explained that he always assumed responsibility for any decision he made, even if it came on the advice of a subordinate. And he would never blame a subordinate* if it turned out to be a mistake.[72]

---

* Weisglass cited a personal example, telling Dennis that once when Sharon's friend Uri Dan was criticizing him in front of Sharon for making a proposal that failed during the Kahan Commission hearings in 1982, Sharon responded by chastising Dan, saying, "Why are you criticizing him. I accepted it, I am responsible, criticize me."

SHARON BECOMES A POLITICIAN

Ariel Sharon's entrée into politics was postponed because of the 1973 war. Immediately after the war, he was forward deployed on the western side of the Suez Canal. Until an initial disengagement agreement, Israel's forces remained on the other side of the canal and there was only a limited demobilization. Sharon remained at the front for a while, and he used his presence there to tell his story of the war to the American and Israeli press, attacking the malfeasance and grievous mistakes of Elazar, Bar-Lev, Gonen, and the government. Although he had legitimate complaints, this, too, was Sharon using his position still in uniform to challenge those above him while also engaging in self-promotion. (True, Bar-Lev and others would answer him in the Israeli press, but the obvious failures—intelligence and military—in a war with a terrible toll lent credence to Sharon's charges. Moreover, he was the one seen as a hero and they were not.)

Once out of uniform, he went back to campaigning for Likud. He was on the Likud party list. While Likud did not win the elections in December 1973, it gained a significant number of seats, and Sharon became a member of the Knesset in the opposition. But being a member of the opposition— and a backbencher at that—meant Sharon could do little. He was not cut out simply to take part in endless meetings and discussions.

Labor continued to dominate the Knesset. In April 1974, the Agranat Commission, the body established to examine the failings in the war, published its findings. When those findings called for the removal of the top military and intelligence officers but not the prime minister or defense minister, reservists led mass demonstrations, and both Golda Meir and Moshe Dayan stepped down. Labor's numerical hold on the Knesset permitted it to select a new party leader who would also become the new prime minister. Yitzhak Rabin became the prime minister, and his Labor Party rival, Shimon Peres, became the defense minister. In 1975, Rabin would ask Sharon to leave the Knesset and become defense advisor to him. For Sharon, the offer rescued him from what he felt was irrelevance.*

---

* His title was shortened to advisor to the prime minister when Shimon Peres objected to his having defense as part of his responsibility.

Sharon's relationship with Rabin had been a good one from the time that Rabin had given him the chance to stay in the military and become a general. At a time when Rabin felt that Peres was constantly trying to undermine him, especially on settlements, he believed that Sharon served him loyally. It was Sharon who helped to produce a compromise with the Gush Emunim on a settlement they tried to establish at Sebastia, near what had been the biblical town of Shomron. This was the eighth settlement that the Gush had tried to establish by occupying an area. Each time, facing ugly resistance, the IDF had dispersed the prospective settlers. Sharon defused the tension and negotiated an outcome in which the Gush agreed that thirty settler families would move to an army site called Camp Kadum. This, of course, was in keeping with Sharon's idea after the 1967 war of moving the training bases to the West Bank and then building accommodations for the families of the officers.* For Sharon, getting a firm hold on the land was the key to being able to keep it—and that was why settlement was crucial.

But settlement required motivation. Security might galvanize Sharon, but that was not an emotional driver for many Israelis to settle in the West Bank or Gaza. With the Gush Emunim, however, there was a religious zeal to restore the Jewish presence in the land of God's patrimony. Sharon understood their motivation and was prepared to champion what they were doing. Prior to becoming Rabin's advisor, Sharon not only supported Gush efforts to settle sites, he actually joined them in one instance and physically protected Rabbi Zvi Yehuda Kook—the spiritual leader of the movement—from Israeli soldiers forcibly removing the settlers.[73]

Sharon continued to stake out a hard-line position on the territories while he worked for Rabin. He advised the prime minister strongly against the territorial withdrawal in the Sinai II agreement. Rabin would not heed this advice, but he still valued Sharon's insights on security.[74] Years later, when Sharon was one of the strongest critics of the Oslo process, Rabin would have him come and talk to him about security issues.

In this sense, both Rabin and Sharon took his position as an advisor very seriously. Sharon did not pull his punches but also did not take his

---

* As described in the Rabin chapter, Rabin thought the controversy over Sebastia/Kadum was crazy and diverted Israel from what was important about its future.

criticisms or policies public so long as he was in the prime minister's office. Three months after Rabin had agreed to the Sinai II accord and gained considerable political, economic, and security commitments from the United States, Sharon proposed a five-point plan for what was needed in Israel. Despite the Sinai II accord—or because of it—Sharon's five points reflected his judgment that Israel was in a precarious state. Sharon proposed that the government announce a national emergency, form a national unity government (NUG) of ten ministers, freeze all talks with Henry Kissinger and further negotiations with the Arabs, prepare the public for war, and carry out massive settlement construction in Judea, Samaria, and Gaza.[75]

Rabin rejected Sharon's plan, setting the stage for Sharon to leave his post. But before departing as Rabin's advisor, he also developed a more specific plan on how and where to build the settlements in the West Bank. In later writing about his tenure with Rabin, he said, "I spent a great deal of time in Samaria and Judea. And being there, I worked out in outline the kind of settlement plan for these areas that I believed was necessary. I knew it was not something which Rabin could ever implement. But who could tell about the future?"[76]

Sharon left as Rabin's advisor in February 1976. He returned to politics but was not inclined to become a backbencher for Likud again. He saw weakness in Labor but also doubted that Begin could ever lead Likud to a victory. He even explored the idea of having a primary in Likud to challenge Begin, but dropped the idea.

Instead, he negotiated over his role in Likud. Eventually he hit a wall in his discussions with Simcha Erlich, who was effectively number two in the party. Erlich saw Sharon as a man without principle, willing to do anything for power—and perhaps anything with power. In fact, his dealings with Sharon convinced him not only that Sharon could not be relied upon but that he would not respect any limits.

Sharon came to believe that if he created his own party, he could become a power broker and emerge in a central position. He created Shlomzion (Peace for Zion), which as he would later recall started fast but soon lost appeal as another new party, DASH (the Democratic Movement for Change), led by Yigael Yadin—an iconic figure in Israel as a world-renowned archaeologist and first head of the IDF—took center stage as an alternative to Labor and Likud. The only noteworthy thing about Shlomzion is that Sharon for a time sought to draw in supporters on the left side of the political spectrum. Sharon pursued what he thought might work politically, not what was ideologically correct.

As Shlomzion sank in the polls, Sharon tried to merge his party with Likud, but that happened only after Begin won the election, when he also offered Sharon a position as minister of agriculture and the head of the cabinet committee on settlements. Ariel Sharon now became the architect of Israeli settlements in the West Bank and Gaza.

MASTER BUILDER

Labor had built settlements from 1967 until 1977. However, they were small, limited in size and population, and largely outgrowths of what had begun as military outposts. The total settler population by the time of Camp David in September 1978 was five thousand. This would be dwarfed by what Sharon had in mind. His plan, of course, was in keeping with Begin and Likud's ideology. Begin's ideology drove his commitment to settling the territories; Sharon's view of Israel's security needs drove his.

He foreshadowed this when he moved the training schools to the West Bank and when he supported the Gush Emunim. The Gush would settle the territories and he would build so that they could.

His plan was guided not by God's patrimony but by his definition of Israel's basic security needs. In explaining his plan to the Begin cabinet in 1977, he presented a large map and laid out the security logic. "I explained that whatever political solution we eventually agreed upon for these territories, we would in any case be facing three major problems: The first was security for the coastal plain with its population centers, its industrial infrastructure, its power stations and airport. Defined by the pre-1967 border, this plain was so narrow as to be essentially indefensible." They needed "to give the coast plain at least minimal depth and strengthen the corridor." That would require settlements on the high controlling terrain. "The second problem was the eastern border itself." What Sharon referred to as the eastern front, involving all of Israel's eastern neighbors (Jordan, Syria, Iraq, and Saudi Arabia), was the most severe military threat Israel faced. Given Israel's small standing forces in the Jordan Valley and along the Jordan River, "a line of settlements along the Jordanian plain from the Beit Shean Valley to the Dead Sea" would be needed. And, the third problem was to be able "to secure Jerusalem as the permanent capital of the Jewish people."[77] He would do that by ringing Jerusalem with a "horseshoe of settlements that would run 10–15 kilometers outside the center." The plan he presented that day would be geared toward building settlements that would keep a hold on these areas and secure them for the future.

Why was civilian settlement in these areas and in large numbers necessary? For Sharon, if there was only a military presence, Israel could be pressured from the outside to retreat from these areas. He would say that the "only way to permanently secure the most strategic terrain in our hands was to live on it." Only that would ensure that "when we found ourselves under pressure . . . we would not be tempted to just give up."[78]

In other words, Sharon anticipated there would be pressure on Israel for withdrawal—no doubt recalling the American pressure that led Israel to withdraw from the Sinai after the Suez War—and he was going to make it difficult to do so. He would build settlements: sixty-four in the West Bank in Begin's first term. Zvi Slonim was a prominent leader of the settlement movement, and the morning after Begin's election in 1977 Sharon showed Slonim his map of settlements for the West Bank. In 2003, Slonim would say, "It is incredible how identical that map was to the map of Israel today."[79]

Like always, Sharon acted on his vision. Interestingly, he also built settlements in the Sinai and Gaza—in both places, security considerations guided him. Both were designed to create barriers to movement by the Egyptians in the event of war. And both he would in time raze.

In the Sinai, of course, it was the peace treaty with Egypt that led to his bulldozing the settlements.* Sharon was trading the settlements for peace. While he would later lament his decision when he was criticizing the Oslo process, Sharon was not only persuasive with Begin, he was the one Begin would call on to evacuate the settlements. In fact, the fierce opposition of the settlers to evacuation is what led Begin to appoint Sharon defense

---

* As described in the chapter on Begin, it was Sharon, the champion of the settlements, who persuaded Begin that he could give up these settlements.

minister. Arye Naor, who was Begin's cabinet secretary and at the time one of his closest aides, said that Begin "feared that settler resistance could lead to bloodshed" and only Sharon "could, perhaps, carry out the evacuation without triggering a violent confrontation."[80]

Begin was right. Sharon would deploy thousands of police and military to prevent settlers who wanted to turn the evacuation into a national trauma from ever getting close to Yamit, the township and focal point of the Sinai settlements. Begin had misgivings about making Sharon defense minister, deciding not to appoint him in 1980 when Ezer Weizman quit the government and Sharon openly campaigned for the job. At one point, Begin was even overheard telling Simcha Erlich that if Sharon were defense minister, he might well send the tanks to surround the prime minister's office—something for which he apologized, explaining he was just joking.

Even if it was just a joke, Begin clearly was hesitant to put Sharon in that position. Many, including Moshe Dayan, warned him about Sharon: "I hear Arik's going to be minister of defense in the new government. I am seriously worried that if he gets the job, he will embroil us in a war in Lebanon. I know him."[81] But Begin's worries about the evacuation trumped his concerns about what Sharon would do as defense minister. And, Dayan's warnings notwithstanding, Begin's views on Lebanon seemed to mirror Sharon's. He, too, was very weary of the terror acts and mortar and rocket fire from the PLO in southern Lebanon. Having been expelled from Jordan in 1970, the PLO had created another state within a state in Lebanon. After a PLO team carried out the Coastal Road massacre, in which thirty-eight Israelis were killed and two hundred wounded, Israel, in March 1978, launched an attack into southern Lebanon and held the territory up to the Litani River. Under great pressure from President Carter, Begin withdrew and the United Nations Interim Force (UNIFIL) was inserted into this area. Not only would UNIFIL prove to be ineffectual, but the PLO would actually operate from its areas, raising the cost to the Israelis of retaliating.

During this period, the Lebanese Civil War was raging and Israel was covertly providing military support to the Phalange/Christian forces in their fight with the largely Muslim opposition. In April 1981, with the Syrians using increasing firepower directly against Christian forces in the Bekaa

Valley, Israel shot down two Syrian helicopters. In response, the Syrians moved surface-to-air missiles (SAMs) into Lebanon, and Begin made clear that Israel would bomb the Syrian SAMs. To avoid a war, the Reagan administration sent Philip Habib as a presidential envoy to the region, with the mission of not just getting the Syrian missiles removed but also producing a cease-fire with the PLO. Israel interpreted the cease-fire to mean no more PLO attacks anywhere, not just from southern Lebanon into Israel. Habib's ongoing shuttles* would succeed neither in getting the Syrian missiles out nor in stopping all PLO terror attacks.[82] Moreover, the PLO used the cease-fire to significantly build up its conventional military presence in southern Lebanon, especially with artillery and Katyusha rockets. For Begin and Sharon, the Habib shuttles and cease-fire were seen as actually protecting the PLO, and thus helped to set the stage for what would be a misguided strategic misadventure in Lebanon for Begin, Sharon, and Israel.

LEBANON AND SHARON'S FALL

This was not an easy time in the US-Israel relationship, and the reason was, at least in part, Sharon.[83] The administration's readiness to treat Israel as a strategic partner was new, but not nearly what Sharon had in mind. He felt Israel was the only country with the military capability to counter the Soviets and their clients in the region, and he offered grandiose plans for Israel becoming a proxy for US force in the wider Middle East, including intervention in Arab states. In return for this, he wanted Israeli "freedom of action and independence from the constraints of subordinating Israeli interests to those of the United States."[84]

Even Alexander Haig—who was the most sympathetic figure toward Israel at the outset of the Reagan administration—was not buying it, and other senior officials viewed Sharon's plans as crazy. Worse, Israeli actions in the region were seen as affecting US relations with the Arab states that the Reagan administration wanted to bring together against the Soviets. As

---

*   While artillery, mortar, and Katyusha fire would stop, terror would not, with attacks in Israel and Europe producing fifteen dead and 250 wounded during the one year that Habib's cease-fire held.

a result, Israel's bombing of the Osirak reactor in Iraq, the air attack against the PLO offices in downtown Beirut during the G7 summit meeting, and Begin's decision to "annex" the Golan Heights all produced American condemnation. In two cases, Osirak and the Golan Heights annexation, the Reagan administration imposed actual penalties: it suspended F-16 deliveries in response to Osirak in June, renewed them in the fall, and then, after the Golan decision in December 1981, suspended not only the F-16 deliveries but also the recently concluded memorandum of understanding on strategic cooperation.

Begin was furious about the suspensions, summoning Samuel Lewis to say that Israel could not be treated as if it was a "banana republic." Begin's anger even led him to think that this was the moment to authorize a far-reaching military plan to resolve the threats from Lebanon. To that end, Begin asked Sharon to brief the cabinet on his military plan for Lebanon— one that involved going to the outskirts of Beirut and removing the PLO once and for all. Sharon said there was no desire to fight the Syrians, but Israel would have to be prepared for Syrian intervention as well. For all the claims later that Begin knew nothing about Sharon's war plans and was misled about how far he intended to go once Israel launched what became Operation Peace for Galilee in June 1982, this meeting lends credence to Sharon's claims that Begin knew everything.

In this meeting, many ministers objected, and Begin dropped the plan for the time being. But the planning and preparation continued, with Sharon visiting Bashir Gemayel, the leader of the Christian Lebanese Forces, in Lebanon three weeks later. He would also meet Habib and Lewis in the coming months, continually telling them that Israel had little choice but to act and making the case for a free and democratic Lebanon—the result, he would argue, would be Gemayel coming to power. Things began to heat up when an Israeli diplomat was killed in Paris by the PLO in April, and Sharon came to see Secretary Haig in May. Sharon would later write that he "had not come to Washington to get American approval for whatever we decided to do but to let them know as friends and allies exactly where we stood."[85] In response, Haig told him that there needed to be an "internationally recognized provocation" to justify any Israeli military action, and that action should not involve the "disproportionate" use of force.[86]

For months, there was chatter in US policy and intelligence circles about Israeli meetings with Gemayel, especially Sharon's. Everything was pointing to a much broader Israeli operation, not just to remove the PLO but to counter the Syrians and remake Lebanon. When Secretary Haig briefed his aides on his meeting with Sharon, he said he sought to douse Sharon's enthusiasm for a wider conflict with broad aims. When the Israeli ambassador to the United Kingdom was shot by Palestinian gunmen on June 3, 1982, Sharon was provided with his trigger for action.

Sharon did not think small. Just like with the settlements, he had a grand plan. In Lebanon, he would defeat and remove the PLO and deter or defeat the Syrian military so Gemayel would be free to make peace with Israel. These twin wins would also make it possible to deal with the Palestinian issue from a position of strength, particularly because radical forces would have suffered such a far-reaching defeat. The Middle East chessboard would thus be reset.

In other words, Operation Peace for Galilee was never only about cleaning out the PLO's presence and artillery deployed in the zone forty to forty-five kilometers north of the Israeli border, which had been the ostensible objective announced publicly when Israel launched its military campaign. It was always more ambitious. Though Simcha Erlich would vote against the cabinet resolution and charge that Sharon was duping everyone to pursue a much wider purpose, Moshe Nissim, the minister of justice, who was also a critic of Sharon's, would later say, "I've got a very great deal against Sharon. But those who say he duped us and misled us are simply distorting. They're trying to justify themselves, to escape criticism, to pretend they didn't know or didn't see when things began to go wrong."[87]

For Nissim, those who "didn't know" did not want to know.* Sharon had an ambitious strategic goal in mind. Interestingly, Haig, who had warned Sharon not to take such a leap, now shifted his position, believing that the IDF's operation and rapid movement to the outskirts of Beirut created a strategic opportunity: "Israel's military incursion also created circumstances in which it was possible, during the fleeting moments in which the

---

* Despite Nissim's belief, Dan Meridor, who was the cabinet secretary in Begin's second term, says Begin felt he was misled by Sharon on the real objectives of the plan.

former equation of power had been overturned, to remove all foreign troops from Lebanon and restore the powers of government to the Lebanese. Beyond that, a settlement in Lebanon would have significant consequences for Arab-Israeli peace: Syria and the PLO, the heart of the Arab opposition to Camp David, had been defeated."[88]

Unfortunately for Haig and Sharon, the secretary of state was alone in the administration in seeing the Israeli military presence around Beirut as a good thing. Haig argued that only if it looked like the United States would not hold the Israelis back would Arafat, who was now trapped in Beirut, feel compelled to leave. But Vice President George H. W. Bush, National Security Advisor William Clark, and Secretary of Defense Caspar Weinberger totally rejected this. The White House spokesman and Weinberger contradicted Haig in public when he seemed to back the Israelis. In private, Bush and Weinberger* conveyed to the Saudis that Israel would not enter West Beirut.[89] Haig would later write that Arafat was signaling he would leave until he heard from the Saudis about the Bush and Weinberger message; once he thought he had room to maneuver, he tried to hold out. That, then, produced the Israeli siege of West Beirut—a siege that would drag on through the summer.[90]

Increasing pressure on Arafat inevitably meant tightening the noose around the residents of West Beirut. Sharon shelled and bombarded the city with air strikes, turned off water and electricity, and sent the IDF in and out of some neighborhoods—all of which portrayed Israel before the world as threatening, and in some cases killing, Lebanese civilians and angering President Reagan and Haig's successor, George Shultz.**

Reagan was unhappy with the humanitarian costs and the Israeli resistance to his calls to stop the constant bombardment of the city and let Habib broker Arafat's departure. From August 2 to 12, Begin insisted to President Reagan that Israel was only returning fire—even as Habib reported that it

---

* Bush and Weinberger would lead a delegation to Saudi Arabia for the funeral of King Khalid at this time and certainly left the impression with the Saudi leadership that the United States would stop the Israelis.

** Haig, frustrated that he could not control the messaging, offered his resignation to Reagan, believing that he could use this as leverage to get his way. Instead, Reagan, who felt that Haig was always threatening to resign when he did not get his way, was ready to see him leave. Shultz would become secretary of state in July 1982.

was impossible for him to talk to anyone or move within the city because of nonstop Israeli firing. As early as August 4, Reagan warned Begin to expect a "drastic change in Israel's relationship with the United States" if the disproportionate bombing of West Beirut did not stop.[91] Following a full-day barrage on August 14, Reagan demanded that the bombing stop or our "entire relationship" would be endangered.[92] After Reagan's threat, the cabinet voted sixteen to two to stop the bombing, and Begin now insisted that any additional air attacks would require his personal approval and not just Sharon's authorization. Some ministers believed at the time that Sharon was trying to subvert Habib's efforts.[93]

If so, he did not succeed. Habib reached an agreement five days later on the details of Arafat's exit. Though Sharon would disagree to the last minute on the PLO fighters being able to take vehicles and personal arms with them, the departure of thousands of Arafat's forces would proceed on September 1. With Bashir Gemayel elected president of Lebanon on August 23, Sharon could see some of his expected gains coming to fruition. The mass expulsion of the PLO would, in his words, be the "first step in what I saw as a process that would lead to a peace treaty between ourselves and the new Lebanese government. Hardly less significant, the PLO's defeat and dispersion also meant that the extremism and incessant violence that organization had always stood for would now be badly discredited . . . and with the PLO crushed, the possibility of a rational dialogue between ourselves and the Palestinians not dedicated to our destruction would be greatly enhanced."[94]

Several developments frustrated Sharon's grand scheme. First, President Reagan unveiled his peace plan the same day as Arafat and the PLO's expulsion. It had not occurred to Sharon that the US response to a two-and-a-half-month siege of Beirut, an Arab capital, might be a peace plan designed to reach out to the Arabs, undercutting Sharon's plans with the Palestinians. Second, Gemayel was assassinated; Sharon's charismatic partner was now dead. Third, Gemayel's forces, the Phalange, rampaged into Sabra and Shatila, two Palestinian refugee camps, and killed the women and children, creating revulsion not just around the world but in Israel too.

After Gemayel's death, Israel sent its forces into West Beirut, ostensibly to stabilize the situation and prevent it from spinning out of control. George Shultz would tell Israel's ambassador to the United States, Moshe Arens, this was a big mistake, as Israel would now be responsible for what happened there.[95] His words became prophetic when the IDF allowed the Phalange forces to go into the two refugee camps, then stayed on the outside and intervened only the next day after the Phalangists had already slaughtered civilians. There was an outcry internationally and in Israel as well, with four hundred thousand turning out to protest the Lebanon War—as it had also turned costly for Israel—and to demand a state commission of inquiry into what had happened in Sabra and Shatila. While Begin initially called the efforts to blame Israel for what the Phalange had done a "blood libel," he would give into the pressure. The Kahan Commission was established to investigate what had taken place.

Sharon argued that Israel had done nothing wrong; there was reason to go into the camps because intelligence suggested that the PLO had left stores of weapons there with fighters, and no one had anticipated that the Phalange might seek revenge against the Palestinians for the assassination of their leader, Gemayel. In any case, he said that it had been the Phalange forces that committed these terrible acts, not Israelis; Israel, therefore, was not responsible. The Kahan Commission would find otherwise, charging Sharon and several senior IDF officers with acts of "omission," not "commission." If Sharon and others did not know, the commission declared that they should have known. It did not buy the argument that no one had anticipated what the Phalange would do—indeed, one minister, David Levy, had predicted the Phalange actions in the cabinet—and, regardless, Sharon and others should have anticipated what would likely happen if the Phalange were let into the camps.

While the commission called for Sharon to resign as defense minister, Begin was not required to replace him—at least in Sharon's mind. But Begin did so, leading Sharon bitterly to say that "this is the only country in the world in which the Minister of Defense is sent home to drive his tractor because of what Christians did to the Muslims."[96] Moreover, he left no doubt about what he felt about Begin's failing to back him: "I regarded what had happened as a betrayal, a real betrayal by people who didn't have the strength to stand up for the things they had been discussing for years, people who understood so well what had to be done but had not had the courage of their convictions."[97]

Begin would not force Sharon out of the government, merely out of the defense ministry. Though disheartened, Sharon chose to stay in the government as a minister without portfolio. For Sharon, having no real responsibility was the worst kind of punishment. But Yisrael Katz, at the time a young activist in the Likud party, came to Sharon and told him that to be effective as a politician, he needed to have a political base, and he asked Sharon to "let me help build you a camp."[98] He proceeded to do so, carving out the right wing of the party and its settler constituency. Sharon stuck with this camp as a way of building his following; he also used it to challenge others in the party (and the government) and to make himself a central player.

With the Lebanon War dragging on, and Israel taking increasing casualties, it was not surprising that Labor would outpoll Likud in the 1984 elections, but it was remarkable that its advantage would be very slight—forty-four to forty-two seats. Sharon, never one to sit on the sidelines, went to the religious parties and their leaders and made promises about meeting their needs if they would not join a Labor-led government in which Likud was left out. His scheming and politicking paid off: once he was able to block Labor from forming a government without Likud, he represented Likud in negotiating with Shimon Peres, the leader of Labor, to form an NUG.* He negotiated the rotation arrangement, whereby Peres would be the prime minister for the first two years of the government and Yitzhak Shamir the foreign minister, and after two years they would swap positions. Peres would say that "Arik, in this, was first rate. Absolute straight-shooter. Whatever we agreed was agreed."[99]

Peres would have several occasions where he was far less happy with Sharon, who had become a minister in the NUG, and the prime minister would insist on apologies for charges Sharon had made against him. Sharon, following the Katz game plan, would be the "authentic, reliable, and unswerving leader of the hawks." This was his base, his following, and they gave him political leverage within Likud. In August 1985, he spoke to a group, saying, "You cannot imagine the hatred for the settlers in Judea and Samaria that comes through at cabinet meetings. They have a 'white paper

---

* Such governments were always his preference, and the corrosive effects of the Lebanon War on the Israeli public only added to his belief in their value.

policy' preventing settlers from taking over more houses in Hebron."[100] Peres was ready to fire him, and Sharon offered an apology. But he would soon be at it again, declaring that Peres's "weak policies" did not rule out the PLO as a negotiating partner and were endangering the peace with Egypt. This time Peres demanded that Sharon say he had confidence in him or he would be fired; Sharon had no support from the other Likud ministers in the government, and so he made the statement that would preserve his position as minister of industry and construction. Again, staying in his position, while he appealed to the right wing, took precedence—even if it required some public groveling.

At the same time, Sharon went about trying to rehabilitate himself more generally before the Israeli public by writing lengthy articles in *Yediot Ahronot,* explaining the Lebanon conflict and putting it in the context of every war that Israel had fought, all of which required tough decisions to secure Israel's future. He described his critics as "nowists," capable of thinking only of today and never of the larger consequences at stake; had they been around in 1948, the "nowists," unlike David Ben-Gurion, would not have declared the state.[101] Sharon's efforts at rehabilitation also included a three-hour lecture at Tel Aviv University—hardly an area of his supporters—to explain the war and show that Israel had no choice but to go beyond the forty to forty-five kilometer zone, and that Begin was involved in every decision.[102]

Rehabilitating himself and appealing to his right-wing base were part of Sharon's ongoing effort to be able to assume a governmental position of real importance. Gaining leverage from the base of the Likud prime minister, Yitzhak Shamir, was his clear aim; Shamir would be prime minister from 1986 to 1992.*

In late 1987, the first intifada erupted; Palestinian youth threw stones and rioted throughout the West Bank and Gaza. Yitzhak Rabin would remain the defense minister in the NUGs during this time, and Sharon would attack both Rabin and Shamir for their inability to squash the intifada, drawing the contrast with his successful experience in Gaza in 1971. Sharon

---

* Shamir would hold this position in two successive NUGs: the first flowing from the rotation agreement, the second following the 1988 election narrowly won by Likud.

pointed out that his policy of coercion and expulsions had worked then: "We gave each of them [the rioters] a little money, a hat, a loaf of bread, and a water bottle and we drove them to the Arava. . . . After that, total peace and quiet descended on Gaza. . . . Believe me, I've got experience."[103]

He wanted to remind Israelis of this experience, not the Lebanon debacle. If allowed, he would stop the intifada. But he would not be allowed, and even though he was a minister in the government, his criticism of Shamir and Rabin did not abate. It even extended beyond the intifada to the Shamir government's peace initiative, presented to the Bush administration in March 1989. When Secretary of State James Baker gave a speech to the American Israel Public Affairs Committee in May 1989 calling on Israel to stop settlement activity, give up the dream of a "greater Israel," and reach out to Palestinians as neighbors who "deserve political rights," Sharon called Baker's words "a slap in the face" and the result of the weakness of the Israeli government's policies and Shamir's peace proposal.[104]

In March 1990, Shimon Peres, the finance minister in this NUG, brought down the government, fully believing he had the votes to form a narrow Labor-led government. While he had the necessary votes in a no-confidence resolution in the Knesset, Sharon, working behind the scenes with the rabbis in the ultraorthodox Agudat party, was able to block the formation of a Labor-led government.* It would take Likud, with Sharon playing the key role, three months to forge a new narrow Likud government, based, as he said, on restoring "the rightist-religious alliance between us and the Orthodox."[105]

Sharon still bore too much of a stigma to become defense minister, but Shamir appointed him the minister of construction and housing. From this post, the bulldozer would be back in action, engineering massive building to meet the needs of the huge influx of Soviet Jewry now free to emigrate to Israel. Once again, there was a need and nothing would stand in Sharon's way from fulfilling this mission. He was ready to take on "mission impossible," and he pressed, pushed, cajoled, exceeded his budget, and handed out

---

* The day of the vote to form the new government, the ninety-six-year-old patriarch of Agudat, Rabbi Shach, mandated that the party should not join a Labor-led government, and two of its members failed to appear for the Knesset vote—thus blocking Peres's effort.

contracts without bids—all with the aim of getting things done. As he would later point out, "It was a period of record construction in our history. We built 144,000 new homes and renovated 22,000 others from top to bottom."[106]

One of his aides at the time said that Sharon felt that destiny had chosen him for this challenge of absorbing hundreds of thousands of new immigrants: "He kept repeating that this was a unique opportunity not only to change the demography of the country but to change the geography. And he did what he said. Beersheba in the south literally doubled its population as a result of his policy. Towns like Carmiel, Safed, Upper Nazereth grew beyond recognition in those two years."[107]

Sharon was meeting the needs of the Soviet émigrés—no doubt winning their support and gratitude in the process—and also affecting the balance of the Arab and Jewish populations in parts of Israel where Jews had less of a presence. To achieve his ends, he cut corners and broke the rules. When the state comptroller issued a report saying he had exceeded his budget by 1.5 billion shekels and criticizing the no-bid process, Sharon had an answer: "I suggest that everyone go out and look at thousands of apartments and houses established across the country. . . . I know what I'm doing and I know what I need to do. More than three hundred fifteen thousand new immigrants arrived in Israel from the beginning of 1990 to 1991—and all of them have a roof over their heads. . . . What other country in the world has done something like that?"[108] Others could criticize him, but he did what was necessary. As always, the ends justified the means.

While most of the building was within the June 4, 1967, lines, he also planned fifteen thousand units in the areas around the perimeter of Jerusalem, stretching extensively into the West Bank. This was a direct challenge to Secretary Baker, who, after the Gulf War, launched a peace effort. But Sharon was on a mission. After the war, the pace of construction in the territories was unlike anything seen since Sharon's initial push in 1977, with 6,435 units, nearly all single-family houses, built in 1991. By way of comparison, 1,410 were built in 1989 and 1,820 in 1990.[109]

Starting in March of 1991, Baker came to Israel at least once a month to try to get peace negotiations launched. Each time he arrived, Sharon would announce the start of a new settlement—something Baker took as a personal affront. Shamir felt the brunt of Baker's anger and would respond by saying he, too, was unhappy about it, but nothing changed. In fact, Sharon declared that any of the new Soviet arrivals "who [don't] want to live in a trailer inside the Green Line can move to a house in Judea and Samaria."[110]

Sharon conveyed an image of caring little about America's reaction—or the damage he might be doing to the government's effort to secure ten billion dollars in loan guarantees from the United States for the absorption of Soviet Jewry.* He was one of the "constraints ministers" at this time, opposing any concessions that Shamir might make to Baker to enable the launching of the Madrid Peace Conference—a conference that would break the taboo on direct talks between Israel and its Arab neighbors and that Sharon declared was "not a peace conference but a war conference."[111]

Baker never met Sharon, but he exacted his revenge. He blocked Sharon from being received officially or formally in Washington when he came for meetings as the minister of construction and housing. Sharon was anxious to see his putative counterpart, Jack Kemp, the secretary of housing and urban development and a well-known friend of Israel. Baker prevented Kemp from seeing Sharon at his office or in any governmental facility. Kemp could agree to see Sharon only at the Israeli embassy—a reminder to the Israeli public that Sharon was not accepted in Washington and that his policies carried a cost.

While that might have tempered his behavior toward the United States later when he became prime minister, he remained firm in his opposition to any peace moves at this time. Not surprisingly, he was a fierce critic of the Oslo process. For him, it was a mistake to deal with the PLO and Arafat. He revisited his theme that Jordan was Palestine, emphasizing that all

---

* The Bush administration would sign off on providing four hundred million dollars in loan guarantees at this time. In return for the four hundred million dollars, Baker and Dennis had negotiated a commitment in writing from David Levy, the foreign minister, demonstrating that none of the loan guarantees would be used for housing in the territories. Dennis would be the one who principally persuaded President Bush to release the four hundred million dollars, arguing that this was a down payment on the much larger request the Israelis would make and Shamir would not be so stupid as to jeopardize the ten-billion-dollar request by not living up to the promises made in the Levy letter. Dennis was wrong, as Sharon acted and Shamir did not stop him.

negotiations on the fate of the Palestinians living in the West Bank and Gaza should be conducted with Jordan.

Notwithstanding his criticism of Oslo and Rabin—Sharon said that Rabin had lost his way—he continued to meet with him and offer his advice on how to make IDF redeployments safer from the standpoint of Israeli security. According to Eitan Haber, "Rabin saw Sharon alone because he valued his views on what made military sense; he would solicit Sharon's opinion and Sharon would say, 'Why are you giving them that hill. It is higher than the next hill. Give them that.' He knew the map like the back of his hand."[112]

Sharon publicly explained his meetings with Rabin, saying, "Our relations are built on a completely different background, they come from another world. In that world, too, there were clashes between us. But we marched together in lockstep, over the decades, on tough missions and in life and death situations. Rabin has completely reversed his positions. I consider this reversal dangerous. But that doesn't affect our relationship."[113]

Still, Sharon's criticism at times was not just over-the-top—it amounted to incitement. In 1995, in giving interviews with the Orthodox religious media, he spoke of Rabin and Peres as being "collaborators" and plotting with Arafat, even suggesting that it might be "hard to speak of treason in connection with Jews, but the essence of their action is no different."[114]

After the assassination, Dalia Rabin, Yitzhak Rabin's daughter, would say that Sharon admitted to her that "there were things said that should not have been said."[115] He would not publicly admit to this, but later he would begin to eulogize Rabin and speak of following his path. At the dedication of the Rabin Center in 1997, he said, "We all want peace but it is hard to reach agreement; therefore, we will have to forfeit something. Although Yitzhak Rabin no longer marches with us, I would like to follow his path."[116]

Here is an early sign that Sharon would alter his position toward peace, especially because he made this statement as the minister of infrastructure in a Netanyahu government. Three months later, in June 1997, he hosted Mahmoud Abbas at his ranch, drawing the ire of some of his settler constituency. In response, he explained that the Palestinians needed to hear what was possible and what wasn't.

When Netanyahu appointed him foreign minister prior to going to Wye River, Sharon announced that he would not shake Arafat's hand, and he did not.* And yet at Wye River, Sharon would negotiate with Abbas and Abu Alaa and make far-reaching concessions on permitting the Palestinians a port in Gaza—so much so that Natan Sharansky would quip, "Arik, shake his hand, you will concede less."**

After Wye River, Abu Alaa would remark that he could do business with Sharon, and Sharon made it clear to American officials that he was ready.*** He would not sacrifice what he felt Israel needed for security purposes but was creative in terms of how to address Palestinian needs at the same time.

Before turning to Sharon's even more decisive victory in February 2001, it is worth noting that his pragmatism as foreign minister would disappear from view when he became the head of Likud after Netanyahu's defeat in 1999. As the head of the opposition, Sharon would be scathing in his criticism of Prime Minister Ehud Barak, especially after the failure of the Camp David talks in July 2000 and the scope of the concessions Barak had been willing to make became known. Sharon's statement on August 15, 2000, is illustrative: "Barak has agreed to cleave in two the heart of the Jewish people; the Old City of Jerusalem. . . . He is ready to concede the Temple Mount. He is trying to soften the blow demanding that Arafat recognize the Jews' right to pray. This very proposal, that Arafat recognize our right to pray at the holy of holies of the Jewish people, is itself debasing and only goes to show to what depths our side has sunk."[117]

Strong words, and words that would seem to explain why Sharon decided to visit the Temple Mount/Haram al-Sharif on September 28, 2000—a visit Palestinians claimed triggered the second intifada, which

---

* At a small dinner meeting that President Clinton hosted, Arafat walked toward Sharon and extended his hand. Gamal Helal, Dennis's closest aide and also President Clinton's Arabic interpreter, leaped in between Arafat and Sharon and shook Arafat's hand.

** Sharansky was at Wye River as a minister in the government.

***In meetings with Dennis, he would explain that he did not think it was possible to bridge the differences on the permanent-status issues, "because we cannot do what the Palestinians want, and they cannot do what we want, but we should strive to produce a long-term interim agreement." In any case, he was open to exploring with Abu Alaa what was feasible.

consisted of suicide bombings and widespread terror within Israeli cities. Uri Dan, Sharon's friend and a journalist, urged him to "wake-up the public" and "make sure that the Temple Mount cannot be used as a bargaining chip." Dan insists that is why Sharon made his visit, literally surrounded by hundreds of Israeli police. Prime Minister Barak disagreed, explaining to US officials that it was a political stunt designed to weaken him and preserve Sharon's position as the head of Likud because Netanyahu was about to return to politics and challenge him for its leadership. Both reasons could be true; Sharon was not willing to see the Temple Mount traded away, and it helped him in Likud as Netanyahu was poised to reenter the political fray.

Sharon's visit to the Temple Mount/Haram al-Sharif probably did not cause the second intifada, but Arafat surely used it as a pretext for the violence.* The intifada had a profound effect in Israel: it soured the Israeli public on making concessions to Palestinians and killed the peace camp in Israel. It also set the stage for Sharon's election.

SHARON BECOMES PRIME MINISTER

In Sharon's election campaign, there was a deliberate effort to reassure the Israeli public that he was seasoned and had mellowed; he was portrayed in the campaign as grandfatherly. On the one hand, he could be counted on to bring security; on the other, it was as if his campaign managers, Reuben Adler and Eyal Arad, worried that the legacy of Lebanon still hung over him. So they coined the slogan "Only Sharon can bring peace." In seeking Sharon's approval to use the slogan, Adler asked Sharon if he knew its implications, and Sharon acknowledged that he did. Adler knew that "that this was not just an election slogan."[118] In fact, this is when Sharon began to speak consistently of "painful concessions" that would be needed for peace.[119]

---

* Arafat was livid after Barak withdrew from the Israeli security zone in southern Lebanon on May 22, 2000—with Hezbollah claiming it had driven the Israelis out and vilifying Arafat in the process. The worst meeting Dennis ever had with Arafat was right after the withdrawal when he was extremely angry, telling Dennis, "The Israelis throw me crumbs while Hezbollah gets everything." Arafat most likely decided then to use violence to pressure the Israelis, no doubt underestimating what would be unleashed on both sides.

Although his overwhelming election victory was the ultimate vindication for Sharon, he was not jubilant. His reaction was sober, and he would tell Uri Dan, "I had the feeling that I was taking on the biggest task that I had ever had in the turbulent history of the state of Israel."[120] In part, this stemmed from the enormity of the challenge and its difficulty, given what he told Dan was "the war of attrition launched by Yasser Arafat. . . . I promised the citizens of Israel that I would restore security and the peace that they deserved."[121] He took this on because, in his words, he was "a specialist in missions that others said were impossible."[122]

But there was something more that explained his mood: he felt a great weight of responsibility, not just to Israel but to the Jewish people. Dubi Weisglass said that after he became prime minister, Sharon called himself "Prime Minister of the Jewish people."[123]

Uri Shani, Prime Minister Sharon's initial chief of staff, agreed, saying Sharon saw "himself as just one link in the chain of Jewish history. His task was to carry it through his term and hand on the burden. He felt it on his shoulders."[124]

Sharon had, in Weisglass's words, reached the "pinnacle." This was "the ultimate position for him," and he had no other ambitions except to fulfill his duties. Sharon understood that his responsibilities were daunting, especially given the intifada, and that he had to rise to the moment; he realized, according to Weisglass, that he had to "accomplish something big." In his mind, it was as if "now God had created this opportunity and he must do something really great with it."[125]

It now becomes clear why Sharon would adopt policies as prime minister that contradicted the positions he had held throughout his career. Put simply, as head of the government, he saw the world through a different lens. His responsibilities were different—broader and heavier. He would often say to the members of Likud when they questioned what he was doing, "What you see from here [as prime minister], you don't see from there." Ruby Rivlin, then the head of the Likud faction in the Knesset, said to Sharon that, if Sharon had been the head of the opposition after the Dolphinarium bombing, he would have demanded the head of a prime minister who said that "restraint is strength." Sharon replied that, true, in the opposition you have one responsibility but as prime minister you have another.[126]

Sharon rose to the challenge and, as always, was ambitious. He was a problem-solver: the tougher the challenge, the more certain he felt the need to tackle it. Early on, he acted in a way that few would have predicted. He sent his son Omri to see Arafat, to create a private channel and show that Sharon was willing to work with him. Even more importantly, shortly after Omri's meeting, Sharon conveyed a far-reaching proposal to Arafat that would have shocked the prime minister's constituency had the Palestinian leader accepted it:

- Israel, within four weeks, would pull its forces back to the pre-intifada lines;
- final status talks would resume within the month;
- Sharon would meet Arafat before the resumption of the final status negotiations, and security coordination talks would begin within three days of the summit;
- Israel would carry out a third further redeployment;
- Israel would refrain from unilateral acts in Jerusalem or building new settlements;
- Israel would also release forty prisoners as a gesture, once Arafat denounced terror and violence and the Palestinian Authority committed to fighting terror and preventing attacks.[127]

Arafat would not act on this offer, instead letting the intifada become far more violent, with suicide bombings increasingly defining the conflict. The Dolphinarium bombing convinced Sharon that nothing was possible with Arafat. He had reached out to Arafat, he had made an offer, and this was the answer. He would convey to the United States that he would accept a resumption of negotiations only if there were seven days of calm first.

Just as he had made a far-reaching offer to Arafat soon after becoming prime minister, he also privately conveyed to President George W. Bush in their first meeting that he was ready for a territorial compromise, as a way of proving his seriousness. He felt the need to do so with the United States.

He was, in the words of his foreign policy assistant Shalom Turgeman, "obsessed with the United States."[128] Several of his former aides repeated that this stemmed from the lessons he had learned from the debacle in Lebanon. He saw the high cost of American opposition to Israeli policies. Another close aide, Lior Schillat, said Sharon was preoccupied with "keeping the US on his side."[129]

His obsession and concerns would lead him, according to Dubi Weisglass, to have sleepless nights before his meetings with President Bush. He did not want to be misunderstood. He worried about his English and would write out the essential points on cards to be sure he got it right. He was extremely nervous before his first visit to meet Bush, wanting the relationship to get off on the right foot. Sharon's anxiety was, undoubtedly, fed by the legacy of Bush's father's administration—and how Sharon had seen himself being treated as a "rogue" leader who did not warrant an official meeting.

Of course, Sharon's own behavior contributed mightily to how he had been seen by the first President Bush. Sharon, at that point, defined Israel's needs and his responsibilities differently. Historically, he had felt that Israel was too dependent on the United States and that America needed to see that Israel, when its security was at risk, would act based on its needs and not America's. While true as a general principle, it was much easier to hold that view when Sharon did not have the ultimate responsibility for Israel's well-being.

As prime minister, everything looked different. His long-standing fears about being too dependent on the United States did not necessarily disappear, but he believed that the United States, the über-power at this time, was so important to Israel that Israeli leaders needed to show they took US concerns into account, even as they sought to minimize any appearance of differences between the two countries. Yes, Sharon would give his October 4, 2001, speech, where he said Israel would not be Czechoslovakia, and the United States and Western powers should not think that they could sacrifice it on the altar of pursuing a partnership with the Arabs in fighting terrorism. But this was a warning at a time when the intifada was raging, and Sharon was responding to President Bush's request to have Shimon Peres, the foreign minister, meet with Arafat—even though Bush had declared a war on terror and bombs were going off in Israel. With acts of terror continuing even after Sharon permitted Peres to see Arafat, Sharon felt the need to signal his limits, and the administration responded by creating a direct channel from the White House to him.[130]

The fact is, Sharon saw America as Israel's only real friend, and his October 4 outburst would be his last such criticism of the United States. The United States was simply too important to Israel, and being prime minister gave him a special responsibility to keep the Americans in lockstep. Indeed, at a time when Israel was confronting the second intifada, Lior Schillat would say that Sharon believed Israel "could not afford to lose the US backing in fighting terror."[131] Dubi Weisglass agreed, saying that Sharon's desire to avoid putting the United States in a position where it felt the need to pressure Israel was at least one factor that accounted for the far-reaching changes in policy that Sharon adopted as prime minister.[132]

Weisglass also pointed out that Sharon for fifty years had had an ambivalent view of the United States; he respected its power and capability, but that respect "was always mixed with suspicion." Throughout this period, Sharon feared the United States would try to push Israel to do what the Arabs wanted it to do. This feeling clearly ran deep—so much so that after the Gulf War, Sharon told Uri Dan he was glad the United States had not removed Saddam Hussein, because "otherwise Israel would have paid an even greater price." In Sharon's view, if the United States had felt guilty about removing an Arab leader, it would have considered itself obliged to "win approval from the Arab world by demanding Israel make large concessions to the Palestinians."[133]

However, Weisglass said the suspicion of the United States (and Bush) changed with the Bush speech of June 24, 2002—a speech where he called for a Palestinian state, but said it could not be built on a foundation of terror and corruption and could not be led by Yasser Arafat. As far back as 1970, Sharon was acknowledging that there would need to be a Palestinian state, only he wanted it in Jordan. Security dictated that position. Once he worked with King Hussein in the 1990s, though, he understood that the answer would not be found in Jordan. Nevertheless, statehood was not thinkable for the West Bank and Gaza until the ideology of terror no longer drove the Palestinians. Peace for Sharon could come only after terror had stopped and truly been renounced. Now, with the Bush speech, Sharon believed—according to Weisglass—that the United States shared Israel's position.

Three factors began to come together to create a context for Sharon to move, and to move in a big, unexpected fashion. First, he was prime minister, and, as such, he defined his responsibilities very differently. He needed to think in terms of Israel's long-term well-being and the well-being of world Jewry. He could not think small or tactically, given these broader responsibilities. Second, Israel's security depended very much on staying on the good side of the United States—by itself, the United States could prevent Israel's isolation. Third, he now felt that America would not betray Israel or surprise it and put it in the corner, because President Bush had demonstrated that he shared Sharon's basic concept. In turn, Sharon believed he must prove to Bush that he was ready to take real steps and not simply play for time or try to frustrate any peace initiative. In fact, he was prepared to go against everything the younger Sharon had stood for, said, and done.

Sharon's Revolutionary Leap

It was Sharon who not only built the settlements, but conceived of where they should be built. His plan was extensive from the beginning and designed to make it difficult to leave the territories. That was his purpose; knowing that Israel would face pressure, he wanted to create a countervailing point of political power domestically.

But it was not just the settlement imperative that drove Sharon's policies. He was tough-minded, with a hard-line political base. In 1982, he said that "terrorism is part of the Palestinian people's character." In 1985, he said the big mistake in Lebanon was "leaving Arafat alive." In 1994, he said, "The agreement with the PLO is a historic, moral and practical error."[134] In 1995, speaking in the Golan Heights, he apologized for "evacuating" the Sinai settlements and said it should not in any way serve as a precedent. A month later, he urged settlers to seize hilltops.[135] In 1998, right after the Wye River Memorandum, he again urged the settlers to go seize hilltops before implementation of the agreement.

In early 1988, in response to the first intifada, Shimon Peres, then the finance minister in the NUG, proposed that Israel withdraw from Gaza. Sharon's response: "This is an unsound suggestion which will lead to intensified violence from the Palestinians, since it is impossible to hermetically seal off the Gaza Strip. If we leave, the terrorists will fire mortars and missiles on Sderot and Ashkelon, just as they did in Lebanon."[136]

Similarly, in an interview with Uri Dan, in which Dan asked him why not withdraw from settlements in isolated places like Gaza, Sharon answered, "Let's take Netzarim, which the Palestinian terrorists continually attack. Why do they do that? Because they understand something that certain Israelis do not want to understand. Netzarim was created to allow us to stop Palestinians from unloading tanks and other war equipment in the port of Gaza. . . . Netzarim had to be created to establish a buffer zone between Gaza and Khan Yunes and give us access to the sea."[137]

Not long before the advent of Oslo, he would make an even blunter, more detailed statement on why withdrawal from Gaza made little sense. In his words, it was a perversion

> voluntarily to cede a part of the national homeland, which no normal nation would do . . . [and] without the bloc of Jewish settlements who is going to block that traffic [of weaponry and terrorists]? They say: "we'll set up barriers and roadblocks . . ." [but] it is just not possible to seal off a territory hermetically. In the past, bands of terrorists have infiltrated Gaza and reached as far as the suburbs of Tel Aviv. But to attack southern Israel, they wouldn't have to leave Gaza at all. A katyusha rocket deployed . . . in central Gaza will easily hit . . . central Ashkelon. What will we do? How will we respond?[138]

Judging from these statements, it is hard to imagine that Sharon would be the one to make the decision to withdraw from Gaza. Yet he would announce this decision less than a year after he said that "the fate of Netzarim is the fate of Tel Aviv"—a statement he had made rejecting the proposal for withdrawing from Gaza from his opponent, Amram Mitzna, in the 2003 election. What changed? A number of things, but, in reality, Sharon had already made a leap—even if a lesser one—before his decision to withdraw from Gaza. He embraced Palestinian statehood in September 2001 and then he embraced the roadmap to peace in May 2003; each represented a departure and each was a response to the United States—and each set the stage for Gaza disengagement.

RECOGNIZING PALESTINIAN STATEHOOD AND THE ROADMAP

On September 23, 2001, Sharon gave a speech at Latrun. His speech, commemorating the battle with some of his old comrades from the Alexandroni Brigade, was about the past and the future. He declared, "The state of Israel wants to give the Palestinians what no one else has heretofore given them—the possibility of establishing a state. Neither the Turks, the English, the Egyptians or the Jordanians gave them such a possibility."[139] No Israeli prime minister had adopted such a public posture.

Why now? It was twelve days after 9/11; the United States was in shock. Bush, in his first call to Sharon after the twin towers came down, had asked him to have Peres meet Arafat. The message was clear: if the United States was to have Arab partners for the war on terror, it needed the Palestinian conflict to be addressed. While Bush would later come to doubt this assumption, he was acting on it at the behest of the State Department at this moment—and Sharon understood that Israel needed to be seen as doing something in response. After initial hesitation, he let Peres meet with Arafat. The Latrun declaration should also be seen in this context. He was taking an initiative, at least rhetorically. Lior Schillat explained that Sharon believed it was a mistake to cede the initiative. Those who did not act would always be reacting—and, Schillat said, for Sharon it was "essential always to be the initiator."[140]

Acting, not reacting, defined him, and it would mark the rest of his tenure as prime minister. He would not let the United States down at a time when it was leading the world in fighting terror. Unfortunately, Palestinian terrorism would continue unabated after he allowed Peres to see Arafat and he made his declaration on supporting Palestinian statehood; this led to his Czechoslovakia speech.*

Still, Sharon had crossed a threshold. There were signs that this was coming. In his inaugural speech as prime minister, he said, "Both our peoples are destined to live together side by side, on this small piece of land. This reality we cannot change. But I do believe that we are capable, if there is a desire on both sides, to veer away from the bitter and bloody path that we are heading towards."[141] Later, on January 14, 2002, in speaking to correspondents, he said, "I'll be 74 in a few weeks. I have no other political ambitions in life. I've done everything; all I want is to achieve a political arrangement that will lead to peace with the Palestinians and the Arab world. That is the last thing I want to do with my life."[142] A year later, in January 2003, he would tell his sons while at the ranch that he "had been given a historic mission that only he could fulfill: to change the face of the Middle East and move to a diplomatic solution."[143]

The second intifada was still ongoing when he made this statement to his sons. But the preceding spring, after several months of gruesome bombings in Israeli cities, he had finally sent the IDF into the West Bank to clean out the terrorist infrastructure. He did not make the decision to do so until after the Park Hotel bombing during a Passover Seder. The bombing killed thirty Israelis and wounded 160, and came at the end of March, a month in which over 130 Israelis had been killed in terror attacks. Even though he had come under fierce criticism from those in his own party, such as Benjamin Netanyahu, for not taking tougher action sooner, Sharon wanted the military to be prepared and to have created a wide domestic consensus for his actions—another lesson he had drawn from Lebanon. Though there would be friction with the United States at the time, given the extent of Israeli military action in West Bank cities, President Bush would back him publicly, saying, "I do believe that Ariel Sharon is a man of peace." Stephen Hadley, who served as Bush's national security advisor, said that Bush had

---

* This showed Sharon could not be taken for granted, and the White House would open a direct communication channel to his office to avoid surprises.

a "gut feeling" about leaders—especially about Sharon—and felt that the Israeli prime minister would want to live up to these words.[144]

In fact he did so, with the Bush administration's roadmap to peace. Surprisingly, when Dubi Weisglass showed Sharon the initial draft of the roadmap, Sharon said, "This is the end of the Zionist project." But in the end, Sharon accepted a version not markedly different. True, he spoke of fourteen reservations when getting Israeli cabinet approval of the roadmap, but there can be little doubt that Sharon was demonstrating his readiness to accept what he had previously rejected. After all, the roadmap called for a freeze on all settlement construction, the end "of the occupation that began in 1967," a "fair solution" to the Palestinian refugee problem, and a "negotiated resolution of the status of Jerusalem."

Sharon accepted the roadmap in principle on May 23, 2003, and faced tremendous opposition from within Likud and the settler movement. He was accused of betrayal, and his defense of his actions speaks volumes about how far he was prepared to go and what was motivating him: "We must reach a political agreement . . . because it is imperative. I also think that the notion that it's possible to keep 3½ million Palestinians under occupation—you may not like the word, but it is under occupation—is bad for Israel, the Palestinians, and the economy of Israel. We must free ourselves from controlling 3½ million Palestinians, whose numbers are not diminishing, and reach a diplomatic agreement."[145]

Here, Sharon raised the issue of demographics and the necessity of ending the occupation—a loaded word for the Likud party, which, going back to Begin's time, had always referred to the territories as "disputed."*

At the Aqaba summit on June 4, 2003, with President Bush, King Abdullah of Jordan, and then prime minister of the Palestinian Authority, Mahmoud Abbas, Sharon repeated this theme and explained explicitly that, for Israel to retain its character, it had an interest in a two-state outcome: "Israel, like others, has lent strong support for President Bush's vision . . . of

---

* Territories that were disputed, not occupied, meant Israel had a legitimate claim to them as well.

two states—Israel and a Palestinian state—living side by side in peace and security. . . . It is in Israel's interest not to govern the Palestinians, but for the Palestinians to govern themselves in their own state. A democratic Palestinian state fully at peace with Israel will promote the long-term security and well-being of Israel as a Jewish state."[146] In the same speech, he added that "we can also reassure our Palestinian partners that we understand the importance of territorial contiguity in the West Bank for a viable Palestinian state."[147] Shalom Turgeman explained that the Americans wanted this in the speech because it was important to the Palestinians, and he and Weisglass worried that Sharon would not accept it. They were surprised when he agreed, saying, "This will keep Israel as a Jewish state. If we see no Palestinians, then we preserve Israel as a Jewish state."[148]

Two days later, Sharon was booed at a Likud Central Committee meeting in which Netanyahu was cheered for saying no to a Palestinian state. Sharon responded by quoting Menachem Begin, saying that the prime minister carries "just a tiny bit more" responsibility and as such he had made these fateful decisions.[149]

Demographics and securing Israel's character were a larger responsibility that the prime minister carried, and Sharon took this responsibility seriously. These factors help account for his support of the roadmap and the seeming transformation in the policies he was now adopting. But there was another factor as well: satisfying the United States. When answering his friend Uri Dan on why he had accepted the roadmap, he said, "First, the desire to support the Bush Administration in its struggle to create peace and democracy in the Middle East [having just removed Saddam Hussein in Iraq]. . . . Second, the desire to avoid at all costs a situation in which Arabs and their sympathizers in the United States could blame Israel for the failure of the Road-Map. Third, and most important, I was given the promise—officially—that Washington would take serious account of our reservations about the proposal, for the entire duration of its effective application."[150]

Each of these points reveal much about Sharon. He would not be on the wrong side of the United States, especially when it was riding high; he would not allow Israel to be put in the corner by hanging back; and he trusted the United States to take his concerns seriously because he was being responsive.

And what were those concerns? That the Bush administration would stick with the idea that statehood for the Palestinians could come only after the infrastructure of terror had been eradicated in the Palestinian Authority, and that each phase of the roadmap could only proceed after the previous one was fully met. Here was a concern that Sharon had expressed at Wye River. In his eyes, it was critical because, as Weisglass explained, Sharon feared that if the Palestinians had a state first and launched terror from it, "Israel would be condemned for retaliating. His experience was that the world would not accept Israeli reprisal actions once a Palestinian state was established, would constrain what Israel could do in response, and that would be untenable for Israel's security."[151]

Bush's acceptance of the necessary sequence, going back to his June 24, 2002, speech, and then embedding it in the roadmap fostered Sharon's trust in the president. He also told President Bush that he was "prepared to make very painful sacrifices in certain areas," but on matters of security, "I have never made concessions in the past, and I won't make them now and I never will."[152]

Security was a constant for Sharon. True, he thought he knew best how to define it, but he had clear limits. Martin Indyk tells the story of Sharon showing him around his ranch after he became prime minister, when Indyk was still serving as the US ambassador to Israel. Sharon was pointing out the "corralling of the sheep" as they were channeled into a small area. He said the June 4, 1967, lines would similarly corral Israel, and that could never be accepted.[153] In effect, Sharon was explaining the limits on the borders that Israel could accept from a strategic standpoint. Shalom Turgeman described how, when looking at the options for evacuating settlements from the West Bank as part of disengagement, Sharon rejected one of the settlements Turgeman and others suggested. While they thought it was small, isolated, and generally not important, Sharon said, "No, it can never be evacuated. It is at the tip of the mountain and it is so narrow that a jeep cannot turn around there and it can block any advance."[154]

Interestingly, Sharon would turn to unilateral disengagement after Abbas resigned and it was clear that the roadmap would not be implemented. Sharon could have stood pat and said that the Palestinians were not fulfilling the roadmap and so the Israelis need not do anything until they do. That, after all, was part of the appeal of the roadmap to Sharon: no negotiations under fire, no Palestinian statehood until the terrorist infrastructure was dismantled, and no movement from phase 1 to phase 2 until all obligations were fulfilled and implemented. So, what changed?

UNILATERAL DISENGAGEMENT

Many factors—both internal and external—explain Sharon's decision and its timing. Not long after Abbas resigned as prime minister of the Palestinian Authority, Weisglass met Secretary of State Condoleezza Rice in Washington, and she told him that "as long as the Bush administration is here, no one will touch the Road-Map, but we will not be here forever." She pointed to the polls in the United States on the upcoming election and spoke of the pressure she was already getting from some European ministers. "The Road-Map is in danger," she said. International pressure would build on Israel to reverse the logic of the roadmap and implement a Palestinian state without first ending terror, and, to head off this possibility, she implored him to "do something—something significant, substantial, something that will rock the boat."[155]

In response, Weisglass returned to Israel and went straight from the airport to see Sharon. Upon hearing Weisglass's account of the meeting, Sharon asked what should be done, and Weisglass offered that "maybe it is time to pull out of Gaza."[156] He argued it would allow Israel to take the initiative and gain strong US backing. In any case, Israel would not remain in Gaza in any permanent arrangement. Sharon's first reaction: "What you are proposing is the end of my service as prime minister."[157] But he then asked Weisglass to put it all in writing—and within a few days, Sharon had taken the idea on, explaining the logic of the initiative to his sons and to the ranch forum.*

---

* The ranch forum was a kind of sounding board for Sharon; his sons and closest friends and associates were part of it. The core of the forum included Eli Landau, Reuven Adler, Uri Dan, Dubi Weisglass, Oded Shamir, Yossi Ginossar, and Rafi Eitan (not the former military chief of staff but a former senior member of Mossad).

Lior Schillat said such a process was typical for Sharon; oftentimes his first reactions were reflexively negative,* but as he would think about what was needed, he would adopt a new position and then argue for it and become even more determined to get it done.[158] In this instance, his chief of staff Uri Shani and campaign manager Eyal Arad were initially against Gaza withdrawal, saying it was political suicide. But Sharon had made up his mind, saying it was better for the IDF, would improve Israel's diplomatic and international standing, and would create more of a chance with the Palestinians.[159]

On November 19, in Rome he met Elliott Abrams, Bush's deputy national security advisor, and laid out his thinking on disengagement. Abrams was taken completely by surprise.[160] On December 18, 2003, Sharon spoke at the annual Herzliya Conference—an annual conference dedicated to Israeli security policy—and presented his concept of unilateral disengagement from the Palestinians. He waited until February to be specific and explain that Israel would evacuate all the settlers and soldiers from Gaza.

Was it the pressure from the United States—and the anticipated pressure of the Europeans in the face of the roadmap going nowhere—that motivated Sharon to take this leap? That is surely part of the story but not all of it. There were developments that also concerned Sharon and fed his natural instinct to act rather than be acted on.

Two developments in the military worried him greatly. As the intifada ground on amid tough Israeli responses, there was a letter from reserve air force pilots in September 2003, in which they wrote that they would not take part in any missions in the West Bank and Gaza. Later, before his Herzliya speech, thirteen reservists in Sayeret Matkal, the most elite of Israel's commando units, announced that they would "no longer participate in the regime of oppression in the territories." For Sharon, this set off serious alarm bells. When one of those in his office tried to minimize the meaning of the letters by saying, "They are just leftists," Sharon reacted angrily, banging his

---

* Schillat described a similar process on the separation barrier—one he had long opposed. But as the costs of the intifada went up, he not only changed his view but would say that Rabin declared it, yet he actually got it done.

hand on the table and shouting, "With some of these people, I have executed the most daring operations of the military."[161]

These fighters mattered to Sharon; they were the pride of the military, and the commandos embodied the very ethic he had socialized within the IDF. If officers or their soldiers should refuse to obey orders, that could put Israel and its democracy at risk. As Shalom Turgeman pointed out, Sharon saw these letters as dangerous harbingers of such a possibility. To preempt any more dissent from the IDF, he felt impelled to show that Israel was doing what it could on peace. Turgeman added that Sharon understood that taking steps on peace would provoke resistance, and Sharon believed that "I might be the last guy that the army will obey."[162] Here again, Sharon displays the self-image of being the only one who can carry these actions out.

In addition to the letters and statements from within the military, Sharon was clearly also motivated by the emergence of the Geneva Accord.* Former Israeli officials and quasi-official Palestinians had produced a draft peace agreement on all the core issues of the conflict, going beyond the parameters presented at the end of the Clinton administration. Sharon had not been a fan of the Clinton parameters, feeling they would lead to borders that would "corral" Israel; they were too restrictive and not defensible in his eyes.** After the official announcement of the agreement in Geneva on December 1, 2003, the two leaders of the Israeli and Palestinian delegations, Yossi Beilin and Yasser Abed Rabbo, traveled to Washington and were received by Secretary of State Colin Powell. The meeting sent a signal that the Bush administration was supportive of the Geneva Accord, making it appear that Rice's warning about coming up with something dramatic applied to forestalling not just international pressure but American pressure as well. All of Sharon's former aides emphasized the impact of the Geneva Accord on him and his need to counter it with an initiative of his own.

---

*   Landau and others argue that the long interview given at this time by four former heads of the Shin Bet, saying the country was heading toward the abyss, also affected Sharon, but none of the aides interviewed by Dennis felt this played much of a role in his decision.

** Dennis would see him not long after he had become prime minister and he would complain about the Clinton parameters.

This, too, was vintage Sharon. Go on the offensive, shift the battlefield and its terrain, force others to react, create surprise, and take the initiative. He seemed to live in fear of being cornered.* He explained to Uri Dan why he made the decision to withdraw from Gaza and implemented it over the fierce opposition of the settler community: "I have only carried out my responsibilities as the head of government for the good of the whole population of Israel. We risked having other plans imposed on us, such as the Saudi Arabian plan or that of the German minister [Joschka] Fischer. Without an initiative on my part, Israel would have had to enter into negotiations that would have ended in an agreement imposed on us from the outside."[163]

In other words, Sharon was saving Israel from being cornered, from being "corralled." Whether responding to protect the military from potentially fragmenting or preempting other, more dangerous, initiatives, Sharon was acting less for positive reasons and more to stop what he saw as threats to Israel. His critics argued there was another, less noble, reason that Sharon suddenly decided to take the initiative and declare his readiness to pull out of Gaza. He was facing a number of police investigations into his conduct and that of his sons,** and Zvi Hendel, a right-wing leader among the settlers, said, "The Disengagement will go as far as the investigations go."[164]

The argument of those like Hendel was that the media and the police, favoring peace moves, would not want to derail Sharon's disengagement initiative with an indictment. In the Middle East, there is a tendency to explain policies one does not like with a conspiracy. There is no denying there were investigations underway, and Sharon's announcement on Gaza in February took place against a backdrop of leaks about the state attorney supporting indictments. But those favoring a "deep state" conspiracy to explain the prime minister's motives ignore his earlier readiness to accept a Palestinian state and the roadmap, which also drew the ire of the right wing in Israel.

---

* It is not just what Sharon told Martin Indyk; Dubi Weisglass remarked that this was a metaphor often used by Sharon.

** Sharon and his sons—Omri and Gilad—were being investigated for illegal fund-raising and false reporting on the amounts raised during the 1999 Likud primary elections, possible conflicts of interest over getting money from Cyril Kern to repay loans connected to the election spending, and the Greek isle affair, in which Gilad was paid large sums in return for what was claimed as governmental help with Greek officials on a project there.

Well before talk of investigations, Sharon had spoken of ending occupation and the consequences, including the demographic ones, of ruling over 3.5 million Palestinians. He made a reference to demography in explaining Gaza withdrawal publicly for the first time: "We must take the initiative. Due to security and demographic issues, some of the Jewish communities in the Gaza Strip will no longer be able to exist."[165]

As prime minister, Sharon had become more preoccupied with demographic trends. Lior Schillat said demography and preserving Israel as a Jewish state began to weigh heavily on Sharon. So much so that he read the work of two of Israel's leading demographers—Arnon Sofaer and Sergio DellaPergola—and his very last meeting before his first stroke in December 2005 was with the Jewish People Policy Institute* to discuss what could be done to strengthen Jewish numbers within Israel.[166]

He was going to preserve Israel as a Jewish state. His arguments in favor of the roadmap were very much connected to ending occupation of Palestinians, not just because it was wrong but because it would preserve the Jewish character of Israel: "Israel has no interest in governing the Palestinians. The Palestinians must govern themselves in their own country. In the long-run, a democratic Palestinian country at peace with Israel will promote the safety and integrity of Israel as a Jewish nation."[167]

Perhaps the most telling Sharon statement about what was at stake in committing to disengagement came from a speech he prepared for the annual event commemorating David Ben-Gurion at Sde Boker, Ben-Gurion's kibbutz. Because Sharon was ill, Ehud Olmert, then the deputy prime minister, read the speech on his behalf. In it, Sharon quoted Ben-Gurion saying, "Let us assume we can conquer the whole of Eretz Israel by force of arms. I'm sure we can. But then what? We will be a single state. But the state will want to be democratic . . . and we will be a minority. . . . When the choice before us was the whole of Eretz Israel but no Jewish state or no Jewish state but not the whole of Eretz Israel, we chose a Jewish state." After quoting

---

* Dennis experienced Sharon's interest in the demographic trends very directly. Dennis was the chairman of the board of the Jewish People Policy Institute at that time, and in the presentation of the annual assessment of Israel and the Jewish people to the cabinet, Sharon asked detailed questions about demographic trends.

this, Sharon then added, "In the near future, leaders of Israel will need to gather their inner strength, all their Zionist faith, in order to determine our destiny with the same remarkable fusion of vision and realism."[168]

Vision and realism defined Sharon. He would come under great attack from the settlers and within Likud. He was never one to back off from a fight, especially one he felt had to be fought and won. But he was no fool; given the domestic political challenges he faced, he sought commitments from the United States that he could use to bolster his arguments and to show that Israel was gaining something even as it withdrew unilaterally from Gaza and four settlements in the West Bank. In fact, policy assurances from the United States became more important because Sharon was getting nothing from the Palestinians in return. In other words, the United States, and not the Palestinian Authority, would be providing compensation, in the form of the Bush-Sharon exchange of letters.

The Bush letter to Sharon dated April 14, 2004, constituted, in Sharon's mind, one of his greatest diplomatic achievements.[169] In it, the United States made clear that the June 4, 1967, lines could not define Israel's final borders, that Palestinian refugees should return to their state and not Israel,* and that Israel should retain the settlement blocs in the West Bank in any peace agreement.[170]

In the Knesset debate on disengagement, Sharon used the Bush assurances, declaring, "Not since the State of Israel was created has there been such strong and broad political support as there is in the President's letter. The letter is an integral part of the disengagement plan. The President of the United States expresses his overwhelming support for the plan. He sees it as a historic step."[171] So, of course, did Sharon.

While he would win the vote within the cabinet and then the Knesset, he would lose the referendum held within the Likud party on the disengagement plan. Yet he proceeded, in part because he understood that the

---

* Euphemistic language was used to refer to the final borders and settlements, with the former being identified as the armistice lines of 1949 and the latter being called the "major population centers" in the West Bank. The Bush letter stated that 1949 armistice lines could not be a stable basis for peace and Israel would retain the major population centers in any peace agreement.

Bush commitments were conditioned on implementing the plan, but also because he said he would do it. On May 23, 2004, speaking at a memorial event at Latrun, he told his old comrades: "You know that when I fight for something that's right, I persevere. That is what I intend to do with the disengagement. It is vital for Israel, and I am going to make it happen."[172]

Still, he did not underestimate the difficulty of proceeding. He knew he was asking those whom he had sent to live in the settlements to leave the lives they had built. In the debate in the Knesset before the vote, Sharon declared, "This is a fateful time for Israel." He would go on to describe both the emotional hardship involved in his decision and why he felt it was necessary to act anyway:

> For me, this decision is unbearably difficult. During my years as a fighter and commander, as a politician, Member of Knesset, as a minister in Israel's governments and as prime minister, I have never faced so difficult a decision. I know the implications and impact of the Knesset's decision on the lives of thousands of Israelis who have lived in the Gaza Strip for many years, who were sent there on behalf of the governments of Israel, and who built homes there, planted trees and grew flowers, and who gave birth to sons and daughters, who have not known any other home. I am well aware of the fact that I sent them and took part in this enterprise, and many of these people are my personal friends. I am well aware of their pain, rage, and despair. However, as much as I understand everything they are going through during these days and everything they will face as a result of the necessary decision to be made in the Knesset today, I also believe in the necessity of taking the step of disengagement in these areas, with all the pain it entails, and I am determined to complete this mission. I am firmly convinced and truly believe that this disengagement will strengthen Israel's hold over territory which is essential to our existence.[173]

Dubi Weisglass wrote that Sharon came to the conclusion that the depth of opposition to settlements internationally, including from the Bush administration, meant that the settlements were a "finished battle," and he had to focus on preserving what Israel must have in terms of settlement blocs.[174]

Sharon met with the Yesha Council members—the umbrella organization of the settlers—and told them, "There was a dream. What we've accomplished is ours, but what we didn't, we won't. I told you at the time when it was possible—go. Bring hundreds of thousands of Israelis to the West Bank [outside the blocs]. It didn't happen. Had this happened, maybe things would be different now. But now it's over. If you don't stand in my way, I will be able to save the large blocs. If you help me, we will succeed. If you continue your sabotage, we'll lose this too."[175]

Sharon was saving what must be saved. Even if the settlers would not give up the dream, even if Sharon would say that some had a "messianic complex," he would not let them prevent him from carrying out the disengagement.* Much like with the Sinai in 1982, he mobilized a massive police and military presence to prevent the settlers from frustrating the withdrawal. The settlers failed to do so. As always, Sharon knew how to carry out an operation—and once again he succeeded.

Few leaders make the transition that Sharon did. It is not hard to explain the factors that led him to take the leap and become the leader who dismantled settlements and withdrew from territory that he had once been responsible for settling. Sharon did not suffer from a messianic complex; he was a realist. He would do what had to be done, no matter the opposition and sometimes because of it. All the factors that led to his belief that he must act to preserve what was important for Israel—American pressure and assurances, the perception of Palestinian irresponsibility, concern about potential problems within the military, worries about demographic trends, the need to be acting and not reacting, the importance of not being cornered—also reinforced his view that he was the only one who could do it.

Yes, making the decision and acting on it fit his self-image. But it also reflected his view of leadership and what is required of leaders. Leaders assume responsibility. They don't shirk it. They don't fear it. Finding Begin once murmuring about the recent losses in Lebanon, Sharon told him,

---

* In his Knesset speech on the vote, he spoke of some settlers having "developed a messianic complex. . . . You ought to remember that before you were born or when you were still small children, there were other days when men endangered their lives day and night and worked and sacrificed, without an iota of any messianic complex."

"Menachem, a leader's role is to make decisions, and good ones, not to cry and complain."[176] Leaders had to be prepared to go it alone. Indeed, by definition, they must brace themselves for those moments and have the courage to face them. There was, in Sharon's words, the "solitude of the leader" and an understanding that others might fear that moment.* He never did.

In many ways, Sharon saw leadership as his calling. He had been saved at Latrun for a reason. He spent a career striving to get to the point where he would make the fateful choices for Israel. He played rough; he bulldozed opposition and former supporters. But he would never fail the test of being up to the challenge and getting the job done. Others might not have had it in them to make big decisions, but for him that simply meant they were not cut out to be leaders. He was. In carrying out disengagement in Gaza, and planning for more in the West Bank, he was securing Israel's future. Much like Yitzhak Rabin, he would not be there to finish what he started. Eival Gilady, the military man responsible for developing Sharon's plan for disengagement in the West Bank, put it best: "He went to sleep two years too soon."**

---

* In a letter to Uri Dan on Dan's seventieth birthday, Sharon wrote, "More than anything else, I remember your presence at my side in the moments that preceded fateful decisions, moments that belong to the 'solitude of the leader.'"

** His critics would say he left a vacuum in Gaza and Hamas filled it, discrediting unilateral Israeli moves. Perhaps, but few in Israel other than the settlers wanted to remain in Gaza—and it is clear that no one is arguing for reoccupying the strip today. As for Sharon, he was not prepared to condition Israel's withdrawal on Palestinians assuming responsibility because he believed they never would. Knowing that, the Bush administration should have stepped in and brokered a handover of security responsibilities to the Palestinian Authority in advance of the Israeli withdrawal. That would have also shown that it was negotiations and Mahmoud Abbas and the Palestinian Authority, not Hamas violence, that produced the Israeli withdrawal. The American role needed to be more than only providing assurances to Sharon; it needed to take advantage of his determination to withdraw to push the Palestinians to develop plans and, with US help, to implement them, securing and governing Gaza following the departure of Israel's settlers and soldiers. Sharon did his part, no doubt also believing that his reputation for toughness would be sufficient to deter threats from Gaza after Israel's withdrawal. If nothing else, it is a reminder that the United States needs to play a pivotal role when Israel acts unilaterally—and the Bush administration, regrettably, failed to do so in this case.

CHAPTER 5

ISRAEL'S FATEFUL CHOICE

I n its relatively short history, Israel has faced critical moments calling for courageous decisions in war and peace. Until now, it has had leaders who were able and willing to rise to the moment. Those leaders did not retreat in the face of daunting challenges; they did not shy away from or try to avoid the decisions that they believed had to be made. High stakes did not paralyze them, even though they knew well that Israel's margin of error was small.

They understood what it took to produce a Jewish state, and they accepted their charge to preserve it. Ariel Sharon believed that he was the last of the generation of founders who would act strategically. He feared his successors were too politically driven and not made of the stuff to make big decisions. That alone was a motivator for him to make the choice on withdrawing from Gaza and deciding to form a new party to be able to withdraw from a significant part of the West Bank.

But he could not complete his mission. His perception of his successors—based on an assumption that their priorities would always be their political needs and not the needs of the state—reflected how little he thought of those who might follow him. It was almost as if he was convinced that they were not even capable of recognizing those moments when historic choices needed to be made. Time will tell whether he was right.

Presently, the Israeli governing coalition does not act like it has to make a big decision anytime soon on Israel's position in the West Bank. In other words, Israel's leaders don't see a looming problem and the imperative of dealing with it. Are they right?

In the Obama administration, the president and his secretary of state, John Kerry, repeatedly warned that the status quo, with Israel occupying Palestinians, was not sustainable. They were not the first to say this. Nearly every US administration since the 1967 war has made this point, starting with the Nixon administration telling Israeli leaders that the situation was destabilizing and could not last. Initially, the argument was that the Arabs, sooner or later, would make the Israelis pay. But since the 1973 war, they have not. Palestinians, on the other hand, sought to do so with two intifadas. Notwithstanding the high price they paid, especially in the second one, Palestinians have responded with rejection and violence to Israeli attempts to find a political solution or take an initiative. As a result, most Israelis find the status quo of occupying Palestinians in the West Bank quite sustainable.

True, the occupation alienates European elites, and hostility is growing on American campuses and among opinion makers. Still, Israel is not suffering isolation, and its economy, as the start-up nation, is the envy of many internationally. Countries from France to China will vote against Israel in international forums but at the same time are anxious to do business with it. Its technology and innovation in so many fields make Israel an attractive place for investment and a good partner on artificial intelligence, cyber, robotics, medicine, agriculture, water development and usage, and many areas of security and arms development.

Diplomatic costs of occupation at this point remain manageable, and Prime Minister Benjamin Netanyahu rightly claims that Israel is not isolated and is succeeding in creating ties and acceptance throughout the globe as never before.* So, the status quo of occupation is sustainable, but it comes at a cost: the erosion of Israel's liberal values and the rule of law, as separate standards for Israelis and Palestinians become more commonplace.

The costs may be intangible, but that does not make them any less real. There is another, more profound, danger: Israel runs the risk of losing its very identity as a Jewish and democratic state, the essence of the Zionist mission.

---

* Under Netanyahu's leadership, Israel has engaged in diplomatic and economic outreach to key Asian, African, and even Arab states.

Its current path leads in only one direction: a binational, Arab-Jewish state. The analysis of Israel's leading demographers make clear that, should Israel continue to occupy the entirety of the West Bank, it will change the demographic balance between Jews and Arabs, with the Jewish majority shrinking to the point where Israel will become one state with two peoples. In such a circumstance, it will have to choose between one law applying to all or two laws and two different standards for two peoples. Therein lies the threat to Israel's character and identity.

For us, the authors, the answer is two states for two peoples. Israel is not, however, headed in that direction. What explains Israel's position of simply drifting toward a reality that will alter its very character and transform it from being the state of the Jewish people with little debate?

For most Israelis, the demographic trends and the danger they pose for the character of the state remain an abstraction. However, the perception of Palestinian hostility, on the one hand, and terrible upheaval in the region, on the other, are very real and not abstract and tend to dominate current thinking. Reality will always trump abstractions and, when looking at the Palestinians, the clear majority of Israelis perceive Hamas as committed to terror against Israel. They also see Mahmoud Abbas and the Palestinian Authority as determined to try to delegitimize the state of Israel. These perceptions have a basis: Hamas, after all, makes no bones about its rejection of Israel's right to exist and portrays violence against Israel as fully legitimate. For his part, Abbas may be against violence, but his periodic speeches denying the historic Jewish connections to the land and to Jerusalem—and even asserting the Holocaust was caused at least in part by Jewish behavior—reflect long-standing anti-Semitic tropes and seemingly challenge the fundamental legitimacy of Israel.

Israelis have experienced terror, and they have seen how their unilateral withdrawals from south Lebanon in 2000 and Gaza in 2005 produced not calm, not security, not peace, but violence. Put simply, Israelis see they gave up land and got rockets in return. Given the widespread conflicts in the region now, the natural tendency of most Israelis is to think about security threats. Indeed, the upheaval in the region (and division and rejection among the Palestinians) makes it hard to focus on Israel's direction or contemplate unilateral Israeli actions designed to preserve a two-state outcome and Israel's identity as a Jewish-democratic state. With radical Islamists, Sunni and Shia, still rejecting Israel's existence, and with a horrific war next door in Syria—marked by few limits, a conscious scorched-earth policy of killing civilians, and an expanding Iranian and Shia militia presence—it is understandable that the Israeli public feels longer-term decisions about Israel's future should wait. Nothing should be done, in their eyes, to alter the current position that the Jordan River is Israel's security border to the east, which Palestinian statehood could call into question.

Moreover, Palestinian statehood seems fanciful even to envision at this point, given the division between the Palestinian Authority (PA) in the West Bank and Hamas's control of Gaza. Even if the Palestinians could agree to such a state, it could not be implemented. And, if a Palestinian state came into being in the foreseeable future, it would almost certainly be a failed state, making the prospects for Israel of having al-Qaeda or ISIS-type groups on its border quite high.

Why risk it seems to be the default position of many in the Israeli public, particularly when the current reality seems sustainable and not especially costly. It is not a surprising or unreasonable position. But that is not the whole explanation. The more fundamental explanation may be that Israel's governing coalition has been dominated by a constituency—very much a settler constituency—that denies there is even a problem or a danger of becoming a binational state. Their arguments are twofold. First, they present alternative demographic numbers and thus claim the so-called demographic fears are wrong. Second, they maintain that Israel can grant autonomy to the Palestinians so they need not be Israeli citizens or have the rights of statehood. Given the weight of these arguments among the right wing in Israel, they need to be addressed and not simply dismissed.

WHAT ARE THE DEMOGRAPHIC FACTS AND THEIR IMPLICATIONS?

For the last decade, one person has stood out among all others in challenging the analysis of those who say that demographic trends require Israel to separate from the Palestinians. Yoram Ettinger, a former member of the

Israeli Foreign Ministry, has been the leading voice in seeking to debunk the demographic argument. He has supported analytical work—though not by demographers—to prove that the Jewish majority is not threatened by demographic trends.* In his words, "The Jewish state is not facing a potential Arab demographic time bomb. In fact, Israel benefits from a robust Jewish demographic tailwind."[1]

Ettinger's analysis is based on several key assertions. First, the Palestinian census numbers of three million in the West Bank are exaggerated, counting Palestinians who live abroad. Second, Israeli demographers who believe in the demographic time bomb make the mistake of double counting the Palestinians who live in East Jerusalem and those who marry Israelis—counting them in the Palestinian Authority and also as part of Israel's population. Third, Palestinian birth rates have declined and Israeli birth rates have grown, making the current population growth very similar. And, fourth, Israel's population has the potential for much greater growth given Jewish immigration (aliyah). As Ettinger observes, Jewish immigration "has persisted since 1882, featuring waves every 20 years. . . . The huge potential of Aliyah—from France, Germany, additional European countries, Russia, Ukraine and Argentina—awaits a pro-active Aliyah policy, which has not been undertaken since the end of Prime Minister Shamir's administration in 1992."[2]

Ettinger sees net migration out of the West Bank and he does not count the two million Palestinians in Gaza in the demographic balance. As a result, he rejects talk of near parity in numbers today, which depends on including the Palestinians in Gaza. We agree with Ettinger on Gaza. Israel withdrew all its settlers and soldiers in 2005. It is simply wrong to say that because Israel imposed a blockade on Gaza, it still occupies the strip. Its blockade of Gaza was adopted only in 2007 after continuing attacks by Hamas and then Hamas's seizure of power from the PA. Absent the hostility, and the building of rockets and tunnels for the purpose of

---

* There are voices on the right that echo his work, such as Caroline Glick, but it is Ettinger who is the intellectual and political spearhead of the efforts to counter the demographic-threat narrative. He has organized groups such as the American-Israel Demographic Research Group to challenge what he calls the fallacy of the Palestinian demographic threat.

attacking Israel, there would be no Israeli quarantine of Gaza. As such, with Israel out of Gaza, it is wrong to count the Gazans in the Israeli-Palestinian population mix.

Since Ettinger deducts 1.1 million from the Palestine census bureau's population numbers, he comes to the conclusion that the total number of Palestinians living in the territories (meaning only the West Bank) is roughly 1.9 million. By contrast,* the Israeli Civil Administration, which manages contact with the Palestinian Authority in the West Bank, uses the three million figure when reporting to the Israeli government and Knesset.[3] The net result is that Ettinger adds the 1.9 million Palestinians in the West Bank to the 1.8 million Arabs living in Israel and says that the 3.7 million Arabs amount to only 35 percent of the population in Israel and the West Bank. For him, the 65/35 split preserves Israel's Jewish character, and his belief on fertility rates and aliyah means that the Jewish majority won't decline.

Two of Israel's most well-known and respected demographers, Arnon Sofaer and Sergio DellaPergola, strongly dispute Ettinger's methodology and numbers. Unlike Ettinger, both are trained demographers. They both believe that Ettinger, whose work is widely cited by the right wing in Israel, is guided by purely political considerations. In Sofaer's words, "The settlers believe this information so they can continue thinking the situation is great."[4]

They point out that, methodologically, Ettinger excludes the Palestinians who study or live abroad but continues to count the Israelis who are not currently living in Israel. Similarly, they say he cites only the Palestinian data that validates his numbers but discredits that which does not—pointing to his use of data from the Palestinian Ministry of Health but not the Palestinian Central Bureau of Statistics.**

DellaPergola goes further and highlights that his own analysis is not based on double counting the Palestinians in East Jerusalem and the West

---

* Ettinger arrives at the 1.1 million deduction by saying 330,000 Palestinians in East Jerusalem are double counted; one hundred thousand Palestinians married to Israelis are also double counted; and that six hundred thousand Palestinians are living outside or have left, and they have had one hundred thousand newborns outside of the West Bank.

** Ettinger argues the former does not count overseas births and the latter does.

Bank. Additionally, he says that Ettinger is wrong on the numbers of Palestinians who have emigrated and live abroad, asserting that the discrepancy "is relatively negligible compared to what Ettinger says." Similarly, he dismisses Ettinger's claims on the fertility rates, declaring that he is "delusional" if he thinks the Palestinians are not growing at a faster pace than Israelis and that this is "the primary driving factor in demographics." In fact, DellaPergola's analysis* continues to show a significant disparity between Arab and Jewish birth rates.[5] Lastly, he questions Ettinger's motives by saying that "since [Ettinger] receives money to say that Israel should never leave the territories, he tries to deny these facts, claiming that in the future the birthrate will change. That's possible. But in the present, it is what it is. He's peddling some imaginary future in an utterly unprofessional way, because he never took a course in demographics."[6]

While the DellaPergola critique is harsh, the actual gap between his and Ettinger's current numbers is not as wide as one might think. DellaPergola, too, thinks the Palestinian census affixing a population of three million to the West Bank is inflated. Unlike Ettinger, his assessment of the East Jerusalem and overseas numbers is such that he comes up with a 2.5 million figure for the Palestinian population in the West Bank alone, six hundred thousand more than Ettinger. Obviously a difference, but in practical terms what it means is that DellaPergola believes that the percentage of Jews to Arabs in Israel and the West Bank is roughly 61/39 today, which is not dramatically different from Ettinger's 65/35. Their real point of difference is what will happen over time, given Ettinger's claim that the fertility rates are now essentially the same, meaning that Israel will keep at least a 65/35 majority of Jews to Arabs, even if they hold on to all of the West Bank and absorb the Arabs in it. DellaPergola charts a very different future,** where

---

* Unlike Ettinger, who claims that the Jewish birth rate actually exceeded the Arab one for the first time in 2016 (at 3.16 to 3.11), DellaPergola says the real numbers are different. He says that Jewish women in Israel have a birth rate of 3, while Israeli Arab women stand at 3.4 and Palestinians in the West Bank at 4.1.

** One indication of the trend lines is that in 1986 the split was 63/37, counting the Palestinians in Gaza in the totals; today, Gaza's population is not included in Ettinger's 65/35 numbers or DellaPergola's 61/39.

what is close to a 6:4 ratio today will move toward parity in the next twenty to twenty-five years.[7]

Uzi Rebhun, a demographer at the Hebrew University and the Jewish People Policy Institute in Jerusalem, suggests there are legitimate questions about Ettinger's projections, but also says that Israeli policy makers should ask themselves what it means for Israel's future if the state is 35 to 40 percent Arab. What, he asks, is the effect on Jewish culture and identity within Israel if the Arab percentage of the population is that great? Without absorbing the Palestinians of the West Bank, he points out, the Arabs in Israel represent 20 percent of Israel's population. This is a number generally consistent with what the percentage of Arabs has been in Israel since the founding of the state. It is a distinctive minority, but one whose numbers do not alter Israel's identity or culture. If, however, their numbers were to nearly double, this would inevitably affect the character of the country.[8]

From this standpoint, one need not even fundamentally challenge Ettinger's current numbers to be worried about the demographic path Israel is on. It is not that Jews in Israel are about to become a minority, which is the argument that many make when they include Gaza in the total. The reality is that when Arabs approach 40 percent of Israel's population, they are less a minority and more a very significant separate national identity within the state. It is hard not to see Israel in binational terms if the Arabs approach or exceed these numbers. Here it is worth noting that when Palestinians under the age of thirty are polled in the West Bank, an increasing number say they prefer the Israelis to remain where they are and simply give them the right to vote.[9] In other words, Palestinians under the age of thirty who favor one state seek full rights of Israeli citizenship. But with some exceptions, the right wing in Israel does not want to grant them that status. So what do right-wing leaders propose?

THE RIGHT WING'S ANSWER FOR THE PALESTINIANS

The right wing in Israel has long opposed Palestinian statehood. Yitzhak Rabin and Ariel Sharon, too, rejected the idea of an independent Palestinian state for a long time, but, given their reading of the choices and the stakes, they changed their minds. There has been no such change of attitude (or heart) on the part of the right wing in Israel. For Rabin and Sharon, the demographic issue became paramount, even as they also believed that the Palestinian national identity would have to gain political expression at some point. For those on the right, the demographic issue has either been denied, as in Ettinger's case, or dismissed as needing to take a back seat to Israel's survival.

Naftali Bennett, a leader of the political right in Israel, rejects a Palestinian state as too threatening to Israel's existence. In his "stability plan," he recognizes that something must be done with the Palestinians in the West Bank, even if he basically accepts Ettinger's demographic numbers.[10] He has no interest in absorbing the vast majority of Palestinians into Israel. Instead, he speaks about providing "autonomy on steroids" for the 96 percent of Palestinians who live in Areas A and B of the West Bank, roughly 40 percent of the territory. The remaining 60 percent of the West Bank—in which about 10 percent of the Palestinian population resides—would, in Bennett's scheme, be annexed by Israel.* He does not want to be governing the vast majority of Palestinians, declaring, "I have no desire to occupy, govern and control the 2 million Arabs that live in Judea and Samaria. I remember what it was like during the First Intifada, and I don't want to control their education, their sewage system and their quality of life."[11]

So, for Bennett, Palestinians will govern themselves with few restrictions in Areas A and B in the West Bank, while Israel will simply absorb the rest of Judea and Samaria (Area C) and the smaller number of Palestinians residing there. By doing this, Bennett believes it is possible to manage the dilemma of not accepting Palestinian statehood, prevent the emergence of a two-tier legal system (one for Israelis and one for Palestinians) within Israel, and avoid any real demographic issues. As he puts it: "Since within the State of Israel you cannot have two levels of people, those Palestinians living in

---

* The interim agreement of 1995 created three areas in the West Bank: Area A, today 18.2 percent of the West Bank, where Palestinians have civil and security responsibility; Area B, today 21.7 percent, where Palestinians have responsibility for civil affairs and day-to-day law and order, while Israel retains overall security responsibility; and Area C, 60.1 percent today, in which Israel has responsibility for everything, civil and security.

Area C—approximately 80,000 people—will be offered full Israeli citizenship, including voting rights." Israel, a country of more than eight million people, cannot, he argues, be endangered demographically by granting citizenship to eighty thousand people. For Bennett, these Palestinians can be "Israeli citizens, Israeli residents or Palestinian citizens."[12]

However, there is a problem with Bennett's population numbers. According to official Israeli data, the number of Palestinians living in Area C is actually 130,000. Moreover, recent research indicates that the number might actually be as high as two hundred thousand Palestinians living in the area that Bennett wants to absorb.[13] Perhaps Bennett would still argue that this number is manageable. And yet, it is probably approaching a point where even he would acknowledge there is a problem.

To be fair, Bennett does not claim that his plan is perfect, just that it is the best possible solution. Until his death in January 2019, Moshe Arens took a different approach. Arens, a more traditional Likudnik, reflected the liberal tradition of Menachem Begin on civil and legal rights. Unlike Bennett, he did not believe that Israel could annex 60 percent of the territory and pretend that the Palestinians would be satisfied with autonomy or self-government in just 40 percent of the West Bank. He also discounted the Jordan option for the Palestinians—in which Palestinians in the West Bank become citizens of Jordan—because "the Jordanians won't hear of it."* His answer for Israel, and for the international critics who charge Israel with occupying Palestinians in the West Bank and denying them rights, was to absorb the Palestinians and give them full rights as citizens in Israel.

For Arens, Israeli sovereignty in the entirety of the West Bank is needed for security reasons, and he argued that the absorption of the Palestinian population would not dilute Israel's democracy. He, too, essentially accepted the Ettinger demographic numbers and believed that Israel could tolerate a Palestinian population that might be in the mid–30 percent range. Unlike Ettinger, however, he acknowledged that this result would create a "situation considerably more difficult" for Israel. In fact, he wrote, annexing the area

---

* Even if they were open to it, what would it mean? Would Jordan be responsible for Palestinian security in the West Bank? Would they manage their economy and exports and imports? What services would they provide?

and its population would "pose a serious challenge to Israeli society," but for him all the alternatives posed an even greater problem.[14]

Others on the right who are more identified with the settler movement, such as Dani Dayan, former head of the Yesha Council and currently Israel's consul general in New York, and Oded Revivi, the mayor of Efrat, basically argue for focusing on coexistence and no longer addressing political issues such as statehood and borders. Dayan argues for dramatically improving the quality of life for Palestinians in the West Bank: doing away with "restrictions on movement," investing heavily in local infrastructure, and removing the barriers that "currently impede Palestinian imports and exports."[15] For his part, Revivi says that his Palestinian neighbors, who live next to Efrat, get along well with those in his municipality. Since the political issues can't be resolved now, and since there is "both an exposed and hidden face" to the conflict, it is better, he says, "to concentrate on strengthening co-existence" through an "authentic discourse with our neighbors." That can lead somewhere, he argues, while political negotiations cannot.[16]

There is, of course, merit to what both Dayan and Revivi propose. There should be more emphasis on coexistence, something long absent from the internal Palestinian discourse. The Palestinians' fear that anything that normalizes relations with the Israelis also normalizes the occupation may be understandable, but their active opposition to any act or move that might promote coexistence with Israelis also makes the Israeli public fundamentally doubt Palestinian purposes. Yes, Palestinians need to know that normalization does not take place in a vacuum, completely removed from the political issues that divide the two sides. And, yes, Israelis need to see that anti-normalization on the Palestinian side is not a strategic goal designed always to put Israel in the docket and delegitimize it.

From that standpoint, both Israelis and Palestinians actually require a believable political process that addresses their mutual concerns. Regrettably, there is no such process and has not been one at least since the Kerry effort that ended in the spring of 2014. The proposals from Bennett, Dayan, and Revivi don't address that reality, reflecting their belief that no process can address the political differences between the two sides and the only answer is to create their preferred outcome. However, since that outcome rejects

Palestinian statehood, Palestinians are deeply suspicious of their suggestions. That is not the only reason for them to be suspicious. The right-wingers' calls for autonomy on steroids or easing the restrictions Palestinians face in traveling or doing business would be far more credible to the Palestinians if Bennett, and others on the right were actually promoting a relaxation of controls on Palestinian day-to-day life or steps that would improve their economy now. All too often, they have done the opposite.

When former defense minister Avigdor Lieberman accepted the Israel Defense Forces (IDF) recommendation that, given acute housing shortages for Palestinians, the walled area immediately adjacent to the West Bank city of Qalkilya should be open for the construction of Palestinian housing, Bennett and others opposed and blocked it. Why? It is in Area C. The new city of Rawabi—designed to promote the living and livelihood of a Palestinian middle class—took far longer to develop than it should have because the Israeli government would not approve either a water line or a road to it, because they would have to go through a narrow strip of Area C. Again, Bennett's party led the opposition.*

One could argue that Bennett opposed each of these moves because they touched Area C, the 60 percent of the West Bank that he wants to annex. But if that is the real story, why is it that Bennett and others on Israel's political right, who claim to favor much greater autonomy, are doing nothing to correct or alleviate the impediments that Israel imposes on the functioning of the Palestinian economy—impediments that Dayan acknowledges? Consider, for example, an illustrative list of impediments that Bennett and his cohort could address and don't: Back-to-back arrangements require the off-loading and then onloading of trucks carrying goods into and out of the West Bank, adding significant time and cost to doing business.** Palestinian goods and materials intended for import or export routinely languish in Israeli ports, raising not just the cost but introducing unpredictability into

---

*   Even now, the city could use more water and more than a one-lane road into it, especially because it is already the second-largest employer outside of the Palestinian Authority in the West Bank and seeks to implement its full plan for twenty-two neighborhoods.

** Yes, such restrictions are security driven, but there are alternative technological means for addressing the Israeli security concerns.

any commercial arrangement. Restrictions remain on what Palestinians can export in general, and trade is largely precluded between the West Bank and Gaza. Israel must approve Palestinian development of industrial zones, and the approvals are extremely difficult to get. Even when given, implementation faces hurdles and delays. Those who seek to invest in the West Bank from the outside face excessive Israeli paperwork, estimated by one expatriate Palestinian businessman as three times what is required for doing business elsewhere in the region. Similarly, to get a line of credit approved for investing in the territories, it takes three weeks when dealing with the Israelis, whereas it takes one week elsewhere. After 2007, Israel imposed new limitations on Palestinian banks, requiring higher levels of cash on hand, which has forced the banks, in the words of one Palestinian banker, to incur the "costs of idle cash" that runs into "tens of millions per year."[17]

Bennett may speak of autonomy on steroids, but Palestinians ask, Wasn't that the theory behind the creation of the Palestinian Authority? Wasn't it created to govern the Palestinians through a transition period? Wasn't Israel to be responsible for overall security, with Palestinians governing everything else? What Palestinians see instead is Israeli control over most aspects of their lives, including areas as simple as daily travel. To be sure, Palestinian terror and the second intifada produced wider Israeli security controls and intrusion. But it is hard to escape the conclusion that many of the continuing economic controls tend to be driven more by habit and inertia than security needs. Most Palestinians would welcome a genuine easing of Israeli controls on commerce and travel, but at this point they are deeply skeptical that any such plans will be translated into reality.*

Moreover, because Bennett's plan excludes Area C, it cuts off an area vital to Palestinian economic development. How real could Palestinian autonomy be if the area crucial for its economic development—not to mention space needed for industry, agriculture, exploiting the minerals of the Dead Sea, housing, and tourism—is cut off from the Palestinian entity? To put this in perspective, the World Bank's assessment in September 2016 was that

---

* Plans for creating "sterile" trucks that could be inspected with scanners were proposed and accepted in the 1990s to replace the back-to-back arrangements, but still have been implemented only in a very limited way.

without any other changes, Palestinians' GDP would increase by 35 percent if they had access to Area C.[18] The operative word here is access, not control.

If nothing else, this raises questions about how real the proposals of Bennett or Dayan on autonomy might be. Even if they are real and the intent is genuine, they ignore that Palestinians actually do have a national identity. What Arens, Bennett, Dayan, Revivi, and others on the right all have in common is the belief that at some point Palestinians will simply learn to accept that they will not have a state or a separate political identity. Similarly, they think that the international community is willing to forget a cause that so many have championed.

The terrible thing is that their assumption might be right if Israel were transformed into a single state with all citizens having equal rights, including voting rights. The postnationalism of European elites might well lead to an embrace of such an outcome. But with the exception of Arens, that is not what those in the right wing have in mind. It is certainly not what we have in mind.

We see a binational state as a prescription for endless conflict. In the Middle East, wherever there is more than one national, sectarian, or tribal identity, one sees a state in conflict. Israelis and Palestinians have separate national identities. It is as if the Israeli right thinks that the Palestinians and the world will accept that they have lost and, with the right economic inducements, the conflict will end.

Unfortunately, for the Palestinians, their national movement has been far better at rejection than at acceptance of reality. Had they been open to settling the conflict—if their leaders had been able to say yes to the Clinton parameters in 2000, Ehud Olmert's plan in 2008, or Barack Obama's proposal in 2014—they could have had a state.

Going back to the Carter administration, the Palestinians missed what the autonomy talks then might have produced. At the time, the Israeli critics of autonomy, including in the Labor Party, said it was a slippery slope to a Palestinian state. In addition, what is often forgotten is that the Israelis, in the autonomy talks with the Egyptians after the assassination of Anwar Sadat, were willing to discuss giving the Interim Self-Governing Authority (ISGA) veto rights over new uses of land. If agreed, the ISGA could have blocked new settlements. Had the Palestinians not rejected the autonomy talks, the landscape of the West Bank might well look very different today, not to mention that a Palestinian state would likely have come into existence long ago.*

But the Palestinians have been the masters of saying no. Resistance and defiance have been the watchwords of the Palestinian national movement. It is easy for us to say what it has cost the Palestinians, but, in their narrative, rejection has preserved the purity of the cause. It has also denied them their rights or the fulfillment of their national aspirations, while preserving their status as victims. Despite the obvious costs to them, Palestinians have not created a new narrative or an explanation for their predicament. On the contrary, they don't admit to missed opportunities or assume any responsibility for their current reality. To imagine that now they will simply submit—and accept that they have lost, Israel will control all the territory, and they can have a theoretical autonomy on steroids—is an illusion.

In saying this, we are not defending the Palestinian position or even arguing that a two-state outcome can be negotiated anytime soon. It cannot, especially with Hamas in control of Gaza. Moreover, succession to Mahmoud Abbas will make the Palestinians even less capable of compromising with the Israelis in any way. Competition for leadership will focus on who can be more extreme or pure in representing the Palestinian cause. Neither a negotiated outcome nor an imposed approach by the Israelis is likely.

Instead, what is most likely is continued drift, with Israel cementing itself more deeply in the West Bank, making the increasing proximity of the settlers and Palestinians hard to untangle. It will feed the growing Palestinian call for one state with equal rights—a throwback to the PLO's call for a secular, democratic state in place of Israel. That, too, is the great irony. The right wing in Israel is basically adopting a position that Palestinians who reject Israel believe in: one state. Of course, Bennett and his compatriots have a different view of the meaning of one state, but their path is based on

---

* After the assassination of Sadat, with the Israeli withdrawal from the Sinai to be completed in several months, Begin and others worried that once Egypt got its land back, it would distance itself from Israel. By breathing life into the autonomy talks, the hope was that Egypt would retain a stake in preserving its relations with Israel.

the illusion that the Palestinians and the international community will accept an outcome in which Palestinians have neither national rights nor equal rights in a binational state. Even in the United States, what happens post-Trump when the Palestinians create the mantra of one person, one vote? Will a post-Trump America dismiss this call? For sure, Democrats, already losing their historic identification with Israel as the sole embodiment of liberal values in the Middle East, will be more open to it. But will Republicans be so quick to dismiss such a mantra?

None of this is inevitable, but the drift toward a future binational reality has to stop. Ya'acov Amidror, Netanyahu's former national security advisor, criticizes the left in Israel for ignoring the real security challenges posed by possible peace with the Palestinians, but he also calls out the right for offering no answer to the demographic drift that threatens the character of the state.[19] He is right to do so. Of course, no one can say for sure when a tipping point will be reached and when separating from the Palestinians no longer remains a viable option. Today, 77 percent of all the settlers in the West Bank live in the blocs—a number that grows to 85 percent if one counts the Jewish neighborhoods in East Jerusalem—so the vast majority are living in areas that would remain a part of Israel in any conceivable peace deal. But with over one hundred thousand settlers living outside the blocs and Prime Minister Netanyahu making clear that in any peace agreement settlers would not be evacuated, the challenges of separation will be difficult and complex. The passage of time and the annual addition of three thousand to four thousand settlers outside the blocs will compound the difficulty. That said, a determined policy to separate can still be implemented. As the clock ticks, however, separation will become a more difficult decision to make and carry out, affecting a larger number of Israelis even more rooted in the territory outside the settlement blocs.

That is why we believe a big decision is needed—a decision that preserves the ability to separate from the Palestinians. Complete separation will be difficult and take time, especially given Palestinian dependency on the Israeli economy for work and goods, but separation is essential if Israel is to retain its character. Several steps will be necessary to make separation possible, all of which will be very difficult in light of the political realities that define Israel today.

- An end to settlement construction to the east of the security barrier. (Because the boundaries of existing settlement blocs are not clearly defined or agreed with the Palestinians, it is better to declare that settlement construction will cease east of the barrier, or on about 92 percent of the West Bank.)
- An end to construction in the Arab neighborhoods in East Jerusalem. (This is needed to preserve separation within Jerusalem.)
- Adoption of legislation to offer financial incentives to those settlers who live east of the barrier and who would move back to the settlement blocs or to within green-line Israel. (Estimates vary, but polling suggests that roughly one-third of the settlers outside the blocs are likely to accept financial incentives or compensation to leave their homes. Preparing a plan now to absorb those settlers is practically necessary and would demonstrate the commitment to separation.)
- A declaration that there will be no Israeli sovereignty to the east of the barrier, even as Israeli security needs must be addressed. Such a declaration would make clear this is Palestinian territory but Israeli security requirements must be met. (An Israeli long-term lease of a narrow strip along the Jordan River could meet what Israel requires for its security. Comparable Palestinian leases of very select facilities in the port of Ashdod and at Ben-Gurion Airport could provide for a sense of mutuality in order to meet the practical and psychological needs of both sides.)
- An acceptance and promotion of an independent Palestinian industrial policy and development of Dead Sea minerals and tourist infrastructure to foster a more self-sufficient economic future for Palestinians.

Taken together, these steps would make clear that Israel is acting to preserve a two-state outcome and to ensure that the blending of populations—Israelis and Palestinians in the West Bank—does not pass a point of no return. These steps may be easy to describe but would be enormously difficult to carry out. The settler constituency is strong politically and will resist, with some on its fringe likely to resist violently. That might weaken the moral authority of settler leaders, but they start with a clear advantage over their counterparts on the left. The left in Israel will favor these steps, but they are fragmented and weak. They will be the most sensitive to occupation and its moral costs, but their numbers are small, and they lack credibility. They are seen by the vast majority of the population as being naive and taken in by the Palestinians—and somehow indifferent to real security threats. It is the mainstream right and center who have to be persuaded.

Tamar Hermann, one of Israel's leading pollsters, points out that presently 62 percent of Israeli Jews now define themselves as right wing. She acknowledges that their definition is loose and many are persuadable, particularly if they are convinced that Israel's security is being credibly addressed.[20] Basically, this tells us that the burden will be very much on Israel's leader to explain how separation is needed to safeguard Israel's identity as a Jewish and democratic state even as its implementation must be carried out in a way that fully addresses Israel's security needs.

It will not be an easy sell given the political weight of settler leaders, but a determined Israeli prime minister can build a consensus by being relentless and framing the stakes as also being about national survival. In other words, Israel's prime minister will need to take a page from Ben-Gurion, Begin, Rabin, and Sharon.

Like them, he or she will face a painful backlash. And like them, he or she will be called to make a fateful decision—the kind Sharon referred to often as involving "the solitude of the leader." It will take enormous political courage to make it. In the chapters on Ben-Gurion, Begin, Rabin, and Sharon, we described their readiness to make tough, courageous decisions and the context that produced them. Can those past decisions and their circumstances provide lessons and guidelines for what it will take to produce this looming fateful choice—one we feel cannot be put off? We hope so.

LESSONS OF ISRAELI LEADERSHIP

There was a commonality to all the instances in which big, fateful decisions were made by Israeli leaders; they all saw the stakes and understood the consequences of not acting, consequences that they believed posed an unacceptable risk to the future of the Zionist enterprise and mission.

With David Ben-Gurion, the cost of not making the decision to declare the state would be that the Jewish state might never exist. Yes, the circumstances were daunting, almost overwhelming: there was the certainty of invasion by all the neighboring Arab state armies, and the leaders of the Jewish forces, Yigael Yadin and Yisrael Galili, said that their soldiers were not prepared and needed more time and weaponry. If that were not enough, Ben-Gurion understood that the new state could not count on outside support and was effectively on its own. He believed, based on Moshe Sharett's report of his conversation with Secretary of State George Marshall, that the United States was opposed to the decision. Yet he also knew that the US arguments against the declaration of statehood were not likely to change in time, and that was the essential point for Ben-Gurion. The risks would always be high. There would always be reasons for not declaring the state, for saying the time was not right. For Ben-Gurion, it was now or never. With the British mandate ending at midnight and the British completing their withdrawal, Ben-Gurion understood there would never again be so clear a justification for declaring the state. Whatever the costs, they were less than seeing the end of the Zionist dream—or so Ben-Gurion believed.

For Menachem Begin, the choice was also historic. He understood he had a chance to make peace with Egypt, the largest Arab state with the largest Arab army. Israel had fought four wars with the Egyptians, and Begin understood that Egypt was the linchpin of any Arab coalition against Israel. Begin also understood that he could not achieve peace with Egypt without withdrawing from the settlements in the Sinai and accepting autonomy for Palestinians, with uncertainty about where autonomy could lead. He had to take on his ideology—and his closest comrades—but he would not forgo what could be gained. Just as importantly, he understood the risks of what might be lost if he chose not to make the decision, including losing US support or Sadat potentially ousted or driven back to a rejectionist camp.*

Like Begin, Yitzhak Rabin saw an opportunity that must not be lost. He did not have the equivalent of Sadat coming to Jerusalem to demonstrate

---

* Even with the Israeli public, Begin might have paid a price for having been nonresponsive to Sadat, who had come to Jerusalem and captured the imagination of the Israeli people.

the opportunity to the public. Instead, he saw a geopolitical tsunami that was producing great change and redefining what was possible internationally. Within the region, the defeat of Saddam Hussein, the weakness of the radicals for the time being, and the leverage of the United States with the Arabs—who were anxious to be on the side of the über-power internationally—all created his belief that he must act or lose the moment. His own feeling that he had a second chance as prime minister added to his sense of possibility and what was at stake, making him determined to produce a breakthrough with the PLO or Syria. He knew the costs would be high but believed that demographic trends and the impact of continuing occupation meant the alternative would surely be worse. He also felt the costs of an opportunity lost would weigh heavily on Israel and provide the radicals, with Iranian backing, the means to make a comeback.

Finally, Ariel Sharon, too, felt Israel must act. He, better than most, understood the costs of withdrawing from Gaza and razing the settlements there and in four small Jewish communities in the West Bank—after all, he had built them. But he felt he must preserve what was essential for Israel. On the one hand, he feared the consequences of Israel not taking the initiative and being cornered by international pressure to give up too much. On the other, he was convinced that Israel must address the demographic challenge. Getting out of Gaza would not solve the demographic danger to preserving Israel as a Jewish-democratic state, but it would buy time to sort out what must be done on the West Bank to ensure Israel's character. Not acting for him was simply not an option, given the consequences of inaction.

All these leaders acted. None was the type to accept drift as an option, even though all knew that the decisions they were making would produce a terrible backlash. To be sure, Ben-Gurion's position and calculus were a little different: it was less about the blowback domestically and more that the cost of declaring statehood was going to be measured in blood. He had no illusions about how high the cost might be, but ultimately fulfilling the Zionist dream required it. While the price was very steep, with 1 percent of the Jewish population in Palestine at the time being killed, it is not an exaggeration to say that without Ben-Gurion's sheer force of will and single-minded commitment to creating the state, it may well not have come into being. His decision to declare statehood reflected that understanding.

For Begin, Rabin, and Sharon the costs might have been different, and more personal, but they were bound to weigh very heavily on each of them. Begin was an ideologue, a deep believer in a set of ideas about Zionism and their meaning. In a speech he gave at the Hebrew University in 1972, he declared that if Israel did not have a right to Hebron, it did not have a right to Tel Aviv or Haifa.* Begin was someone deeply committed to the concepts of law and legitimacy, and this statement revealed his belief that Israel needed to have rights to historic Palestine up to the Jordan River or it would essentially lose its rights to any of the territory. Yet Palestinian autonomy might set Israel on a slippery slope that could defy this core belief, and leaders in the Gush Emunim settler movement were not hesitant to call Begin on it. They called him a traitor. For someone like Begin, for whom principle was sacred and for whom comradeship mattered so profoundly, this was bound to cause a great wound. So much so that it led him to speak of the Gush, formerly his great supporters, as having a messianic complex.

Begin understood what was coming and made his painful choice. Sharon, too, knew what was coming. He was different from Begin in that, for him, it was never about ideology. He was the ultimate pragmatist. But it was about principle, and the guiding principle for him was the state of Israel comes first. Sharon understood he had to take on the very groups he had championed, tearing down the same settlements he had developed and built. He, too, would be called a traitor, a charge that had already led to the assassination of Rabin.

For both Sharon and Rabin, the risks were not just psychological and political. Rabin, in a private discussion shortly after he was elected, explained that the steps he would ultimately take on the West Bank might lead to a civil war.[21] He was dismissive of personal threats to him, even as violent demonstrations full of depictions of him in a Nazi uniform or wearing a kaffiyeh like Arafat's increasingly took place. He would not be deterred from what he felt the state of Israel needed to do, even if he might pay the price for it. After the assassination of Rabin, Sharon knew that the threats to him over Gaza withdrawal were not idle. But, like Rabin, they would not stop him. Both men had put their lives on the line as soldiers, and they carried

---

* Dennis, then a student, attended the speech.

the burden of having ordered others to do so as well; many of their forces had paid the ultimate price. Rabin and Sharon had lived their lives in the service of the state, and as prime ministers they put the future of Israel first, whatever the personal price.

Consider the lessons for leadership that emerge from the stories and policies of Ben-Gurion, Begin, Rabin, and Sharon. To begin with, they shared one common trait: they all defined leadership the same way. Leadership meant being responsible and assuming responsibility, and not letting that burden fall to others. It meant leading, not following the public, which also required explaining the realities and the stakes to Israelis. It meant being able to see risks clearly and understand which ones had to be run and not avoided. It meant being willing to make very lonely decisions. It meant persevering in the face of terrible opposition. It meant being willing to face the consequences, personal and political, for acting. That is what leaders do.

Real leaders, in the words of presidential historian Doris Kearns Goodwin, have "an ambition for self that becomes something larger."[22] They all had that. They all also shared an unrelenting mental toughness. Where did that come from? Goodwin, in her book on leadership, profiled Abraham Lincoln, Theodore and Franklin Roosevelt, and Lyndon Johnson, and explored how they had faced deep personal adversity and overcome it.[23] For these four Israeli leaders, it is hard to exaggerate the adversity they had faced and how it had both readied and steeled them to overcome challenges. Ben-Gurion persevered, from the daunting conditions he faced arriving in Palestine in 1906 to managing and organizing the Yishuv in the face of the Arab revolt, the British White Paper, and the Holocaust. Begin was arrested and put in a Soviet prison, and his parents and brother were murdered by the Nazis. Rabin and Sharon fought in the War of Independence, where so many of their closest comrades were killed. Sharon also had to cope with the personal tragedies of losing his first wife in a car accident and firstborn son at the age of ten to an accidental gunshot in his front yard.

To face profound adversity, endure, and overcome it requires not just mental toughness but also resilience—another trait Goodwin defines as common to leaders. Ben-Gurion, Begin, Rabin, and Sharon were surely resilient. They also shared one other attribute: a profound sense of duty. No doubt, that contributed to their capacity to see what was important and to act on it. Of course they could be tactically agile, especially as circumstances changed, but they did not lose sight of what they defined as a strategic necessity—all else was secondary. They were certainly not indifferent to the political realities and they faced them, trying to minimize the costs of their decisions. All understood the importance of explaining their decisions, not hiding them or obfuscating what they intended and why. They saw leadership as elevating the discussion, as a way of explaining the stakes and transforming the political climate. Yes, they wanted to politically survive, but not to hold power for its own sake. As such, when they saw the stakes and the need for action, their decisions reflected what they believed leadership and their responsibilities as prime ministers required of them.

One other factor contributed to their ability to act and exercise the power of their position. Israel, as a very young state, has institutions that are not deeply rooted. From Ben-Gurion's time, the power of the prime minister as the crucial decision-maker was real. The Knesset, the Supreme Court, the media, the political parties, the military and security establishment, and the fact that every government is made up of a coalition of multiple parties create some limitations on the power of the prime minister. The prime minister does have to answer to the Knesset and in one way or another is affected by these other institutions. But even governments with very narrow majorities are capable of making big decisions if the prime minister acts as a leader. Yitzhak Rabin passed the interim agreement in the Oslo process—the agreement that effectively brought the Palestinian Authority to every city in the West Bank—even though he had a majority of one in the Knesset. Ariel Sharon, even though he lost the referendum within his party on withdrawal from Gaza, proceeded anyway. Decisiveness on the part of the prime minister is instrumental to being able to make big decisions; institutions and coalition governments tend to preclude such decisions by prime ministers only if they are not ready to take those steps in the first place. In other words, when prime ministers assume the real mantle of leadership, the institutions of the state are unlikely to prevent their making historic leaps.

Can Israel's leaders now or in the near future measure up to this standard of leadership? No one who becomes Israel's prime minister faces a simple set of challenges, practically or politically. Given the real threats that Israel confronts in the region, it takes character, toughness, intelligence, and judgment to do the job. Benjamin Netanyahu, in July 2019, will become the longest-serving prime minister ever, longer than Ben-Gurion, and it takes more than political smarts to have served so long. Certainly, he knows how to maneuver in Israel's political hothouse. But he has also unmistakably managed Israel through challenging times, including great upheaval in the Arab world. He has carefully worked out delicate relationships with a number of Israel's Arab neighbors, understanding that practical cooperation is more important than public disclosure. He has also adopted a policy toward the war in Syria designed to deal with the most serious strategic threats posed to Israel from the expansion of the Iranian Quds Force and its Shia militia proxies in the country. While not being able to blunt this presence, Netanyahu has sought to build Israeli deterrence against it both directly and indirectly through the Russians.* Unquestionably, he has managed to reduce conflict with the Russians, even as his efforts to persuade Vladimir Putin have produced only limited results in containing the spread and growth of the Iranian military infrastructure in Syria.

The point is that Netanyahu has been effective in dealing with threats as well as opportunities with the Arabs. His decisions in this regard are clearly important for Israel strategically. Can we say the same about his approach to dealing with the Palestinians? No. He has presided over the current path that threatens to turn Israel into a binational state. Both publicly and privately he has said that Israel will not become a binational state. Yet his policies belie his claims and lead in that direction. He might well claim that he is resisting pressure from the right to build more outside of the blocs and to annex parts of Area C. And, of course, he has done that, justifying his decision to hold back such moves by explaining that, even with the Trump administration—which is not prone to criticizing Israeli policies—this would create problems.

---

* The more than one hundred strikes carried out by the Israeli military against Quds Force, Hezbollah, and Assad regime targets—strikes that have not generally been acknowledged—is a testament to this.

Still, even if the building outside the blocs is smaller than it would be if Naftali Bennett or others on the right, such as Yisrael Katz, were prime minister, the growth continues each year. Since Netanyahu became prime minister in 2009, the numbers outside the blocs have grown from less than sixty thousand to more than one hundred thousand. The higher the number, the harder it is going to be to prevent the geographic intertwining of populations that will doom any possibility of separation. (The growth of the Palestinian population in Area C is certain to compound the difficulty of separating Israelis and Palestinians demographically.) Netanyahu seems to think that his politics won't permit anything more than what he is now doing. But if that is so, then Israel will become a binational state, despite what Netanyahu has said as prime minister.

Perhaps, he has changed his views on a single state and, much like others on the right, believes that the world will learn to live with Palestinians having a form of self-rule under broad Israeli control. Or perhaps he hopes that if he equivocates long enough another solution will emerge—for example, a confederal arrangement with Jordan that permits Israel to retain maximum territory and absorb a minimal number of Palestinians. Such an agreement would essentially divide the West Bank with Jordan and have the Palestinians become part of the Hashemite kingdom or be a state within a confederation with Jordan.

As Moshe Arens pointed out, however, the Jordanians continue to reject any such arrangement and there is no real sign that their opposition will change. Or maybe Prime Minister Netanyahu believes he still has time and just needs to form a different government with centrist parties. Of course, he had that chance in 2016 with the Zionist Union and its leader, Isaac Herzog, and chose, after negotiating over the formation of the government, not to take it.

So the real question with Netanyahu and his possible successors is, Do they understand that the current path is leading to a binational state? Or do they seek to deny this reality, either because they don't believe it or as a way of avoiding a historic decision certain to generate extreme opposition from the right wing and the settler constituency? During his first term as prime minister in 1997, Netanyahu at one point privately said that he would make the kind of decisions Ben-Gurion made; should he make the decisions needed to ensure that separation remains possible with the Palestinians, he would fulfill that statement. Indeed, were Ben-Gurion prime minister today, he would act to guarantee Israel's Jewish, democratic character.*

Of course, Ben-Gurion, Begin, Rabin, and Sharon are not around today. They were all there for the founding of Israel and fought for its survival. They lived through the period characterized by the genuine fragility of the state. Maybe that made them see the choices through a different lens—a lens in which the new Jewish state did not have the luxury of avoiding basic, hard choices. Maybe, as a result, Israel is past the point where it will have heroic leaders. Regardless, given the difficulty of choosing to act unilaterally to separate from the Palestinians, Israel's current or next leaders may well need outside help to take this leap. In theory, the United States could offer such help; it has in the past. Indeed, even with leaders who were heroic, there was always an interest in trying to manage the costs or demonstrate that there were gains that offset them to help convince the Israeli public about the wisdom of the choices being made.

What America Can Do to Ease the Burden of Choice

Looking back, it is interesting that Begin, Rabin, and Sharon all counted on US assistance and assurances or commitments. In each case, the United States made it easier for them to make their decisions, providing a financial and security cushion and added justification. In finalizing the Egypt-Israel peace treaty—which turned the Camp David Accords, with its provisions for the Palestinians, into a formal peace agreement—President Carter promised to help underwrite the costs of building two new air bases in the Negev to replace those being given up in the Sinai. He also committed, for the first time, to provide annual assistance to Israel of three billion dollars—which in the first year, given the costs of the base relocation, amounted to roughly 4.5 billion dollars. Additionally, since Israel was surrendering the oil wells in

---

* Recall his statement, also quoted by Sharon, that Israel could have taken the land to the Jordan River but chose not to do so because then the Jews would have been a minority and could not have had a Jewish-democratic state.

the Sinai it had been exploiting, Carter promised that if Egypt did not supply Israel's oil needs, the United States would guarantee that Israel's needs were met. All these commitments, which were made as Carter closed the deal with Begin in March 1979, allowed Begin to point to the gains he was producing and what he would be giving up if he failed to conclude the peace treaty.

Begin likely would have done the deal anyway, given the stakes, but there is little doubt these commitments made it easier for him to take his historic leap. For his part, Rabin understood that if and when a peace with the Palestinians or the Syrians was reached, the United States would address Israel's security and economic needs. He knew how important US policy assurances and security assistance had been when he concluded the Sinai II accord in 1975. Not surprisingly, for the much bigger historic moves on peace he was contemplating, Rabin began to anticipate what might be necessary, especially if Israel withdrew from the Golan Heights: early warning and surveillance, next-generation fighter aircraft, and missile defense. The price tag would be high, but President Clinton was receptive, understanding the significance of what Rabin was prepared to do.

Sharon was no different, except in his case the US assurances and pay-offs would take the place of anything he would get from the Palestinians for withdrawing from Gaza. Sharon believed that the Bush-Sharon letter was one of Israel's greatest diplomatic achievements. It certainly helped sustain Sharon's commitment to see the Gaza withdrawal through after he lost the referendum on it in his own party.

In other words, even heroic leaders, in making their historic choices, needed US diplomatic support, assurances, and financial and security assistance. With leaders today whose experience and frame of reference is so different from the founders' generation, it is hard to imagine that they would take any such leaps without serious American commitments to safeguard Israel's future and boost the leaders politically.

So, what might the United States do? It could provide commitments and cash. The US commitments need to help Israel's prime minister show the strategic benefits he or she is gaining by making this choice and how it serves Israel's long-term well-being. With this in mind, the United States could promise that

- Israel would not need to take any other or new initiatives, so long as Palestinians remained unable or unwilling to offer or make any concessions on peace;

- it would block any resolution Israel opposed at the United Nations Security Council;

- it would work with the Europeans and others to gain their public support for Israel's unilateral moves to ensure separation, including new commitments collectively to fight delegitimization efforts and the Boycott, Divestment and Sanctions movement;

- it would press the Europeans to announce that Palestinians and Arabs need to take steps to respond to the Israeli actions and criticize them in public if they are not responsive—something Europeans have not previously done;*

- it would seek to get Arab leaders to engage in public outreach to Israel, perhaps by organizing a three-way meeting of senior Arab, Israeli, and American officials to discuss common security threats, first in Washington and then in Jerusalem;

- it would push for broad international recognition of Israel as the nation-state of the Jewish people, a consideration made more important to Israelis as Palestinians seek to deny that the Jews are a people and have a right to a state; and

- it would renew a systematic dialogue on preserving Israel's qualitative military edge, one that has lapsed in the Trump administration.

None of these promises would constitute a departure from traditional American policies. While they would resonate in Israel, they might not prove politically potent enough for Israel's prime minister to feel he or she could take the leap. Two other possible American offers—both significant departures from past American positions—could help give the prime minister the political tailwind to act.

---

* This would also be the moment to coordinate with the European Union on conditioning additional assistance to the Palestinians only if the Palestinian Authority began to build a rule of law and take on corruption.

First, assuming the administration believed that Israeli negotiations with the Palestinians were either unlikely to emerge soon or produce anything if they did, the United States could decide to recognize a border Israel might establish in the West Bank. That border would define the settlement blocs close to the green line on roughly 5 percent of the territory, and the United States would recognize the blocs as part of sovereign Israel. The United States would state that its recognition did not preclude compensation for the Palestinians—territorial and otherwise—when they would enter negotiations in good faith, or even that the boundaries of blocs might be modestly altered in those talks. Unquestionably, this would be a big political move for the United States and should not be undertaken without serious discussions with Arab leaders and Palestinians first. But it might well be worth it if the alternatives look bleak and this is what it would take to get Israel's prime minister to act unilaterally to ensure separation and preserve a two-state option.

A second possible policy departure, which would not have the broader regional implications of recognizing Israel's annexation of the blocs, could be an American willingness to provide "cash" to help cover some of the costs of providing financial incentives to settlers to resettle, either in the blocs or within green-line Israel. While not having the same impact as US recognition of the blocs, US willingness to help finance resettlement would strengthen the Israeli prime minister's hand in managing the costs and explaining the decision. Of course, for an American administration to be seen as paying to resettle those that American presidents had opposed settling in the first place would not be an easy or simple decision—and Congress might not be so willing to approve it. But if it could tip the scales in helping the Israeli prime minister make a historically difficult move that preserves a two-state outcome, it could be worth at least considering.

All of these commitments, offers, or assurances would be positive and part of an effort to encourage whomever the prime minister is to make this historic decision. There should also be another side to the effort to urge Israel's leaders to act. American officials, from the administration and Congress, need to have conversations with their Israeli counterparts about a future in which there is only one state and Palestinians have launched a campaign internationally calling for one person, one vote. With that future looking more likely than the alternatives—unless there is a change in Israeli policy—Israel's prime minister, other ministers, members of the Knesset, and the Israeli public need to hear about how such an eventuality might affect future US policy. Truth be told, it is hard to believe that under such circumstances the level of American support for Israel—material and political—will remain what it has become over time. Indeed, even under presidents such as Obama, who was willing to be publicly critical of Israel, the level of material support, especially on security, never wavered. But that may no longer be the case in the event that a one-state reality emerges, with Palestinians then demanding full rights as citizens, including the right to vote.

In light of the possible implications of such a development, the discussions should not be limited only to American officials. The leaders of the American Jewish community need to engage in their own candid conversations with Israelis. They, too, must level with Israeli leaders and address the likely impact in the United States, and within the Jewish community, of Israel becoming a binational state, but with the Palestinians not being given equal rights. Israelis tend to be dismissive of those Jews in the diaspora who are critical of Israel's policies but who don't live there or have their kids serve in the military. That is legitimate.

However, what we are calling for is not criticism but an honest discussion of what is likely to happen in America should Israel not act to preserve its character and separate from the Palestinians. Jewish leaders, too, have a stake in Israel preserving its basic Zionist character; it is very much part of their ethos and belief system. In addition, they well know that Jewish identity in America has, at least in part, been influenced by the ability to identify with Israel. Should that become more difficult, it would certainly produce a critical loss of support for Israel in the Jewish community, especially among the younger Jewish demographic that embraces more progressive, liberal values. Whether this would have a larger impact on the future of the Jewish communal life in America is unclear, but it is possible.

Perhaps the right wing in Israel believes that the evangelical Christians and the Orthodox Jewish community are the only support they need in America to preserve the relationship and the level of US support. If so, they are kidding themselves. That is not the base that has actively lobbied Congress and produced strong congressional support for Israel. What's more, a base that narrow will ensure that Israel loses its bipartisan support, which is what has made Israel an American—not a Republican or Democratic—interest. Sooner or later the political pendulum will swing, and losing broad-based support would come back to haunt Israel.

The point is that for Israel's leaders to make a truly tough political decision and face the consequences in Israel, they will probably need help from America. That help must come not only in the form of assurances and inducements but also with candid discussions by US officialdom and Jewish leaders with their Israeli counterparts. Israeli leaders must hear the likely consequences of not making the choice.

Admittedly, it is hard to imagine those conversations taking place with the Trump administration. It is not at all clear that the president or his senior officials have thought much about whether Israel retains its dual Jewish-democratic character. To be fair, should their peace plan materialize and lead to a renewal of diplomacy and hope, it would likely blunt the drift toward a binational state outcome. The chances of that appear slim at this point.

In the meantime, Jewish leaders should begin their honest conversations with Israelis, if for no other reason than to start a conditioning process in the hope of igniting greater awareness of what is at stake. With Prime Minister Netanyahu or his successors, it is necessary to pose the questions: Are you concerned about Israel becoming a binational state? If so, what are you doing to prevent it? If not, why not? What makes you believe it will not materialize? At a minimum, this might actually trigger a serious policy discussion within Israel about its future before it is too late.

Conclusion

WE DECIDED TO write this book because we see Israel fast approaching one of those hinge points in history where a decision is needed to preserve the country's character. Though we both have long worked on promoting peace between Israel and the Palestinians (and the Arabs), we have no illusions that a peace deal is possible with the Palestinians in the near term. Even if they had a more forthcoming Israeli government to work with, the Palestinians would be unlikely to be responsive. Palestinian weakness and division, the lack of legitimacy of its leaders, Hamas control in Gaza, and succession politics all rule out their ability to conclude a deal with Israel, much less implement it. That is not an argument for doing nothing to try to improve coexistence and the realities on the ground—here Dayan and Revivi are surely right. Moreover, not giving up on diplomacy is also necessary because to do so would create a vacuum, and vacuums in the Middle East are always filled by the most extreme forces. We need to preserve the possibility of peace, not make it more remote.

As important as it is to preserve the possibility of peace, the even greater urgency may be to preserve the possibility of separation. Israeli separation from Palestinians may be more about a divorce than peacemaking. Of course, it could contribute to peacemaking by creating international pressure on Palestinians and Arabs to be responsive to Israel's steps. It might be used to restart a diplomatic process and perhaps even restore the sense of possibility that both sides have lost.

We certainly believe that it is best to try to make Israeli moves to preserve separation as part of a larger package, producing, at least, steps in response by Arab states. Ultimately, however, these moves are necessary lest Israel, by default, lose its Jewish or democratic identity.

Preventing that is what motivated us, two lifelong supporters of Israel, to ask what can be done now to stop the slide toward one state. We understand well the threats that Israel faces on the outside. We, too, believe that Israel must remain strong, have defensible borders, retain overriding security responsibilities for the area, and be able to defend itself by itself—especially when the signs of US wariness about regional involvements appear even stronger under Trump than Obama. We also believe that, in practical terms, the Jordan River must remain Israel's security border, even if the packaging of how that is done should take into account Palestinian political needs. States accept certain limitations on their sovereignty as part of security arrangements—why else do the United Kingdom and Germany have US bases on their territory?

Fortunately, the steps Israel needs to take to preserve separation as an option do not endanger or create doubts about Israel's security. Not building outside of the settlement blocs and forswearing sovereignty to the east of the barrier do not raise security concerns—they raise domestic political challenges. Unfortunately, avoiding those challenges will endanger Israel's future.

If nothing else, Israelis and those who care about Israel should at least debate what is at stake. David Ben-Gurion, Menachem Begin, Yitzhak Rabin, and Ariel Sharon faced up to moments of truth. There is a looming moment of truth in Israel, and the actions of these former prime ministers and their examples of leadership offer a guide for dealing with it. They showed the importance of recognizing the stakes and the costs of inaction—and they also proved that they could enlist the help of the United States as they made their fateful choices. Our hope is that Israel's leaders now will find the wisdom and the courage to draw from their examples and make their own fateful choice.

Acknowledgments

No book is ever solely the work of the author or authors. This book is no exception. We began discussing it in 2016 and were fortunate to have wonderful research support from many talented research and editorial assistants at the Washington Institute for Near East Policy. None of that would have been possible without the support of Rob Satloff, the director of the institute. Rob has always fostered an environment not just of serious analytical work but also collegiality. He runs the Washington Institute brilliantly, and we are deeply indebted to him, the director of research Patrick Clawson, and those who have served as president and chairpersons of its board during this process: Martin Gross, Shelly Kasten, and James Schreiber. All have been enthusiastic supporters of our work, and for that we are deeply appreciative.

We also want to express our gratitude to a remarkable group of younger scholars and practitioners, who did so much to identify and locate original and secondary sources: Mitchel Hochberg and Eitan Sayag contributed much early in the research process. Lia Weiner deserves special thanks for all the work she did for both of us. William Ellison, Aviva Weinstein, Madison Rinder, and Basia Rosenbaum were truly instrumental, doing not only research and fact-checking but also taking care of supporting our administrative needs as well. To William, Aviva, Madison, and Basia, we say thank you.

There are also a number of research interns we would like to thank for their fact-checking, alignment of endnotes, and endless trips to the library: Harry Aaronson, Emma Colbran, Tali Edid, Matt Gang, Jennifer Gurev, Jared Kraay, Yael Krifcher, Moritz Lutgerath, M. Z. Morgenstern, Margaux Nijkerk, and Lexi Scheen. We also deeply appreciate Jason Warshof's editorial and substantive advice on the Ben-Gurion and Begin chapters; he was of immense help.

We were given access to the Ben-Gurion archive at Sde Boker, and that proved to be a useful resource. Dror Bar-Yosef of the Menachem Begin library also deserves our thanks for his assistance and helpful suggestions. We would also like to thank Louise Fisher at the Israel State Archives.

Others deserve our thanks as well. Dov Seidman's suggestions on explaining why Israel faces a fateful choice helped to sharpen the last chapter. Mike Herzog also carefully reviewed the last chapter, and his comments were particularly helpful and much appreciated. Similarly, Uzi Rebhun of the Jewish People Policy Institute and the Hebrew University in Jerusalem provided guidance and insight that was especially useful in framing the discussion on the demographic issue. In addition, Itamar Rabinovich's recommendations on sources and substance proved very useful. In particular, his recounting of the meeting between Ben-Gurion and de Gaulle in 1960 added a wonderful finishing touch to the Ben-Gurion chapter.

Dennis wants to thank a number of people who gave very generously of their time in lengthy interviews: Ehud Olmert, Oren Magnezy, Dror Moreh, Lior Schillat, Shalom Turgeman, and Dov "Dubi" Weisglass. Their insights into Sharon and the choices he made were invaluable. Similarly, Martin Idyk offered some very helpful observations about meeting Sharon during Sharon's early months as prime minister. David is also grateful to several people for their help and support in enhancing his understanding of Begin: Aharon Barak, Benny Begin, and Dan Meridor. He also very much appreciates those who took the time to read his chapters and offered invaluable advice: UCLA political scientist Steve Spiegel, Emory University diplomatic historian Kenneth Stein, and Dan Meridor. There are others whose advice was extremely helpful: Moshe Halbertal, Yehudah Mirsky, and Rina Hakimian.

We also owe much to Peter Osnos, the founder of PublicAffairs and now a consultant to Hachette Book Group, and Clive Priddle, publisher of PublicAffairs. Peter and Clive have been enthusiastic supporters of the book and made very helpful comments on the draft manuscript. We are especially indebted to Clive for his masterful edits; together with Brynn Warriner and Liz Dana, Clive sharpened the chapters and made them more readable. And, of course, Esther Newberg deserves our collective thanks, as she once again proved she has no peer as a literary agent. She brought our plans for the book to Peter's attention early on and set us on a wonderful collaborative track with Peter and Clive.

As always, our families supported our doing this book, knowing full well that both of us would be preoccupied for an extended period of time. They tolerated our excitement as we discovered little-known facts about Ben-Gurion, Begin, Rabin, and Sharon and reported to them how relevant these tidbits were to the thread of the story we were writing. More importantly, they shared our conviction that telling the story of past big decisions just might help to inspire a recognition that such leadership is required if Israel is to avoid losing its Jewish-democratic character. Dennis is particularly grateful to his wife, Debbie, who suggested the title for the book, and his children Gabe, Rachel, and Ilana—all of whom posed challenging questions that helped to sharpen his own thinking and improved the final product. Ilana in particular also provided very thoughtful and candid advice on the Sharon chapter. Thankfully, Debbie has also taught them to tell him what he needs to hear, not necessarily what he wants to hear. David wants to thank his family: Varda and his three children, Jonathan (Tani), Josh, and Elliana. They remain joys in his life. He is grateful for their love, support, and understanding.

NOTES

Chapter 1   David Ben-Gurion: Ben-Gurion's Unswerving Road to Statehood

1. Amos Oz, "David Ben-Gurion," *Time,* April 13, 1998, http://content.time.com/time /subscriber/article/0,33009,988160,00.html.

2. Anita Shapira, *Ben-Gurion: Father of Modern Israel* (New Haven, CT: Yale University Press, 2014), 65.

3. Ibid., 2; Michael Bar-Zohar, *Ben-Gurion: A Biography* (Tel Aviv: Magal Books, 1978), 1.

4. Bar-Zohar, *Ben-Gurion,* 2; Shimon Peres, *Ben-Gurion: A Political Life* (New York: Schocken Books, 2011), 11.

5. Bar-Zohar, *Ben-Gurion,* 4–5.

6. Peres, *Ben-Gurion,* 11; Bar-Zohar, *Ben-Gurion,* 5.

7. Robert St. John, *Ben-Gurion: The Biography of an Extraordinary Man* (Garden City, NY: Doubleday & Company, 1959), 20.

8. Hillel Halkin, *Jabotinsky: A Life* (New Haven, CT: Yale University Press, 2014), 45; St. John, *Ben-Gurion,* 20.

9. Bar-Zohar, *Ben-Gurion,* 6; St. John, *Ben-Gurion,* 20.

10. Peres, *Ben-Gurion,* 13.

11. "Aliya," Israel Ministry of Foreign Affairs, August 20, 2001, http://mfa.gov.il /MFA/MFA-Archive/2001/Pages/Aliya.aspx; "From Haven to Home: 350 Years of Jewish Life in America: A Century of Immigration, 1820–1924," Library of Congress, www.loc .gov/exhibits/haventohome/haven-century.html.

12. Shapira, *Ben-Gurion,* 19–20.

13. Bar-Zohar, *Ben-Gurion,* 26; Shapira, *Ben-Gurion,* 20.

14. Ilan Troen, "The Transformation of Zionist Planning Policy: From Rural Settlements to an Urban Network," *Planning Perspectives* 3 (1988), 3–23, www.tandfonline.com /doi/abs/10.1080/02665438808725649.

15. Bar-Zohar, *Ben-Gurion,* 28.

16. Ibid.

17. Ibid., 29; Avigdor Levy, ed., *Jews, Turks, Ottomans: A Shared History, Fifteenth Through the Twentieth Century* (Syracuse, NY: Syracuse University Press, 2002), 101, 214.

18. Bar-Zohar, *Ben-Gurion,* 29.

19. Benny Morris, *Righteous Victims: A History of the Zionist-Arab Conflict, 1881–1999* (New York: Alfred A. Knopf, 1999), 83.

20. David Ben-Gurion, *Israel: A Personal History*, trans. Nechemia Meyers and Uzy Nystar (New York: Funk & Wagnalls, 1971), 40; Shapira, *Ben-Gurion*, 41.

21. Lord Balfour, "Balfour Declaration," in *Israel in the Middle East: Documents and Readings on Society, Politics and Foreign Relations, Pre-1948 to the Present*, ed. Itamar Rabinovich and Jehuda Reinharz (Waltham, MA: Brandeis University Press, 2008), 29.

22. Bar-Zohar, *Ben-Gurion*, 38.

23. Ibid.

24. Shapira, *Ben-Gurion*, 58–60.

25. Ibid., 60; Shabtai Teveth, *Ben-Gurion: The Burning Ground 1868–1948* (Boston: Houghton Mifflin, 1987), 142.

26. Benny Morris, *Righteous Victims: A History of the Zionist-Arab Conflict, 1881–1999* (New York: Alfred A. Knopf, 1999), 83.

27. Shapira, *Ben-Gurion*, 84; Morris, *Righteous Victims*, 35.

28. Bar-Zohar, *Ben-Gurion*, 47; Shapira, *Ben-Gurion*, 84.

29. David Ben-Gurion, *My Talks with Arab Leaders*, trans. Misha Louvish (New York: The Third Press, 1973), 7.

30. Ibid.

31. Bar-Zohar, *Ben-Gurion*, 59; Peres, *Ben-Gurion*, 45.

32. Shabtai Teveth, *Ben-Gurion and the Holocaust* (New York: Harcourt Brace & Company, 1996), xxxvii.

33. Daniel Gordis, *Menachem Begin: The Battle for Israel's Soul* (New York: Random House, 2014), 11; Shapira, *Ben-Gurion*, 39; "Chaim Weizmann's Acetone Patent Turns 100," Weizmann Compass, September 27, 2015, www.weizmann.ac.il/WeizmannCompass/sections/people-behind-the-science/chaim-weizmann%E2%80%99s-acetone-patent-turns-100.

34. Teveth, *Ben-Gurion and the Holocaust*, xxxiv.

35. Ibid.

36. Ibid., xxxv.

37. Ibid.

38. Ibid., xiii.

39. Ibid., xxxvi.

40. Ibid., xiii.

41. Ibid., xxxvi.

42. Ibid., xlv.

43. Ibid., xiv, xxxvi.

44. Ibid., xxxvi–xxxvii.

45. Ibid., xxxviii.

46. Ibid., xxxix.

47. Bar-Zohar, *Ben-Gurion*, 101.

48. Ibid., 52.

49. Peres, *Ben-Gurion*, 65.

50. Ibid.

51. E. M. Epstein, "The Political Significance of Land Purchase," December 31, 1937, Center for Israel Education, http://israeled.org/resources/documents/jewish-national-fund/.

52. Halkin, *Jabotinsky*, 2, 41, 164; Bar-Zohar, *Ben-Gurion*, 63.

53. Avi Shlaim, *The Iron Wall: Israel and the Arab World* (London: Penguin Books, 2000), 11–14.

54. Daniel Kupfert Heller, *Jabotinsky's Children: Polish Jews and the Rise of the Right-Wing Zionism* (Princeton, NJ: Princeton University Press, 2017), 25.

55. Shapira, *Ben-Gurion*, 77.

56. Halkin, *Jabotinsky*, 182.

57. Mark Tessler, *A History of the Israeli-Palestinian Conflict*, 2nd ed. (Bloomington: Indiana University Press, 2009), 891.

58. Ben-Gurion, *My Talks with Arab Leaders*, 8, 310; Shapira, *Ben-Gurion*, 86–87, 110, 112, 114.

59. Teveth, *Ben-Gurion: The Burning Ground*, 458–459.

60. Anita Shapira, *Israel: A History*, trans. Anthony Berris (Waltham, MA: Brandeis University Press, 2012), 76.

61. Teveth, *Ben-Gurion: The Burning Ground*, 468.

62. Ibid.

63. Ibid., 460; Ben-Gurion, *My Talks with Arab Leaders*, 15.

64. Ben-Gurion, *My Talks with Arab Leaders*, 15.

65. Teveth, *Ben-Gurion: The Burning Ground*, 465; Ben-Gurion, *My Talks with Arab Leaders*, 15.

66. Ben-Gurion, *My Talks with Arab Leaders*, 18–19.

67. Ibid., 16.

68. Teveth, *Ben-Gurion: The Burning Ground*, 465–466.

69. Ibid., 466.

70. Ben-Gurion, *My Talks with Arab Leaders*, 31.

71. Ibid.

72. Teveth, *Ben-Gurion: The Burning Ground*, 478.

73. Ben-Gurion, *My Talks with Arab Leaders*, 43.

74. Ibid.

75. Ibid.

76. Ibid.

77. Ibid., 44.

78. Ibid., 54.

79. Ibid., 539.

80. Ibid.

81. Ibid.

82. Ibid., 544.

83. Ibid., 542.

84. Ben-Gurion, *My Talks with Arab Leaders*, 66, 69.

85. Shapira, *Ben-Gurion*, 99–104.

86. Teveth, *Ben-Gurion: The Burning Ground*, 159.

87. Shapira, *Ben-Gurion*, 90; Teveth, *Ben-Gurion: The Burning Ground*, 159.

88. Shapira, *Ben-Gurion*, 99.

89. Ibid., 103; Bar-Zohar, *Ben-Gurion*, 78.

90. Shapira, *Ben-Gurion*, 102, 105.

91. Bar-Zohar, *Ben-Gurion*, 87.

92. Ibid.

93. Teveth, *Ben-Gurion: The Burning Ground,* 529.

94. Ibid., 530.

95. Bar-Zohar, *Ben-Gurion,* 87.

96. Teveth, *Ben-Gurion: The Burning Ground,* 531; "Moshe Sharett," Israel Ministry of Foreign Affairs, www.mfa.gov.il/mfa/aboutisrael/state/pages/moshe%20sharett.aspx.

97. Teveth, *Ben-Gurion: The Burning Ground,* 531.

98. Bar-Zohar, *Ben-Gurion,* 87.

99. Teveth, *Ben-Gurion: The Burning Ground,* 535.

100. Ibid., 542.

101. Ibid., 550.

102. Ibid., 540.

103. Ibid., 551–552.

104. Ibid., 569.

105. Ibid., 611.

106. Ibid., 547.

107. Ibid., 546–548.

108. Ibid., 587.

109. Ibid.

110. Ibid., 543.

111. Bar-Zohar, *Ben-Gurion,* 91–92.

112. Teveth, *Ben-Gurion: The Burning Ground,* 591.

113. Bar-Zohar, *Ben-Gurion,* 91.

114. Ibid., 91–92.

115. Ibid., 93.

116. Teveth, *Ben-Gurion: The Burning Ground,* 633, 636, 638.

117. Ibid., 681.

118. Ben-Gurion, *Israel: A Personal History,* 53.

119. Ibid.

120. Yitzhak Avnery, "Immigration and Revolt: Ben-Gurion's Response to the 1939 White Paper," in *David Ben-Gurion: Politics and Leadership in Israel,* ed. Ronald W. Zweig (New York: Frank Cass, 1991), 102.

121. Ben-Gurion, *Israel,* 52.

122. Teveth, *Ben-Gurion: The Burning Ground,* 674.

123. Ibid., 668.

124. Ronald W. Zweig, ed., *David Ben-Gurion: Politics and Leadership in Israel* (New York: Frank Cass, 1991), 100.

125. Teveth, *Ben-Gurion: The Burning Ground,* 674.

126. Bar-Zohar, *Ben-Gurion,* 100.

127. Jonathan D. Sarna, "Louis D. Brandeis: Zionist Leader," *Brandeis Review* 2 (Winter 1992), 22.

128. Bar-Zohar, *Ben-Gurion,* 103.

129. Shapira, *Ben-Gurion,* 121.

130. Tom Segev, *David Ben-Gurion: A State at All Costs* (Jerusalem: Keter Books, 2017), 339.

131. Teveth, *Ben-Gurion: The Burning Ground*, 768–769.

132. Ibid., 768–769, 771, 780.

133. Segev, *David Ben-Gurion*, 335.

134. Teveth, *Ben-Gurion: The Burning Ground*, 679–680.

135. Ibid., 851.

136. Ibid., 844.

137. Segev, *David Ben-Gurion*, 331.

138. Ibid., 335.

139. Ibid.

140. Ibid., 348.

141. Teveth, *Ben-Gurion: The Burning Ground*, 674.

142. Ibid., 679.

143. Ben-Gurion, *Israel*, 52.

144. Teveth, *Ben-Gurion: The Burning Ground*, 871.

145. Shapira, *Ben-Gurion*, 141.

146. Teveth, *Ben-Gurion and the Holocaust*, xxxiv.

147. Segev, *David Ben-Gurion*, 354.

148. Teveth, *Ben-Gurion: The Burning Ground*, 871.

149. Ibid., 873.

150. Segev, *David Ben-Gurion*, 356.

151. Bar-Zohar, *Ben-Gurion*, 128.

152. Ibid., 131.

153. Ibid.

154. Ibid., 132.

155. Ibid., 129.

156. Ibid., 129–130.

157. Ibid.

158. Ibid., 130.

159. Ibid., 134, 136.

160. Benny Morris, *1948: The First Arab-Israeli War* (New Haven, CT: Yale University Press, 2008), 36.

161. Bar-Zohar, *Ben-Gurion*, 134; Peres, *Ben-Gurion*, 95.

162. David Ben-Gurion, "Speaking at Paris Conference, Sunday Afternoon, 3 pm 18th August," 1946, David Ben-Gurion Archives, Ben-Gurion University of the Negev, Beersheba, Israel.

163. Allis Radosh and Ronald Radosh, *A Safe Haven: Harry S. Truman and the Founding of Israel* (New York: Harper Perennial, 2010), 189.

164. Ibid.

165. Bar-Zohar, *Ben-Gurion*, 136.

166. Ibid.

167. Ibid.

168. Ibid., 138.

169. Ibid.; Ben-Gurion, *Israel*, 58.

170. Ben-Gurion, *Israel*, 56.

171. Bar-Zohar, *Ben-Gurion*, 143–144.

172. Shapira, *Ben-Gurion,* 149.

173. Ibid.

174. Ibid.

175. Bar-Zohar, *Ben-Gurion,* 143–144.

176. Ibid.

177. Peres, *Ben-Gurion,* 39.

178. Ibid., 146.

179. Ibid.

180. Ibid., 144.

181. Ibid., 148–149.

182. Segev, *David Ben-Gurion,* 336.

183. Bar-Zohar, *Ben-Gurion,* 148.

184. Ben-Gurion, *Israel,* 84.

185. Howard M. Sachar, *Israel and Europe: An Appraisal in History* (New York: Vintage, 2000), 71–75.

186. Ben-Gurion, *Israel,* 65.

187. Ibid., 64–65.

188. Ibid., 54–55.

189. Ibid.

190. Morris, *1948,* 30.

191. Mirian Joyce Haron, "The British Decision to Give the Palestine Question to the United Nations," *Middle Eastern Studies* 17, no. 2 (April 1981): 241, www.jstor.org /stable/4282830?seq=1#page_scan_tab_contents.

192. Ibid.

193. Morris, *1948,* 32.

194. Bar-Zohar, *Ben-Gurion,* 141; David Ben-Gurion, "Statement of Mr. D. Ben Gurion," in *The Jewish Plan for Palestine (1947): Memoranda and Statements Presented by the Jewish Agency for Palestine to the United Nations Special Committee on Palestine* (Atlanta, GA: Center for Israel Education, 2014), https://israeled.org/wp-content/uploads /2014/10/1947-Jewish-Plan-for-Palestine.pdf.

195. Ibid., 21.

196. Ibid., 2–3.

197. Ibid., 24.

198. Ibid., 17.

199. Ibid., 28.

200. Ibid., 53.

201. Ibid., 82.

202. Peres, *Ben-Gurion,* 99–100.

203. Segev, *David-Ben Gurion,* 385.

204. Ibid.

205. Peres, *Ben-Gurion,* 100.

206. Segev, *David Ben-Gurion,* 378.

207. Avi Shlaim, *The Politics of Partition: King Abdullah, the Zionists, and Palestine 1921–1951* (Oxford: Oxford University Press, 1999), 101.

208. Ben-Gurion, *Israel,* 61.

209. Golda Meir, *My Life* (New York: Dell Publishing, 1976), 216.

210. Shlaim, *The Politics of Partition*, 101–103.

211. Ben-Gurion, *Israel*, 65.

212. Shapira, *Israel*, 158.

213. Morris, *1948*, 101–103.

214. Ben-Gurion, *Israel*, 72.

215. Ibid., 82–83.

216. Segev, *David Ben-Gurion*, 389.

217. Morris, *1948*, 121.

218. Cohen, *Supreme Command*, 160.

219. Ben-Gurion, *Israel*, 66.

220. Bar-Zohar, *Ben-Gurion*, 151.

221. Ibid., 151–152.

222. Ben-Gurion, *Israel*, 66.

223. Ibid.

224. Morris, *1948*, 129.

225. Ibid., 130.

226. Ben-Gurion, *Israel*, 158.

227. Morris, *1948*, 116.

228. Salam Fayyad, interview by David Makovsky, Ramallah, 2012.

229. Moshe Sharett, "Mivrak El David Ben-Gurion, Tel Aviv" [Wire to David Ben-Gurion, Tel Aviv], in *Moshe Sharett: Rosh HaMemshala HaSheni—Mivhar Teudot MiPirkey Hayav (1894–1965)*, ed. Louise Fischer (Jerusalem: Israel State Archives, 2007), 334.

230. "Memorandum of Conversation, by Secretary of State, Washington, May 12, 1948," in *Foreign Relations of the United States, 1948: The Near East, South Asia, and Africa*, vol. 5, part 2, ed. Herbert A. Fine and Paul Claussen (Washington: United States Government Printing Office, 1976), 973, https://history.state.gov/historicaldocuments/frus1948v05p2/d252.

231. Ibid.

232. Transcript of the Provisional Government Meeting (May 12, 1948), 55.

233. Ibid.

234. Radosh and Radosh, *A Safe Haven*, 327–328.

235. Ibid., 326–327.

236. Ibid., 327.

237. Ibid., 328.

238. Gabriel Sheffer, *Moshe Sharett: Biography of a Political Moderate* (Oxford: Oxford University Press, 1996), 326.

239. Ibid., 325.

240. Bar-Zohar, *Ben-Gurion*, 159.

241. Meir, *My Life*, 216–218.

242. Ibid., 216–217.

243. Ibid., 218.

244. Ibid.

245. Ibid.

246. Sheffer, *Moshe Sharett*, 326.

247. Meir, *My Life*, 221.

248. Ibid.

249. Bar-Zohar, *Ben-Gurion*, 159–160.

250. Morris, *Righteous Victims*, 214.

251. Transcript of the Provisional Government Meeting (May 12, 1948), 46.

252. Ibid.

253. Ibid., 48.

254. Ben-Gurion, *Israel*, 89.

255. Transcript of the Provisional Government Meeting (May 12, 1948), 63, 67.

256. Ibid., 65.

257. Ibid., 70.

258. Bar-Zohar, *Ben-Gurion*, 160.

259. Transcript of the Provisional Government Meeting (May 12, 1948), 70.

260. Ibid., 75.

261. Ibid., 73.

262. Ibid., 75.

263. Ibid., 74.

264. Martin Kramer, "The May 1948 Vote That Made the State of Israel," *Mosaic*, April 2, 2018, https://mosaicmagazine.com/essay/2018/04/the-may-1948-vote-that-made -the-state-of-israel/.

265. Bar-Zohar, *Ben-Gurion*, 161.

266. Ben-Gurion, *Israel*, 76–77.

267. Bar-Zohar, *Ben-Gurion*, 162–163.

268. Ben-Gurion, *Israel*, 93.

269. Teveth, *Ben-Gurion and the Holocaust*, xxxiv.

Chapter 2   Menachem Begin: The Thin Line: Menachem Begin and the Justice of a Cause

1. Avi Shilon, *Menachem Begin: A Life* (New Haven, CT: Yale University Press, 2012), 6; Daniel Gordis, *Menachem Begin: The Battle for Israel's Soul* (New York: Random House, 2014), 3.

2. Gordis, *Menachem Begin*, 2.

3. Ibid., 1.

4. Ibid., 8.

5. Shilon, *Menachem Begin*, 3, 5.

6. Ibid., 1, 13.

7. Ibid., 4.

8. Ibid.

9. Ibid., 8; Gordis, *Menachem Begin*, 6.

10. Gordis, *Menachem Begin*, 6.

11. Shilon, *Menachem Begin*, 9.

12. Lawrence Wright, *Thirteen Days in September: Carter, Begin, and Sadat at Camp David* (New York: Knopf, 2014), 46.

13. Gordis, *Menachem Begin*, 8.

14. Shilon, *Menachem Begin*, 5.

15. Ibid., 7, 9.

16. Ibid., 9.

17. Ibid., 10.

18. Shilon, *Menachem Begin,* 10.

19. Ibid., 11–12.

20. Yaacov Shavit, *Jabotinsky and the Revisionist Movement 1925–1948* (New York: Routledge, 2013), 220.

21. Shilon, *Menachem Begin,* 12.

22. Ibid., 13; Gordis, *Menachem Begin,* 20.

23. Gordis, *Menachem Begin,* 16; "Menachem Begin Biographical," in *Les Prix Nobel,* ed. Wilhelm Odelberg (Stockholm: Nobel Foundation, 1979), www.nobelprize.org/prizes /peace/1978/begin/biographical/.

24. Gordis, *Menachem Begin,* 16.

25. Ibid., 17.

26. Menachem Begin, *The Revolt* (New York: Nash Publishing, 1977), 32–33.

27. Shilon, *Menachem Begin,* 19.

28. Gordis, *Menachem Begin,* 127.

29. Ibid., 23.

30. Yehuda Avner, "The Great Emancipator," *Jerusalem Post,* May 16, 2007, www.jpost .com/Opinion/Op-Ed-Contributors/The-great-emancipator.

31. Shilon, *Menachem Begin,* 19–20.

32. Ibid., 20.

33. Ibid.

34. Gordis, *Menachem Begin,* 25.

35. Uri Avnery, "Menachem Begin: The Reality," *WorldView,* June 1978, 10, https:// carnegiecouncil-media.storage.googleapis.com/files/v21_i006_a002.pdf.

36. Ibid.

37. Shilon, *Menachem Begin,* 29.

38. Menachem Begin, *White Nights: The Story of a Prisoner in Russia* (New York: Harper & Row, 1957), 91, 102.

39. Begin, *The Revolt,* 16.

40. Shilon, *Menachem Begin,* 35.

41. Gordis, *Menachem Begin,* 35–36.

42. Shilon, *Menachem Begin,* 38.

43. Begin, *The Revolt,* 28–29.

44. Ibid., 42–43.

45. Ibid., 54.

46. Ibid., 284–285.

47. Shilon, *Menachem Begin,* 51.

48. Begin, *The Revolt,* 84.

49. Ibid.

50. Shilon, *Menachem Begin,* 49.

51. Begin, *The Revolt,* 55–56.

52. Bruce Hoffman, *Anonymous Soldiers: The Struggle for Israel, 1917–1947* (New York: Vintage, 2015), 127.

53. Shilon, *Menachem Begin*, 42.

54. Ibid., 79.

55. Ibid., 76.

56. Begin, *The Revolt*, 133.

57. Ibid.

58. Shapira, *Ben-Gurion*, 188.

59. Begin, *The Revolt*, 221.

60. Shilon, *Menachem Begin*, 92.

61. Begin, *The Revolt*, 220.

62. Ibid., 225.

63. Gordis, *Menachem Begin*, 58.

64. Begin, *The Revolt*, 335.

65. Morris, *Righteous Victims*, 126.

66. Segev, *David Ben-Gurion*, 339.

67. Cohen, *Supreme Command*, 166.

68. Begin, *The Revolt*, 175.

69. Ibid., 176.

70. Shilon, *Menachem Begin*, 130.

71. Gordis, *Menachem Begin*, 116.

72. *Israel in Statistics 1948–2007* (Jerusalem: Central Bureau of Statistics, 2009), www .cbs.gov.il/statistical/statistical60_eng.pdf; "Jews from Arab Lands," World Jewish Congress, www.worldjewishcongress.org/en/issues/jews-from-arab-lands.

73. Shilon, *Menachem Begin*, 181.

74. Ibid., 164.

75. Ibid., 168.

76. Ibid., 168–169.

77. Ibid., 169.

78. Ibid., 170–171.

79. Ibid., 147.

80. Ibid.

81. Ibid.

82. Ibid., 151.

83. Gordis, *Menachem Begin*, 115.

84. Dennis Ross, *Doomed to Succeed: The U.S.-Israel Relationship from Truman to Obama* (New York: Farrar, Straus and Giroux, 2015), 84.

85. Michael Oren, *Six Days of War: June 1967 and the Making of the Modern Middle East* (New York: Oxford University Press, 2002), 79–81.

86. Gordis, *Menachem Begin*, 129.

87. Ibid., 128.

88. Dan Meridor, interview by David Makovsky, Jerusalem, May 14, 2018.

89. "Government Meeting on June 19, 1967, Morning and Afternoon," June 19, 1967, declassified memorandum of conversation, p. 29, Israel State Archives, Jerusalem.

90. Yigal Allon, "Israel: The Case for Defensible Borders," *Foreign Affairs,* October 1976, www.foreignaffairs.com/articles/israel/1976-10-01/israel-case-defensible-borders; "Dayan Suggests Israel Keep West Bank," *New York Times,* April 6, 1971, www.nytimes .com/1971/04/06/archives/dayan-suggests-israel-keep-west-bank.html.

91. Wael R. Ennab, *Population and Demographic Developments in the West Bank and Gaza Strip until 1990* (New York: United Nations Conference on Trade and Development, June 28, 1994), http://unctad.org/en/docs/poecdcseud1.en.pdf; Paul Rivlin, "Demographics between the Mediterranean and the River Jordan," in *Middle East Economy* 7, no. 6 (July 23, 2017), https://dayan.org/content/demographics-between-mediterranean-and-river-jordan.

92. "Meeting of the Committee of Ministers for Security Affairs," June 15, 1967, declassified memorandum of conversation, p. 25, Israel State Archives, Jerusalem.

93. Ibid., 30.

94. "Government Meeting on June 19, 1967, Morning and Afternoon," June 19, 1967, declassified memorandum of conversation, pp. 39–40, Israel State Archives, Jerusalem.

95. "Meeting of the Committee of Ministers for Security Affairs," June 15, 1967, declassified memorandum of conversation, p. 29, Israel State Archives, Jerusalem.

96. "Government Meeting on June 19, 1967, Morning and Afternoon," June 19, 1967, declassified memorandum of conversation, p. 34, Israel State Archives, Jerusalem.

97. "Meeting of the Committee of Ministers for Security Affairs," June 15, 1967, declassified memorandum of conversation, p. 31, Israel State Archives, Jerusalem.

98. Ibid., 3.

99. Gordis, *Menachem Begin,* 130.

100. Netanel Lorch, ed., *Major Knesset Debates, 1948–1981: Seventh Knesset 1969–1973, Eighth Knesset 1974–1977* (Lanham, MD: University Press of America, 1993), 1980, http://jcpa.org/wp-content/uploads/2012/02/KnessetDebatesVol5.pdf.

101. Jimmy Carter, *Keeping Faith: Memoirs of a President* (Fayetteville: University of Arkansas Press, 1995), 298.

102. Don Peretz, "The Earthquake: Israel's Ninth Knesset Elections," *Middle East Journal* 31, no. 3 (Summer 1977): 252, www.jstor.org/stable/4325643.

103. "Menachem Begin," Central Intelligence Agency, July 7, 1977, declassified November 13, 2013, www.cia.gov/library/readingroom/docs/1977-07-07.pdf.

104. Gordis, *Menachem Begin,* 164.

105. "Israel Prepares for an Election," Central Intelligence Agency, February 18, 1977, declassified July 3, 2006, www.cia.gov/library/readingroom/docs/1977-02-18.pdf.

106. Kenneth W. Stein, *Heroic Diplomacy: Sadat, Kissinger, Carter, Begin and the Quest for Arab-Israeli Peace* (London: Routledge, 1999), 198.

107. "25. Memorandum of Conversation, Washington, April 4, 1977, 11:10 am–12:30 pm," in *Foreign Relations of the United States, 1977–1980,* vol. 8, *Arab-Israeli Dispute, January 1977–August 1978,* ed. Adam M. Howard (Washington: United States Government Printing Office, 2013), 169, https://history.state.gov/historicaldocuments/frus1977-80v08/d25.

108. Ibid., 173.

109. Ibid.

110. Stein, *Heroic Diplomacy,* 199.

111. "52. Memorandum of Conversation, Washington, July 19, 1977, 11:15 am–1:10 pm," in *Foreign Relations of the United States, 1977–1980,* vol. 8, *Arab-Israeli Dispute, January 1977–August 1978,* ed. Adam M. Howard (Washington: United States Government Printing Office, 2013), 340–342, https://history.state.gov/historicaldocuments/frus1977-80v08/d52.

112. Ibid., 347.

113. Yehuda Avner, *The Prime Ministers: An Intimate Narrative of Israeli Leadership* (New Milford, CT: Toby Press, 2010), 438–439.

114. Ibid., 436.

115. Ibid.

116. "64. Telegram from Secretary of State Vance to the White House and the Department of State, Alexandria, August 2, 1977," in *Foreign Relations of the United States, 1977–1980,* vol. 8, *Arab-Israeli Dispute, January 1977–August 1978,* ed. Adam M. Howard (Washington: United States Government Printing Office, 2013), 381, https://history.state .gov/historicaldocuments/frus1977-80v08/d64.

117. "64. Telegram from Secretary of State," 382.

118. "80. Memorandum of Conversation, Jerusalem, August 9, 1977, 5:40 pm," in *Foreign Relations of the United States, 1977–1980,* vol. 8, *Arab-Israeli Dispute, January 1977– August 1978,* ed. Adam M. Howard (Washington: United States Government Printing Office, 2013), 432, https://history.state.gov/historicaldocuments/frus1977-80v08/d80.

119. "81. Memorandum of Conversation, Jerusalem, August 10, 1977, 9:45 am–12:10 pm," in *Foreign Relations of the United States, 1977–1980,* vol. 8, *Arab-Israeli Dispute, January 1977–August 1978,* ed. Adam M. Howard (Washington: United States Government Printing Office, 2013), 448, https://history.state.gov/historicaldocuments/frus1977-80v08 /d81.

120. Carter, *Keeping Faith,* 298.

121. Stuart E. Eizenstat, *President Carter: The White House Years* (New York: Thomas Dunne Books, 2018), 472.

122. "Meeting: Dayan—Tuhamy," October 18, 1977, declassified [in Hebrew], p. 3, Israel State Archives, Jerusalem, www.archives.gov.il/en/archives/#/Archive /0b0717068001c167/File/0b07170684cd6be2/Item/0907170685119160.

123. Ibid.

124. Ibid., 4.

125. Ibid.

126. See also "Report of Our Delegation from the Hassan—Tuhamy—Dayan Meeting," December 6, 1977, declassified, p. 2, Israel State Archives, Jerusalem, www.archives .gov.il/en/archives/#/Archive/0b0717068001c167/File/0b07170684cd6be2/Item /0907170684cef931.

127. Ambassador Samuel Lewis, interview by Peter Jessup, August 9, 1998, in *Foreign Affairs Oral History Project* (Arlington, VA: Association for Diplomatic Studies and Training, 1998), 66, www.adst.org/OH%20TOCs/Lewis,%20Samuel%20W.toc.pdf.

128. "Meeting: Dayan—Tuhamy," 7.

129. "107. Memorandum of Conversation, Washington, September 21, 1977, 11:10 am–12:10 pm," in *Foreign Relations of the United States, 1977–1980,* vol. 8, *Arab-Israeli Dispute, January 1977–August 1978,* ed. Adam M. Howard (Washington: United States Government Printing Office, 2013), 550, https://history.state.gov/historicaldocuments /frus1977-80v08/d107.

130. "109. Memorandum of Conversation, Washington, September 22, 1977, noon–12:40 pm," in *Foreign Relations of the United States, 1977–1980,* vol. 8, *Arab–Israeli Dispute, January 1977–August 1978,* ed. Adam M. Howard (Washington: United States Government

Printing Office, 2013), 563, https://history.state.gov/historicaldocuments/frus1977-80v08/d109.

131. "117. Memorandum of Conversation, New York, September 29, 1977, 10:55 am," in *Foreign Relations of the United States, 1977–1980,* vol. 8, *Arab-Israeli Dispute, January 1977–August 1978,* ed. Adam M. Howard (Washington: United States Government Printing Office, 2013), 622, https://history.state.gov/historicaldocuments/frus1977-80v08/d117.

132. "124. Memorandum of Conversation, New York, October 4, 1977, 6:55 pm," in *Foreign Relations of the United States, 1977–1980,* vol. 8, *Arab-Israeli Dispute, January 1977–August 1978,* ed. Adam M. Howard (Washington: United States Government Printing Office, 2013), 652–654, https://history.state.gov/historicaldocuments/frus1977-80v08/d124.

133. Ibid., 671.

134. Carter, *Keeping Faith,* 301.

135. "Romania Leader Mediated Sadat's '77 Peace Trip to Israel, Begin Says," Reuters, November 14, 1987, http://articles.latimes.com/1987-11-14/news/mn-5138_1_sadat-begin-peace.

136. Gordis, *Menachem Begin,* 159.

137. Aryeh Naor, interview by David Makovsky, Israel, May 2018.

138. "Memorandum of Conversation: Prime Minister Menahem Begin and Foreign Minister Moshe Dayan with Ambassador Lewis," November 3, 1977, declassified, p. 1, Israel State Archives, Jerusalem.

139. Anwar Sadat, "Speech to the Inaugural Session of the People's Assembly," November 9, 1977, Anwar Sadat Chair for Peace and Development, University of Maryland, https://sadat.umd.edu/sites/sadat.umd.edu/files/Excerpts%20from%20a%20Speech%20to%20the%20People%E2%80%99s%20Assembly.pdf.

140. Lewis, interview, 67.

141. "73. Statement to the Knesset by President Sadat, 20 November 1977," Israel Ministry of Foreign Affairs, https://mfa.gov.il/mfa/foreignpolicy/mfadocuments/yearbook3/pages/73%20statement%20to%20the%20knesset%20by%20president%20sadat-%2020.aspx?ViewMode=Print.

142. "74. Statement to the Knesset by Prime Minister Begin, 20 November 1977," Israel Ministry of Foreign Affairs, www.mfa.gov.il/mfa/foreignpolicy/mfadocuments/yearbook3/pages/74%20statement%20to%20the%20knesset%20by%20prime%20minister%20begi.aspx.

143. Moshe Dayan, *Breakthrough: A Personal Account of the Egypt-Israel Peace Negotiations* (New York: Alfred A. Knopf, 1981), 91.

144. Gerald M. Steinberg and Ziv Rubinovitz, *Menachem Begin and the Israel-Egypt Peace Process: Between Ideology and Political Realism* (Bloomington: Indiana University Press, 2019), 84.

145. "155. Telegram from the Embassy in Egypt to the Department of State, Cairo, November 23, 1977," in *Foreign Relations of the United States, 1977–1980,* vol. 8, *Arab-Israeli Dispute, January 1977–August 1978,* ed. Adam M. Howard (Washington: United States Government Printing Office, 2013), 769, https://history.state.gov/historicaldocuments/frus1977-80v08/d155.

146. Ibid., 774.

147. Aharon Barak, interview by David Makovsky, Herzliya, Israel, May 16, 2018.

148. Ibid.

149. Dan Meridor, interview by David Makovsky, Jerusalem, Israel, May 14, 2018.

150. Dayan, *Breakthrough*, 95.

151. "Meeting: Dayan—Tuhamy," 4.

152. "177. Memorandum of Conversation, Washington, December 16, 1977, 9–10 am," in *Foreign Relations of the United States, 1977–1980*, vol. 8, *Arab-Israeli Dispute, January 1977–August 1978*, ed. Adam M. Howard (Washington: United States Government Printing Office, 2013), 863, https://history.state.gov/historicaldocuments/frus1977-80v08/d177.

153. Ibid., 865.

154. Ibid., 866.

155. Ibid., 868–869.

156. "178. Memorandum of Conversation, Washington, December 17, 1977, 7:05–8:35 pm," in *Foreign Relations of the United States, 1977–1980*, vol. 8, *Arab-Israeli Dispute, January 1977–August 1978*, ed. Adam M. Howard (Washington: United States Government Printing Office, 2013), 874, https://history.state.gov/historicaldocuments/frus1977-80v08/d178.

157. Ibid., 881.

158. Ibid., 875.

159. Ibid., 878, 887.

160. Shilon, *Menachem Begin*, 291.

161. Ibid., 886.

162. "181. Telegram from the Embassy in Egypt to the Department of State, Cairo, December 27, 1977," in *Foreign Relations of the United States, 1977–1980*, vol. 8, *Arab-Israeli Dispute, January 1977–August 1978*, ed. Adam M. Howard (Washington: United States Government Printing Office, 2013), 898, https://history.state.gov/historicaldocuments/frus1977-80v08/d181.

163. Ibid., 899.

164. Ibid., 902.

165. "103. Statement to the Knesset by Prime Minister Begin Presenting Israel's Peace Plan, 28 December 1977," Israel Ministry of Foreign Affairs, www.mfa.gov.il/MFA/ForeignPolicy/MFADocuments/Yearbook3/Pages/103%20Statement%20to%20the%20Knesset%20by%20Prime%20Minister%20Beg.aspx.

166. "The Sixty-First Meeting of the Ninth Knesset," December 28, 1977, 992.

167. Aryeh Naor, *Begin in Power: A Personal Testimony* (Tel Aviv: Yedioth Ahranoth, 1993), 63–66.

168. "198. Memorandum of Telephone Conversation, January 18, 1978, 2:07–2:17 pm," in *Foreign Relations of the United States, 1977–1980*, vol. 8, *Arab-Israeli Dispute, January 1977–August 1978*, ed. Adam M. Howard (Washington: United States Government Printing Office, 2013), 952, https://history.state.gov/historicaldocuments/frus1977-80v08/d198.

169. William B. Quandt, *Camp David: Peacemaking and Politics* (Washington, DC: Brookings Institution Press, 2016), 167.

170. Zbigniew Brzezinski, *Power and Principle: Memoirs of the National Security Adviser, 1977–1981* (New York: Farrar, Straus and Giroux, 1985), 242.

171. Avner, *The Prime Ministers,* 478.

172. Carter, *Keeping Faith,* 319.

173. Lewis, interview, 86.

174. Avner, *The Prime Ministers,* 480–481.

175. Ibid., 481.

176. Ibid.

177. Carter, *Keeping Faith,* 320.

178. Lewis, interview, 83.

179. Avner, *The Prime Ministers,* 482.

180. "Transcript of the Meeting in Cairo (March 30–31, 1978)," April 2, 1978, p. 2, Ministry of Justice, Israel State Archives, Jerusalem.

181. Ibid.

182. Ibid.

183. Barak, interview.

184. Carter, *Keeping Faith,* 320–321.

185. "172. Briefing by Legal Adviser Rosenne on the Egyptian Plan, 11 July 1978," Israel Ministry of Foreign Affairs, http://mfa.gov.il/MFA/ForeignPolicy/MFADocuments/Yearbook3/Pages/172%20Briefing%20by%20Legal%20Adviser%20Rosenne%20on%20the%20Egypt.aspx.

186. Cyrus Vance, *Hard Choices: Critical Years in America's Foreign Policy* (New York: Simon & Schuster, 1983), 215.

187. Ibid., 216.

188. Carter, *Keeping Faith,* 324.

189. Vance, *Hard Choices,* 217.

190. Carter, *Keeping Faith,* 365.

191. Elyakim Rubinstein, interview by David Makovsky, Jerusalem, May 13, 2018.

192. Brzezinski, *Power and Principle,* 252.

193. Carter, *Keeping Faith,* 355.

194. Ibid., 359.

195. Ibid., 367.

196. Ibid., 374.

197. Ibid., 379.

198. Ibid., 388.

199. Ibid., 357.

200. Ibid.

201. Ibid., 371.

202. Wright, *Thirteen Days in September,* 223.

203. Carter, *Keeping Faith,* 399; Dayan, *Breakthrough,* 171.

204. Barak, interview.

205. Quandt, *Camp David,* 247–248.

206. Wright, *Thirteen Days in September,* 310.

207. "Consultations of the Israeli Delegation to Camp David," September 17, 1978 [in Hebrew], p. 4, Israel State Archives, Jerusalem, www.archives.gov.il/archives/#/Archive/0b0717068002f74b/File/0b07170680d07489/Item/0907170684c11869.

208. Ezer Weizman, *The Battle for Peace* (New York: Bantam Books, 1981), 369.

209. Ibid., 372.

210. Quandt, *Camp David,* 248.

211. Carter, *Keeping Faith,* 405.

212. *Camp David 25th Anniversary Forum* (Atlanta, GA: Carter Center, September 17, 2003), 33–35, www.cartercenter.org/resources/pdfs/peace/conflict_resolution/camp_david_forum_03.pdf.

213. "Remarks of the President, President Anwar al-Sadat of Egypt, and Prime Minister Menahem Begin of Israel at the Conclusion of the Camp David Meeting on the Middle East," *American Presidency Project,* September 17, 1978, http://www.presidency.ucsb.edu/ws/index.php?pid=29787.

214. Menahem Begin, letter to Amos Oz, printed in *Yediot Aharonot* on May 29, 1987.

215. Shilon, *Menachem Begin,* 309.

216. Ibid.

217. Sally Quinn, "Fighter in the Promised Land, Geula Cohen and the New Zionism," *Washington Post,* October 11, 1978, www.washingtonpost.com/archive/lifestyle/1978/10/11/fighter-in-the-promised-land-geula-cohen-and-the-new-zionism/1ac2c81a-edc5-43c8-8f6f-e429de5814b0/.

218. Netanel Lorch, ed., *Major Knesset Debates, 1948–1981: Ninth Knesset 1977–1981* (Lanham, MD: University Press of America, 1993), 2266, http://jcpa.org/wp-content/uploads/2012/02/KnessetDebatesVol6.pdf.

219. Quinn, "Fighter in the Promised Land."

220. Lorch, *Major Knesset Debates, 1948–1981: Ninth Knesset 1977–1981,* 2247.

221. Ibid., 2272–2273.

222. Ibid., 2274.

223. "Military Expenditure (% of GDP)," World Bank, https://data.worldbank.org/indicator/MS.MIL.XPND.GD.ZS.

224. Meridor, interview.

Chapter 3   Yitzhak Rabin: Mr. Security Accepts the PLO and Oslo

1. Henry Kissinger, *White House Years* (New York: Simon & Schuster, 1979), 355.

2. Itamar Rabinovich, *Yitzhak Rabin: Soldier, Leader, Statesman* (New Haven, CT: Yale University Press, 2017), 6–7.

3. Yitzhak Rabin, *The Rabin Memoirs* (Berkeley: University of California Press, 1996), 4.

4. Rabin, *The Rabin Memoirs,* 5.

5. Ibid., 6.

6. Ibid.

7. Rabinovich, *Yitzhak Rabin,* 6.

8. Rabin, *The Rabin Memoirs,* 7.

9. Ibid.

10. Ibid.

11. Ibid., 8.

12. Ibid., 19.

13. Ibid., 10.

14. Ibid., 14.

15. Ibid., 16.

16. Ibid., 20.

17. Ibid.

18. Ibid., 25–26.

19. Ibid., 32.

20. Ibid., 28.

21. Quoted in Rabinovich, *Yitzhak Rabin*, 20–21.

22. Yitzhak Rabin, "On the Road to Peace," December 1993, appendix G in *The Rabin Memoirs*, 411.

23. Yitzhak Rabin, "I, Military I.D. Number 30743, Yitzhak Rabin," address to the US Congress, July 26, 1994, http://www.rabincenter.org.il/Items/01099/RabinAddressto U.S.Congress.pdf.

24. Rabin, *The Rabin Memoirs*, 28.

25. Ibid, 45.

26. Ibid.

27. Rabinovich, *Yitzhak Rabin*, 47.

28. Quoted in Rabinovich, *Yitzhak Rabin*, 38.

29. Rabin, *The Rabin Memoirs*, 120–121.

30. Quoted in Efraim Inbar, *Rabin and Israel's National Security* (Washington, DC: Woodrow Wilson Center Press, 1999), 11.

31. Ibid., 15.

32. Ibid., 174.

33. Ibid., 85.

34. Quoted in Yoram Peri, afterword to *The Rabin Memoirs*, by Yitzhak Rabin (Berkeley: University of California Press, 1996), 352–353.

35. Quoted in Inbar, *Rabin and Israel's National Security*, 174.

36. Quoted in Peri, afterword to *The Rabin Memoirs*, 347.

37. See Itamar Rabinovich discussion, Rabinovich, *Yitzhak Rabin*, 110–111.

38. See Ross, *Doomed to Succeed*, 132–133

39. Conversation with Avineri, quoted in Peri, afterword to *The Rabin Memoirs*, 348.

40. Quoted in Inbar, *Rabin and Israel's National Security*, 46.

41. Inbar, *Rabin and Israel's National Security*, 31.

42. Quoted in Rabinovich, *Yitzhak Rabin*, 117.

43. See the documentary, *Rabin in His Own Words*, directed by Erez Laufer (Santa Monica, CA: Menemsha Films, 2015).

44. Rabin, *The Rabin Memoirs*, 332.

45. Ibid., 332–333.

46. Ibid., 334.

47. Ibid.

48. Quoted in Inbar, *Rabin and Israel's National Security*, 23.

49. Inbar, *Rabin and Israel's National Security*, 24.

50. See Ross, *Doomed to Succeed*, 140.

51. Quoted in Inbar, *Rabin and Israel's National Security*, 24–25.

52. Quoted in Peri, afterword to *The Rabin Memoirs*, 353.

53. Ibid., 355.

54. Inbar, *Rabin and Israel's National Security*, 104.

55. Ibid., 105.

56. Rabinovich, *Yitzhak Rabin*, 158.

57. Interview with Haber quoted in Peri, afterword to *The Rabin Memoirs*, 355.

58. Inbar, *Rabin and Israel's National Security*, 106.

59. Quoted in Rabinovich, *Yitzhak Rabin*, 165.

60. Rabin, *The Rabin Memoirs*, 64.

61. Ibid., 122.

62. Ibid., 123.

63. Quoted in Robert Slater, *Rabin: 20 Years After* (Glil Yam, Israel: Kotarim International Publishing, 2015), 212; interview with Yitzhak Rabin, *Al Hamishmar*, November 16, 1973.

64. Ross, *Doomed to Succeed*, 130.

65. Rabin, *The Rabin Memoirs*, 258.

66. Ibid., 274.

67. Ibid., 317.

68. Quoted in Rabinovich, *Yitzhak Rabin*, 91.

69. Inbar, *Rabin and Israel's National Security*, 44.

70. Baker had Dennis reach out to Shamir aide Eli Rubenstein to make this point.

71. Quoted in Rabinovich, *Yitzhak Rabin*, 165–166.

72. Inbar, *Rabin and Israel's National Security*, 26–27.

73. "Excerpts of PM Rabin Knesset Speech—DOP—21-Sep-93," Israel Ministry of Foreign Affairs, http://mfa.gov.il/MFA/MFA-Archive/Pages/EXCERPTS%20OF%20 PM%20RABIN%20KNESSET%20SPEECH%20-DOP-%20-%2021-Sep.aspx.

74. "1. Address to the Knesset by Prime Minister Rabin Presenting His Government, 13 July 1992," Israel Ministry of Foreign Affairs, http://www.mfa.gov.il/mfa/foreignpolicy /mfadocuments/yearbook9/pages/1%20%20address%20to%20the%20knesset%20by%20 prime%20minister%20rabin.aspx.

75. "101. Address by Prime Minister Rabin at the National Defense College, 12 August 1993," Israel Ministry of Foreign Affairs, http://mfa.gov.il/MFA/ForeignPolicy/MFA Documents/Yearbook9/Pages/101%20Address%20by%20Prime%20Minister%20 Rabin%20at%20the%20Nationa.aspx.

76. Quoted in Rabinovich, *Yitzhak Rabin*, 182.

77. Quoted in Peri, afterword to *The Rabin Memoirs*, 364.

78. Inbar, *Rabin and Israel's National Security*, 161–162.

79. Ibid., 164.

80. Ibid., 165.

81. Yitzhak Rabin, Nobel Prize acceptance speech, December 10, 1993.

82. "Excerpts of PM Rabin Knesset Speech—DOP—21-Sep-93."

83. Yitzhak Rabin, remarks to peace rally, November 4, 1995.

84. Rabin, "On the Road to Peace."

85. Yitzhak Rabin, statement to the Knesset on Gaza-Jericho agreement, May 11, 1994.

86. Yitzhak Rabin, address at the Levi Eshkol Creativity Awards, October 6, 1994.

87. Bill Clinton, speech, Brookings Institution, Washington, DC, March 9, 2017.

88. Yitzhak Rabin, speech to the Knesset on ratifying the Israeli-Palestinian interim agreement, October 5, 1995.

89. Meeting with Dennis in February 1995, when he was the American peace envoy under Clinton.

90. Martin Indyk, *Innocent Abroad: An Intimate Account of American Peace Diplomacy in the Middle East* (New York: Simon & Schuster, 2009), 28.

91. Inbar, *Rabin and Israel's National Security,* 111.

Chapter 4   Ariel Sharon: A Leader Who Tells the Settlers to Give Up the Dream

1. Nir Hefez and Gadi Bloom, *Ariel Sharon: A Life* (New York: Random House, 2006), 23.

2. Ariel Sharon with David Chaneff, *Warrior: An Autobiography* (New York: Simon & Schuster, 1990), 10.

3. Ibid., 15.

4. Ibid., 12.

5. Quoted in Hefez and Bloom, *Ariel Sharon,* 22.

6. Sharon, *Warrior,* 23.

7. Ibid.

8. Quoted in Hefez and Bloom, *Ariel Sharon,* 22.

9. Hefez and Bloom, *Ariel Sharon,* 32.

10. Ibid., 34.

11. Sharon, *Warrior,* 20.

12. Quoted in Hefez and Bloom, *Ariel Sharon,* 275–276.

13. Hefez and Bloom, *Ariel Sharon,* 302.

14. Ibid., 114.

15. Sharon, *Warrior,* 210.

16. Oren Magnezy, interview by Dennis Ross, November 17, 2017.

17. Quoted in Hefez and Bloom, *Ariel Sharon,* 6–7.

18. Sharon, *Warrior,* 56–58.

19. Hefez and Bloom, *Ariel Sharon,* 12.

20. Uri Dan, *Ariel Sharon: An Intimate Portrait* (New York: Palgrave Macmillan, 2006), 13.

21. Sharon, *Warrior,* 64.

22. Dan, *Ariel Sharon,* 13.

23. Ibid., 14.

24. David Landau, *Arik: The Life of Ariel Sharon* (New York: Alfred A. Knopf, 2014), 24–25.

25. Dan, *Ariel Sharon,* 19.

26. Hefez and Bloom, *Ariel Sharon,* 53.

27. Sharon, *Warrior,* 88.

28. Ibid., 90.

29. Ibid.

30. Ibid., 91.

31. Ibid., 96.

32. Ibid., 120.

33. Ibid., 76.

34. Landau, *Arik,* 37.

35. Ibid.

36. Ibid., 44.

37. Ibid., 42.

38. Ibid., 45.

39. Ibid., 46.

40. Moshe Dayan, *Story of My Life: An Autobiography* (New York: William Morrow, 1976), 243.

41. Landau, *Arik,* 49.

42. Ibid., 50.

43. Sharon, *Warrior,* 162.

44. Landau, *Arik,* 52.

45. Yitzhak Rabin with Dov Goldstein, *Service Notebook* [in Hebrew], vol. 1 (Tel Aviv: Maariv Book Guild, 1979), 118.

46. Quoted in Landau, *Arik,* 55.

47. Landau, *Arik,* 58–59.

48. Hefez and Bloom cite the research of Colonel Ami Gluska (*Ariel Sharon,* 96).

49. Landau, *Arik,* 59.

50. Sharon, *Warrior,* 208.

51. Ibid., 208–209.

52. Ibid., 210.

53. Sharon, *Warrior,* 220.

54. Ibid., 225.

55. Ibid., 227.

56. Sharon, *Warrior,* 247.

57. Ibid.

58. Sharon, *Warrior,* 269.

59. Ibid., 270.

60. Landau, *Arik,* 92.

61. Ibid., 98.

62. Ibid., 95.

63. Sharon, *Warrior,* 301–302.

64. Ibid., 308.

65. Landau, *Arik,* 112.

66. Ibid., 133.

67. Quoted in Landau, *Arik,* 133.

68. Landau, *Arik,* 134–135.

69. Ibid., 99

70. Dov Weisglass, interview with Dennis Ross, Israel, January 7, 2018.

71. Sharon, *Warrior,* 250.

72. Weisglass, interview.

73. Landau, *Arik,* 147.

74. Ibid., 146.

75. Hefez and Bloom, *Ariel Sharon,* 184.

76. Sharon, *Warrior,* 347.

77. Ibid., 357–358.

78. Ibid., 210–211.

79. Landau, *Arik,* 157.

80. Landau, *Arik,* 170.

81. Ibid., 169.

82. Sharon, *Warrior,* 433.

83. Ross, *Doomed to Succeed,* 186–190.

84. Howard Teicher and Gayle Radley Teicher, *Twin Pillars to Desert Storm: America's Flawed Vision in the Middle East from Nixon to Bush* (New York: William Morrow, 1993), 143.

85. Sharon, *Warrior,* 451.

86. Ibid.

87. Landau, *Arik,* 184.

88. Alexander M. Haig Jr., *Caveat: Realism, Reagan, and Foreign Policy* (New York: Macmillan, 1984), 318.

89. Ross, *Doomed to Succeed,* 193–194.

90. Ibid., 194.

91. Ronald Reagan, *An American Life* (New York: Pocket Books, 1990), 425–426.

92. Ibid., 427–428.

93. Landau, *Arik,* 196.

94. Sharon, *Warrior,* 495–496.

95. Ross, *Doomed to Succeed,* 200–201.

96. Landau, *Arik,* 214.

97. Sharon, *Warrior,* 523.

98. Landau, *Arik,* 216.

99. Ibid., 221.

100. Ibid., 229.

101. Ibid., 232–234.

102. Ibid.

103. Ibid., 243.

104. Ibid., 253.

105. Ibid., 259.

106. Dan, *Ariel Sharon,* 169.

107. Landau, *Arik,* 273.

108. Hefez and Bloom, *Ariel Sharon,* 298.

109. Landau, *Arik,* 262.

110. Hefez and Bloom, *Ariel Sharon,* 295.

111. Ibid., 296.

112. Landau, *Arik,* 284.

113. Ibid., 282.

114. Ibid., 287.

115. Ibid., 291.

116. Ibid., 321.

117. Ibid., 339.

118. Ibid., 360.

119. Ibid., 447.

120. Dan, *Ariel Sharon,* 167.

121. Ibid.

122. Ibid.

123. Weisglass, interview.

124. Landau, *Arik,* 359.

125. Weisglass, interview.

126. Landau, *Arik,* 374.

127. Ibid., 368.

128. Shalom Turgeman, interview, Tel Aviv, January 21, 2018.

129. Lior Schillat, interview, Jerusalem, January 8, 2018.

130. Ross, *Doomed to Succeed,* 310.

131. Schillat, interview.

132. Weisglass, interview.

133. Dan, *Ariel Sharon,* 133.

134. Hefez and Bloom, *Ariel Sharon,* 323.

135. Landau, *Arik,* 290.

136. Hefez and Bloom, *Ariel Sharon,* 274.

137. Dan, *Ariel Sharon,* 174.

138. Landau, *Arik,* 280.

139. "Sharon: Israel Wants to Give Palestinians Possibility of a State," *Haaretz,* September 24, 2001, www.haaretz.com/1.5406469.

140. Schillat, interview.

141. "Inauguration Speech of Prime Minister Ariel Sharon in the Knesset, 7-Mar-2001," Israel Ministry of Foreign Affairs, http://mfa.gov.il/MFA/PressRoom/2001/Pages/Inauguration%20Speech%20of%20Prime%20Minister%20Ariel%20Sharon.aspx.

142. Quoted in Hefez and Bloom, *Ariel Sharon,* 371.

143. Hefez and Bloom, *Ariel Sharon,* 413.

144. Stephen Hadley, interview with Dennis Ross, see Ross, *Doomed to Succeed,* 316.

145. Quoted in Hefez and Bloom, *Ariel Sharon,* 423.

146. "Remarks by Leaders at Mideast Summit," *New York Times,* June 4, 2003, www.nytimes.com/2003/06/04/international/middleeast/remarks-by-leaders-at-mideast-summit.html.

147. Ibid.

148. Turgeman, interview.

149. Hefez and Bloom, *Ariel Sharon,* 426.

150. Dan, *Ariel Sharon,* 218.

151. Weisglass, interview.

152. Dan, *Ariel Sharon,* 223.

153. Martin Indyk, discussion with Dennis Ross, New York City, November 2017.

154. Turgeman, interview.

155. Dov Weisglass, *Ariel Sharon: Prime Minister, from a Personal Perspective* (Tel Aviv: Yediyot Ahronoth Books and Chemed Books, 2012), unpublished English translation, 209.

156. Weisglass, interview.

157. Weisglass, *Ariel Sharon,* 210.

158. Schillat, interview.

159. Weisglass, *Ariel Sharon,* 209.

160. Elliott Abrams, interview by Dennis Ross, Washington, DC, January 2018.

161. Weisglass, interview.

162. Turgeman, interview.

163. Dan, *Ariel Sharon: An Intimate Portrait,* 236.

164. Quoted in Hefez and Bloom, *Ariel Sharon,* 446.

165. Quoted in Landau, *Arik,* 463.

166. Schillat, interview.

167. Weisglass, *Ariel Sharon,* 199.

168. Landau, *Arik,* 461.

169. Weisglass, *Ariel Sharon,* 240.

170. See Dennis's discussion of the Bush-Sharon letters in Ross, *Doomed to Succeed,* 323–325.

171. Landau, *Arik,* 486.

172. Ibid., 491.

173. Ariel Sharon, "Prime Minister Ariel Sharon's Address to the Knesset—The Vote on the Disengagement Plan," October 25, 2004, trans. from Hebrew, in *Israel's Disengagement Plan: Renewing the Peace Process* (Jerusalem: Israel Ministry of Foreign Affairs, 2005), 35, http://mfa.gov.il/MFA_Graphics/MFA%20Gallery/Documents/disengagement2.pdf.

174. Weisglass, *Ariel Sharon,* 270.

175. Ibid., 271.

176. Dan, *Ariel Sharon,* 128.

Chapter 5   Israel's Fateful Choice

1. Yoram Ettinger, "Jewish-Arab Demography Defies Conventional Wisdom," *in-FOCUS* (Spring 2018), www.jewishpolicycenter.org/2018/04/11/jewish-arab-demography -defies-conventional-wisdom/.

2. Ibid.

3. Yoram Ettinger, "Jewish-Arab Demography"; Sue Surkes, "Palestinians Will Breach West Bank Settlement Fences, Arab MK Predicts," *Times of Israel,* March 26, 2018, www .timesofisrael.com/palestinians-will-breach-west-bank-settlement-fences-arab-mk-predicts/.

4. Ariel Ben Solomon, "Experts Clash over Palestinian Demographic Statistics," *Jerusalem Post,* January 1, 2015, www.jpost.com/Middle-East/Experts-clash-over-Palestinian -demographic-statistics-386443.

5. Elhanan Miller, "Right-Wing Annexation Drive Fueled by False Demographics, Experts Say," *Times of Israel,* January 5, 2015, www.timesofisrael.com/right-wing -annexation-drive-fueled-by-false-demographics-experts-say.

6. Miller, "Right-Wing."

7. See Yehoshafat Harkabi, "Fateful Choices for Israel," lecture, Claremont McKenna College, Claremont, CA, 1986, In *Essays on Strategy and Diplomacy* (Claremont, CA: College Press, 1987).

8. Uzi Rebhun, interview by Dennis Ross, May 10, 2018.

9. Sarah Glazer, "The Israeli-Palestinian Conflict," *CQ Researcher,* April 13, 2018, http://library.cqpress.com/cqresearcher/document.php?id=cqresrre2018041300.

10. Naftali Bennett, "'My Stability Plan Offers Only Partial Self-Determination but Will Allow the Palestinians to Thrive': Naftali Bennett's Bottom-Up Peace Plan," *Fathom Journal,* December 2017, http://fathomjournal.org/my-stability-plan-is-only-partial-self -determination-but-will-allow-the-palestinians-to-thrive-naftali-bennetts-bottom-up -peace-plan/.

11. Bennett, "My Stability Plan."

12. Ibid.

13. Dov Lieber, "MKs Knock IDF for Not Knowing How Many Palestinians Live Where," *Times of Israel,* June 8, 2016.

14. Moshe Arens, "Is There Another Option?" *Haaretz,* June 2, 2010, www.haaretz .com/1.5128357.

15. Dani Dayan, "Peaceful Nonreconciliation Now," *New York Times,* June 8, 2014, www.nytimes.com/2014/06/09/opinion/peaceful-nonreconciliation-now.html.

16. Oded Revivi, presentation to the Jewish People Policy Institute, Jerusalem, October 2017; Oded Revivi, "Who Said 'Occupied'?" *Jerusalem Post,* February 27, 2016, www .jpost.com/Opinion/Who-said-occupied-446284.

17. Kamal Husseini, interview by Dennis Ross; paper given to author; conversations with former Palestinian prime minister Salam Fayyad, Samer Khouri, a Palestinian businessman living outside the West Bank with investments in it and throughout the Middle East, and Zvi Eckstein, professor of economics at IDC, Herzliya.

18. *Economic Report to the Ad Hoc Liaison Committee, September 2016* (Washington, DC: World Bank, September 2016).

19. Ya'acov Amidror, "Israel's Inelegant Options in Judea and Samaria: Withdrawal, Annexation, and Conflict Management," April 23, 2017, https://besacenter.org /mideast-security-and-policy-studies/israel-options-judea-samaria.

20. Tamar Hermann, presentation at the Washington Institute for Near East Policy, February 5, 2019.

21. Private discussion with Dennis after the Baker visit in July 1992.

22. Quoted in Peggy Noonan, "How to Find a Good Leader," *Wall Street Journal,* November 1, 2018, www.wsj.com/articles/how-to-find-a-good-leader-1541111329.

23. Doris Kearns Goodwin, *Leadership: In Turbulent Times* (New York: Simon & Schuster, 2018).

BIBLIOGRAPHY

Abrams, Elliott. Interview by Dennis Ross. Washington, DC. January 2018.

"Aliya." Israel Ministry of Foreign Affairs. August 20, 2001. https://mfa.gov.il/MFA /MFA-Archive/2001/Pages/Aliya.aspx.

Allon, Yigal. "Israel: The Case for Defensible Borders." *Foreign Affairs,* October 1976. www .foreignaffairs.com/articles/israel/1976-10-01/israel-case-defensible-borders.

Amidror, Ya'acov. "Israel's Inelegant Options in Judea and Samaria: Withdrawal, Annexation, and Conflict Management." *BESA Center,* April 23, 2017. https://besacenter.org /mideast-security-and-policy-studies/israel-options-judea-samaria/.

Arens, Moshe. "Is There Another Option?" *Haaretz,* June 2, 2010. www.haaretz.com /1.5128357.

Avner, Yehuda. "The Great Emancipator." *Jerusalem Post,* May 16, 2007. www.jpost.com /Opinion/Op-Ed-Contributors/The-great-emancipator/.

———. *The Prime Ministers: An Intimate Narrative of Israeli Leadership.* New Milford, CT: Toby Press, 2010.

Avnery, Uri. "Menachem Begin: The Reality." *WorldView,* June 1978. https://carnegiecouncil -media.storage.googleapis.com/files/v21_i006_a002.pdf.

Avnery, Yitzhak. "Immigration and Revolt: Ben-Gurion's Response to the 1939 White Paper." In *David-Ben Gurion: Politics and Leadership in Israel.* Edited by Ronald W. Zwieg. New York: Frank Cass, 1991.

Balfour, James. "Balfour Declaration." In *Israel in the Middle East: Documents and Readings on Society, Politics and Foreign Relations, Pre-1948 to the Present.* Edited by Itamar Rabinovich and Jehuda Reinharz. Waltham, MA: Brandeis University Press, 2008.

Bar-Zohar, Michael. *Ben-Gurion: A Biography.* Tel Aviv: Magal Books, 1978.

Barak, Aharon. Interview by David Makovsky. Herzliya, Israel. May 16, 2018.

Begin, Menachem. Letter to Amos Oz. Printed in *Yediot Aharonot.* May 29, 1987.

———. *The Revolt.* New York: Nash Publishing, 1977.

———. *White Nights: The Story of a Prisoner in Russia.* New York: Harper & Row, 1957.

Ben-Gurion, David. "Diary Entry, December 10, 1938." David Ben-Gurion Archives, Ben-Gurion University of the Negev, Beersheba, Israel.

———. *Israel: A Personal History.* Translated by Nechemia Meyers and Uzy Nystar. New York: Funk & Wagnalls, 1971.

———. *My Talks with Arab Leaders.* Translated by Misha Louvish. New York: The Third Press, 1973.

———. "Speaking at Paris Conference, Sunday Afternoon, 3 pm 18th August." 1946. David Ben-Gurion Archives, Ben-Gurion University of the Negev, Beersheba, Israel.

———. "Statement of Mr. D. Ben Gurion." In *The Jewish Plan for Palestine (1947): Memoranda and Statements Presented by the Jewish Agency for Palestine to the United Nations Special Committee on Palestine.* Atlanta, GA: Center for Israel Education, 2014. https://israeled.org/wp-content/uploads/2014/10/1947-Jewish-Plan-for-Palestine.pdf.

Bennett, Naftali. "'My Stability Plan Offers Only Partial Self-Determination but Will Allow the Palestinians to Thrive': Naftali Bennett's Bottom-Up Peace Plan." *Fathom Journal,* December 2017. http://fathomjournal.org/my-stability-plan-is-only-partial-self-determination-but-will-allow-the-palestinians-to-thrive-naftali-bennetts-bottom-up-peace-plan/.

Brzezinski, Zbigniew. *Power and Principle: Memoirs of the National Security Adviser, 1977–1981.* New York: Farrar, Straus and Giroux, 1985.

Camp David 25th Anniversary Forum. Atlanta, GA: The Carter Center. September 17, 2003. www.cartercenter.org/resources/pdfs/peace/conflict_resolution/camp_david_forum_03.pdf.

Carter, Jimmy. *Keeping Faith: Memoirs of a President.* Fayetteville: University of Arkansas Press, 1995.

"Chaim Weizmann's Acetone Patent Turns 100." Weizmann Institute of Science: Weizmann Compass, September 27, 2015. Accessed August 30, 2018. www.weizmann.ac.il/WeizmannCompass/sections/people-behind-the-science/chaim-weizmann%E2%80%99s-acetone-patent-turns-100.

Clinton, Bill. Speech at the Brookings Institution. Washington, DC. March 9, 2017.

Cohen, Eliot A. *Supreme Command: Soldiers, Statesmen, and Leadership in Wartime.* New York: Anchor Books, 2003.

"Consultations of the Israeli Delegation to Camp David." September 17, 1978 [in Hebrew]. Israel State Archives, Jerusalem. www.archives.gov.il/archives/#/Archive/0b0717068002f74b/File/0b07170680d07489/Item/0907170684c11869.

Dan, Uri. *Ariel Sharon: An Intimate Portrait.* New York: Palgrave Macmillan, 2006.

Dayan, Dani. "Peaceful Nonreconciliation Now." *New York Times,* June 8, 2014. www.nytimes.com/2014/06/09/opinion/peaceful-nonreconciliation-now.html.

Dayan, Moshe. *Breakthrough: A Personal Account of the Egypt-Israel Peace Negotiations.* New York: Alfred A. Knopf, 1981.

———. *Story of My Life: An Autobiography.* New York: William Morrow, 1976.

"Dayan Suggests Israel Keep West Bank." *New York Times,* April 6, 1971. www.nytimes.com/1971/04/06/archives/dayan-suggests-israel-keep-west-bank.html.

"Economic Report to the Ad Hoc Liaison Committee." *World Bank,* September 2016. www.worldbank.org/en/country/westbankandgaza/publication/economic-monitoring-report-to-the-ad-hoc-liaison-committee-september-2016.

Eizenstat, Stuart E. *President Carter: The White House Years.* New York: Thomas Dunne Books, 2018.

Ennab, Wael R. *Population and Demographic Developments in the West Bank and Gaza Strip until 1990.* New York: United Nations Conference on Trade and Development. June 28, 1994. http://unctad.org/en/docs/poecdcseud1.en.pdf.

Ettinger, Yoram. "Jewish-Arab Demography Defies Conventional Wisdom." *Jewish Policy Center,* Spring 2018. www.jewishpolicycenter.org/2018/04/11/jewish-arab-demography-defies-conventional-wisdom/.

Fayyad, Salam. Interview by David Makovsky. Ramallah. 2012.

Foreign Relations of the United States, 1977–1980, Volume 8, *Arab-Israeli Dispute, January 1977–August 1978.* Edited by Adam M. Howard. Washington, DC: United States Government Printing Office, 2013.

"From Haven to Home: 350 Years of Jewish Life in America: A Century of Immigration, 1820–1924." Library of Congress. Accessed February 7, 2019. www.loc.gov/exhibits /haventohome/haven-century.html.

Galili, Ziva, and Boris Morozov. *The Emigration of Zionist Convicts from the Soviet Union, 1924–1934.* New York: Routledge, 2006.

Glazer, Sarah. "The Israeli-Palestinian Conflict." *CQ Researcher,* April 13, 2018. http://library .cqpress.com/cqresearcher/document.php?id=cqresrre2018041300.

Goodwin, Doris Kearns. *Leadership: In Turbulent Times.* New York: Simon & Schuster, 2018.

Gordis, Daniel. *Menachem Begin: The Battle for Israel's Soul.* New York: Random House, 2014.

"Government Meeting on June 19, 1967, Morning and Afternoon." June 19, 1967. Declassified Memorandum of Conversation. Israel State Archives, Jerusalem.

Haaretz Service. "Sharon: Israel Wants to Give Palestinians Possibility of a State." *Haaretz,* September 24, 2001. www.haaretz.com/1.5406469.

Haig Jr., Alexander M. *Caveat: Realism, Reagan, and Foreign Policy.* New York: Macmillan, 1984.

Halkin, Hillel. *Jabotinsky: A Life.* New Haven, CT: Yale University Press, 2014.

Harkabi, Yehoshafat. "Fateful Choices for Israel." Lecture at Claremont McKenna College, Claremont, CA, 1986. In *Essays on Strategy and Diplomacy.* Claremont, CA: College Press, 1987.

Haron, Mirian Joyce. "The British Decision to Give the Palestine Question to the United Nations." *Middle Eastern Studies* 17, no. 2 (April 1981): 241–248. www.jstor.org /stable/4282830?seq=1#page_scan_tab_contents.

Hassanein, Haisam. *Beyond Security: Steps Toward Warmer Egypt-Israel Relations.* Policy Note 49. Washington, DC: Washington Institute for Near East Policy, 2018. www .washingtoninstitute.org/policy-analysis/view/beyond-security-steps-toward-warmer -egypt-israel-relations.

Hefez, Nir, and Gadi Bloom. *Ariel Sharon: A Life.* New York: Random House, 2006.

Heller, Daniel Kupfert. *Jabotinsky's Children: Polish Jews and the Rise of Right-Wing Zionism.* Princeton, NJ: Princeton University Press, 2017.

Hoffman, Bruce. *Anonymous Soldiers: The Struggle for Israel, 1917–1947.* New York: Vintage, 2015.

Husseini, Kamal. "Banking Constraints in West Bank, ILS Cash Surplus, Liquidity Issue with Israeli Correspondent Banks, Threat of De-risking by Israeli Respondent Banks." Paper given to author.

———. Interview by Dennis Ross. Israel.

Inbar, Efraim. *Rabin and Israel's National Security.* Washington, DC: Woodrow Wilson Center Press, 1999.

Indyk, Martin. Discussion with Dennis Ross. New York City. November 2017.

———. *Innocent Abroad: An Intimate Account of American Peace Diplomacy in the Middle East.* New York: Simon & Schuster, 2009.

Israel in Statistics 1948–2007. Jerusalem: Central Bureau of Statistics, May 2009. Accessed August 20, 2018. www.cbs.gov.il/statistical/statistical60_eng.pdf.

"Israel Prepares for an Election." Central Intelligence Agency. February 18, 1977. Declassified July 3, 2006. www.cia.gov/library/readingroom/docs/1977-02-18.pdf.

"Jews from Arab Lands." World Jewish Congress. Accessed August 20, 2018. www.world jewishcongress.org/en/issues/jews-from-arab-lands.

Kissinger, Henry. *White House Years.* New York: Simon & Schuster, 1979.

Kramer, Martin. "The May 1948 Vote That Made the State of Israel." *Mosaic,* April 2, 2018. https://mosaicmagazine.com/essay/2018/04/the-may-1948-vote-that-made-the -state-of-israel/.

Landau, David. *Arik: The Life of Ariel Sharon.* New York: Alfred A. Knopf, 2014.

Levy, Avigdor, ed. *Jews, Turks, Ottomans: A Shared History, Fifteenth Through the Twentieth Century.* Syracuse, NY: Syracuse University Press, 2002.

Lewis, Ambassador Samuel. Interview by Peter Jessup. August 9, 1998. In *Foreign Affairs Oral History Project.* Arlington, VA: Association for Diplomatic Studies and Training, 1998. www.adst.org/OH%20TOCs/Lewis,%20Samuel%20W.toc.pdf.

Lieber, Dov. "MKs Knock IDF for Not Knowing How Many Palestinians Live Where." *Times of Israel,* June 8, 2016. www.timesofisrael.com/mks-knock-idf-for-ignorance -on-palestinian-demographics/.

Lorch, Netanel, ed. *Major Knesset Debates, 1948–1981: Ninth Knesset 1977–1981.* Lanham, MD: University Press of America, 1993. http://jcpa.org/wp-content/uploads/2012 /02/KnessetDebatesVol6.pdf.

———. *Major Knesset Debates, 1948–1981: Seventh Knesset 1969–1973, Eighth Knesset 1974–1977.* Lanham, MD: University Press of America, 1993. http://jcpa.org/wp -content/uploads/2012/02/KnessetDebatesVol5.pdf.

Magnezy, Oren. Interview by Dennis Ross. Israel. November 17, 2017.

"Meeting: Dayan-Tuhamy." October 18, 1977. Declassified [in Hebrew]. Israel State Archives, Jerusalem. www.archives.gov.il/en/archives/#/Archive/0b0717068001c167 /File/0b07170684cd6be2/Item/0907170685119160.

"Meeting of the Committee of Ministers for Security Affairs." June 15, 1967. Declassified Memorandum of Conversation. Israel State Archives, Jerusalem.

Meir, Golda. *My Life.* New York: Dell Publishing, 1976.

"Memorandum of Conversation: Prime Minister Menahem Begin and Foreign Minister Moshe Dayan with Ambassador Lewis." November 3, 1977. Declassified. Israel State Archives, Jerusalem.

"Memorandum of Conversation, by Secretary of State, Washington, May 12, 1948." In *Foreign Relations of the United States, 1948: The Near East, South Asia, and Africa,* vol. 5, part 2. Edited Herbert A. Fine and Paul Claussen. Washington, DC: United States Government Printing Office, 1976. https://history.state.gov/historicaldocuments /frus1948v05p2/d252.

"Menachem Begin." Central Intelligence Agency. July 7, 1977. Declassified November 13, 2013. www.cia.gov/library/readingroom/docs/1977-07-07.pdf.

"Menachem Begin Biographical." *Les Prix Nobel.* Edited by Wilhelm Odelberg. Stockholm: Nobel Foundation, 1979. Accessed November 6, 2018. www.nobelprize.org/prizes /peace/1978/begin/biographical/.

Meridor, Dan. Interview by David Makovsky. Jerusalem, Israel. May 14, 2018.

"Military Expenditure (% of GDP)." *World Bank.* Accessed January 10, 2019. https://data
.worldbank.org/indicator/MS.MIL.XPND.GD.ZS?locations=IL.

Miller, Elhanan. "Right-Wing Annexation Drive Fueled by False Demographics, Experts Say." *Times of Israel,* January 5, 2015. www.timesofisrael.com/right-wing
-annexation-drive-fueled-by-false-demographics-experts-say/.

Morris, Benny. *1948: The First Arab-Israeli War.* New Haven, CT: Yale University Press,
2008.

———. *Righteous Victims: A History of the Zionist-Arab Conflict, 1881–1999.* New York:
Alfred A. Knopf, 1999.

"Moshe Sharett." Israel Ministry of Foreign Affairs. www.mfa.gov.il/mfa/aboutisrael/state
/pages/moshe%20sharett.aspx.

Naor, Aryeh. *Begin in Power: A Personal Testimony.* Tel Aviv: Yedioth Ahranoth, 1993.

———. Interview by David Makovsky. Israel. May 2018.

Noonan, Peggy. "How to Find a Good Leader." *Wall Street Journal,* November 1, 2018.
www.wsj.com/articles/how-to-find-a-good-leader-1541111329.

"172. Briefing by Legal Adviser Rosenne on the Egyptian plan, 11 July 1978." Israel Ministry of Foreign Affairs. http://mfa.gov.il/MFA/ForeignPolicy/MFADocuments
/Yearbook3/Pages/172%20Briefing%20by%20Legal%20Adviser%20Rosenne%20
on%20the%20Egypt.aspx.

"103. Statement to the Knesset by Prime Minister Begin Presenting Israel's Peace Plan,
28 December 1977." Israel Ministry of Foreign Affairs. www.mfa.gov.il/MFA
/ForeignPolicy/MFADocuments/Yearbook3/Pages/103%20Statement%20to%20
the%20Knesset%20by%20Prime%20Minister%20Beg.aspx.

Oren, Michael. *Six Days of War: June 1967 and the Making of the Modern Middle East.* New
York: Oxford University Press, 2002.

Oz, Amos. "David-Ben Gurion." *Time,* April 13, 1998. http://content.time.com/time
/subscriber/article/0,33009,988160,00.html.

Peres, Shimon. *Ben-Gurion: A Political Life.* New York: Schocken Books, 2011.

Peretz, Don. "The Earthquake: Israel's Ninth Knesset Elections." *Middle East Journal* 31,
no. 3 (Summer 1977): 251–266. www.jstor.org/stable/4325643.

"The Political Significance of Land Purchase." Center for Israel Education. Accessed January 23, 2019. https://israeled.org/resources/documents/jewish-national-fund/.

Quandt, William B. *Camp David: Peacemaking and Politics.* Washington, DC: Brookings
Institution Press, 2016.

Quinn, Sally. "Fighter in the Promised Land, Geula Cohen and the New Zionism." *Washington Post,* October 11, 1978. www.washingtonpost.com/archive/lifestyle/1978/10/11
/fighter-in-the-promised-land-geula-cohen-and-the-new-zionism/1ac2c81a-edc5
-43c8-8f6f-e429de5814b0/.

Rabin in His Own Words. Directed by Erez Laufer. Santa Monica, CA: Menemsha Films,
2015.

Rabin, Yitzhak. Address to the General Assembly of the Council of Jewish Federations.
Montreal. November 18, 1993.

———. Address to Knesset. Jerusalem. September 21, 1993.

———. Address to the Knesset by Prime Minister Rabin Presenting his Government. Jerusalem. July 13, 1992.

———. Address at the National Defense College. Washington, DC. August 12, 1993.

———. *Al Hamishmar.* November 16, 1973.

———. "I, Military I.D. Number 30743, Yitzhak Rabin." Address to the US Congress. Washington, DC. July 26, 1994.

———. Nobel Prize acceptance speech. Oslo. December 10, 1993.

———. "Our Tremendous Energies from a State of Siege." Address at the Levi Eshkol Creativity Awards. Tel Aviv. October 6, 1994.

———. *The Rabin Memoirs.* Berkeley: University of California Press, 1996.

———. Remarks to peace rally. Tel Aviv. November 4, 1995.

———. Speech to the Knesset on ratifying the Israeli-Palestinian interim agreement. Jerusalem, October 5, 1995.

———. Statement to the Knesset on Gaza-Jericho agreement. Jerusalem. May 11, 1994.

Rabin, Yitzhak, and Dov Goldstein. Service Notebook [in Hebrew], vol. 1. Tel Aviv: Maariv Book Guild.

Rabinovich, Itamar. *Yitzhak Rabin: Soldier, Leader, Statesman.* New Haven, CT: Yale University Press, 2017.

Radosh, Allis, and Ronald Radosh. *A Safe Haven: Harry S. Truman and the Founding of Israel.* New York: Harper Perennial, 2010.

Reagan, Ronald. *An American Life.* New York: Pocket Books, 1990.

Rebhun, Uzi. Interview by Dennis Ross. Israel. May 10, 2018.

"Remarks by Leaders at Mideast Summit." *New York Times,* June 4, 2003. www.nytimes .com/2003/06/04/international/middleeast/remarks-by-leaders-at-mideast-summit .html.

"Remarks of the President, President Anwar al-Sadat of Egypt, and Prime Minister Menahem Begin of Israel at the Conclusion of the Camp David Meeting on the Middle East." *The American Presidency Project.* September 17, 1978. www.presidency.ucsb.edu /ws/index.php?pid=29787.

"Report of Our Delegation from the Hassan-Tuhamy-Dayan Meeting." December 6, 1977. Declassified. Israel State Archives, Jerusalem. www.archives.gov.il/en/archives/# /Archive/0b0717068001c167/File/0b07170684cd6be2/Item/0907170684cef931.

Revivi, Oded. Presentation to the Jewish People Policy Institute. Jerusalem. October 2017.

———. "Who Said 'Occupied'?" *Jerusalem Post,* February 27, 2016. www.jpost.com /Opinion/Who-said-occupied-446284.

Rivlin, Paul. "Demographics between the Mediterranean and the River Jordan." *Middle East Economy* 7, no. 6 (July 23, 2017). https://dayan.org/content/demographics -between-mediterranean-and-river-jordan.

"Romania Leader Mediated Sadat's '77 Peace Trip to Israel, Begin Says." *Reuters,* November 14, 1987. http://articles.latimes.com/1987-11-14/news/mn-5138_1_sadat-begin -peace.

Ross, Dennis. *Doomed to Succeed: The U.S.-Israel Relationship from Truman to Obama.* New York: Farrar, Straus and Giroux, 2015.

Rubinstein, Elyakim. Interview by David Makovsky. Jerusalem, Israel. May 13, 2018.

Sachar, Howard M. *Israel and Europe: An Appraisal in History.* New York: Vintage Books, 2000.

Sadat, Anwar. "Speech to the Inaugural Session of the People's Assembly." November 9, 1977. Anwar Sadat Chair for Peace and Development, University of Maryland. https://

sadat.umd.edu/sites/sadat.umd.edu/files/Excerpts%20from%20a%20Speech%20 to%20the%20People%E2%80%99s%20Assembly.pdf.

Said, Edward W. *The Question of Palestine.* New York: Vintage Books, 1992.

Sarna, Jonathan D. "Louis D. Brandeis: Zionist Leader." *Brandeis Review* 2 (Winter 1992): 22–27.

Schillat, Lior. Interview by Dennis Ross. Jerusalem, Israel. January 8, 2018.

Segev, Tom. *David Ben-Gurion: A State at All Costs.* Jerusalem: Keter Books, 2017.

"74. Statement to the Knesset by Prime Minister Begin—20 November 1977." Israel Ministry of Foreign Affairs. www.mfa.gov.il/mfa/foreignpolicy/mfadocuments/yearbook3 /pages/74%20statement%20to%20the%20knesset%20by%20prime%20minister%20 begi.aspx.

"73. Statement to the Knesset by President Sadat, 20 November 1977." Israel Ministry of Foreign Affairs. www.mfa.gov.il/mfa/foreignpolicy/mfadocuments/yearbook3 /pages/73%20statement%20to%20the%20knesset%20by%20president%20 sadat-%2020.aspx.

Shapira, Anita. *Ben-Gurion: Father of Modern Israel.* New Haven, CT: Yale University Press, 2014.

———. *Israel: A History.* Translated by Anthony Berris. Waltham, MA: Brandeis University Press, 2012.

Sharett, Moshe. "Wire to David Ben-Gurion, Tel Aviv." *Moshe Sharett: The Second Prime Minister: A Variety of Reports from His Life (1894–1965).* Translated from "Mivrak El David Ben-Gurion, Tel Aviv." *Moshe Sharett: Rosh HaMemshala HaSheni—Mivhar Teudot MiPirkey Hayav (1894–1965).*

Sharon, Ariel. Inauguration Speech of Prime Minister Ariel Sharon in the Knesset, Jerusalem, March 7, 2001.

———. Prime Minister Ariel Sharon's Address to the Knesset—The Vote on the Disengagement Plan, Jerusalem, October 25, 2004.

Sharon, Ariel, and David Chaneff. *Warrior: An Autobiography.* New York: Simon & Schuster, 1990.

Shavit, Yaacov. *Jabotinsky and the Revisionist Movement 1925–1948.* New York: Routledge, 2013.

Sheffer, Gabriel. *Moshe Sharett: Biography of a Political Moderate.* Oxford: Oxford University Press, 1996.

Sheref, Zeev. *Three Days.* Garden City, NY: Doubleday, 1962.

Shilon, Avi. *Menachem Begin: A Life.* New Haven, CT: Yale University Press, 2012.

Shlaim, Avi. *The Iron Wall: Israel and the Arab World.* London: Penguin Books, 2000.

———. *The Politics of Partition: King Abdullah, the Zionists, and Palestine 1921–1951.* Oxford: Oxford University Press, 1999.

"The Sixty-First Meeting of the Ninth Knesset." December 28, 1977.

Slater, Robert. *Rabin: 20 Years After.* Glil Yam, Israel: Kotarim International Publishing, 2015.

Solomon, Ariel Ben. "Experts Clash over Palestinian Demographic Statistics." *Jerusalem Post,* January 1, 2015. www.jpost.com/Middle-East/Experts-clash-over -Palestinian-demographic-statistics-386443.

Spitzer, Yannay. "Pogroms, Networks, and Migration: The Jewish Migration from the

Russian Empire to the United States 1881–1914." September 17, 2013. http://eh.net/eha /wp-content/uploads/2013/11/Spitzer.pdf.

St. John, Robert. *Ben-Gurion: The Biography of an Extraordinary Man.* Garden City, NY: Doubleday & Company, 1959.

Stein, Kenneth W. *Heroic Diplomacy: Sadat, Kissinger, Carter, Begin, and the Quest for Arab-Israeli Peace.* London: Routledge, 1999.

Steinberg, Gerald M., and Ziv Rubinovitz. *Menachem Begin and the Israel-Egypt Peace Process: Between Ideology and Political Realism.* Bloomington: Indiana University Press, 2019.

Teicher, Howard, and Gayle Radley Teicher. *Twin Pillars to Desert Storm: America's Flawed Vision in the Middle East from Nixon to Bush.* New York: William Morrow, 1993.

Tessler, Mark. *A History of the Israeli-Palestinian Conflict.* 2nd ed. Bloomington: Indiana University Press, 2009.

Teveth, Shabtai. *Ben-Gurion: The Burning Ground 1868–1948.* Boston: Houghton Mifflin, 1987.

———. *Ben-Gurion and the Holocaust.* New York: Harcourt Brace & Company, 1996.

"Transcript of the Meeting in Cairo (March 30–31, 1978)." April 2, 1978. Ministry of Justice, Israel State Archives, Jerusalem.

Transcript of the Provisional Government Meeting (May 12, 1948).

Troen, Ilan. "The Transformation of Zionist Planning Policy: From Rural Settlements to an Urban Network." *Planning Perspectives* 3, no. 1 (1998): 3–23. www.tandfonline.com /doi/abs/10.1080/02665438808725649.

Turgeman, Shalom. Interview by Dennis Ross. Israel. January 21, 2018.

Vance, Cyrus. *Hard Choices: Critical Years in America's Foreign Policy.* New York: Simon & Schuster, 1983.

Weisglass, Dov. *Ariel Sharon: Prime Minister, from a Personal Perspective.* Translated by Yael Nussbaum. Tel Aviv: Yediyot Ahronoth Books and Chemed Books, 2012.

———. Interview by Dennis Ross. Israel. January 7, 2018.

Weizman, Ezer. *The Battle for Peace.* New York: Bantam Books, 1981.

Wren, Christopher S. "Military Talk Begun by Israel and Egypt." *New York Times,* January 12, 1978. www.nytimes.com/1978/01/12/archives/military-talk-begun-by-israel-and -egypt-weizman-flies-to-aswan-to.html.

Wright, Lawrence. *Thirteen Days in September: Carter, Begin, and Sadat at Camp David.* New York: Knopf, 2014.

INDEX

Dennis Ross is an American diplomat and author. He is the William Davidson distinguished fellow at the Washington Institute for Near East Policy and distinguished professor in the practice of diplomacy at Georgetown University. He has served as the director of policy planning in the State Department under President George H. W. Bush, the special Middle East coordinator under President Bill Clinton, and special assistant to President Obama on the National Security Council staff for the central region. Ambassador Ross has published extensively on the former Soviet Union, arms control, and the greater Middle East, including most recently *Doomed to Succeed: The U.S.-Israel Relationship from Truman to Obama*. He has authored many op-eds in the *New York Times, Washington Post, Wall Street Journal,* and other papers and magazines. He writes monthly columns for two Middle Eastern publications: *Al Majalla* and *Asharq Al-Awsat*. He lives in Bethesda, Maryland.

David Makovsky is the Ziegler distinguished fellow at the Washington Institute for Near East Policy and director of the project on the Middle East peace process. He is also an adjunct professor in Middle East studies at Johns Hopkins University's Paul H. Nitze School of Advanced International Studies. In 2013–2014, he worked in the Office of the US Secretary of State, serving as a senior advisor to the special envoy for Israeli-Palestinian negotiations. He is coauthor, with Dennis Ross, of the 2009 *Washington Post* best seller *Myths, Illusions, and Peace: Finding a New Direction for America in the Middle East*. His commentary on the peace process and the Arab-Israeli conflict has appeared in the *New York Times, Washington Post, Los Angeles Times, Wall Street Journal, Financial Times, Foreign Affairs,* and *Foreign Policy*. He appears frequently in the media to comment on Arab-Israeli affairs, including *PBS NewsHour*. He lives in Silver Spring, Maryland.

PublicAffairs is a publishing house founded in 1997. It is a tribute to the standards, values, and flair of three persons who have served as mentors to countless reporters, writers, editors, and book people of all kinds, including me.

I. F. STONE, proprietor of *I. F. Stone's Weekly*, combined a commitment to the First Amendment with entrepreneurial zeal and reporting skill and became one of the great independent journalists in American history. At the age of eighty, Izzy published *The Trial of Socrates*, which was a national bestseller. He wrote the book after he taught himself ancient Greek.

BENJAMIN C. BRADLEE was for nearly thirty years the charismatic editorial leader of *The Washington Post*. It was Ben who gave the *Post* the range and courage to pursue such historic issues as Watergate. He supported his reporters with a tenacity that made them fearless and it is no accident that so many became authors of influential, best-selling books.

ROBERT L. BERNSTEIN, the chief executive of Random House for more than a quarter century, guided one of the nation's premier publishing houses. Bob was personally responsible for many books of political dissent and argument that challenged tyranny around the globe. He is also the founder and longtime chair of Human Rights Watch, one of the most respected human rights organizations in the world.

·   ·   ·

For fifty years, the banner of Public Affairs Press was carried by its owner Morris B. Schnapper, who published Gandhi, Nasser, Toynbee, Truman, and about 1,500 other authors. In 1983, Schnapper was described by *The Washington Post* as "a redoubtable gadfly." His legacy will endure in the books to come.

Peter Osnos, *Founder*